Going Public

Going Public
New Strategies of Presidential Leadership

Second Edition

Samuel Kernell
University of California, San Diego

PRESS

A Division of Congressional Quarterly Inc.

Printed in the United States of America

Second Printing

Library of Congress Cataloging in Publication Data

Kernell, Samuel, 1945-
    Going public: new strategies of presidential leadership / Samuel
Kernell. — 2nd ed.
        p.   cm.
    Includes index.
    ISBN 0-87187-635-3 (hardback) — ISBN 0-87187-614-0 (softback)
    1. Presidents—United States.   2. Presidents—United States—Press
conferences.   3. Communication in politics—United States.
I. Title.
JK518.K46   1992
353.03'23—dc20   92-25581
                                                              CIP

Nothing is so unbelievable that oratory cannot make it acceptable.
—Cicero

One thought receiving wide expression [is] that the politician of tomorrow must become an "actor."
—Jack Gould, *New York Times,* June 25, 1951

Too many good people have been beaten because they tried to substitute substance for style.
—Adviser to Jimmy Carter, December 1976

Contents

Tables and Figures   ix

Preface   xiii

1 Introduction: Going Public in Theory and in Practice   1
Presidential Theory   2
Presidential Practice   4

2 How Washington and Presidents Have Changed   9
Institutionalized Pluralism: The Bargaining Community   10
Public Opinion and Institutionalized Pluralism   17
Individualized Pluralism: The Emerging Community   23
Going Public and Individualized Pluralism   29
Presidential Selection Reforms: Outsiders in the White House   33
The Politics of Divided Government   39
Conclusion   45

3 The President and the Press   53
The Bargaining President and the Press   55
Emergence of the Washington Press as an Institution   57
The FDR System: Hard News, Openly Conveyed   65
Press Relations under Truman and Eisenhower   70
The Kennedy System: Press Relations in an Era of Direct
    Communication   71
The Kennedy System as a Model for Presidents Who Go Public   76
George Bush's Adaptation of the Kennedy System   79
The Modern Trajectory of Presidential-Press Relations   80

4 The Growth of Going Public   89
Trends in Going Public   91
The Incremental Growth of Going Public   106
Conclusion   114

5 **President Reagan and His First Three Budgets**   121
  Reagan as an Outsider   122
  Reagan's Three Budgets   124
  Going Public and Leadership: The Lessons of Reagan's Budgets   146

6 **Opinion Leadership and Foreign Affairs**   157
  Rally Events and Presidential Popularity   160
  Rally Events and Opinion Leadership   164
  The Truman Doctrine Speech: A Case Study   168
  Conclusion   182

7 **The Politics of Popularity**   189
  Popularity and Public Relations   191
  Thinking Strategically about Popularity   199
  Presidential Popularity and Economic Performance   217
  Conclusion   220

8 **Conclusion: The Prospects for Leadership**   227
  Adaptive Responses to Presidents Going Public   228
  Public Policy and Going Public   234

  Appendix   247

  Index   257

Tables and Figures

Tables

2-1 Presidential Survey of Public Opinion on Reallocation of
Jobs under the Works Progress Administration, 1936   20

3-1 Turnover among Washington Correspondents, Selected Years,
1864-1932   59

3-2 Presidential News Conferences with White House
Correspondents, 1929-1984   74

4-1 Calendar of Presidential "Reports to the Nation" on
National Television, Jan. 1953-Dec. 1991   94

4-2 Presidential Television from Kennedy to Bush, First 19
Months in Office   98

4-3 President Bush's "Minor" Addresses, September 1991   100

5-1 Performance Ratings of President Reagan, 1982-1983
(Percent)   140

6-1 Public Concern over Foreign Policy before and after Truman
Doctrine Speech   172

6-2 Distribution of Public Support for Foreign Aid Requests in
Truman Doctrine Speech (Percent)   173

6-3 Relationship between Approval of President Truman and
Support for His Foreign Aid Requests (Percent)   174

6-4 Relationship between Approval of President Truman and
Support for Aid to Greece, Controlling for Education and
Presidential Vote (Percent and Number Who Favor Aid to
Greece among Respondents Who Heard or Read about the
President's Speech)   176

6-5 Educational Differences in Support for the Truman
Doctrine (Percentage Points)   177

6-6   Relationship between Familiarity with Truman Doctrine
      Speech and Response to Forbid-Communist-Party Question
      (Percent and Number of Respondents)   179

6-7   Relationship between Familiarity with Truman Doctrine
      Speech and Anticommunist Opinion, Controlling for
      Education and Participation (Percent Who Favor
      Forbidding Communist Party)   180

6-8   Relationship between Response to Forbid-Communist-Party
      Question and Support for Aid to Greece and Turkey
      (Percent and Number of Respondents)   182

7-1   Group Preferences in Selection of Unemployment
      and Inflation as the Most Important Problem,
      1974-1987 (Percent)   210

7-2   Relative Importance of Unemployment and Inflation in the
      Annual *Economic Report of the President,* 1962-1992   213

7-3   Average Popularity Rating of Presidents by Partisan Group   215

7-4   Relative Effects of Unemployment and Inflation on
      Presidential Popularity among Party Groups   219

A-1   Effects of Political Conditions on Presidential Popularity
      among Party Groups: Eisenhower, Kennedy, and Johnson   251

A-2   Effects of Political Conditions on Presidential Popularity
      among Party Groups: Nixon, Ford, Carter, and Reagan   252

A-3   Long-term and Mean Effects of Political Conditions on
      Presidential Popularity among Party Groups: Eisenhower,
      Kennedy, and Johnson   253

A-4   Long-term and Mean Effects of Political Conditions on
      Presidential Popularity among Party Groups: Nixon, Ford,
      Carter, Reagan, and Bush   254

Figures

3-1   Growth of the Washington Press Corps, 1864-1987   69

4-1   Presidential Addresses, 1929-1990 (Yearly Averages for
      First Three Years of First Term)   92

4-2   Public Appearances by Presidents, 1929-1990 (Yearly
      Averages for First Three Years of First Term)   102

4-3   Days of Political Travel by Presidents, 1929-1990
      (Yearly Averages for First Three Years of First Term)   105

4-4   Households with Radios and Televisions, Cable TV and
      VCRs, 1930-1990 (Percent)   108

4-5   The Declining Presidential Audience, 1969-1992   114

5-1   Public Opinion on the Effects of Reaganomics on
      Personal Finances, March 1981-March 1983   133

6-1   President Bush's Popular Support as a Product of
        Rally Events   159
6-2   Support for FDR among Income Subgroups: 1937-1942   165
7-1   Relationship between Vote Share and Popularity of
        Incumbent Presidents Seeking Reelection, 1948-1984
        (Percent)   204

Preface

Going public is a class of activities that presidents engage in as they promote themselves and their policies before the American public. Some examples of going public are a televised press conference, a special, prime-time address to the nation, a speech before a business convention on the West Coast, a visit to a day care center, and a White House ceremony to decorate a local hero that is broadcast via satellite to the hometown television station. What these various activities have in common is that they are intended principally to place presidents and their messages before the American people in a way that enhances their chances of success in Washington. Going public draws heavily upon techniques developed over the years in election campaigning; but in going public, the ultimate object of the president's designs is not the American voter, but fellow politicians in Washington.

The possibility that the president might at times appeal for the public's support in dealings with Congress occurred to James Madison. In *Federalist* No. 49 Madison argued against a constitutional provision that would allow any of the branches of the federal government to redress constitutional imbalance by appealing "to the people" for reform.

Citing recent occurrences in various state legislatures, Madison began by stipulating that if any branch were likely to be guilty of "aggrandizement," it would be the popular one, Congress. Though presidents "are generally the objects of jealousy; *and their administration is always liable to be discolored and rendered unpopular"* [emphasis added], members of Congress by virtue of being "more numerous," and having "connections of blood, of friendship, and of acquaintance, embrace a great proportion of the most influential part of society." Simply stated, Congress can trump any effort by the president to enlist public opinion.

Near the end of *Federalist* No. 49, Madison allowed the possibility that "the executive power might be in the hands of a peculiar favorite of the people." Against this he reverted to the distinction, common in his day, between the public's *passions* and its *reason*. Public appeals excite the passions so that the outcome, he concluded, "could never be expected to turn on the true merits of the question." In short, Madison had nothing much good to say about going public. Of course, his extraordinary precognition concerned political circumstances far different from those today that lead one to examine going public as a presidential strategy.

Today, over 200 years later, the matter warrants reassessment. No longer a subject only of speculation, modern presidents routinely appear before the American public on evening television on all kinds of issues ranging from national crises to the commemoration of a presidential library. Like Madison, I find the most interesting appeals to be those that involve the president's dealings with Congress. Because the president's success in publicly advancing his policies presupposes his own strong standing in the country, I also give considerable attention to the things presidents do to gain the public's favor.

The second edition further explores the use and effectiveness of going public, analyzing President Bush's media strategies, the link between opinion leadership and foreign affairs, and the rally phenomenon, in which presidents receive increased public support during times of international crisis, such as the Persian Gulf War.

The Plan of the Book

I begin by examining presidential power in the context of political relations in Washington. The president's influence with other, more or less autonomous politicians depends upon his ability to satisfy their needs and exploit their vulnerabilities. In the first chapter I develop a rationale for the rise of going public as a presidential strategy tailored to the ever-changing political relations in Washington. As other politicians' needs and expectations are changing, so too must the president's.

Alternative models of political relations in Washington that should be the most conducive to bargaining and going public are set forth in Chapter 2. It is not too surprising to find that different forms of influence thrive in quite different kinds of political communities. Paying special attention to changes in Congress and its relations with the presidency, I argue that within the past half century, political Washington has come to look less like institutionalized pluralism (which is conducive to bargaining) and more like individualized pluralism (which is conducive to going public). Presidents more freely go public nowadays because it is a strategy better adapted to modern politics.

In Chapter 3, I continue this analysis of presidential leadership as a function of evolving community relations, this time by chronicling presidential-press relations throughout the twentieth century. This inquiry reveals some of the specific political circumstances that gave rise to presidents adopting technologies of direct communications between the White House and the country—the *sine qua non* of going public.

Having established a rationale for the going public phenomenon, I next present the evidence that presidents do indeed increasingly rely upon public relations to build support for their policies in Washington. Chapter 4 presents 50-year trends that document the growing practice of going public, highlighting President Reagan's use of the televised address and President Bush's unprecedented number of domestic trips.

To appreciate the extent to which going public is altering the character of presidential leadership, one must examine firsthand the president's choice to go public or to bargain and its ramification on the choices of others. More than any other recent president, Reagan was ideally suited by experience, temperament, and ideology to capitalize on going public, and in Chapter 5, I analyze the strategies he employed in promoting his budgets in Congress during his first three years in office.

As presidents rely more heavily upon public strategies, their success in Washington will depend vitally upon the reactions of ordinary citizens. In Chapters 6 and 7, I shift the discussion from Washington relations to public opinion. We begin by considering the rally phenomenon, in which the public frequently responds to international crises by upgrading its assessment of the president's job performance. Typically, however, the president's public leadership rests on more than job performance ratings. Rather, it requires that the approval of the president's performance be transferred to support for his policies. In Chapter 6, I consider a model of this type of opinion change and then examine the effects of one specific presidential appeal—the Truman Doctrine speech of 1947. The way the American public did (and did not) respond to President Truman's appeal for emergency aid for Europe offers instruction to present-day presidents similarly interested in molding public opinion.

A president must not only be able to rally his supporters, he must also maintain the public's backing. Beyond the platitude "maintain peace and prosperity," the sizable literature on presidential popularity offers little strategic advice to presidents in this endeavor. In Chapter 7, I analyze the alternative ways a *strategic* president might seek to win and maintain the public's favor. Finally I conclude by considering some of the implications of going public on the continued evolution of community relations in Washington.

Because going public involves direct appeals to the American people, I think it is of value to be able to *see* and *hear* how presidential press conferences and direct communications from the White House have evolved from Franklin D. Roosevelt to present times. Drawing on historical newsreel and broadcast news footage, as well as interviews, I have prepared a half-hour videocassette for use in the classroom. Speeches and events of particular interest include Roosevelt's Fireside Chats, the Truman Doctrine speech, Nixon's "Silent Majority" speech, and Kennedy's first televised press conferences. This videotape is available from the publisher.

Acknowledgments

The proximate motivation to sit down and write the first edition of this book was Ronald Reagan. It was his success in 1981 that so confirmed and clarified my own views on the direction of presidential leadership. A fellowship at the Hoover Institution (and in particular the cookie hour banter there) gave me the needed time and additional inspiration to write *Going Public*. I am also grateful to the National Science Foundation, which supported the statistical analysis of public opinion in Chapter 7.

The revision of this text was prompted by the thoughtful comments and criticism generously offered by numerous colleagues over the past six years. In many respects, my conversations and correspondence with them have been as satisfying as writing the book.

Much of the text assumes the form of argument, but more of it is engaged in presenting statistical analysis and marshaling other kinds of evidence. Hardly any of these data originate with me. At various times I have called upon colleagues for assistance in obtaining hard-to-come-by facts and figures. The following individuals, some of whom I have never met, were most charitable in helping me obtain important material to sustain my argument: Roger Davidson, Denis Steven Rutkus, and Sula Richardson at the Congressional Research Service; Laura Kapnick at CBS News; Dianne Colonitas at Gallup; Teri Luke at A. C. Nielsen Company; and fellow scholars Richard Brody, Michael Baruch Grossman, Susan Webb Hammond, Martha Joynt Kumar, William Lammers, Richard W. Steele, and Jeffrey Tulis.

For the second edition, I'd like to acknowledge the contributions of Joe Foote, who gave me television ratings data he had employed in his fine book, *Television Access and Political Power*; Diane Buono at A. C. Nielsen Company, who updated Foote's series to include President Bush; and Gerald Rafshoon, who in interviews offered telling insights into President Carter's media strategy.

I'm grateful to Conrad, Herblock, and Jim Morin, whose cartoons of President Bush's public strategies are reproduced here. These cartoons aptly— and humorously—demonstrate that going public is a strategy fully appreciated by contemporary editorialists. Finally, students from my presidency class helped classify the public activities of President Bush in order to update the trends in public activities reported in Chapter 4.

Introduction:
Going Public in
Theory and Practice⸻⸻ 1

When President Bush delivered his State of the Union address to the joint assembly of the mostly Democratic Congress in January 1992, he assumed what has become a familiar stance with Congress:

> I pride myself that I am a prudent man, and I believe that patience is a virtue. But I understand that politics is for some a game. . . . I submit my plan tomorrow. And I am asking you to pass it by March 20. And I ask the American people to let you know they want this action by March 20.
> From the day after that, if it must be: The battle is joined.
> And you know when principle is at stake, I relish a good fair fight.

Once upon a time, these might have been fighting words, but in this era of divided government, with the legislative and executive branches controlled by different parties, and presidents who therefore routinely enlist public support in their dealings with other Washington politicians, such rhetoric caused hardly a ripple in Congress.

By 1992, presidential appeals for public support had, in fact, become commonplace. Jimmy Carter delivered four major television addresses on the energy crisis alone and was about to give a fifth when his pollster convinced him that he would be wasting his time. Richard Nixon employed prime-time television so extensively to promote his policies on Vietnam that the Federal Communications Commission (FCC) took an unprecedented step when it applied the "fairness doctrine" to a presidential appeal and granted critics of the war response time on the networks.[1] (In the past, the FCC had occasionally invoked the "equal time" rule during presidential campaigns.) More than any other of Bush's predecessors, Ronald Reagan excelled in rallying public opinion behind presidential policies, but by the end of his second term, he had worn out his welcome with the networks, who stood to lose at least $200,000 in advertising each time he delivered one of his prime-time addresses. They instituted an independent assessment of the likely newsworthiness of the president's address, thereby managing to pare down the frequency of Reagan's televised speeches.[2]

I call the approach to presidential leadership that has lately come into vogue at the White House "going public." It is a strategy whereby a president promotes himself and his policies in Washington by appealing to the American public for support. Forcing compliance from fellow Washingtonians by going over their heads to appeal to their constituents is a tactic not unknown during the first half of the century, but it was seldom attempted. Theodore Roosevelt probably first enunciated the strategic principle of going public when he described the presidency as the "bully pulpit." Moreover, he occasionally put theory into practice with public appeals for his Progressive reforms. During the next 30 years, other presidents also periodically summoned public support to help them in their dealings with Congress. Perhaps the most famous such instance is Woodrow Wilson's ill-fated whistle-stop tour of the country on behalf of his League of Nations treaty. Another historic example is Franklin D. Roosevelt's series of radio "fireside chats," which were designed less to subdue congressional opposition than to remind politicians throughout Washington of his continuing national mandate for the New Deal.

These historical instances are significant in large part because they were rare. Unlike President Nixon, who thought it important "to spread the White House around," [3] these earlier presidents were largely confined to Washington and obliged to speak to the country through the nation's newspapers. The concept and legitimizing precedents of going public may have been established during these years, but the emergence of presidents who *routinely* do so to promote their policies in Washington awaited the development of modern systems of transportation and mass communications. Going public should be appreciated as a strategic adaptation to the information age.

The regularity with which recent presidents have sought public backing for their Washington dealings has altered the way politicians both inside and outside the White House regard the office. The following chapters of this book present numerous instances of presidents preoccupied with public relations, as if these activities chiefly determined their success. Cases are recounted of other Washington politicians intently monitoring the president's popularity ratings and his addresses on television, as if his performance in these realms governed their own behavior. Also examined are testimonials of central institutional figures, such as the Speaker of the House of Representatives, citing the president's prestige and rhetoric as he explains Congress's actions. If the public ruminations of politicians are to be believed, the president's effectiveness in rallying public support has become a primary consideration for those who do business with him.

Presidential Theory

Going public merits study because presidents now appeal to the public routinely. But there is another reason as well. Compared with many other aspects of the modern presidency, going public has received scant attention in the scholarly literature. In part this can be attributed to its recent arrival in the president's repertoire, but by itself this explanation is inadequate. Although going public had not become a keystone of presidential leadership in the 1950s and 1960s when much of the influential scholarship on the subject was written, sufficient precedents were available for scholars to consider its potential for presidential leadership in the future.

Probably the main reason going public has received so little attention in the scholarly literature is its fundamental incompatibility with bargaining. Presidential power is the "power to bargain," as Richard E. Neustadt taught a generation of students of the presidency.[4] When Neustadt gave this theme its most evocative expression in 1960, the "bargaining president" had already become a centerpiece of pluralist theories of American politics. Nearly a decade earlier, Robert A. Dahl and Charles E. Lindblom had described the politician in America generically as "the human embodiment of a bargaining society." They made a special point to include the president in writing that despite his possessing "more hierarchical controls than any other single figure in the government ... like everyone else ... the President must bargain constantly." [5] Since Neustadt's landmark study, other major works in the field have reinforced and elaborated on the concept of the bargaining president.[6]

Going public violates bargaining in several ways. First, it rarely includes the kinds of exchanges necessary, in pluralist theory, for the American political system to function properly. At times, going public will be merely superfluous—fluff compared with the substance of traditional political exchange. Practiced in a dedicated way, however, it can threaten to displace bargaining.

Second, going public fails to extend benefits for compliance, but freely imposes costs for noncompliance. In appealing to the public to "tell your senators and representatives by phone, wire, and Mailgram that the future hangs in balance," the president seeks the aid of a third party—the public—to force other politicians to accept his preferences.[7] If targeted representatives are lucky, the president's success may cost them no more than an opportunity at the bargaining table to shape policy or to extract compensation. If unlucky, they may find themselves both capitulating to the president's wishes and suffering the reproach of constituents for having resisted him in the first place. By imposing costs and failing to offer benefits, going public is more akin to force than to bargaining. Nelson W. Polsby makes this point when he says that members of Congress may "find themselves ill disposed toward a president who prefers to deal indirectly with them [by going public] through what they may interpret as coercion rather than face-to-face in the spirit of mutual accommodation." [8] The following comment of one senator may well sum up commonly felt sentiments, if not the actions, of those on Capitol Hill who find themselves repeatedly pressured by the president's public appeals: "A lot of Democrats, even if they like the

President's proposal, will vote against him because of his radio address on Saturday." [9]

Third, going public entails public posturing. To the extent that it fixes the president's bargaining position, posturing makes subsequent compromise with other politicians more difficult. Because negotiators must be prepared to yield some of their clients' preferences to make a deal, bargaining proverbially proceeds best behind closed doors. Consider the difficulty Ronald Reagan's widely publicized challenge "My tax proposal is a line drawn in dirt" posed for subsequent budget negotiations in Washington.[10] Not only did the declaration threaten to cut away any middle ground on which a compromise might be constructed, it also probably stiffened the resolve of the president's adversaries, some of whom would later be needed to pass the administration's legislative program.

Finally, and possibly most injurious to bargaining, going public undermines the legitimacy of other politicians. It usurps their prerogatives of office, denies their role as representatives, and questions their claim to reflect the interests of their constituents. For a traditional bargaining stance with the president to be restored, these politicians would first have to reestablish parity, probably at a cost of conflict with the White House.[11]

Given these fundamental incompatibilities, one may further speculate that by spoiling the bargaining environment, going public renders the president's future influence ever more dependent upon his ability to generate popular support for himself and his policies. The degree to which a president draws upon public opinion determines the kind of leader he will be.

Presidential Practice

The distinction between bargaining and going public is a theme one hears more and more often from presidents and those who deal with them. No president has enlisted public strategies to better advantage than did Ronald Reagan. Throughout his tenure, he exhibited a full appreciation of bargaining and going public as the modern office's principal strategic alternatives. The following examples from a six-month survey of White House news coverage show how entrenched this bifurcated view of presidential strategy has become. The survey begins in late November 1984, when some members of the administration were pondering how the president might exploit his landslide victory and others were preparing a new round of budget cuts and a tax reform bill for the next Congress.

November 29, 1984. *Washington Post* columnist Lou Cannon reported the following prediction from a White House official: "We're going to have confrontation on spending and consultation on tax reform." The aide explained, "We have somebody to negotiate with us on tax reform, but may not on budget cuts." [12] By "confrontation" he was referring to the president's success in appealing to the public on national television, that is, in going public. By "consultation" he meant bargaining.

January 25, 1985. The above prediction proved accurate two months later when another staffer offered as pristine an evocation of going public as one is likely to find: "We have to look at it, in many ways, like a campaign. He [Reagan] wants to take his case to the people. You have a constituency of 535 legislators as opposed to 100 million voters. But the goal is the same—to get the majority of voters to support your position." [13]

February 10, 1985. In a nationally broadcast radio address, President Reagan extended an olive branch inviting members of Congress to "work with us in the spirit of cooperation and compromise" on the budget. This public statement probably did little to allay the frequently voiced suspicion of House Democratic leaders that such overtures were mainly intended for public consumption. One Reagan aide insisted, however, that the president simply sought to reassure legislators that "he would not 'go over their heads' and campaign across the country for his budget without trying first to reach a compromise." [14] In this statement the aide implicitly concedes the harm public pressure can create for bargaining but seeks to incorporate it advantageously into the strategic thinking of the politicians with whom the administration must deal by not foreswearing its use.

March 9, 1985. After some public sparring, the administration eventually settled down to intensive budget negotiations with the Republican-led Senate Finance Committee. Failing to do as well as he would like, however, Reagan sent a message to his party's senators through repeated unattributed statements to the press that, if necessary, he would "go to the people to carry our message forward." [15] Again, public appeals, though held in reserve, were threatened.

March 11, 1985. In an interview with a *New York Times* correspondent, a senior Reagan aide sized up his president: "He's liberated, he wants to get into a fight, he feels strongly and wants to push his program through himself.... Reagan never quite believed his popularity before the election, never believed the polls. Now he has it, and he's going to push ... ahead with our agenda." [16]

May 16, 1985. To avoid entangling tax reform with budget deliberations in Congress, Reagan, at the request of Republican leaders, delayed unveiling his tax reform proposal until late May. A couple of weeks before Reagan's national television address on the subject, White House aides began priming the press with leaks on the proposal's content and promises that the president would follow it with a public relations blitz. In the words of one White House official, the plan was to force Congress to make a "binary choice between tax reform or no tax reform." [17] The administration rejected bargaining, as predicted nearly six months earlier by a White House aide, apparently for two strategic reasons. First, Reagan feared that in a quietly negotiated process, the tax reform package would unravel under the concerted pressure of the special interests. Second, by taking the high-profile approach of "standing up for the people against the special interests," in the words of one adviser, tax reform might do for Republicans what social security did for Democrats—make them the majority party.[18]

During these six months when bargaining held out promise—as it had during negotiations with the Senate Finance Committee—public appeals were held in reserve. The White House occasionally, however, threatened an appeal in trying to gain more favorable consideration. On other occasions, when opponents of the president's policies appeared capable of extracting major concessions—House Democrats on the budget and interest groups on tax reform, for example—the White House disengaged from negotiation and tried through public relations to force Congress to accept his policies. Although by 1985 news items such as the preceding excerpts seemed unexceptional as daily news, they are a recent phenomenon. One does not routinely find such stories in White House reporting 20 years earlier when, for example, John Kennedy's legislative agenda was stalled in Congress.

Clearly, going public appears to foster political relations that are quite at odds with those traditionally cultivated through bargaining. One may begin to examine this new phenomenon by asking, what is it about modern politics that would inspire presidents to go public in the first place?

Notes

1. Newton N. Minow, John Bartlow Martin, and Lee M. Mitchell, *Presidential Television* (New York: Basic Books, 1973), 84-87.
2. Peter J. Boyer, "Networks Refuse to Broadcast Reagan's Plea," *New York Times,* February 3, 1988.
3. Robert B. Semple, Jr., "Nixon Eludes Newsmen on Coast Trip," *New York Times,* August 3, 1970, 16.
4. Richard E. Neustadt, *Presidential Power* (New York: John Wiley and Sons, 1980).
5. Robert A. Dahl and Charles E. Lindblom, *Politics, Economics, and Welfare* (New York: Harper and Row, 1953), 333.
6. Among them are Aaron Wildavsky, *The Politics of the Budgetary Process* (Boston: Little, Brown, 1964); Graham Allison, *The Essence of Decision* (Boston: Little, Brown, 1971); Hugh Heclo, *The Government of Strangers* (Washington, D.C.: Brookings Institution, 1977); and Nelson W. Polsby, *Consequences of Party Reform* (New York: Oxford University Press, 1983).
7. From Ronald Reagan's address to the nation on his 1986 budget. Jack Nelson, "Reagan Calls for Public Support of Deficit Cuts," *Los Angeles Times,* April 25, 1985, 1.
8. Nelson W. Polsby, "Interest Groups and the Presidency: Trends in Political

Intermediation in America," in *American Politics and Public Policy,* ed. Walter Dean Burnham and Martha Wagner Weinbey (Cambridge: MIT Press, 1978), 52.

9. Hedrick Smith, "Bitterness on Capitol Hill," *New York Times,* April 24, 1985, 14.

10. Ed Magnuson, "A Line Drawn in Dirt," *Time,* February 22, 1982, 12-13.

11. See David S. Broder, "Diary of a Mad Majority Leader," *Washington Post,* December 13, 1981, C1, C5; David S. Broder, "Rostenkowski Knows It's His Turn," *Washington Post National Weekly Edition,* June 10, 1985, 13.

12. Lou Cannon, "Big Spending-Cut Bill Studied," *Washington Post,* November 29, 1984, A8.

13. Bernard Weinraub, "Reagan Sets Tour of Nation to Seek Economic Victory," *New York Times,* January 25, 1985, 43.

14. Bernard Weinraub, "Reagan Calls for 'Spirit of Cooperation' on Budget and Taxes," *New York Times,* February 10, 1985, 32. On Democratic suspicions of Reagan's motives see Hedrick Smith, "O'Neill Reflects Democratic Strategy on Budget Cuts and Tax Revisions," *New York Times,* December 6, 1984, B20; and Margaret Shapiro, "O'Neill's New Honeymoon with Reagan," *Washington Post National Weekly Edition,* February 11, 1985, 12.

15. Jonathan Fuerbringer, "Reagan Critical of Budget View of Senate Panel," *New York Times,* March 9, 1985, 1. Senate Majority Leader Robert Dole told reporters that if the president liked the Senate's final budget package he would campaign for it "very vigorously . . . going to television, whatever he needs to reduce federal spending." Karen Tumulty, "Reagan May Get Draft of Budget Accord Today," *Los Angeles Times,* April 4, 1985, 1.

16. Bernard Weinraub, "In His 2nd Term, He Is Reagan the Liberated," *New York Times,* March 11, 1985, 10.

17. David E. Rosenbaum, "Reagan Approves Primary Elements of Tax Overhaul," *New York Times,* May 16, 1985, 1.

18. Robert W. Merry and David Shribman, "G.O.P. Hopes Tax Bill Will Help It Become Majority Party Again," *Wall Street Journal,* May 23, 1985, 1. See also Rosenbaum, "Reagan Approves Primary Elements of Tax Overhaul," 14. Instances such as those reported here continued into summer. See, for example, Jonathan Fuerbringer, "Key Issues Impede Compromise on Cutting Deficit," *New York Times,* June 23, 1985, 22.

How Washington and Presidents Have Changed _____ 2

The incompatibility of bargaining and going public presents a pressing theoretical question. Why should presidents come to favor a strategy of leadership that appears so incompatible with the principles of pluralist theory? Why, if other Washington elites legitimately and correctly represent the interests of their clients and constituents, would anything be gained by going over their heads? The answers to these questions are several and complex, having to do with the ways Washington and presidents have changed. All in all, bargaining has shown declining efficiency, and opportunities to go public have increased.

Some would account for the rise of going public by resorting to the imperative of technology as an explanation. Certainly, advances in transportation and communications have been indispensable to this process, but they have not been sufficient in themselves to alter political relations in such a contradictory way. Others who have noticed that recent presidents frequently prefer public relations to negotiation with members of Congress blame the presidential selection reforms of the late 1960s and the 1970s. The system of nominating presidential candidates through primaries (along with federal campaign financing) produces presidents with weak ties to core constituent groups within their parties and with little experience in Washington politics. They do, however, have a lot of experience in campaigning. Rather than negotiate with other institutional elites, these presidents are more inclined to pursue the same public strategies that placed them in the White House. Though this explanation has merit, it, too, is insufficient. If presidential selection reforms had simply been grafted onto traditional political arrangements, they might explain the inclination of recent presidents to go public, but they would not account for the success of that strategy. For traditional pluralist explanations of the presidency, Ronald Reagan's 1981 accomplishments—passing major cuts in social programs while cutting taxes and sharply increasing military spending—pose a serious anomaly.

There is another, more fundamental reason for the discrepancy between theory and current practice. Presidents have preferred to go public in recent years perhaps because the strategy offers a better prospect of success than it did in the past. Politicians in Washington may no longer be as tractable to bargaining as they once were. We are in an era of divided government, with Democrats in control of Congress and Republicans holding the presidency. Each side frequently finds political advantage in frustrating the other. On such occasions, posturing in preparation for the next election takes precedence over bargaining.

The decoupling of voters from political parties across the nation, which makes possible the occurrence of divided government, has also had more pervasive consequences for political relations among politicians in Washington. Weaker leaders, looser coalitions, more individualistic politicians, and stronger public pressure are among the developments reworking political relations in Washington that may inspire presidents to embrace a strategy of leadership antithetical to that prescribed by theory.

Institutionalized Pluralism: The Bargaining Community

In the early 1950s Dahl and Lindblom developed a theoretical rationale for America's particular brand of pluralism. In *Politics, Economics, and Welfare* they helped establish a framework for the study of American politics that would guide scholars for the next generation. They described the practice of politics in such a way as to make the appearance of a bargaining president inevitable.

> The politician is, above all, the man whose career depends upon the successful negotiation of bargains. To win office he must negotiate electoral alliances. To satisfy his electoral alliance he must negotiate alliances with other legislators and with administrators, for his control depends upon negotiation. Most of his time is consumed in bargaining. This is the skill he cultivates; it is the skill that distinguishes the master-politician from the political failure.[1]

For what structure of politics is bargaining ideally suited? It is one in which political elites, and for the most part only elites, matter. The citizenry is offered limited and occasional avenues of participation—through periodic elections and membership in such mediating associations as unions, voluntary societies, and churches. Politics need to be structured this way so that elites retain the flexibility to bargain and the certainty that once an accord is reached it will not be undone. The citizenry's interests are not ignored, however. Partitioned geographically, citizens participate vicariously through their elected representatives; partitioned functionally, they participate through interest groups and the agencies for whom they are clients.

In this pluralistic system each politician must be reckoned with not only according to the strength of his or her constituency but also according to the institutional resources provided by his or her office. Through intensive constitutionalism, the Founding Fathers sought to mitigate the plebiscitary tendency of democracy by giving officeholders legitimacy apart from their representative role. They succeeded and bestowed on Washington what has evolved into the pronounced institutional character of its politics.

In the absence of some overriding criterion, such as party fidelity, authority within institutions is generally distributed by seniority. Everywhere, senior partners matter more than junior partners, and transients for whom Washington is a way station to some private career count for little. These, in Hugh Heclo's words, are "the low credit risk in a high credit market." [2] From time to time some politicians will graduate to new roles as seniority rules are triggered to fill vacancies at the top. Others will try to rise to higher office by expanding their electoral constituency. Some of these, inevitably, will be defeated, along with others who merely sought reelection. And many of those forced off the career ladder will elect to leave Washington altogether.

Elections may be commended by democratic theory, but from the local vantage of a bargaining society they mostly pose disruptions. By generating turnover, they raise uncertainty for bargaining. A politician at risk in the next election will have greater interest in receiving credit than in extending it. But recognizing his precarious existence, his potential trading partners may see themselves giving something for nothing. This leaves, of course, little common ground for transacting business. Beyond this, campaigns and elections are unwanted distractions from the real business of politicians in Washington. Under the pressure of reelection, some community members may be tempted to hector or to make excessive demands of unaccommodating bargaining partners, or otherwise to behave in ways that make future negotiation and compromise more difficult.

The same disruptive tendencies are true of public opinion more generally. To function smoothly, a bargaining society must insulate itself against short-term swings in popular sentiment. Appreciating this, the Founding Fathers minimized the influence of the citizenry through staggered elections, which would require that "public passions" be sustained for a long time before they could influence the policies of each branch of government. And by differentiating constituencies into states and by delegating to these subdivisions specific constitutional prerogatives, they sought to give minorities a sufficient toehold to resist short-lived majorities.

A Washington ideally suited for bargaining should therefore be a stable and a somewhat insular community in which even a new president may be viewed as an interloper. It must be this way if the circumscribed avenues of mutual adjustment through negotiation are to work effectively. The system also needs to be this way to accommodate the local political economy. Negotiation occurs within a market where dissimilar goods and services are bartered. Identifying mutually attractive exchanges takes time, and once a transaction is opened it may not be consummated immediately. Indebtedness is commonplace; unspecified IOUs may not be called in for years.

I call this system "institutionalized pluralism" for several reasons. First, political exchange occurs within a dense institutional milieu that allocates resources among actors and identifies the relevant bargaining partners. Second, a stable bargaining society may be expected to institutionalize informal rules of the marketplace that regulate behavior and reduce uncertainty. Perhaps the most sacred commandment is "Honor one's commitments." Variants of this are tailored to each role. To the lobbyist it means never lie by knowingly giving legislators incorrect information on which they may base a vote or seek to persuade others. For the correspondent it means never publish material provided off the record or directly attribute background information to the source. Playing it straight with one's colleagues does not require that a participant reveal true preferences at the bargaining table, but it does require that once a bargain is agreed to, the politician strive to fulfill his or her part of it.

Another commandment is "Don't use force," for the simple reason that force usually will not work. Dahl and Lindblom noted, "The politician does not often give orders. He can rarely employ unilateral controls. Even as a chief executive or a cabinet officer he soon discovers that his control depends upon his skill in bargaining." [3] Even if politicians or bureaucrats enjoy hierarchical superiority over another or in some other way could unilaterally preempt another's choice, they should hesitate to use this advantage. That force begets counterforce is a law of political physics. A politician may be able to avoid compensation one day, but he cannot ensure himself against retribution the next.

Besides, collectively, a politician's peers in Washington have efficient ways of judging and punishing individuals who violate trust or fail to honor the standards of mutual accommodation. Each politician carries a reputation, a continuously updated record of all the qualities that are relevant to others as they contemplate doing business with him or her. Senator A may double-cross Senator B, but in doing so, he or she may be sure that some community members are watching and still others will soon learn about it. Depending upon the seriousness of the violation, concerted sanctions might be applied. Collective enforcement of community norms will generally be unnecessary, however. Other actors' pursuit of simple self-interest will suffice. The violator will naturally suffer ostracism proportionate to his or her transgression. What other senators, for instance, would be cheerfully willing to work with Senator A? If they were willing to deal with Senator A at all, it would be on their terms and with the requirement that his or her end of the bargain must first be fulfilled.

The local culture may also contain a variety of functional folkways and mores that restrain contravention of tacit rules. One such venerable understanding allows senators and representatives when back home to rail against Congress, the other party, and its leadership as much as they feel necessary to satisfy appetites of constituents; but in Washington, such displays are inappropriate. Having been exposed only to public rhetoric before arriving in Washington as a freshman in the 1950s, Clem Miller marveled at the "cocoon of good feeling" that enveloped Congress.[4]

Reciprocity is so vital to a bargaining society that it is deeply ingrained in the normative order. Writing about the Senate of the mid-1950s, Donald R. Matthews observed, "It is not an exaggeration to say that reciprocity is a way of life in the Senate." As a senator's administrative assistant told him, "My boss ... will—if it doesn't mean anything to him—do a favor for any other Senator. It doesn't matter *who* he is. It's not a matter of friendship, it's just a matter of I won't be an S.O.B. if you won't be one." [5]

Trust and fellow-feeling will at times give rise to more focused and ambitious reciprocity arrangements. Whether because of shared goals or complementary resources or both, two politicians may come to recognize the mutual gain possible through a continuing relationship. The bargain may never be explicitly stated, much less negotiated, and no ledger of indebtedness kept. Instead, a simple understanding to work together exists until one party decides the relationship is too costly and ends it. Bargains in the form of relationships occur most naturally among proximate participants who share interests—among congressional committee members, for instance, or between an agency head and the representative of a clientele group the agency serves. The time-honored practice of "cue giving" between pairs of like-minded members of Congress during floor voting is a minor instance of this.

Protocoalitions

The president is doubtless the bargaining community's most prominent member. But even the consummate bargainer in this high office can participate in only a small fraction of the transactions that must occur daily in Washington to form governing coalitions. Exchange is thus a necessary and ubiquitous activity of Washington elites. It does not, however, proceed randomly.

Institutionalized pluralism promotes a two-tiered process of coalition building. The higher-level, presidential coalition can be distinguished by its greater size, the diversity of its membership, the specificity of its goals, and its fragility. Presidential coalitions are usually temporary associations, forming and dissolving around a single issue or bill. Arrived at in an ad hoc fashion, they rarely survive the resolution of the issue in question.

The building of lower-level coalitions, or protocoalitions, follows predictable lines by adhering to a couple of political principles. First, it spans the constitutionally mandated policy course from enactment to implementation. Because institutional barriers confine communication, exchange proceeds more easily and commonly within rather than between organizations.[6] Well-known examples of protocoalitions are Senate Majority Leader Lyndon Johnson's Democratic troops, Wilbur Mills's Ways and Means Committee, the Justice Department's civil rights lawyers under Nixon, even Eisenhower's military-industrial complex, if there was such a thing. Second, those building protocoalitions seek out mutual needs and complementary resources. The proverbial "iron triangles" among agencies, clienteles, and congressional committees are so called because they follow the policy course, spanning institutional boundaries as they do so and incorporating dissimilar yet compatible partners. These dense networks of political exchange form the subcommunities of institutionalized pluralism.

Many protocoalitions may be ad hoc and short lived, but those that matter most tend to be constructed more coherently and durably. They arise not from some fleeting issue but from kindred interest or the continuing need of proximate participants to work together. For example, the agency heads in the Department of Agriculture, subcommittee members of the House and Senate Agriculture committees, and the Washington representatives of the numerous farm groups must cooperate if they are to satisfy the interests of their common client—America's farmers. Rarely are these entities self-sufficient. Iron triangles notwithstanding, a protocoalition typically must join with others if its bill is to be passed or its policy implemented effectively. Leaders of protocoalitions arise if for no other reason than to conduct these external relations.

Activities and transactions among these groups may be far more consequential for the president's own success than any business he might conduct with them directly. Limits on his time, energy, and resources may prevent a president from intruding even when he recognizes the damage their transactions may have on his own designs. More often than not, the president must look on as an interested bystander. These protocoalitions define his options; they may prescribe particular combinations of coalition partners; they may even dictate the substance of exchange. Once the protocoalition pacts are concluded, they come to the president as givens from which he will try to stitch together a larger, more institutionally expansive coalition.

The President's Place in Institutionalized Pluralism

Constructing coalitions across the broad institutional landscape of Congress, the bureaucracy, interest groups, courts, and state governments requires a politician who possesses a panoramic view and commands the resources necessary to engage the disparate parochial interests of Washington's political elites. Only the president enjoys such vantage and resources. Traditional presidential scholarship leaves little doubt as to how they should be employed. Nowhere has Dahl and Lindblom's framework of the bargaining society been more forcefully employed than in Richard E. Neustadt's classic *Presidential Power*, published in 1960. Neustadt observes,

> Status and authority yield bargaining advantages. But in a government of "separated institutions sharing powers," they yield them to all sides. With the array of vantage points at his disposal, a President may be far more persuasive than his logic or his charm could make him. But outcomes are

not guaranteed by his advantages. There remain the counter pressures those whom he would influence can bring to bear on him from vantage points at their disposal. Command has limited utility; persuasion becomes give-and-take. . . .

The President's advantages are checked by the advantages of others. Continuing relationships will pull in both directions. These are relationships of mutual dependence. A President depends upon the men he would persuade; he has to reckon with his need or fear of them. They too will possess status, or authority, or both, else they would be of little use to him. Their vantage points confront his own; their power tempers his.[7]

Bargaining is thus the essence of presidential leadership, and pluralist theory explicitly rejects unilateral forms of influence as usually insufficient and ultimately costly. The ideal president is one who seizes the center of the Washington bazaar and actively barters with fellow politicians to build winning coalitions. He must do so, according to this theory, or he will forfeit any claim to leadership.

A president has the potential for symbiosis. Protocoalitions provide him with economy: he need not engage every coalition partner; talking to their leaders will do. In return the president provides protocoalitions with much needed coordination although, as Neustadt points out, presidential activity guarantees no more than that the president will be a "clerk." Clearly, however, institutionalized pluralism offers the virtuoso bargainer in the White House the opportunity for real leadership.

For years critics complained that autocratic committee chairmen, indifferent party leaders, and the conservative coalition of Republicans and Southern Democrats prevented Democratic presidents from achieving their ambitious policy goals. Yet institutionalized pluralism requires the president to keep company with these "obstacles" if he is to succeed. Leaders of lower-level coalitions may extract a steep price for cooperation, and at times they may defeat him outright. Still, as difficult as a Lyndon Johnson, a Wilbur Mills, a Wilbur Cohen at Social Security, or a J. Edgar Hoover might have been when he got his back up, each was indispensable as a trading partner. The reason is not difficult to see. Consider what these men had to offer: a majority leader who could strike a deal with the president on compromise legislation and then return to the chamber floor and deliver the critical votes necessary for its passage; a committee chairman who spoke so authoritatively for his committee that its markup sessions were spent detailing the language of an agreement reached earlier; or an agency head who, once persuaded, effectively redirected his organization's activities. A president simply has insufficient authority to command his way to success and insufficient time and energy to negotiate individually with everyone whose cooperation he needs.[8]

Bargaining Techniques

Perhaps the best way to specify more concretely how presidents behave under institutionalized pluralism is to list some of the things they have traditionally done when they have run into trouble with Congress. The doors of the Oval Office would fling open and scores of representatives and senators—some reluctantly, others with shopping lists in hand—would traipse through to hear the president's case. When large blocks of votes needed to be shifted, compromise positions were readied by White House aides with an eye toward giving the president the margin of victory at the least expense. As the vote date neared and the requisite number of converts shrank, fence-sitters would be singled out for special treatment. Outstanding IOUs would be called in and fresh ones tendered as the president courted ambivalent legislators with promises of goods and services for their constituencies.

These and many of the other tactics traditionally part of the presidential repertoire are essentially private transactions among elite negotiators. Beyond understanding the character of the game, the president must also sense the needs of the potential partners in the coalition and discover the most cost-effective exchange. What constitutes the "right stuff" for bargaining presidents has been a frequent subject of rich description. Douglass Cater's offering is typical:

> A President has to have an acute awareness of the resistances that exist to any step he takes. The elements of his essential knowledge can be picayune: that he must communicate with a certain committee chairman in the mornings because he is too drunk by afternoon—any afternoon—to be coherent; that a certain bureaucrat is so buttressed by interest-group support that he can regularly defy the occupant of the White House, Democrat or Republican; that a certain issue has grown so mired in lobbyist intrigue that it is irredeemable. If he is to be any good, a President must have a mental catalogue of the movers and shakers in the Washington community, their habits and habitats. He needs to know the crotchets of M. De Gaulle of France, Mr. Meany of AFL-CIO, Mr. Reston of the *New York Times,* and many, many others.[9]

Subtlety and fine tuning in bargaining are vital to conserve resources in such situations. The president's bargaining chips are limited, but demand for their expenditure is insatiable.

No president has understood the requirements of institutionalized pluralism better than Franklin Roosevelt. Occasionally there were lapses, but usually the congruence between the actions expected and Roosevelt's practice was remarkable—so much so that at times the model of the bargaining president appears to be little more than a generalization of Roosevelt's style. In his actions alone, every aspect of bargaining can be illustrated. I shall resist the temptation to add to the already voluminous Roosevelt hagiography, but not before considering an example of the paragon at work. In a memo dated September 16, 1941, Roosevelt instructs his aide Marvin McIntyre in the art of grooming congressmen:

> I have been disturbed about things I am hearing very frequently about "the Hill." You have probably heard the same. A large number of Senators and Congressmen, who should be and usually are our friends, have been saying

entirely too frequently that they get no cooperation from the White House; that no one in the White House will talk to them unless we want their votes. A new refrain is that the only way to get attention from the Administration is to vote against it a few times.

I do not think there is too much basis for these complaints. As you well know, a large portion of the favors they ask for we cannot give them. But I do think we should create a medium for them to register their complaints—and I want you to do that job.

I certainly do not mean that you should be a liaison man with the Hill. . . . But you should be the man in the White House whom Senators and Congressmen can talk to. It does not matter so much that they don't get what they want. If they can tell their colleagues and friends "I told Marvin McIntyre at the White House so and so" that will be a psychological advantage. If they can also say "Marvin McIntyre told me so and so", they will soon have a feeling their advice is being listened to.

I think the way to get this started is to do it in a very casual manner. If you could start telephoning two or three of your Congressional friends a day just to ask how they are and what they know, word will soon get around that Marvin McIntyre will listen to them. In a few weeks or so, the casual phone calls will soon develop into an iron-clad system. [Emphasis in original.][10]

The moral of Roosevelt's instruction to his aide was that the president's success rests upon satisfying others' needs.

Public Opinion and Institutionalized Pluralism

Public pressure has little place in the community I have described. To be effective it would generally need either to emanate from a dominant economic interest of the constituency or client, such as the tobacco industry in North Carolina, or to be an otherwise pervasive and strongly held value, such as anti-gun control sentiments among hunters in Montana. Presumably, representatives who know their districts, or agency heads or lobbyists who understand their clients, will represent the values of the constituency, thereby making grass-roots expression redundant. Writing about the Senate of the 1940s and 1950s, William S. White asserted, "Constituent pressure . . . is rarely the *cause* of any Senator's action." White recalled a conversation with Senator Theodore Francis Green of Rhode Island, who was at the time receiving hate mail from some of his state's McCarthyites. Pointing to "shoals of postcards," White asked, " 'What about all these, Senator?' 'Old disgusting little things, aren't they?' he said in a bored fastidious drawl, using the very end of his fingernail to flick his communications into the wastebasket. That closed the subject with him." [11]

Of interest group tactics during the same period, David Truman observed, "Skillful interest groups . . . make limited use of letters, telegrams, and petitions," and cited comments in a trade association publication that one or two personal contacts were "of far greater value than a hundred letters or telegrams from persons unknown to the legislator." [12]

Given such conditions, a president who goes public would only undercut the abilities of other Washington elites to act as representatives—and these are people with whom he must deal. Moreover, to the degree that the community is insulated, the strategy would not work. In denying elites their place at the bargaining table, the mobilization of public opinion becomes little more than an abrasive. One can see this in a 1944 survey of members of Congress that found them by and large resentful of the Roosevelt administration's occasional use of public opinion polls to buttress its case before Congress. One midwesterner responded, "A poll is supposed to represent the people; the Congressman represents them; he should know what the people think." He added, "Polls are in contradiction to representative government." Others interviewed concurred that polls were injurious.[13] Mobilizing public opinion might succeed occasionally, but in a setting of institutionalized pluralism, where reciprocity is normative and memory long, its regular use as a strategic device can sow only ill will and ultimately reap failure.

Public Opinion and Bargaining Presidents

Not all the tactics and resources available to bargaining presidents are private. Among Washington's political elites, the president is, after all, the only one chosen by the national electorate. Even some nineteenth-century presidents—the manufactured products of political machines who delivered their State of the Union messages to Congress via courier—found occasions between elections to solicit popular support.

Going public is sufficiently well precedented that statements of the pluralist theory of presidential leadership must take it into account. According to this view, however, if public pressure is to be applied, it must be insinuated into the bargaining process. Timely leaks of information—as age-old as they appear modern—have long made the president's bargaining posture more defensible to those outside Washington and hence more formidable to those inside. Trial balloons floated by presidents or their associates have also been a favorite technique to test the political winds before embarking on a new policy course. More direct public pressure has at times taken the form of personal overtures to sympathetic constituencies and organizations to voice their grievances to their representatives who would deny the president's policies. But in pluralist theory each of these public tactics is appropriate for the bargaining president only to the degree that it helps clarify the stakes and heighten others' appreciation of the need to bargain with him.

Consistent with the dictates of institutionalized pluralism, bargaining presidents of an earlier era rarely relied upon public strategies. With some, this shows up in their skepticism toward public opinion surveys. Harry Truman stated flatly, "I never paid any attention to the polls myself," arguing that they "did not represent facts but mere speculation."[14] Franklin Roosevelt, a president with a stronger public mandate to draw upon, showed more interest in surveys. Before scientific surveys were available, Roosevelt's staff monitored public opinion as best it could in other ways. The White House mail was continuously tallied, and the editorial stances of the nation's newspapers were routinely reported to Roosevelt in summary form.[15] Sometimes Roosevelt more actively sought out such information, as in late 1936 when he asked each state director of the National Emergency Council to assess public opinion toward an announced reallocation of jobs under the Works Progress Administration. The results of this canvass are displayed in Table 2-1. That the directors' reading of public opinion strongly correlated with the editorial positions of local papers is evidence of the poor state of knowledge about public opinion in the presurvey era.

After polling came into vogue, the Roosevelt administration occasionally commissioned official surveys. Except at elections, the president was usually more concerned with the views of specific publics who might be adversely affected by his policies than with any summary of national opinion.[16] According to Richard W. Steele,

> He saw public attitudes not as a mandate for initiatives generated outside the White House, but as potential obstacles to courses he had already decided upon. Since the President's interest in the public's views stemmed largely from his concern for preserving or strengthening Administration power, the information he sought was issue oriented, and especially attuned to the attitudes of those Americans whose opinions were most intense, and usually most negative, toward a given policy. Thus midwesterners came in for special attention in regard to their attitudes toward intervention; mothers, and women in general, concerning draft extension; farmers in regard to farm policy; Poles and Catholics in regard to relations with Russia, and so forth. This also helps explain Roosevelt's strong interest in the generally hostile views of the press and the business community. *The opposition of these publics could encourage obstructionism in Congress.... If the President could get by these formidable groups without generating excessive criticism, he had a good chance of success....* Roosevelt's conception of the public's role tended to focus his attention on the opinions of the powerful and hostile. [Emphasis added.][17]

President Roosevelt occasionally went public to improve his position in Washington. Before World War II he delivered fireside chats directing public attention to his legislative agenda. Only once, however, did he succumb to the temptation to exhort the citizenry to pressure Congress. Using the ages of current Supreme Court members as an excuse, Roosevelt tried in 1937 to increase their number by six. This instance, the "court packing" proposal of 1937, ended in a fiasco.[18] Compared with today's presidents, Roosevelt enlisted public strategies sparingly. His game remained in Washington. His interest in public opinion was motivated by a need to anticipate and, when possible, to neutralize the representatives of interested publics who might oppose his programs.

Nowhere is the value of public opinion to a bargaining president more systematically explored than in Neustadt's study of presidential power. On the importance of public prestige, he writes:

Table 2-1   Presidential Survey of Public Opinion on Reallocation of Jobs under the Works Progress Administration, 1936

States	Actual curtailment to Dec. 15, 1936[1] (%)	Possible further reductions for Jan., Feb., Mar. 1937[1] (%)	Reaction of Workers	Reaction of Public	Reaction of Press
Ala.	0	5	none	none	none
Ariz.	13	20	none	none	none
Ark.	8	0	none	favorable	favorable
Calif.	1	0	unfavorable	none	none
Colo.	20	14	unfavorable	none	favorable
Conn.	8	0	unfavorable	favorable	favorable
Fla.	2.25	10.6	none	favorable	none
Ga.	6.4	5	unfavorable	favorable	favorable
Idaho	0	0	unfavorable	none	favorable
Ill.	0	0	unfavorable	none	none
Ind.	5	0	unfavorable	unfavorable	none
Iowa	6	0	unfavorable	unfavorable	unfavorable
Kan.	10	0	unfavorable	unfavorable	unfavorable
Ky.	0	0	none	none	none
La.	7	0	none	none	none
Maine	0	0	favorable	favorable	favorable
Md.	8	0	unfavorable	none	none
Mass.	0	7	unfavorable	favorable	favorable
Mich.	9	0	unfavorable	favorable	favorable
Minn.	7	0	unfavorable	50-50	favorable
Miss.	9.04	6.9	unfavorable	favorable	favorable
Mo.	3	0	none	none	none
Mont.	20	0	unfavorable	unfavorable	unfavorable
Neb.	10	0	unfavorable	unfavorable	unfavorable
Nev.	0	0	none	none	none
N.H.	0	0	unfavorable	unfavorable	unfavorable
N.J.	4	0	unfavorable	favorable	favorable
N.M.	7.9	9.4	none	none	none
N.Y.	5.5	0	unfavorable	50-50	50-50
N.C.	0	12	none	favorable	favorable
N.D.	0	0	unfavorable	unfavorable	unfavorable
Ohio	8	0	unfavorable	none	none
Okla.	0	0	unfavorable	none	none
Ore.	0	0	none	none	none
Pa.	10	0	unfavorable	unfavorable	unfavorable
R.I.	5.4	0	unfavorable	favorable	favorable
S.C.	3	4	unfavorable	unfavorable	unfavorable
S.D.	49.5	0	unfavorable	unfavorable	unfavorable
Tenn.	13	0	unfavorable	none	none
Texas	1.9	2.8	unfavorable	favorable	favorable
Utah	10.3	0	unfavorable	none	none
Vt.	15	0	unfavorable	none	none
Va.	0	10	none	none	none
Wash.	0	0	none	none	none
W.Va.	1	7	none	none	none
Wis.	0	10	none	none	none
Wyo.	0	0	unfavorable	none	none

[1] Based on employment as of September 1, 1936.

SOURCE: Franklin D. Roosevelt Personal Collection, National Emergency Council box, Franklin Delano Roosevelt Library, Hyde Park, New York.

> The Washingtonians who watch a President ... have to think about his standing with the public outside of Washington. They have to gauge his popular prestige. Because they think about it, public standing is a source of influence for him, another factor bearing upon their willingness to give him what he wants.
>
> It works on power just as reputation does through the mechanism of anticipated reactions ... they anticipate reactions from the public. Most members of the Washington community depend upon outsiders to support them or their interests. The dependence may be as direct as votes, or it may be as indirect as passive toleration. Dependent men must take account of popular reaction to *their* actions. What their publics may think of them becomes a factor, therefore, in deciding how to deal with the desires of a President. His prestige enters into that decision; their publics are part of his. Their view from inside Washington of how outsiders view him thus affects their influence with them.[19]

Elsewhere Neustadt argues that presidents must husband their prestige just as they would their reputation and bargaining chips. Still, politics remains the exclusive domain of Washingtonians. Public opinion never does more than passively color the bargaining context. Within this intentionally confined role for public opinion, Neustadt concedes only that strong popular support purchases the president some leeway in his dealings with other elites.

Moreover, he does not consider that the president might abandon negotiation (or even threaten to) and take his case directly to the American people. But if Washington politicians are dependent on public opinion and so sensitive to a popular president's standing that some may recoil at being identified as his adversary, why should they not be all the more accommodating when the president summons public opinion to his side? If, as Neustadt suggests, elections allow the president's prestige to be insinuated into the bargaining society, why do they not also open the community to the president's active solicitation of popular support?

Neustadt offers two reasons. First, the public is normally inattentive. Only when events and conditions press upon the nation and the welfare of citizens does the president win an audience.[20] (Washington's insulation from short-term swings in public opinion is thus complemented by the country's inattention to elite relations.) Second, as a substitute for bargaining, going public amounts to little more than the application of force and necessarily violates the interdependence and reciprocity that make bargaining possible. It assumes a status akin to "command"—Neustadt's term for the unilateral application of authority—which he argues is usually costly and indicates previous failure to achieve one's goal through persuasion.[21]

Two Early Cases of Going Public

Dramatic, even heroic, instances of going public have tended historically to occur against a backdrop of prior failure. Consider briefly what are perhaps the two outstanding twentieth-century instances when presidents have gone public to pressure Congress.

The first is President Woodrow Wilson's attempt to force Senate ratification of his version of the League of Nations Treaty. Unwilling to accept any of the reservations to the treaty being promulgated by Republican Majority Leader Henry Cabot Lodge and a Foreign Relations Committee stacked with "irreconcilables and strong reservationists," President Wilson decided as "a last resort" to abandon Washington and take his case to the American public.[22] His travel schedule would have been grueling even for a healthy man, which Wilson was not. The trip began on September 3, 1919, and ended with his stroke on October 3. During the month he logged in over 8,000 miles, made 37 speeches, and endured countless hand-shaking gatherings. For all of his "resolve to overpower his opposition," his effort won him no new support in Washington, and by most accounts it stiffened opposition.[23] Going public broke Wilson politically as well as physically.

A second instance, though it too began in adversity, yielded a far different outcome. The Truman Doctrine speech is widely credited not only with securing President Truman his emergency aid legislation for Greece and Turkey but also with laying the groundwork for the more comprehensive Marshall Plan that shortly followed. In this instance the public appeal rested not on a prior failure of bargaining but on its remote chance of success before an isolationist, Republican-dominated Congress. Seeking counsel from Republican Senate leader Arthur Vandenberg, Truman reportedly was advised that he would first have to "scare hell out of the country" if he hoped to persuade Congress to pass his emergency aid program.[24]

Describing the new world order as comprising the forces of freedom on one side and those of totalitarianism on the other, the statement President Truman delivered to the joint session of Congress on March 12, 1947, was plainly hortatory.[25] Congress responded with an enthusiastic standing ovation. Although the ripples of elite and public opinion that followed over the next several weeks were less than uniformly supportive, it soon became apparent that most of the public and Congress were lining up behind the president's program. By early summer Truman's proposals for Greece and Turkey had become U.S. policy, and the more comprehensive Marshall Plan was headed toward enactment.

These two instances of going public differ in a way that helps to explain their dissimilar results. President Wilson sought through public pressure to force the Senate to accept his version of the League. Wilson's form of going public has become a familiar modern activity for which there are few historical examples. President Truman's effort was less confrontational. Only after conferring with congressional leaders and being warned to take a strong public stance did he begin to draft his address. President Truman and those members of Congress who counseled him perhaps foresaw potential opposition in the country that could be preempted only by an appeal that would generate a more favorable climate of public opinion. The speech identified no individuals or blocs of politicians in Washington as opponents. In strategic terms Truman's act of going public was part of a larger bargain in which he agreed to try to make this internationalist posture more palatable to the country and to shoulder responsibility for any adverse reactions in return for support from members of Congress who were rarely his allies. Wilson failed miserably; Truman succeeded brilliantly. Both men's standing in history has been heavily influenced by their performance in going public.

However much they differ, these two cases do share an important feature. In both instances negotiation alone had or would have failed. Historically, public strategies have been employed after other avenues proved insufficient. This still may be true.

The reciprocity of exchange and the complementarity of tasks between presidents and protocoalitions—especially when the latter equitably represents the interests of the nation—render institutionalized pluralism the look of a finely regulated clock. The synchronization of such a system of cogs and escapements would gratify those Newtonian mechanics whom we call our Founding Fathers. Of course, the American political system has never really achieved such clockwork performance. At best the model of institutionalized pluralism offers a rough approximation of reality, making recognizable some of its less obvious features. According to most students of American politics and not a few politicians, however, it illuminates even less about American politics today than at any time during the past half century. A consensus is emerging that at both levels—protocoalitional and presidential—leadership based on reciprocity and negotiation is in increasingly short supply.

Individualized Pluralism: The Emerging Community

If institutionalized pluralism depicts a society whose members are bound together by calculated fealty to a network of protocoalitions and a dense normative system for which bargaining is the prescribed behavior, for what kind of political community should going public be an appropriate strategy? It is one constituted of independent members who have few group or institutional loyalties and who are generally less interested in sacrificing short-run, private career goals for the longer-term benefits of bargaining. Social pluralism and institutional fragmentation guarantee that exchange will remain a ubiquitous activity, but egocentric traders will rarely subscribe to the kinds of commitments and tacit understandings that allow bargains to assume the form of relationships. Instead, these politicians will generally prefer immediate, explicit, and tangible exchanges.

A protocoalition's success in securing its members' collective interest is a function of its internal integration. When members agree on goals, or at least are prepared to subordinate their private interests, when they adhere to reciprocity agreements and endure personal apprenticeship, and when they invest in their leaders the authority and flexibility to negotiate with other leaders, the protocoalition achieves the internal coherence that makes it both a formidable and yet an attractive trading partner to others in Washington.

Conversely, protocoalitions containing egocentric members will suffer internally and will be less able to secure collective goals in the marketplace.

Weak protocoalitions reinforce the propensity of members toward independence. Unsustained by collective rewards, members must resort to their own devices to find their political fortunes. Unfettered by the commitments strong protocoalitions require, members are free to pursue private career goals. Because it is both burden and freedom, self-reliance creates uncertainty, which prompts many politicians to assume a continuous campaign footing. They spend proportionately more time cultivating clients and constituents than they do cementing relations with their Washington colleagues. Governing and campaigning lose their distinctiveness. This is as true for the ongoing polling and communications activities of the White House as it is for the same activities in a freshman representative's office. The result of this pervasive free agency is a more erratic community—one less well regulated by its internal mechanisms of exchange and less shock resistant to short-term perturbations of public opinion.

How might so different a system of political relations come to replace institutionalized pluralism? One can think of many possible reasons, any of them potentially sufficient and all of them probably true, which ensuing chapters will analyze as the appropriate data are introduced. For now, I will simply state the possible causes for the rise of individualized pluralism. First, the growth of the modern welfare state has both increased the size of the community and created large, interested constituencies outside of Washington. Second, modern communications and transportation have brought Washington prominently to the attention of the nation so that over-the-shoulder inspection by constituents and clients can easily contaminate the transactions of politicians. Third, and perhaps most important, the decay of institutionalized pluralism has been abetted by the decline of political parties in the country and in Washington. This decline has meant the erosion of affinity relations among political elites within and across institutions that made exchange easier and occasionally unnecessary.

Each of these possible causes has created opportunities for those in Washington to be more independent. How precisely they have affected strategic behavior will differ from one office to the next, but the expansion of federal services, the ability to send, as well as the probability of receiving, messages to and from targeted constituencies, and the fading of party feeling have thoroughly altered the way Washington politicians view their own and others' political options.[26] Nowhere should such self-awareness be more acute than in the White House.

For a president seeking to construct broad-based coalitions, the implications of individualized pluralism are profound. From his vantage, the leveled political topography offers fewer clues about where precisely his efforts at coalition building should begin. Instead of a subcommunity of leaders with solid reputations and convertible credits, the president finds himself surrounded by a larger number of weaker leaders who titularly preside over shaky protocoalitions. It is not that these people are uninterested in trading. To the contrary, success with the president should help them secure their position with their colleagues. The problem is that in the absence of local hierarchies where a few members authoritatively represent many others, the president quickly discovers that he needs to trade with many more participants, unsure as he does so which will or even can deliver on their promises. It is an unmanageable prospect, one that guarantees overload and multiplies the chances of failure. What is Neustadt's bargaining president to do in such a setting? It is conundrum without solution.

A president who feels effective in going public, however, will find frequent opportunities for leadership in a Washington of free agency and emaciated protocoalitions. The sensitivity of self-reliant politicians to public opinion is their vulnerability and the key to his influence. By campaigning around the country, the president can create uncertainty for them while offering refuge in their support for his policies. By giving up bargaining with individuals and instead working with politicians' preferences *en masse,* a president achieves comparative economy.

From Institutionalized to Individualized Pluralism

A change from institutionalized to individualized pluralism appears to be occurring rapidly on every front from the takeover of bureaucracies by issue specialists to the loss of leadership in Congress.[27] Appropriately, the causes are compound, some general, like those described above, and others specific to the institution. Articles and books on the subject, often carrying worried if not apocalyptic overtones, proliferate from think tanks and commercial presses. One is hard pressed to identify a recent development in Washington that someone has not credited with contributing to the decay of institutionalized pluralism. They may all be correct.

An anthology suggestively entitled *The New Congress*[28] examines several such developments, showing how pervasive the phenomenon is. Throughout the book, the case mounts against the hegemony of institutionalized pluralism. Thomas Mann singles out the heightened career concerns of members of Congress: "The forces fueling the individualistic tone of the present-day Congress remain strong.... Senators and representatives are in business for themselves." As a consequence, "they all are likely to view themselves first and foremost as individuals, not as members of a party or as part of a president's team." [29]

In the next contribution Michael Robinson offers a reason: "Compared with the class of 1958, the class of 1978 was three times more likely to make heavy use of the congressional recording studio, three times more likely to regard the House TV system as 'very useful,' three times more likely to have relied 'a lot' on TV in the last election." From these findings Robinson concludes that "although these figures pertain to campaign style more than legislative character, one may infer that the increasingly greater reliance on the media for nomination, election, status in the Congress, and reelection is one sign of a new congressional character—one more dynamic, egocentric, immoderate, and, perhaps, intemperate." [30] In short, many members of Congress today are themselves successfully going public.

Robinson's use of the class of 1958 nicely complements Douglass Cater's earlier observations. Writing in 1959, Cater was among the first to spot this new-style member of Congress. "There has *begun to emerge* in the halls of Congress a new type of politician conditioned to the age of mass media and more keenly aware of the uses of publicity. He is not apt to be a member of . . . the 'Inner Club,' where emphasis is still put on seniority and skill in negotiation" [emphasis added]. In fact, "usually he is lacking in direct influence among his colleagues." [31] One does not find such unfavorable judgments of the senator or representative who goes public today.

Roger Davidson begins his chapter in *The New Congress* by noting that the new, less cooperative, and certainly less submissive member of Congress described by Mann, Robinson, and Cater has created "persistent pressures . . . to expand the number of available workgroups and the overall number of seats and leadership posts." He then catalogues the proliferation of subcommittees and assignments, the growth of informal working groups, and the multiplication of staffs and budgets. Leadership posts were so numerous in the 96th Congress, Davidson points out, that "all but two Democratic senators and nearly half of all Democratic representatives chaired a committee or subcommittee." [32] Only a quarter of the Democratic members held these positions in the mid-1950s. Davidson notes that to accommodate the diffusion of power, additional institutional innovations, such as the practice of referring bills to several committees rather than only to one, have occurred to give more subcommittees an opportunity to get their hands on the president's program.

New Institutional Arrangements in Congress

In recent Congresses, new organizational forms have arisen to compete with the old. Two that give ample expression to the centrifugal forces at work are caucuses, or working groups, and political action committees (PACs). Each caucus and committee in its own way competes with the party leaders of Congress for influence and seeks to redirect its members' attention and loyalties beyond the institution to particular publics. I shall describe them not so much because they threaten to replace existing structures but because they show how Congress as an institution is adapting to the Washington community of individualized pluralism.

Today's venerable Democratic Study Group (DSG) was founded in 1959 by a cadre of liberal northern House Democrats who were frustrated with the dominance of southern conservatives in the chamber's leadership positions. By offering an alternative legislative program and by providing a mechanism for bloc voting that in turn leveraged liberals' negotiating positions with the leadership; the DSG has been credited with moving the legislative agenda in a liberal direction. Because of its large, diverse membership, its million-dollar annual budget, and the promotion of its liberal members to positions of House leadership, the Democratic Study Group has today lost much of its certitude as an alternative voice within the institution.[33] In recent years, however, a plethora of new caucuses has arisen to continue the legacy of the DSG.

With well over a hundred voluntary associations to choose from, members typically affiliate with a half dozen or so of these organizations. Many of these caucuses have achieved the status of legislative service organizations, which entitles them to staff and office space on Capitol Hill. Most of the caucuses created before 1971 concentrated on broad issues; those formed since then have assumed a decidedly parochial cast. According to some scholars, these caucuses provide many of the same services as their counterpart interest groups with whom they cooperate closely.[34] The Congressional Arts Caucus reveals how particularistic these would-be protocoalitions can be. Its single goal, passage of the National Heritage Resources Act, would make it possible for artists and authors to deduct from their taxes the full market value of any of their works they donate to charitable organizations.[35] Apparently, no interest or issue is too esoteric to deserve organizational embodiment.

Even were they so inclined, these organizations, founded upon affinity of interest rather than proximity of organizations in the policy-making process, are ill suited to negotiate agreement among competing interests. Whatever bargains a caucus may make will count for little unless its members are well placed on the relevant committees. To the degree the Arts Caucus, for instance, fails to include the members of the House Ways and Means and Senate Finance committees, it is deficient. Moreover, to the degree it includes members not on these committees, it is inefficient. Whatever their standing as functioning coalitions, committees remain the vital juncture of the legislative process.

Caucuses are also deficient as protocoalitions because they are casual, voluntary associations that lack the rewards or sanctions necessary to induce members to adhere to collective goals. Even when a consensus on policy and tactics emerges and the caucus negotiates as a bloc with other leaders or with the president, its effectiveness remains limited. Everyone recognizes that each member of the caucus retains independent judgment about the relative merits of whatever deals its leaders are able to achieve and that the consensus could unravel at any moment. Consequently, rather than serving as building blocks to coalitions, these caucuses commonly assume a less critical role as clearinghouses of position papers.

The rapid increase in the number of congressional caucuses has been more than matched by the rise of political action committees. In the six elections from 1974 through 1990, the number of PACs grew from 608 to 4,172. During this period their contributions to House and Senate races increased from $12 million to $150 million.[36]

Before the passage of the Federal Election Campaign Act in 1971, private groups participated openly in political campaigns at great risks. Some, such as unions and professional associations (the American Medical Association, for example), had flexed their financial muscle from time to time, but others, such as corporations, had shied away from overt participation for fear of running afoul of ambiguous election laws. The campaign finance reforms that began in 1971 have changed all that. All organizations, and particularly corporations, now have clear guidelines for participating in congressional elections.

The first PACs registered with the Federal Election Commission (FEC) were largely the traditional organized contributors, principally the unions. With each subsequent election, however, more and more businesses have joined. Many, if not most, corporate donations go to incumbents and are motivated more by defensive consideration than by any aspiration to alter the ideological disposition of Congress. A smaller share, but still a large amount, of PAC money goes to influence members, if not elections. Challengers and vulnerable incumbents are frequently invited to disclose their preferences on issues of concern to the PAC, and here is where the parochial character of this money leaves its greatest imprint. Rep. David Obey's assertion that "ten thousand dollars may come against you from one group because of a single vote" is supported by the experiences of many members of Congress.[37]

Contrary to the unflattering stereotype of the unctuous lobbyist, representatives of interest groups have traditionally spurned the unrefined tactics portrayed in Obey's remark. When some occasionally succumbed to the temptation to lubricate the legislative process with financial contributions, they were often caught and punished. One of the most frequently recounted instances occurred in 1956 when President Eisenhower, citing the natural gas industry's heavy-handed use of campaign funds, vetoed a gas deregulation bill that he was on record as favoring.[38] Memory was long, and such instances did not need to be repeated frequently. The opposite message was conveyed in 1982 when, after spreading nearly a million dollars among 300 candidates, the National Automobile Dealers Association easily won a congressional veto of the Federal Trade Commission's proposed "full disclosure" regulation for used cars.[39]

Under institutionalized pluralism the *modus operandi* of lobbyists was quiet diplomacy. "Never lie" and "don't threaten" were their operational codes. Quiet diplomacy has not disappeared, but increasingly it gives way to more direct, public strategies of influence. These include inspiring pressure from the constituency as well as targeting the group's PAC contributions.

One of the last groups to catch on to the opportunities of individualized pluralism was the national Chamber of Commerce. For years the chamber was one of the more staid, even stolid, inside players on Capitol Hill. After watching its legislative success rate drop with each successive Congress, however, it adopted an aggressive public relations strategy. Today, the chamber has its own public affairs television network called Biznet, which produces weekly programs that are fed from Washington to cable and independent broadcast stations around the country. These programs do not hesitate to advise viewers of what they need to do to protect their interests in Congress.[40]

Well-heeled corporate groups are not the only participants to take full advantage of the new opportunities for influence. One recent survey of 175 lobbying groups found that while the great majority said they were doing more of almost all kinds of lobbying activity, the greatest increases have occurred in the realm of going public. Of the 27 classes of lobbying identified in the study, "talking with people from the press and media" scored the greatest gains. A close second were reported increases in "mounting grass roots campaigns" and "inspiring letter-writing or telegram campaigns." [41] Savings and loan associations, environmentalists, anti-gun control organizations, and Mothers Against Drunk Driving have all won quick victories with grass-roots strategies of influence.

Judged against the requirements of institutionalized pluralism, political action committees and caucuses are functionally primitive entities. Serving only to articulate generally narrow positions on issues, these organizations are neither well designed for nor much interested in brokering the diverse interests brought into play by policy proposals. With them, the first-tier function of interest aggregation traditionally performed by protocoalitions is absent. From the vantage of the White House, caucuses and PACs threaten to "balkanize the political process." [42]

These new organizations will not replace congressional parties and standing committees, but they have weakened these traditional groups as protocoalitions. The "new Congress" has added a veneer, so that the typical representative and senator today are associated with more congressional organizations, both formal and informal, than ever before. Yet the paradoxical result has been a depreciation of institutions and an elevation of individual politicians as coalitional matter.

Going Public and Individualized Pluralism

The present-day susceptibility of relations within Washington to public opinion manifests itself in a variety of ways. The influence of single-issue constituencies has been abetted by the discovery that by defeating one targeted incumbent a clear message will be sent to others. Issues also blow into Washington more quickly and in less-filtered form. During the 97th Congress, for example, President Reagan's supply-side program, with its unprecedented deficits, was being enacted while a majority in each house appeared ready to endorse a constitutional amendment requiring a balanced budget. And off to the side, a large bipartisan huddle was forming to carry forward the recently arrived "flat tax" rate reform.[43]

In a recent appraisal of coalition politics within Congress during the past 30 years, Barbara Sinclair makes the same connection between internal organization and the effect of external forces: "Instead of a policy process dominated by powerful, conservative committee chairmen, one in which crucial decisions were made in secret and thus were relatively insulated from public influence, we now see a process characterized by extreme individualism, one in which open, public decision making often hinders compromise." [44] When asked by a reporter about changes in Congress, Reagan lobbyist Kenneth Duberstein echoed this conclusion and gave it recent origin: "It's not been like Lyndon Johnson's time, being able to work with 15 or 20 Congressmen and Senators to get something done. For most issues you have to lobby all 435 Congressmen and almost all 100 Senators." [45] As a result, "how Congress performs its legislative role," continues Sinclair, "depends much more upon the character of the environmental forces impinging upon its members than upon its internal organization." [46]

The President's Calculus

The limited goods and services available for barter to the bargaining president would be quickly exhausted in a leaderless setting where every coalition partner must be dealt with individually. When politicians are more subject to "environmental" forces, however, other avenues of presidential influence open up. No politician within Washington is better positioned than the president to go outside of the community and draw popular support. With protocoalitions in disarray and members more sensitive to influences from beyond Washington, the president's hand in mobilizing public opinion has been strengthened. For the new Congress—indeed, for the new Washington generally—going public may at times be the most effective course available.

Under these circumstances, the president's prestige assumes the currency of power. It is something to be spent when the coffers are full, to be conserved when low, and to be replenished when empty. As David Gergen remarked when he was President Reagan's communications director, "Everything here is built on the idea that the President's success depends on grassroots support." [47] Such a president must be attentive to the polls, but he will not be one who necessarily craves the affection of the public. His relationship with it may be purely instrumental, and however gratifying, popular support is a resource the expenditure of which must be coolly calculated.

Bargaining presidents require the sage advice of politicians familiar with the bargaining game; presidents who go public need pollsters. Compare the relish with which President Nixon was reported by one of his consultants to have approached the polls with the disdain Truman expressed. "Nixon had all kinds of polls all the time; he sometimes had a couple of pollsters doing the same kind of survey at the same time. He really studied them. He wanted to find the thing that would give him an advantage." [48] The confidant went on to observe that the president wanted poll data "on just about anything and everything" throughout his administration.

Indicative of current fashion, Carter, Reagan, and Bush have had in-house pollsters taking continuous—weekly, even daily—readings of public opinion.[49] They have vigilantly monitored the pulse of opinion to warn of slippage and to identify opportunities for gain. Before adopting a policy course, they have assessed its costs in public support. These advisers' regular and frequently unsolicited denials that they affected policy belie their self-effacement.

To see how the strategic prescriptions of going public differ from those of bargaining, consider the hypothetical case of a president requiring additional votes if he is to prevail in Congress. If a large number of votes is needed, the most obvious and direct course is to go on prime-time television to solicit the public's active support. Employed at the right moment by a popular president, the effect may be dramatic. This tactic, however, has considerable costs and risks. A real debit of lost public support may occur when a president takes a forthright position. There is also the possibility that the public will not respond, which damages the president's future credibility. Given this, a president understandably finds the *threat* to go public frequently more attractive than the *act*. To the degree such a threat is credible, the anticipated responses of some representatives and senators may suffice to achieve victory.

A more focused application of popular pressure becomes available as an election nears. Fence-sitting representatives and senators may be plied with promises of reelection support or threats of presidential opposition. This may be done privately and selectively, or it may be tendered openly to all who may vote on the president's program. Then there is the election itself. By campaigning, the president who goes public can seek to alter the partisan composition of Congress and thereby gain influence over that institution's decisions in the future.

All of these methods for generating publicity notwithstanding, going public offers fewer and simpler stratagems than does its pluralist alternative. At the heart of the latter lies bargaining, which above all else involves choice: choice among alternative coalitions, choice of specific partners, and choice of the goods and services to be bartered. The number and variety of choices place great demands upon strategic calculation, so much so that pluralist leadership must be understood as an art. In Neustadt's schema, the president's success ultimately reduces to intuition, an ability to sense "right choices." [50] Going public also requires choice, and it leaves ample room for the play of talent. (One need only compare the television performance of Carter and Reagan.) Nonetheless, public relations appears to be a less obscure matter. Going public promises a straightforward presidency—its options fewer, its strategy simpler, and consequently, its practitioner's behavior more predictable.

Thus there is a rationale for modern presidents to go public in the emerging character of Washington politics. As Washington comes to depend on looser, more individualistic political relations, presidents searching for strategies that work will increasingly go public. So far, I have said little about the individual in the White House or the personal character of leadership. To consider these ingredients important does not violate any of the assumptions made here. Rationality does not leave choice to be determined strictly by the environment. To the degree occupants of the Oval Office differ in their skills and conceptions of leadership, one may expect that similar circumstances will sometimes result in different presidential behavior.

Perhaps, as has frequently been suggested, presidents go public more today because of who they are. What did Jimmy Carter and Ronald Reagan have in common? The answer is their lack of interest in active negotiation with fellow politicians and their confidence in speaking directly to the voters.

The Calculus of Those Who Deal with the President

Those Washingtonians who conduct business with the president observe his behavior carefully. Their judgment about his leadership guides them in their dealings with him. Traditionally, the professional president watchers have asked themselves the following questions: What are his priorities? How much does he care whether he wins or loses on a particular issue? How will he weigh his options? Is he capable of winning?

Each person will answer these questions about the president's will and skill somewhat differently, of course, depending upon his or her institutional vantage. The chief lobbyist for the United Auto Workers, a network White House correspondent, and the mayor of New York City may size up the president differently depending upon what they need from him. Nonetheless, they arrive at their judgments about the president in similar ways. Each observes the same behavior, inspects the same personal qualities, evaluates the views of the same recognized opinion leaders—columnists and commentators, among others—and tests his or her own tentative opinions with those of fellow community members. Local opinion leaders promote a general agreement among Washingtonians in their assessments of the president. Their agreement is his reputation.[51]

A president with a strong reputation does better in his dealings largely because others expect fewer concessions from him. Accordingly, he finds them more compliant; an orderly marketplace prevails. Saddled with a weak reputation, conversely, a president must work harder. Because others expect him to be less effective, they press him harder in expectation of greater gain. Comity at the bargaining table may give way to contention as other politicians form unreasonable expectations of gain. Through such expectations, the president's reputation regulates community relations in ways that either facilitate or impede his success. In a world of institutionalized pluralism, bargaining presidents seldom actively traded upon their prestige, leaving it to influence Washington political elites only through their anticipation of the electorate's behavior. As a consequence, prestige remained largely irrelevant to other politicians' assessments of the president.[52] Once presidents began going public and interjecting prestige directly into their relations with fellow politicians, and once these politicians found their resistance to this pressure diminished because of their own altered circumstances, the president's ability to marshal public opinion soon became an important ingredient of his reputation. New questions were added to traditional ones. Does the president feel strongly enough about an issue to go public? Will he follow through on his threats to do so? Does his standing in the country run so deep that it will likely be converted into mail to members of Congress, or is it so shallow that it will expire as he attempts to use it?

In today's Washington, the answers to these questions contribute to the president's reputation. As a consequence, his prestige and reputation have lost much of their separateness. The community's estimates of Carter and Reagan rose and fell with the polls. Through reputation, prestige has begun to play a larger role in regulating the president's day-to-day transactions with other community members. Grappling with the unclear causes of Carter's failure in Washington, Neustadt arrived at the same conclusion:

> A President's capacity to draw and stir a television audience seems every bit as interesting to current Washingtonians as his ability to wield his formal powers. This interest is his opportunity. While national party organizations fall away, while congressional party discipline relaxes, while interest groups proliferate and issue networks rise, a President who wishes to compete for leadership in framing policy and shaping coalitions has to make the most he can out of his popular connection. Anticipating home reactions, Washingtonians . . . are vulnerable to any breeze from home that presidential words and sights can stir. If he is deemed effective on the tube they will anticipate. That is the essence of professional reputation.[53]

The record supports Neustadt's speculation. In late 1978 and early 1979, with his monthly approval rating dropping to less than 50 percent, President Carter complained that it was difficult to gain Congress's attention for his legislative proposals. As one congressional liaison official stated, "When you go up to the Hill and the latest polls show Carter isn't doing well, then there isn't much reason for a member to go along with him." [54] A member of Congress concurred: "The relationship between the President and Congress is partly the result of how well the President is doing politically. Congress is better behaved when he does well. . . . Right now, it's almost as if Congress is paying no attention to him." [55]

Presidential Selection Reforms: Outsiders in the White House

Campaigning and governing have always tended to draw upon the same conceptions of politics. Studying the former helps one comprehend the latter. In the nineteenth century, presidential candidates resulted from negotiations among political machines that came together at conventions to identify an acceptable candidate their state organizations could work for. Acceptability had something to do with electability and a lot to do with the perceived fairness of the candidate in distributing patronage to their locale. Frequently, aspiring politicians with established national reputations were ruled out because of their inevitable association with party organizations in one region of the country. This explains why conventions were commonly deadlocked, and unknowns, or dark horses, occasionally emerged with the nomination. In office these presidents were typically weak, which suited the needs of the state party organizations: they wanted someone at the patronage levers who would follow established protocol in distributing the federal largesse.

Twentieth-century bargaining presidents have been activists who were expected to lead their party to victory, rather than simply head the ticket, and to build coalitions in government. Just as in governing, these presidents succeeded as candidates by stitching together the disparate elements of their party. With state delegations to the convention handpicked by party leaders and bound to them by unit rules, aspiring presidential candidates sought the support of those who were, in the words of Thomas B. Reed, turn-of-the-century Speaker of the House and nemesis to reformers, "guided by the base desire to win." [56] Writing in 1968, Nelson W. Polsby and Aaron B. Wildavsky described this process of presidential nomination:

> Decision-making at conventions is ordinarily coordinated by a process of bargaining among party leaders. Each leader represents a state party or faction within a state which is independently organized and not subject to control by outsiders. . . . In order to mobilize enough nationwide support to elect a President, party leaders from a large number of constituencies must be satisfied with the nominee. [57]

During the middle decades of the twentieth century, a highly popular military hero was nominated, but presidential candidates mostly came from a class of politicians with established political careers—careers increasingly located in Washington, particularly in the Senate. Leadership through bargaining was the leitmotif of that era's presidents.

In these last decades of the twentieth century, these political arrangements appear to be giving way to those in which coalition building proceeds less through mediating organizations and elite negotiation and more through the direct mobilization of national constituencies. No aspect of the presidency has escaped this tendency. It is as true for how candidates seek the nomination and campaign in the general election as it is for how they behave once in the White House.

How the Reforms Changed Presidential Nominations

Until the 1972 Democratic convention adopted the proposed reforms of the McGovern-Fraser Commission, the convention system of nominating candidates had remained largely untouched during the twentieth century. Since then, reforming the presidential selection procedures has become a quadrennial political exercise as candidates have begun their campaigns by seeking to alter the rules under which they would compete for the nomination. The rules of the game have become an important part of the game itself.

The cumulative effect of these reforms has been to transfer the nomination of the party's candidate from party leaders at the convention to the mass electorate in primary elections and caucuses. One telltale indicator of this change can be found in the number of delegates who come to the convention already bound to a particular candidate. In 1960, committed delegates constituted 20 percent of all Democratic delegates and 35 percent of all Republican delegates. By 1980 these figures stood at 71 and 69 percent respectively.[58] This change reflects several specific reforms. The number of primaries was on the rise before the 1972 reforms, but increased sharply after state parties were required to open delegate selection procedures. From 1960 to 1992, the number of states holding primaries more than doubled to 39. Other reforms beefed up the primaries as the arena in which the nomination took place. Under the new rules, primary voters would choose candidates rather than anonymous slates of delegates, and delegates selected in primaries would be bound to their declared candidate at least for the first ballot at the convention. Finally, the winner-take-all primary was replaced with some form of proportional distribution of delegates according to the candidates' shares of the popular vote. This has inspired nationally unknown candidates to enter and stay in the race.[59]

In addition to these primary reforms, other reforms were also at work dismantling the convention system. State parties that did not opt for a primary were required to open their caucuses to all party members and to democratize delegate selection procedures. No longer could a state's delegation be selected well before election season, nor could it be led into the convention bound by a unit rule to some state party leader. As a result, delegates began showing up at the convention having little familiarity with, much less loyalty to, state party leaders. Instead, they gave their allegiance to a particular candidate or cause they wanted the convention to embrace.[60]

Further eroding the parties' presence were rules that, though falling short of strict quotas, insisted that more minorities, women, and young people be included in each state's delegation. Because most elected officeholders are white males over 30, this meant that many of them would no longer be attending the convention. From 1960 to 1980, the percentage of Democratic senators attending their party's convention fell from 68 to 17 percent, and for representatives, from 45 to 11 percent.[61]

Elected politicians were not the only losers under the reforms. Representatives of core constituency groups—most notably union leaders within the Democratic party—saw their influence dwindle piecemeal with reform. Their position further deteriorated with the enactment of new campaign finance laws that gave federal matching money to candidates for the nomination who could raise $5,000 in small contributions from each of 20 or more states and who agreed to abide by ceilings on campaign spending. This loosened the dependency of all candidates on the parties' core constituent groups for organizational and financial support.[62] More to the point, candidates who had little hope of winning endorsement from these groups could, nonetheless, raise and spend as much money as necessary to compete in the primaries.

Added together, these reforms ended any semblance of the nominating convention as a forum where the leaders of the party's constituencies came together to select the party's standard-bearer from the ranks of Washington-based politicians. In its place the reforms substituted a multiphased popularity contest with low entrance barriers. Many more candidates began showing up, · few of whom would have stood a chance under the old convention arrangements. That some of these long-distance runners have won their party's nomination and the presidency and that others did well enough to ruin the chances of more conventionally styled candidates contribute independently to modern presidential leadership. Our presidents are, after all, the products of the system that selects them.

During the prereform era, the parties would occasionally find irresistible someone like Dwight Eisenhower whose fame and reputation rested on a nonpolitical career. More often, however, candidates were drawn from the mainstream of the party and frequently from among well-positioned members of the Washington political community. Others, "outsiders" even if technically Washington residents, stood not a chance. Having established national visibility in conducting televised hearings into organized crime in the early 1950s, Democratic Senator Estes Kefauver won virtually every presidential primary he entered in 1952, and yet largely because of a suspect reputation among the Washington elite, he managed to move no closer than his party's vice-presidential nomination.[63] Kefauver was clearly a man ahead of his time.

By the time Jimmy Carter and Ronald Reagan came to Washington, outsiders were no longer being shunted aside. Back-to-back, these two men were the first in memory to assume the Oval Office without any experience in Washington. Jimmy Carter's statement in his memoirs, "We came to Washington as outsiders . . . we left as outsiders," signifies how thoroughly the selection reforms have altered presidential recruitment.[64] Not even General Eisenhower had such impeccable credentials for boasting his nonpolitical rearing.

A candidate achieves his outsider status less by his non-Washington residency than by his standing within the party or governmental establishment. What precisely this establishment means is left to the candidate to define. It may be as specific as Eugene McCarthy's Lyndon Johnson or as general as Reagan's "bumbling bureaucrats" and "spendthrift politicians" who occupy the "puzzle palaces on the Potomac." For a Democrat to succeed as a credible outsider, organized labor must be included in the establishment. Generally, the strategy plays better when one is competing against a front-runner who occupies a credible "insider's" position. In 1972 George McGovern took apart Senator Edmund Muskie in the early primaries and Senator Hubert Humphrey in the later ones. Both appeared to have labor's support. In 1984 Gary Hart could not have campaigned nearly so well on the ambiguous platform of "new ideas" and being "less beholden" if his adversary had not been so conspicuously "more beholden" to the "old ideas" of the Democratic establishment.

The 1992 campaign for the Democratic nomination followed much the same script. Of the five candidates who competed in the first state primary in New Hampshire, only two then held public office in Washington. And two of the candidates—Paul Tsongas and Jerry Brown—held no office at all. Over the next six weeks, the two Washington-based politicians dropped out, then a former senator. Neither of the finalists—Bill Clinton or Jerry Brown—was tainted with having previously held public office in Washington.

The presidential selection system constitutes a strategic environment that enhances certain skills and resources while penalizing others. In addition to its direct effect on current candidates' fortunes, it shapes the kinds of presidents elected by influencing the career decisions and stylistic adaptations of potential candidates in the future. Politicians on the sideline go to school on the experiences of candidates in the arena. Eugene McCarthy's "victory" over President Johnson in the New Hampshire primary in 1968 instructed George McGovern and numerous other Democratic aspirants about the new opportunities provided by the expanding primary system. McGovern in turn demonstrated that a virtual unknown six months before the convention could capture the nomination. Jimmy Carter reinforced this lesson in 1976 and strengthened it by showing that such a candidate could also go on to win the general election in November. Similarly, in 1976 Ronald Reagan taught future candidates that in a world of primaries, incumbency no longer shields a sitting president from a primary challenge. When Patrick Buchanan, a former Reagan speechwriter and television commentator who had never run for elective office, announced his plans to enter the New Hampshire primary in 1992, Washington pundits carefully deliberated the damage his candidacy might inflict on Bush's reelection chances.

Outsiders as Presidents

Fresh from an extended and successful stint of campaigning, an outsider will enter the White House probably as uninterested in playing the bargaining game as he is ill prepared. For him, whether to promote his policies in Washington by attending to a great many transactions with other elites or by going over their heads to enlist popular support with a television appeal may be an easy choice.

Bargaining, however, is not dead. In the modern Washington characterized by individualized pluralism, presidents will continue to receive many invitations to the bargaining table. Beyond familiarity with the formal procedures and informal folkways that govern exchange even today, successful bargaining requires of the president a keen sense of the needs and preferences of those whom he seeks to influence. Bargaining may, however, surpass the capacities of the outsider president. Recognizing future bargaining partners and figuring out what a particular bargain might look like may seem trivial, but experience shows that both may escape White House occupants. When President Carter canceled 19 water projects without consulting fellow Democrats on Capitol Hill, did he appreciate the political costs he was inflicting upon others and eventually upon himself? Given the self-congratulatory aplomb with which he announced his decision, one suspects not. Several of these projects had been long-sought goals of Sen. Russell Long and Louisiana's House delegation. Senator Long was chair of the important Senate Finance Committee through which much of the White House's legislative program was destined to pass, and where in fact some of it came to rest.[65]

No less important and probably even more demanding for the outsider in the White House is awareness of an opportunity to bargain when it presents itself. At the least, the president must understand that his formal responsibilities and prerogatives are convertible in barter. In addition, he must know the customary routines of exchange that have grown up in Washington over the years to reduce the uncertainty of coalition building for all participants. Without such knowledge even an avid negotiator might quickly become overwhelmed.[66] The inability of outsiders in the White House to recognize these routines not only constitutes lost opportunity but also may assume real political costs.

President Carter, for example, repudiated the vestigial practice of replacing the other party's federal district attorneys with local partisans recommended by the district's Democratic members of Congress. The questionable legitimacy of such blatant partisanism muted the outcry among House and Senate Democrats, but those adversely affected by the decision no doubt recognized that they alone bore the costs of the president's unilateral action. Another political custom, seemingly costless to the president but invaluable to his party's members of Congress, has been that of allowing the local representative to claim some credit by announcing new federal programs in the district. The Carter administration, in contrast, issued periodic press releases from the White House that summarily listed new programs.[67]

I have dwelt on President Carter's shortcomings for a reason. Although other presidents have from time to time failed to enlist routine exchange systems, Carter did so more consistently and more flagrantly. Even taking into account the centrifugal forces at work in present-day Washington, the large Democratic majorities in Congress offered Carter the luxurious prospect that even uninspired, routine bargaining would reap great legislative rewards. As it was, his legislative accomplishments are generally judged to have been modest. Even his victories appeared grudgingly delivered by the Democratic congressional leaders. The explanation, of course, is his path to the White House.

One would be hard pressed to find a better illustration of the outsider's propensity for going public than the following colloquy between House

Speaker Thomas P. O'Neill, Jr., and President Carter during a pre-inauguration briefing in Plains, Georgia.

> O'Neill: Mr. President, I want you to understand something. Some of the brightest men in America are in this Congress of the United States. Don't make the mistake of underestimating them. . . . We want to work together, but I have a feeling you are underestimating the feeling of Congress and you could have some trouble.
>
> Carter: I'll handle them just as I handled the Georgia legislature. Whenever I had problems with the Georgia legislature I took the problems to the people of Georgia.[68]

Whatever the emerging job requirements or the partisan disposition of Washington, the style of presidential leadership will largely reflect the skills and experiences of the person in office. A president who developed his political skills in the chambers and corridors of Congress will understandably find it exasperating to deliver salutations to a television camera. Similarly, the outsider whose career success is founded largely upon the stylized public presentation of self will derive greater gratification and even stimulation from traveling around the country delivering speeches and appearing on television than in following the private, daily, all-too-mysterious rituals of cultivating support from other politicians. That today's Washington elites are less responsive to such methods only adds to modern presidents' distaste for them. Whenever the advantages of the recruitment process for outsiders prove decisive, going public will enjoy favored status within the White House.

The Politics of Divided Government

One of the most prominent, if underrecognized, political developments over the past several decades is the emergence of divided party control of government. The 1956 presidential election was the first in this century to result in split party control of the presidency and Congress. The pattern thus established of electing a Republican president and Democratic majorities in one or both houses of Congress has been repeated in five of the eight subsequent presidential elections, and since 1968 in five of six elections. The single exception occurred in 1976, an election that the Democratic nominee, Jimmy Carter, barely won against an unelected incumbent, Gerald Ford, and easily lost four years later.

Midterm congressional elections have always tended to go against the president's party. Occasionally during the first half of the century this midterm bias was strong enough to give the opposition party temporary control of one or both houses of Congress, but unified party control was restored in the next presidential election. In recent years, midterm elections have consistently reinforced divided government by increasing the opposition party's majority control of Congress.

In order to understand how divided government can influence a president's leadership strategies, we must first consider how it generally alters relations throughout the Washington community. With politicians increasingly loosened from the once dominant network of mutual dependency, political parties have not been portrayed here as prominent features of the Washington landscape. Nonetheless, every politician seeking reelection needs to provide constituents with two levels of products: local goods and services as well as information about his or her stand on national issues that concern them. Neither of these can easily be supplied alone. That a politician requires the ongoing cooperation of colleagues to provide goods and services is apparent. Less clear is the fact that communication is costly and may be just as difficult to achieve alone. Even a long-standing incumbent who has assiduously plied his or her constituency with goods and services may remain unknown to half or more of the electorate. And fewer still will be familiar with their representative's positions on national issues. Narrow self-interest therefore impels politicians to seek association with a party, through which information on their positions on public issues can be efficiently transmitted to voters. Evidence of the value of party as a cue to voters—even self-proclaimed independent voters—can be found in the minuscule number of unaffiliated candidates ever elected to Congress. Because the electoral fortunes of politicians are, at least in part, bound to the public's opinion of their party, they have a stake in its success. And because one party's gain at the ballot box is the other's loss, they have a comparable stake in the other party's failure.

When party control of Congress and the presidency is unified, leaders from both branches of government have a special incentive to resolve disagreements harmoniously. Whatever their policy differences, party members negotiate with one another, recognizing that each will be judged for the party's collective performance. If the governing party's leaders were to allow internal disagreements to erupt into public discord, they would be flirting with defeat in the next election. Instead, they engage in quiet diplomacy to reach the compromises necessary to unify the party and give it an attractive record for the next campaign. In this circumstance, going public will frequently be unnecessary and, as an application of force, might well upset party harmony. Members of the governing party team in the legislative and executive branches therefore have a strong incentive to resolve their differences discreetly.

But when party control of Congress and the presidency is divided, a much different dynamic arises, with public conflict frequently replacing cooperation. One problem has to do with reconciling the distant policy preferences that arise more between parties than within them. More importantly, under divided government opposing politicians can gain electoral advantage by frustrating and embarrassing the other side, even if this thwarts their own policy goals. During the 102d Congress, the majority Democrats rejected President Bush's overtures for concessions on bills expanding civil rights protection and extending unemployment benefits, preferring instead to send him repeatedly popular legislation he had publicly committed himself to veto.[69]

Conflict and confrontation can serve a party's electoral purposes even when its policy goals are the casualty. In 1985, as Richard Cheney, then House Republican whip, stated: "Polarization often has very beneficial results. If everything is handled through compromise and conciliation, if there are no real issues dividing us from the Democrats, why should the country change and make us the majority?" [70] Under divided government, the desire to achieve policy goals through give-and-take at the bargaining table yields to the strategic dictates of the next election.

The following two cases exemplify presidents contemplating bargaining with an opposition Congress. They are more than forty years apart and the presidents opted for different strategies, but the moral is the same.

Case 1: Truman Spurns Cooperation and Succeeds

After the 1946 midterm election in which the Republicans captured control of Congress for the first time since the 1920s, President Truman faced an outpouring of unsolicited advice from mostly Republican politicians and newspaper editorial writers urging him to cooperate with Congress. Some even championed novel institutional arrangements such as regularly scheduled "summit" meetings between the Democratic president and the Republican congressional leaders to hash out policy accords.

Observing from a distance the pressure being exerted on the uncertain president, James Rowe, a former White House assistant to Roosevelt, wrote Truman a lengthy, unsolicited memo entitled "Cooperation or Conflict?" [71] He sought to dissuade the president from agreeing to formal mechanisms of cooperation with the opposition Congress, arguing that they were just Republican schemes to ensnare the president. Truman found Rowe's argument persuasive and followed its advice in his relations with Congress.[72]

The premise of Rowe's argument was that the main business of an opposition Congress is to prepare for the next election. Investigations of administration decisions, contentious confirmation hearings, and passage of popular bills fashioned to elicit the president's veto were some of the devices available to an opposition Congress. With 11 of the last 12 Congresses laboring under divided government, these activities have become the familiar routines of politics. But at the time this memo was written, the country had not experienced divided government for 14 years (and then only briefly), so these were viewed as troubling prospects. There was not much the president could do, Rowe advised, but grin and bear it.

What the president could do—and this was the thrust of Rowe's argument—was to avoid being suckered into naively negotiating with Congress. With each side maneuvering the other into a position to be exploited, summit resolution becomes a sharp game in which the president plays with several distinct disadvantages stemming from the institutional characteristics of the legislature and the executive. First is the presidency's "extremely public nature," which "leaves no room whatever for the private give-and-take, the secrecy and anonymity of compromise, which is the essence of negotiation. . . . The presidency is rigid—when its incumbent speaks the world soon knows exactly what he said." Second, in agreeing to negotiate, "the president yields his one source of strength—the backing of public opinion for his point of view. He brings that opinion to his view only by means of public statements. But reaching agreement with [the opposition] . . . means sitting around the conference table with them and indulging in bargaining and negotiation with them. The agreements would be made public as a combined product and the people would not know which were the contributions—or the concessions—of the . . . President." Third, the president has the ability to deliver on his agreements, but congressional leaders do not or can easily claim not to. Once a compromise is reached, they can return to the bargaining table for more concessions to gain votes from members holding out. In the end, "cooperation is a one way street."

So what is the president to do? "Unlike majority presidents [in unified government] who are able to do business with their party . . . minority presidents are forced to fall back on their chief weapon—the marshalling of public opinion." Rowe identified two types of opportunity especially appropriate for going public: veto messages and press conferences. Today, in an era of jet transportation and television, these avenues of public persuasion seem rather timid and unimaginative, but they were the principal opportunities available to a president in the 1940s. He was being urged to confront the opposition Congress not because the prospects for going public were bright but rather because those for bargaining were bleak.

In his dealings with the Republican 80th Congress, President Truman followed Rowe's advice. He selectively vetoed legislation on which he could take forceful and politically attractive positions. Foremost, he refused to bow to pressure to engage in summit diplomacy. In public statements, he proposed popular social policies to Congress, daring it to reject them. And in 1948 he called the Republican Congress back into special session and presented it with popular social legislation, not in expectation of making policy but in order to create potent issues for his fall reelection campaign. Indeed, these activities laid the groundwork for the famous, come-from-behind victory in which he instructed future presidents on how to make an obstructionist Congress the campaign issue.

Case 2: President Bush Cooperates and Fails

In the fall of 1990, as President Bush sat staring at the teleprompter, waiting to deliver only his third prime-time appeal to the American people, he may well have wondered how he landed in his predicament. He was about to promote a deficit reduction budget package of increased taxes and reduced spending that more closely resembled the program of congressional Democrats

OPERATION CONGRESS STORM

Paul Conrad Copyright 1991, Los Angeles Times
Reprinted by permission

than his own. The legislation did not contain his long-sought reductions in capital gains taxes, but it did include a tax hike for wealthy, mostly Republican taxpayers. And yet here was the president about to shoulder responsibility for it with the American people.

An unpleasant irony for Bush was that he had worked hard to reach this uncomfortable moment. First, he had to sacrifice his earlier image of resoluteness in order to get budget negotiations moving. The Democrats had insisted that the president retract his 1988 campaign slogan, "Read my lips: no new taxes," before they would participate in any discussions that might result in new taxes. The president tried to minimize the political fallout by slipping the concession into a press release that buried "tax revenue increases" among a list of topics open to negotiation.

Throughout the summer of meetings, Bush had refrained from publicly criticizing the Democratic Congress, lest he drive its members away from the bargaining table. However, this necessitated surrendering his advantage on the public stage, which Rowe had advised Truman was the strongest card available to a president facing an opposition Congress.

One can therefore sympathize with Bush's predicament as he began his television address, feigning enthusiasm for the budget compromise. No wonder his appeal was brief and tepid, without impact in the country or Congress. This, his first solicitation of the public's support—"Tell your Congressmen and Senators you support this deficit reduction agreement"— did little to stem the "avalanche" of mail opposed to some feature of the legislation. The only indicator to register any movement after the speech was the further weakening of the president's job-performance rating in the opinion polls.

The less numerous and inflexible congressional Republicans had been largely ignored in developing the budget compromise. With little investment in the product, and fearing that, as members of the president's party, they would be tagged with responsibility for the tax increases in the upcoming congressional election, these Republicans were the first to bolt. Many congressional Democrats strategically followed the Republicans in highly public criticism of the budget compromise. Within 72 hours of the president's national appeal, the package of taxes and spending that had taken all summer to hammer out collapsed.

With congressional Republicans in open revolt, President Bush was stuck with a dilemma. He could allow the provisions of the current law to kick in and automatically reduce the deficit with severe, across-the-board cuts in discretionary spending or he could return to the negotiating table to develop a package that would attract stronger Democratic support. He opted for the latter, but not without a lot of bickering within the administration that spilled over into the press. The collective consternation was brought on by the realization that the bipartisan compromise no one in the White House was enthusiastic about would become the administration's new bargaining position from which an even less attractive, more Democratic policy would be fashioned.

As soon as the new package was signed, President Bush left town to repair his relations with congressional Republicans by helping in their reelection campaigns. He conjured up the image of himself as a Reaganesque outsider—"God, I'm glad to be out of Washington"—and painted congressional Democrats, his erstwhile trading partners, as "America's biggest and most entrenched special interest." And he adopted what his aides called a "Harry Truman style" by claiming the budget had been held "ransom" by Congress, and in the future he was "absolutely going to hold the line on taxes." [73]

There was little confidence among fellow partisans, however, that the president could switch from cooperation to confrontation so easily. A "senior Republican strategist" summed up the matter to one news correspondent this way: "They're going to sign off on the budget deal, then try to pin it on the Democrats, say George Bush didn't do it and expect the voters to believe this whole budget was an immaculate conception. . . . It's not going to be easy."

Republican congressional candidates also viewed this as a dubious strategy. Of the hundred or so who had made campaign commercials with Bush earlier in the fall, only a few chose to air them. Many canceled the president's visit to their district, and some of those who required his presence to raise campaign funds with the party faithful stayed in Washington on "pressing business." Sometimes matters did not improve even when the president succeeded in joining a candidate on stage. Surely the following introduction offered by a House Republican from Oklahoma was well intended: "George Bush on his worst day is a whole lot better than Michael Dukakis on his best day." The *coup de grace* came while the president was stumping in Vermont for another House Republican incumbent. Seeking maximum distance from the president, who was seated within a stone's throw, the candidate addressed the audience: "Ask yourselves, why did this President, last May, decide that the issue he had run on and won on now had to be laid on the table as a point of negotiations? We're talking about his pledge on taxes."

The Most Effective Strategy

Congress and the presidency are different kinds of institutions, mostly having to do with the number of principals involved. The modern institutional presidency has a staff of thousands, but only one individual is able to commit the institution. This gives that person special credibility and prominence when staking out policy positions either publicly or privately. When members of Congress take positions, they speak as one voice among many. Even when the institution's leaders take a position on an issue, which they do only infrequently, it assumes the form of a prediction or a reading of the unrevealed preferences of the collectivity. Especially in this era of individualized pluralism, congressional leaders cannot often commit their institution to a course of action.

While this difference gives the president a comparative advantage in going public, it becomes a disadvantage in negotiations between these institutions. Just as Rowe advised Truman, and as Bush had to learn for himself, only the president is obliged to honor his commitment. If he backs away from an agreement, he is reneging. If congressional leaders fail to deliver their members' votes, they can be faulted for ineffectiveness but not bad faith. In the politics of the 1990 budget accord, George Bush stumbled onto every mine field James Rowe had warned Truman about nearly half a century earlier. The moral of these two cases is clear. Under divided government, the president should engage Congress distantly, in full view of the public. In subsequent chapters we shall examine evidence showing that the arrival of divided party control of government has led incumbent presidents to increase their level of public activities, presumably aware of the implications of dealing with an opposition Congress.

Conclusion

We have considered several major developments in national politics as causes for the rise of going public as a presidential strategy: political relations in Washington that no longer permit a limited set of bargains to carry the day; presidential selection reforms that allow ordinary voters to determine nominations rather than state party organizations; and the rise of divided party control of government. Although on the surface these developments appear quite different and suggest a multiplicity of possible causes, they share a common root: the declining influence of political parties on the electorate. Since the 1960s, fewer voters identify with one of the two major parties. At times over the intervening years, the number of self-proclaimed "independents" has actually surpassed the number of party identifiers. But loyalties are fading even among partisans, who are more likely to defect at the ballot box than did their counterparts during the several decades when institutionalized pluralism reigned. As a result of weakening loyalty, local and state party organizations have atrophied and in many communities are extinct.

This attitude among the electorate has filtered into Washington. Politicians can no longer depend on their party's performance for their personal success and have made a strategic turn to self-reliant individualism. With voters' choices up for grabs, mobilization has been of less importance. State party organizations consequently have had less to offer and a weaker claim for control of party affairs. Since the 1940s the parties' national committees had been steadily weakening, and in the late 1960s the nominating convention was reformed to strip state organizations of the control they once had. Delegates were to be selected in primaries or highly public and open caucuses, and at the convention the majority of a state delegation could no longer control all of its delegates. Among those who benefited from parties' decline, of course, were those self-styled outsiders who would never have received their party's endorsement.

Many plausible explanations have been advanced for the rise of divided government, and a discussion of them would lead us far afield. However, the simple fact that divided government in Washington is the result of voters choosing candidates from both parties similarly ties this cause of going public to weakening of party loyalties.

From what has been said thus far, bargaining and going public appear to have little in common. Bargaining thrives when numerous protocoalitions represented by authoritative leaders are present and when the actors do not have to worry that deals will disintegrate because of short-term shifts in public opinion. Going public becomes the preferred course when protocoalitions are weak, when individual politicians are susceptible to public pressures, and when politicians in the White House appreciate the requirements of television better than the needs of committee chairs.

Institutionalized pluralism prescribes that presidents bargain, and individualized pluralism that they go public. But these settings are abstractions—their starkness intended to clarify the evolution of Washington politics during the past half century; presidents in the real world retain choice in their leadership. Bargaining continues to be a ubiquitous activity in today's Washington, just as going public was occasionally the choice of presidents of an earlier era. What has changed significantly is the balance of incentives and constraints that influences strategic choice and the kinds of politicians in the Oval Office who make them. After carefully considering their options in confronting opposition Congresses and less reliable coalition partners, contemporary presidents will choose going public over bargaining more often than did their predecessors.

The next chapter continues to explore presidential leadership as a reflection of the community within which the president works. Specifically, it examines the historical transformation of Washington from a community of institutionalized pluralism to one of individualized pluralism in the context of twentieth-century relations between the president and the press. The evolution of these relations, containing all the elements of old and new Washington, was instrumental in bringing about this alternative style of presidential leadership.

Notes

1. Robert A. Dahl and Charles E. Lindblom, *Politics, Economics, and Welfare* (New York: Harper and Row, 1953), 333.
2. Hugh Heclo, *The Government of Strangers* (Washington, D.C.: Brookings Institution, 1977), 194.
3. Dahl and Lindblom, *Politics, Economics, and Welfare,* 333.
4. Clem Miller, *Member of the House* (New York: Charles Scribner's Sons, 1962), 93.
5. Donald R. Matthews, *U.S. Senators and Their World* (Chapel Hill: University of North Carolina Press, 1960), 100-101.
6. From this perspective Richard F. Fenno has described the House Appropriations Committee as a coalition. Although the collective goals of the committee—to protect the Treasury and to preserve the House's influence—are rooted in institutional needs, its coalitional features are no less significant. Richard F. Fenno, *Power of the Purse* (Boston: Little, Brown, 1966), 191-264.
7. Richard E. Neustadt, *Presidential Power,* 28-29. Copyright © 1980. Reprinted by permission of John Wiley and Sons, Inc. Compare with Dahl and Lindblom's earlier observation: "The President possesses more hierarchical controls than any other single figure in the government; indeed, he is often described somewhat romantically and certainly ambiguously as the most powerful democratic executive in the world. Yet like everyone else in the American policy process, the President must bargain constantly—with Congressional leaders, individual Congressmen, his department heads, bureau chiefs, and leaders of nongovernmental organizations" (Dahl and Lindblom, *Politics, Economics, and Welfare,* 333).
8. Peter Sperlich questions whether the president has sufficient time, energy, and resources to bargain his way to coalitions even when authoritative leaders are available. Peter Sperlich, "Bargaining and Overload: An Essay on *Presidential Power,*" in *Perspectives on the Presidency,* ed. Aaron Wildavsky (Boston: Little, Brown, 1975), 406-430.
9. Douglass Cater, *Power in Washington* (New York: Vintage, 1964), 75.
10. Franklin Delano Roosevelt Library, Hyde Park, New York; PSF: McIntyre, 1-4. The memo continued:

> In this connection, there is something else I wish you would do. Up to now Jim Rowe [Justice Department official and Roosevelt confidant] has been clearing all nominations with the Democratic National Committee and on the Hill. For your very private information, there is too much friction between the Committee and the Senators on patronage. I want you to handle the Treasury and Justice nominations with Flynn and the Senators. I think I shall let Jim Rowe continue to handle the independent agencies. After you have cleared these nominations for

a while, perhaps you can be a mollifying influence and bring the Committee and the Senators more into harmony.

Let Jim Rowe know about this so he can shift over his arrangements with the Committee, Treasury and Justice to you.

11. William S. White, *The Citadel* (New York: Harper and Brothers, 1956), 135-153.
12. David B. Truman, *The Governmental Process* (New York: Alfred A. Knopf, 1951), 391.
13. Martin Kriesberg, "What Congressmen and Administrators Think of the Polls," *Public Opinion Quarterly* 9 (Fall 1945): 333-337. Concluding from this and other sources, historian Richard Jensen states, "The threat [of polls] was a short-circuiting of the representative form of government. It was one thing for Roosevelt, in his capacity as party leader and candidate to appeal for support. It was quite another to use the agencies of government to mold public opinion and thereby to force Congress to relinquish its authority to set policy" (Richard Jensen, "Public Opinion Polls: Early Problems of Method and Philosophy," Paper delivered at the Oxford Conference on History and Theory of the Social Sciences, Oxford, England, July 23, 1977, 14.)
14. *Memoirs by Harry S Truman: Years of Trial and Hope,* vol. 2 (Garden City, N.Y.: Doubleday and Co., 1956; reprint New York: New American Library, 1965), 207-208.
15. Leila A. Sussman, "FDR and the White House Mail," *Public Opinion Quarterly* 20 (Spring 1956): 5-15.
16. A case in point occurred in 1943 when farm organizations announced their opposition to the president's farm subsidy program. The White House responded by commissioning private surveys on farmers' views of his agricultural policies. On finding that by and large farmers had no idea what his policies were, Roosevelt used the results to refute farm group leaders' claims that their constituents opposed his program. Richard W. Steele, "The Pulse of the People: Franklin D. Roosevelt and the Gauging of American Public Opinion," *Journal of Contemporary History* 9 (October 1975): 210-212.
17. Ibid., 125. Newton N. Minow, John Bartlow Martin, and Lee M. Mitchell present Franklin Roosevelt as more actively mobilizing national opinion than argued by Steele. See their *Presidential Television* (New York: Basic Books, 1973), 29-32.
18. Befitting the lapse, the court packing case is one of the few instances when FDR failed to sound out congressional leadership before announcing his plan at a press conference. There are many good accounts of this event. One that does a good job conveying the surprise and consternation of Roosevelt's usual supporters at his "high handed" tactics is Joseph Alsop and Turner Catledge, *The 168 Days* (New York: Doubleday and Co., 1938).
19. Neustadt, *Presidential Power,* 64-65.
20. Ibid., 74-75.
21. Neustadt's use of the word "command" to mean the unilateral use of authority to alter others' behavior without compensation has entered the presidential literature as the chief alternative to bargaining as a mode of influence.
22. Alexander L. George and Juliette L. George, *Woodrow Wilson and Colonel House* (New York: J. Day Co., 1956), 290-292.
23. John Morton Blum, *Woodrow Wilson and the Politics of Morality* (Boston: Little, Brown, 1956), 189-191.
24. David S. McLellan and John W. Reuss, "Foreign and Military Policies," in *The Truman Period as a Research Field,* ed. Richard S. Kirkendall (Columbia: University of Missouri Press, 1967), 55-57. Curiously, this widely cited quotation is absent from Vandenberg's memoirs. It is ironic that Neustadt treats the Truman

Doctrine speech, which was perhaps the most successful use of public opinion in the postwar era to gain the president leverage vis-à-vis other political elites in Washington, as a prime example of pluralist exchange. He notes that Truman and others rallied the public to the subsequent Marshall Plan, but this was necessarily preceded, he argues, by elite exchange. Neustadt, *Presidential Power*, 36-40.

25. Truman in his memoirs vividly describes his rewriting of the "half hearted" draft from the State Department: "The key sentence, for instance, read, 'I believe that it should be the policy of the United States. . . .' I took my pencil, scratched out 'should' and wrote in 'must'. . . . I wanted no hedging in this speech. This was America's answer to the surge of expansion of Communist tyranny. It had to be clear and free of hesitation or double talk" (Harry S Truman, *Memoirs,* vol. 2, 105-109). For further discussion of the writing of the Truman Doctrine speech, see Chapter 6.

26. See on each of these points, respectively, Morris P. Fiorina, *Congress: Keystone of the Washington Establishment* (New Haven: Yale University Press, 1977); Austin Ranney, *Channels of Power* (Washington, D.C.: American Enterprise Institute, 1983); and Martin P. Wattenberg, *The Decline of Political Parties* (Cambridge: Harvard University Press, 1984).

27. For similar treatment of the bureaucracy, see Hugh Heclo, "Issue Networks and the Executive Establishment," in *The New American Political System,* ed. Anthony King (Washington, D.C.: American Enterprise Institute, 1978), 87-124; and Nelson W. Polsby, *Consequences of Party Reform* (New York: Oxford University Press, 1983), 90-104.

28. Thomas E. Mann and Norman J. Ornstein, eds., *The New Congress* (Washington, D.C.: American Enterprise Institute, 1981). See also Eric L. Davis, "Legislative Reform and the Decline of Presidential Influence on Capitol Hill," *British Journal of Political Science* 9 (October 1979): 465-479; and Bruce I. Oppenheimer, "Policy Effects of U.S. House Reform: Decentralization and the Capacity to Resolve Energy Issues," *Legislative Studies Quarterly* 5 (February 1980): 5-30.

29. Thomas E. Mann, "Elections and Change in Congress," in *The New Congress,* ed. Mann and Ornstein, 53. On announcing his retirement from the Senate after 51 years in Congress, Sen. Jennings Randolph was asked what major changes in politics he had seen. Randolph responded, "There is a lack of discipline in the Senate—a deterioration every year I've been here. I just don't understand it" (Marjorie Hunter, "From Roosevelt's Outings to Reagan's Greetings," *New York Times,* October 5, 1984, B10). See also, Steven V. Roberts, "Senate's New Breed Shuns Novice Role," *New York Times,* November 26, 1984, 1; and Alan Ehrenhalt, "In the Senate of the '80s, Team Spirit Has Given Way to the Rule of Individuals," *Congressional Quarterly Weekly Report,* September 4, 1982, 2175-2182.

30. Michael Robinson, "Three Faces of Congressional Media," in *The New Congress,* ed. Mann and Ornstein, 93. For confirmation of Robinson's reference, see Julia Malone, "Party 'Whips' Lose Their Snap to TV and Voters Back Home," *Christian Science Monitor,* June 27, 1984, 16; and Bob Michel, "Politics in the Age of Television," *Washington Post,* June 4, 1984, 27.

31. Douglass Cater, *The Fourth Branch of Government* (Boston: Houghton Mifflin, 1959), 65.

32. Roger Davidson, "Subcommittee Government: New Channels for Policy Making," in *The New Congress,* ed. Mann and Ornstein, 109.

33. For the early history of the Democratic Study Group, see Mark F. Ferber, "The Formation of the Democratic Study Group," in *Congressional Behavior,* ed. Nelson W. Polsby (New York: Random House, 1971), 249-269. Dennis Farney

reports the DSG's efforts to overcome its recent complacency in "Democratic Study Unit in Ferment," *Wall Street Journal,* April 25, 1984, 54.

34. Susan Webb Hammond, Arthur G. Stevens, Jr., and Daniel P. Mulhollan, "Congressional Caucuses: Legislators As Lobbyists," in *Interest Group Politics,* ed. Allan J. Cigler and Burdett A. Loomis (Washington, D.C.: CQ Press, 1983), 285-287.

35. Michael Kinsley, "The Art of Deduction: Writer's Loophole," *Wall Street Journal,* March 11, 1983, 21.

36. Norman J. Ornstein et al., *Vital Statistics on Congress, 1984-1985 Edition* (Washington, D.C.: American Enterprise Institute, 1984), 86-87. Data for 1984 are from Federal Election Commission, "PAC Support of Incumbents Increases in '84 Elections" (May 19, 1985), 1-3.

37. Quoted in J. David Gopoian, "What Makes PACs Tick? An Analysis of the Allocation Patterns of Economic Interest Groups," *American Journal of Political Science* 28 (May 1984): 259-281.

38. For an account of this incident, see White, *The Citadel,* 144-146.

39. Defending the Senate's action Sen. Larry Pressler inadvertently made the critic's point: "We got 69 votes, and we might have been able to top out at 80. With that many votes I don't think you can attribute it to campaign contributions alone" (Albert R. Hunt, "Special-Interest Money Increasingly Influences What Congress Enacts," *Wall Street Journal,* July 26, 1982, 13).

40. In addition to contributing heavily to probusiness (almost exclusively Republican) candidates, the chamber has sought to coordinate the political donations of smaller business PACs. In 1982 it produced a closed-circuit show called "See How They Run," which reviewed 50 key races for 150 PAC managers around the country. Much of the information reported here on the Chamber of Commerce comes from the program titled "Congress and the Media" from the series "Congress: We the People," PBS network, 1984. See also "Running with the PACs," *Time,* October 25, 1982, 20-26.

41. Kay Lehman Schlozman and John T. Tierney, "More of the Same: Washington Press Group Activity in a Decade of Change," *Journal of Politics* 45 (May 1983): 351-377. Indicative of the growing fashion of enlisting public relations on Capitol Hill are executive seminars conducted by Congressional Quarterly with such unabashed titles as "Understanding Public Relations and the Washington News Media: Getting Your Message across to Congress" (from a conference listing in *Washington Post,* September 23, 1985, Business Calendar section, 19).

42. According to Stuart Eizenstat, Carter's domestic affairs adviser, "PACs balkanize the political process" ("Running with the PACs," 21).

43. Alvin Rabushka and Pauline Ryan, *The Tax Revolt* (Stanford: Hoover Institution, 1982); and Robert Hall and Alvin Rabushka, *Low Tax, Simple Tax, Flat Tax* (New York: McGraw-Hill, 1983). Another example is the unanimous House support in 1983 for legislation that would force absent parents to make child support payments. Earlier in the session Rep. Barbara Kennelly, the bill's sponsor, could attract little interest among her colleagues on the Ways and Means Committee. Once public opinion polls began showing that female voters across the country were sensitive to this issue, it did not take long for the bandwagon to fill up. "Members want to be able to go home and say, 'I've done something for women,' " stated Representative Kennelly (Steven V. Roberts, "Political Survival: It's Women and Children First," *New York Times,* December 6, 1983, 10).

44. Barbara Sinclair, "Coping with Uncertainty: Building Coalitions in the House and the Senate," in *The New Congress,* ed. Mann and Ornstein, 220. At the 1976 convention of the American Society for Public Administration, Dean Rusk

observed, "In the 1950s and 1960s we handled sensitive foreign affairs policy questions with the Congress by dealing with the 'whales'—Rayburn, Vinson, men like that. They could make commitments. Now it is as if we were dealing with 535 minnows in a bucket" (from a statement to the plenary session, Panel of Former Cabinet Officers, National Convention of the American Society for Public Administration, Washington, D.C., April 1976).

45. Steven R. Weisman, "No. 1, the President Is Very Result Oriented," *New York Times,* November 12, 1983, 10.
46. Sinclair, "Coping with Uncertainty," 220.
47. Sidney Blumenthal, "Marketing the President," *New York Times Magazine,* September 13, 1981, 110.
48. Cited in George C. Edwards III, *The Public Presidency* (New York: St. Martin's Press, 1983), 14.
49. B. Drummond Ayres, Jr., "G.O.P. Keeps Tabs on Nation's Mood," *New York Times,* November 16, 1981, 20.
50. Neustadt, *Presidential Power,* especially chap. 8; and Sperlich, "Bargaining and Overload."
51. This discussion of reputation follows closely that of Neustadt in *Presidential Power,* (New York: John Wiley and Sons, 1980), chap. 4.
52. Neustadt observed that President Truman's television appeal for tighter price controls in 1951 had little visible effect on how Washington politicians viewed the issue. This is the only mention of a president going public in the original eight chapters of the book. Neustadt, *Presidential Power,* 45.
53. Ibid., 238.
54. Cited in Gary C. Jacobson, *The Politics of Congressional Elections* (Boston: Little, Brown, 1983), 179-180. Jacobson goes on to note, "Carter did not enjoy broad public support during most of his presidency ... [and when] he was most popular early in his term ... he was unable to turn public support into political influence."
55. Statement by Rep. Richard B. Cheney cited in Charles O. Jones, "Congress and the Presidency," in *The New Congress,* eds. Thomas E. Mann and Norman J. Ornstein (Washington, D.C.: American Enterprise Institute, 1981), 241.
56. William A. Robinson, *Thomas B. Reed, Parliamentarian* (New York: Dodd, Mead, 1930), 100-101.
57. Nelson W. Polsby and Aaron B. Wildavsky, *Presidential Elections,* 2d ed. (New York: Charles Scribner's Sons, 1968), 80-81.
58. Polsby, *Consequences of Party Reform,* 64.
59. Polsby describes the reforms and convincingly argues their effects on the kinds of presidents elected in *Consequences of Party Reform.*
60. William Cavala, "Changing the Rules Changes the Game: Party Reform and the 1972 California Delegation to the Democratic National Convention," *American Political Science Review* 68 (March 1974): 27-42.
61. As a result of special rule changes that reserved at-large delegate seats for members of Congress, in 1984 these figures shot up to 63 percent for representatives and 62 percent for senators. "At Washington West, Clout and Compromise," *Congressional Quarterly Weekly Report,* July 21, 1984, 1745.
62. Richard B. Cheney, "The Law's Impact on Presidential and Congressional Election Campaigns," in *Parties, Interest Groups, and Campaign Finance Laws,* ed. Michael J. Malbin (Washington, D.C.: American Enterprise Institute, 1980), 238-248. On growing PAC participation in presidential elections, see Sara Fritz, "Changing Rules in Game of Politics Shaping Races," *Los Angeles Times,* December 22, 1983, 1.

63. Joseph Bruce Gorman, *Kefauver: A Political Biography* (New York: Oxford University Press, 1971), 80-106. For an account of the rise of Kefauver as an overnight television personality, see G. D. Wiebe, "Responses to the Televised Kefauver Hearings," *Public Opinion Quarterly* 16 (Summer 1952): 179-200.

64. Jimmy Carter, *Keeping the Faith* (New York: Bantam Books, 1982). For a more detailed treatment of the rise of outsiders, see Samuel Kernell, "Campaigning, Governing, and the Contemporary Presidency," in *The New Direction in American Politics,* ed. John E. Chubb and Paul E. Peterson (Washington, D.C.: Brookings Institution, 1985), 117-141.

65. Haynes Johnson, *The Absence of Power* (New York: Viking, 1980), 159-161.

66. Sperlich complains that Neustadt demands too much bargaining activity from the president and argues that more presidential influence comes from deference than Neustadt is willing to concede. Neither Neustadt nor Sperlich considers that bargaining is made more efficient by the routines of exchange and through political parties as protocoalitions. See Sperlich, "Bargaining and Overload."

67. Johnson, *Absence of Power,* 166-167.

68. Ibid., 22. Two months later they were having the same dialogue but in public. Hedrick Smith reports: " 'It upsets me when they say, "we'll bring it to the people," ' the stentorian white-haired speaker declared. 'That's the biggest mistake Carter could ever make' " ("Congress and Carter: An Uneasy Adjustment," *New York Times,* February 18, 1977, B16).

69. In both instances, the president eventually relented to mounting public pressure and signed essentially Democratic bills.

70. Walter J. Olezek, "The Context of Congressional Policy Making," in *Divided Democracy,* ed. James A. Thurber, (Washington, D.C.: CQ Press, 1991), 99.

71. James H. Rowe, Oral History Interview, 1969 and 1970, Harry S. Truman Library, Appendix.

72. "Oral History of the Truman White House" 1980, Harry S. Truman Library.

73. David E. Rosenbaum, "In Appeal for Support for Budget, President Calls Plan Best for Now," *New York Times,* October 3, 1990, A1.

74. Michael Oreskes, "Advantage: Democrats," *New York Times,* October 29, 1990, A14; and Maureen Dowd, "From President to Politician: Bush Attacks the Democrats," *New York Times,* October 30, 1990, A13.

The President
and the Press————————————— 3

On May 18, 1937, with some 200 reporters packed around the president's desk in the Oval Office, Franklin Roosevelt opened his normal Tuesday press conference by saying,

> Off the record, wholly off the record. I wanted to tell you a story that I think you ought to know because it does affect the press of the country. . . . As you know, I have always encouraged, and am entirely in favor of, absolute freedom for all news writers. That should be and will continue to be the general rule in Washington.[1]

He then pulled out the latest pink sheet (the color signifying "not for publication") from the McClure Syndicate to approximately 270 member newspapers, and began to read:

> Unchecked. A New York specialist high in the medical field is authority for the following, which is given in the strictest confidence to editors: Toward the end of last month Mr. Roosevelt was found in a coma at his desk. Medical examination disclosed the neck rash which is typical of certain disturbing symptoms. Immediate treatment of the most skilled kind was indicated, with complete privacy and detachment from official duties. Hence the trip to southern waters, with no newspapermen on board and a naval convoy which cannot be penetrated.
>   The unusual activities of Vice President Garner are believed to be in connection with the current situation and its possible developments. "Checking has been impossible."[2]

Then Roosevelt read another pink-sheet item that reported on a conversation at a private New York dinner party in which an official of American Cyanamid called the president "a paranoiac in the White House"; he declared that "a couple of well placed bullets would be the best thing for the country, and that he would buy a bottle of champagne as quick as he could get it to celebrate the news." In the ensuing conversation with reporters, the president revealed that the editor responsible for the stories was Richard Waldo. Waldo, who is better remembered for having originated the Good Housekeeping Seal of Approval, was not a Washingtonian and clearly must have felt he had little to lose by taking on the president.[3] After about 15 minutes, Roosevelt closed the discussion by reminding the reporters, "It is all off the record; all strictly in the family and nothing else." [4]

Institutionalized pluralism requires continuous face-to-face negotiations among partisan participants and inculcates strong norms of propriety. Cordial relations are functional. This incident reveals, however, that politics in this former era—especially when outsiders were involved—could be just as virulent as anything the egoism of individualized pluralism can produce. As startling as the episode must have been to the men and women gathered around the president's desk, it is, nonetheless, indicative of the FDR system of presidential-press relations, examined later in this chapter. It also shows how the normative order of the day dealt with deviant behavior.

Consider first that Roosevelt made his remarks "in confidence" to the regular assemblage of the Tuesday press conference. No effort was made to recruit sympathetic reporters. Nor did he have to resort to any hidden-hand strategies; the standard dictum "off the record" sufficed. Yet if Roosevelt did not wish his remarks to become news, why did he tell newspaper reporters? Two motives are possible. First, it is apparent on careful reading of his statement that FDR sought retribution against McClure's editor—not at his own hands, but at those of the Washington press corps. When asked, he did not hesitate to reveal the culprit's name. Roosevelt's fellow community members did not let him down.

Organically integrated societies commonly banish those guilty of serious violations of community norms, and Washington was no exception. The White House correspondents could not run Waldo out of town, but they could strip him of standing. Some tried to have him expelled from the National Press Club. When brought before the club's board of governors to answer charges, Waldo threatened to sue everyone present. According to one account, "The board members naturally hesitated." Although no formal action was taken, Waldo left the club.[5] The confidentiality of the president's remarks kept the story off the pages of the nation's newspapers and successfully summoned forth community sanctions.

A second, probably less immediate reason for giving this off-the-record information to reporters may have been to elicit the press corps' sympathy. Setting White House correspondents against this New York editor strengthened Roosevelt's ties with them and loosened theirs with distant editors. With most of the nation's newspapers and chains on record opposing his election in 1932 and again in 1936, Roosevelt made a special effort to generate good will among the working press in Washington. He largely succeeded. In consequence, Roosevelt enjoyed a more productive relationship with the press corps, over a longer time, than any president before or since.[6]

The Bargaining President and the Press

As traditionally conceived, presidential leadership flows through quiet diplomacy and is generally ill served by public pressure on bargaining partners. Why, then, should favorable press relations have been important to Roosevelt? The reason is that news contributes to pluralist leadership and affects the way elite relations are conducted. Close ties to the working press were, in fact, more highly valued in Roosevelt's time than they are today.

The universal "law of anticipated reactions" dictates that politicians in Washington will pay attention to their publics in deciding what stance to take with the president. Before scientific surveys were widely available, a politician's mail and the newspapers of the constituency substituted for public opinion. A favorable press may have only fostered an illusion of support, but frequently it sufficed. Also, prominent journalists serve as important opinion leaders in establishing the president's reputation. In Roosevelt's time the appraisals of David Lawrence, Walter Lippmann, Arthur Krock, and others were given close scrutiny by Washingtonians; others who would later take on this responsibility include James Reston, Richard Strout, Joseph Kraft, and David Broder.

The bargaining president can use press coverage in a variety of ways to improve his position. By making an issue newsworthy, he can force other negotiators to deal with it.[7] The president may selectively release information that enhances his position and diminishes the position of his bargaining partner. By assuming a firm public posture on an issue, he can stake out a negotiating stance that everyone recognizes cannot be easily abandoned. The president can float a trial balloon from which he may identify coalition partners and test potential avenues of compromise. Many of these activities have precedents reaching far back into the nineteenth century. Unlike purely public strategies of leadership, none requires a communications infrastructure that gives the president instant access to millions of citizens, and all are directed toward the bargaining table.

To appreciate why pluralist arts are sometimes publicly practiced, one must understand the rationale of the constitutional structure and how news serves the presidency. Montesquieu's proposition that unchecked power is inherently corrupt preoccupied the Founding Fathers as they deliberated a new constitutional order. Reasoning that in a democracy, tyranny requires collusion, they dispersed governmental authority wherever possible. The result was, and is, autonomous institutions with formal relations among them. On reading the Constitution, the capital's planner, Pierre L'Enfant, concluded, "No message to nor from the President is to be made without a sort of decorum." Accordingly, there was little reason to place the Capitol and the White House on the same hill.[8]

Despite continuous interaction today, the institutional distance created between Congress and the presidency 200 years ago has not been greatly shortened. Even as informal, face-to-face negotiation occurs, it is commonly preceded and facilitated by the preparatory public activities institutional distance encourages. As Douglass Cater has noted, "Unofficial communication between the executive and legislative branches of government—and within each branch—goes on regularly through the press, well in advance of official communications." [9] Woodrow Wilson was surely correct when, as president, he observed, "News is the atmosphere of politics." [10] This is why a devout bargainer like Franklin Roosevelt would be so attentive to the Washington press corps.

The conspicuous deficiency of professional good will between modern presidents and the Washington press has prompted some historians and journalists whose careers spanned the administrations of Franklin Roosevelt and Richard Nixon to reexamine the "secret" of Roosevelt's success. These chroniclers give the Great Depression and the New Deal much of the credit. [11] Never before during peacetime, they have written, had the country looked so intently to Washington to solve its problems.

For reporters, the rise of Washington as the center of the nation's politics meant that Washington by-lines suddenly commanded front-page space. For the president, the times posed unprecedented responsibilities and opportunities. Roosevelt sought the cooperation of more elites than any president since Lincoln. Beyond Capitol Hill, old-line agencies had to be made compliant, if not enthusiastic, about implementing the many New Deal programs. Interest groups had to be attracted to the programs. In a few instances, such as the formation of the Tennessee Valley Authority, altogether new constituencies had to be mobilized. [12] The federal courts—from those in the districts to the Supreme Court—had to be converted from the sanctity of the Constitution's contract clause that threatened to paralyze much of the administration's interventionist economic program. [13] Because the president needed to enlist so many persons dispersed throughout government, Washington correspondents could play a major role in helping Roosevelt sell the New Deal.

The urgency of the times explains what brought the presidency and the Washington press together, but it fails to account fully for the productive relationship that ensued. The rest of the explanation lies in the convergence of interests between a newly professional press corps and the presidency. The kind of relationship revealed in the news conference of May 18, 1937, served the emerging needs of both the president and the press.

From the late nineteenth century to Franklin Roosevelt's inauguration, Washington correspondents evolved from an amorphous collection of visiting editors, reporters on temporary assignment, and disguised job seekers to a stable community of professional journalists. [14] This professional development held consequences for a president seeking influence. Where Roosevelt excelled—and where his predecessors distinctly did not—was in recognizing correspondents' *professional* stake in a particular kind of news conveyed in a particular way. From his first day in office, Roosevelt understood this—better, one can add, than some of the correspondents' editors, who could not fathom why their reporters were toeing Roosevelt's line rather than that of their home paper.

To appreciate how the mutual interests of the president and the press formed a basis for reciprocity, one needs to understand the modern evolution of the Washington press corps. Because the institutional development of Congress has been well plotted in the political science literature,[15] it in large measure informs one's conception of the workings of institutionalized pluralism. What is largely unknown is that the development of the press corps since the late nineteenth century—a far less well documented story—follows a parallel course and similarly contributes to the transformation of Washington into a community of institutional actors.

This is also an ideal arena for examining the refinement of bargaining leadership because presidential exchange with the press appears thoroughly, though subtly, rooted in the institutional needs of each participant. When a president cuts a quick deal with the head of a powerful committee, one is afforded only a brief and superficial glimpse of the bargaining arts. Anyone anywhere can horse trade. By contrast, the workings of tacit, ongoing reciprocity agreements described below show how pluralist leadership is embedded in the institutional milieu.

Finally, this historical survey introduces key elements in the breakdown of institutionalized pluralism. Better than any other pairing in Washington, the modern evolution of presidential-press relations describes the recent transformation of the Washington community and the rise of presidents who routinely go public.

Emergence of the Washington Press as an Institution

Early Professionalization

Shortly after Henry Adams arrived in Washington in 1868 to pursue a career in journalism, he followed the established protocol of paying respects to the president. Adams's visit to the White House was uneventful, but that it happened at all reveals a lot about the size and pace of the Washington community in the late 1860s. "In four-and-twenty hours," reported Adams, a young man "could know everybody; in two days, everybody knew him." [16]

President Andrew Johnson could take an informal approach to press relations because there were fewer correspondents in those days and they were not so interested in him. Whereas about four-fifths of modern reporting of Congress and the presidency is devoted to the latter, the opposite pattern was the case throughout most of the nineteenth century. A study of Washington reporting in the newspapers of one midwestern city found closer scrutiny of congressional committees than of the presidency.[17] To discern the origins of the Washington press corps, one must therefore look to Capitol Hill.

The press corps had gained official recognition during the late 1850s when control over credentials to the House and Senate press galleries was turned over to a committee of correspondents, and registered journalists began to be listed in each year's official *Congressional Directory*. In 1868, 58 reporters were so listed. By Adams's death in 1918, the number had more than quadrupled.

Growth contributed to the professionalization of the Washington press corps, but as long as growth was accompanied by high turnover, the Washington assignment remained little more than a revolving door. Above all, professionalization required a stable membership. Though it is impossible to state definitively what increased stability and promoted professionalization at the turn of the century, biographical sketches and circumstantial evidence contained in gallery listings suggest several influences. One is that the number of papers that pulled out of the press gallery declined sharply after the turn of the century.[18] Also, one suspects that veteran correspondents were valued for their personal contacts with officials. These contacts increasingly became a resource that gave Washington correspondents an advantage over their would-be replacements.[19]

By the early 1900s, reporters viewed Washington as an attractive assignment. Correspondents were sent to Washington often after years of service on local and state political beats. When they returned home, they frequently did so to become their paper's managing editor. The Washington assignment had become an important step in career advancement.[20] The status of the Washington correspondent must have been secure by the 1920s when press chronicler Silas Bent remarked, "The corps of correspondents there represents the very flower of the American press." [21]

Another, more significant development that stabilized careers was the practice of writing for more than one paper. Begun as early as the 1870s, this custom resulted in consistently lower turnover rates for correspondents. Turnover declined sharply from the close of the Civil War to the election of Franklin Roosevelt (see Table 3-1). In 1864-1866, when all reporters worked for only one paper, 75 percent of the correspondents left Washington before the next session of Congress convened. By 1876, 15 percent of the gallery reporters listed in the *Congressional Directory* associated themselves with two or more papers, and turnover was down to 52 percent. By 1914, 35 percent of the listed reporters had multiple clients, and turnover was 34 percent. Turnover rates for correspondents between Congresses had been reduced to 22 percent by the early 1930s.

The trend toward working for multiple papers probably had a greater effect on career stability and professionalization than the numbers alone suggest. Many of the papers constituting multiple clients for a reporter came from smaller communities far from Washington and were only marginally interested in Washington coverage beyond that available from the wire services. Without being able to share the expenses of a correspondent with

Table 3-1 Turnover among Washington Correspondents, Selected
Years, 1864-1932

	1864- 1866	1876- 1878	1890- 1892	1900- 1902	1914- 1916	1930- 1932
Turnover (%)						
Departing	75	52	37	34	34	22
New[1]	70	59	36	34	35	26
Distribution of all correspondents, by clients (%)[2]						
Single paper	100	85	66	62	51	48
Syndicate	0	0	15	9	14	30
Multiple papers	0	15	19	29	35	22
Total number of correspondents	51	132	151	159	200	351
Percent leaving over two-year period, by client						
Single paper	75	56	41	40	44	22
Syndicate	—	—	26	29	38	25
Multiple papers	—	30	31	22	17	18

[1] New additions in gallery listings from first to second year.
[2] Calculated for first year of pair.
SOURCES: *Congressional Directory* for each year indicated.

other papers, they probably would not have long maintained a Washington
bureau. Also, multiple papers were a form of diversification through which
reporters were able to reduce uncertainty. The more papers reporters could
sign on, the less their dependence upon any one of them. Newspapers became,
then, a market for correspondents, and the relationship changed from
employer to client.[22]

Diversification and the establishment of client relationships fostered
professionalism and set it on a course that would in time shape presidential-
press relations. One conspicuous consequence was the posture of journalists
toward politicians. In the past when newspapers were as much party organs as
they were business enterprises, correspondents served the party in the news
they wrote. Absolute fidelity to the editorial position of the home paper was a
prerequisite to assignment. Client relationships, however, required flexibility
on the part of reporters. While they perhaps had to be willing to color reports
with whatever slant a paper's editor wanted, correspondents could ill afford to
be too partisan lest they lose their appeal to other current and potential clients.
Too close an association with a particular party line reduced correspondents'
marketability. The more neutral the stance reporters could maintain, the
better their market position.

In the 1920s Washington correspondents began writing about them-selves—a self-absorption characteristic of blossoming professionalism. These articles and books are revealing in depicting correspondents largely shorn of personal partisanship. If they, as a class, held their subjects in any special regard, it was most likely one of cynicism. In 1927 Silas Bent wrote:

> Newspaper men are seldom men of strong convictions; their work seems somehow to militate against that. It is nothing unusual to see a Washington correspondent shift without the slightest jar from a newspaper of one political complexion to another of the opposite camp. . . . [H]ad it happened during the last century [it] would have provoked, almost certainly, cries of turncoat.[23]

All professions strive to legitimize practice with creed, and the Washing-ton press corps was no exception. At the same time that increasing numbers of Washington correspondents were working for multiple clients, growing syndi-cates, or neutral wire services, the concept of objective reporting came into vogue. The job of Washington correspondents, J. Frederick Essary explained in 1928, "demands of them scrupulous fairness and as near literal accuracy as may be possible, within human limitations, in the matter which is daily spread before their millions of readers." [24] Walter Lippmann was an early exponent of this "progressive" creed. In 1960 he served again as a bellwether for a new doctrine when he addressed the National Press Club and called for reporters to abandon mindless objectivity in favor of interpretation. From the 1920s through the 1950s, however, objective journalism reigned as the dominant ideology of the profession.[25]

Other trappings of professionalism, such as collegiality and collusive efforts to control the work environment, were also much in evidence during this era. There are many examples of the former, including the practice of "blacksheeting": reporters would informally divide up coverage of Washington events and share the carbon copies of their articles for others to rewrite for their home papers.[26] The formal expression of professional collegiality was the formation of professional societies, such as the Gridiron Club, the Press Gallery Correspondents Association, the National Press Club, and the White House Correspondents Association.

Creed, collegiality, and the recognition of collective goals all helped distinguish Washington correspondents as a separate and resourceful entity in the Washington community. Professional trappings would soon begin to alter the relations of these correspondents with the president.

Early Presidential-Press Relations

The nineteenth-century progenitor of the presidential press conference was the private interview, offered first by President Andrew Johnson (1865-1869) to selected reporters. Sensing that the public was reading published interviews more closely than his speeches, Johnson made it a practice during his impeachment trial to rebuke charges from Congress by summoning a sympathetic correspondent to the White House. Most of Johnson's nineteenth-century successors submitted to an occasional private interview.[27]

President William McKinley (1897-1901) attended to press relations more conscientiously than most of his predecessors. During important White House meetings reporters were frequently permitted to wait in an anteroom for interviews with the president's visitors. McKinley's staff also routinely gave reporters the president's speaking schedule and advance copies of his addresses. Personally, however, McKinley remained aloof, and any direct contact with the press was left largely to chance. Ida M. Tarbell describes White House coverage during the McKinley years.

> It is in "Newspaper Row," as the east side of the great portico is called, that the White House press correspondents flourish most vigorously. Here they gather by the score on exciting days and ... watch for opportunities to waylay important officials as they come and go. Nobody can get in or out of the Executive Mansion without their seeing him, and it is here most of the interviews, particularly with Cabinet officers, are held....
>
> It is part of the unwritten law of the White House that newspaper men shall never approach the President as he passes to and fro near their alcove or crosses the portico to his carriage, unless he himself stops and talks to them. This he occasionally does.[28]

McKinley left ample room for innovation in this realm to his successor—the man who called the presidency "the bully pulpit."

Theodore Roosevelt (1901-1909) was probably the first president to appreciate the value of public opinion in leading Washington. Certainly, he was the first to cultivate close ties with Washington correspondents and consequently was the first important transitional figure in presidential-press relations. In his age, before "direct communication" via radio and television, public relations and press relations were operationally largely the same. Roosevelt succeeded with the former because he was able to dictate such favorable terms with the latter.

According to David S. Barry, a prominent correspondent of the era and a Roosevelt favorite, the difference between Theodore Roosevelt and all the presidents who preceded him was that he read papers' treatment of the news more than their editorials. Roosevelt "knew the value and potent influence of a news paragraph written as he wanted it written and disseminated through the proper channels." [29]

On his first day in office, Roosevelt summoned several represen-tatives of the wire services and enunciated a set of ground rules that would give the press unprecedented access to the White House but leave him with a large measure of control over what was printed. The president insisted that, above all, information given in confidence must remain confidential. "If you ever hint where you got [the story]," Roosevelt warned, "I'll say you are a damn liar." [30] Anyone who broke this rule would be banned from the White House and denied access to legitimate news. Historian George

Juergens describes how Roosevelt maintained this hierarchical relation with the press.

> He divided newsmen into distinct groups of insiders and outsiders, and was unforgiving in banishing those he felt, justifiably or not, had betrayed him. The fact that he could get away with such high-handedness goes far to explain why he received the favorable coverage he did. It did a journalist's career no good to be on the outside, not to know what was going on. The reporter had every reason to play along if that was the price for being informed. Of course the coercion only worked because of the unequal relationship between Roosevelt and a not yet fully mature press corps. Reporters in a later era, conscious of their own prerogatives, would not have tolerated a president telling them who could have access to the news and on what terms. But this was a different game played by different rules.[31]

Theodore Roosevelt's approach to press relations may have greatly increased accessibility to the White House, but it also posed serious problems for the rapidly professionalizing correspondents. By retaining control over which stories could be reported and how, the president preempted journalistic discretion, a prerogative Congress had surrendered by the mid-nineteenth century. Looking back on Roosevelt's administration a decade later, Washington correspondents found intolerable his division of the White House press into "insiders and outsiders." [32] This practice created uncertainty, obviously for the outsiders because they were missing the stories, but also for the insiders because they could so easily be demoted to the ranks of the outcasts. Among professionals whose careers depended upon their access to political news, this could, of course, be devastating, which is precisely why the stringent rules were seldom violated.

Finally, Roosevelt, who sported a strict and complex ethical code, excoriated reporters who wrote for papers that held distinctly different editorial positions. As far as he was concerned, these men had "sold their ethics." It could be cause for banishment.[33] Roosevelt may have been a fan of the news business, as his biographers attest, but his attitude reveals a fundamental lack of appreciation for the emerging professional requirements of the Washington correspondent. This stance appears all the more arbitrary (and hence revealing) since it served no apparent strategic purpose.

Roosevelt could dictate the rules because, as Juergens noted, he was working with a still poorly professionalized press. Washington correspondents had neither a strong sense of their rights nor any means for enforcing them. During the next two decades, both of these deficiencies would be corrected.

The other important transitional figure in the development of presidential-press relations was Woodrow Wilson (1913-1921).[34] Like Roosevelt, a Progressive facing a conservative Washington, he also recognized the value of public opinion and sedulously set out to establish favorable relations with the press. In this case, the talent was missing, and instead of substantive reciprocity, the result was procedural reform.

Wilson extended to the press most of the prerogatives that Roosevelt had held back. Continuing Roosevelt's practice of frequent meetings, he opened them to all correspondents. The response, he discovered somewhat to his chagrin, was overwhelming. At one of his early conferences more than 200 reporters—many of whom had never participated in a presidential interview— packed themselves into the Oval Office. This and his other meetings with the press proved to be unhappy affairs. Wilson considered reporters dullards, and they sensed his condescension. After two years of discomfort for all involved, Wilson quietly abandoned the weekly gatherings.

However unsatisfying for either party, those regular, open conferences yielded another significant advancement for the press corps. Roosevelt's small entourage of insiders, or "fair haired boys," as they would later be remembered, posed no problem for his rules of confidentiality, but Wilson's news conferences opened the door to violations. In 1913 a significant breach occurred. After Wilson had given his views "off the record" on current conditions in Mexico, the story appeared the next day on the front pages of several newspapers.[35] Recognizing the threat this incident posed to the future of the open conference, a group of reporters from the most respected papers and wire services met informally with the president's secretary, Joseph Tumulty, to rectify the situation. Out of their meeting came an agreement whereby the White House press corps would assume full responsibility for policing the president's news conference. Shortly thereafter, the White House Correspondents Association was formed with the mandate to establish standards of professional behavior and to regulate attendance at the conferences. Assuming collective responsibility, the profession gained control over its members and superseded White House regulation.

The next three presidents—Harding, Coolidge, and Hoover—experienced difficulties in the press relations they inherited from Roosevelt and Wilson. Each began well enough with a friendly announcement of frequent and open conferences. Within a few months, however, the press relations of each fell on hard times. Warren G. Harding (1921-1923) even caused some correspondents to voice concern over his incompetence with the freewheeling press conference format. When he finally made the anticipated egregious misstatement, which necessitated a White House retraction and a State Department disclaimer, Harding's aides decided the informal press conference was too risky. Subsequently, they insisted that all questions be written and submitted in advance. The correspondents complied, although privately many complained. With follow-up questions disallowed, spontaneity was lost, and the conferences became dull. Many reporters quit attending.

Calvin Coolidge (1923-1929) kept the written questions and added new stringencies. Correspondent Willis Sharp laid out the Coolidge ground rules.

> The correspondents may not say that they saw the President. They may not quote the President. They may not say that an official spokesman said what the President said. The information or views he gives out are supposed to be

presented to the public without any indication of official responsibility. The correspondents are supposed to present these views as if they had dropped from heaven, and are wholly unprotected when, as has happened, Mr. Coolidge finds it expedient to repudiate them. As a climax the correspondents are forbidden to mention that a question asked at the conferences was ignored.[36]

He went on to report "murmuring among the correspondents," who especially disliked the requirement that the president could not be directly quoted without permission. This rule had been in place since President Wilson's conferences, but no president hid behind the "White House spokesman" as frequently as Coolidge. Again, the White House press complied, but in magazine articles some correspondents began to ridicule the practice. "The White House spokesman" became "the Presidential Larynx" and "the Figure of Speech." [37] For the first time, the press began to impose costs on an unaccommodating president.

By the time Herbert Hoover (1929-1933) was inaugurated, the complaints of the press about Coolidge's rules were widely known and shared by other Washington elites who had to transact business with him.[38] So when Hoover announced at his first press conference that he would liberalize the attribution rules and consult with the White House Correspondents Association on ways to improve the news conference, his remarks evoked jubilation from the press. Their glee was short-lived, however. None of the reforms were instituted, none of the promised consultations held.

Instead, Hoover managed to strain press relations further when he failed to acknowledge the great majority of questions submitted by the press and began favoring sympathetic journalists with choice stories. Twenty-five years earlier Theodore Roosevelt had gotten away with this practice, but by this time the correspondents had a clear sense of their collective interests. They retaliated. Hoover's favorites were dubbed the "White House Pen Men's Association." According to James E. Pollard, "Other [than the favored] correspondents were affronted and they not only refrained from writing favorably about Mr. Hoover but were impelled to write things that hurt him." [39] Singling out the president's favorite insider, one journalist sniped, "If Hoover is defeated, a large share of his unpopularity can be attributed to Mark Sullivan." [40] Theodore Roosevelt and Woodrow Wilson were transitional figures in advancing presidential-press relations; Harding, Coolidge, and Hoover proved to be demonstration cases of the implications for a president's options of the developing professionalism of the press.

Early Competition and Collective Interests

As the market between papers and correspondents emerged, reporters competed tacitly with one another for choice clients, chiefly by competing for choice stories. Correspondents' growing independence from home editors increased their dependence on news sources—presidents included. Competition creates losers as well as winners, however, and unconstrained competition could be hazardous for budding careers.

The collective interests of the Washington press corps favored open news conferences over private presidential interviews. The reason was simple. Open news conferences gave no reporter undue advantage over another or permitted a president to divide and conquer. Within the first three decades of the century, the long-term, collective interests of the group achieved precedence over the short-term, competitive desires of its individual members, a mark of professionalization. In describing the professional needs of today's journalists, Anthony Smith explains how, once established, standardized outlets for news are perpetuated:

> The tensions within the news gathering process help to accentuate the dependence upon recognized channels and therefore the power of those channels over the shaping of news itself. Competition between reporters of different newspapers working at the same beat will ensure that they will not want to miss press conferences, announcements, or social functions at which principal makers of news or providers of information may be present. Competition will make them dissatisfied with the shared channels but will tend to entrench those channels in their importance.[41]

This explains why during Wilson's administration senior correspondents rushed in to protect the open conference when it appeared that a breach of confidentiality might end it; also why reporters chafed under Harding's "written questions" rule and Coolidge's refusal to allow attribution. Finally, it explains why Hoover was publicly derided when he showed favoritism in giving stories to correspondents. These professionals had a vested, collective interest in the integrity of the open press conference. The press conference became sacrosanct, not because it satisfied the competitive urges of journalists but precisely because it denied them.

As the Washington press corps evolved into a corporate entity, its members attained standing within the Washington community that few could have hoped to achieve acting alone. Writing about this era in 1937, Leo Rosten observed, "Their help is sought by persons and organizations trying to publicize an issue; their displeasure is avoided. They are aware by virtue of the deference paid to them and the importance attached to their dispatches, that they are factors of political consequence."[42]

The FDR System: Hard News, Openly Conveyed

This chapter opened with a press conference that took place in 1937, early in the second term of President Roosevelt's administration (1933-1945). By most estimates the honeymoon between the president and the press corps had long ended. Still, it was evident that the mutual respect and professional intimacy begun at Roosevelt's first press conference four years earlier remained firm. Years later, near the end of his presidency, reporters would still attribute their continuing amity to the relationship he spawned in 1933.[43] By the mid-1950s, they were writing about it nostalgically.

When Roosevelt began his first news conference in 1933, he, like Wilson 20 years earlier, was met by a throng of more than 200 reporters anxiously awaiting word as to how he planned to conduct business. Roosevelt began by announcing that he was dispensing with written questions. He then identified four classes of information that would be presented in these "delightful family conferences": (1) occasional direct quotations permitted only through written authorization from the White House; (2) press conference comments attributed to the president "without direct quotations"; (3) background information to be used in stories without a reference to the White House; and (4) "off the record" remarks not to be repeated to absent reporters. To administer the policy of authorized direct quotations and other relations with the press, Roosevelt appointed the White House office's first press secretary, Stephen Early.

When the conference ended, the correspondents applauded, the first time ever according to some veterans.[44] One seasoned reporter called it "the most amazing performance the White House has ever seen. The press barely restrained its whoopees ... the reportorial affection for the president is unprecedented. He has definitely captivated an unusually cynical battalion of correspondents." [45] *Editor and Publisher,* the semiofficial scribe and gossip of the profession, was unrestrained:

> Mr. Roosevelt is a great hit among newspapermen at Washington. I rubbed my ears and opened my eyes when I heard hard-boiled veterans, men who had lived through so many administrations and been so disillusioned that there are calluses in their brain, talk glibly about the merits of the White House incumbent. If Mr. Roosevelt fails the craft, by any false word or deed, he will break a hundred hearts that have not actually palpitated for any political figure in many a year.[46]

That first day Roosevelt gave them what they had sought for more than a decade: assurance of hard news, openly conveyed. The president had made his pact with the Washington press corps.

Roosevelt strengthened the press conference in other ways. He met with the press frequently and routinely; only rarely did he depart from his biweekly, Tuesday-Friday schedule. By the time of his death in April 1945, Roosevelt had invited correspondents into the Oval Office on 998 occasions. Equally important to White House reporters, he used these conferences as occasions to make significant announcements. Reporters came expecting hard news. "He never sent reporters away empty-handed ... [they] are all for a man who can give them several laughs and a couple of top-head dispatches in a twenty minute visit." [47] The White House correspondents not only appreciated the choice stories he saved for these gatherings, they also praised his "timing" and packaging in ways that enhanced an item's newsworthiness.[48] Frequently over the years, Roosevelt would go so far as to suggest how a story should be written, and rarely did the press find this spoon-feeding unpalatable.

For a talented pluralist president like Roosevelt, these delightful family conferences offered ample opportunity to employ his considerable interpersonal skills. The president was usually a model of cordiality. Even his harshest critics in the press corps freely conceded that they were treated fairly at these conferences.[49] Whenever Roosevelt complained about a particular article, he would frequently blame the paper's editor, who he tactfully asserted must have put the correspondent up to it.[50] This technique reduced tension and gave the reporter a convenient way of dissociating himself from his paper's editorial stance.

Even the editors who occasionally traveled to Washington to observe these conferences to see "what had gotten into" the reporters were defenseless against the president's charm. Writing on an incident that took place shortly before Roosevelt's death, Walter Davenport described how one group of editors responded to the Roosevelt treatment.

> Now they [the editors] had come to Washington to be the guests of their reporters at one of America's own peculiar institutions—a Presidential press conference. They were just that—visitors. Outside, they might shout until windows broke but here they were bound by rule and precedent to be silent. Only an accredited correspondent may ask questions or make comment. . . . They stood closely grouped, tight-lipped, skeptical, narrow-eyed, as though alerted against the widely advertised charm. That is, at first. Gradually they softened, relaxed. At one of the President's early sallies . . . they grinned. Before it was over, the grin had become a chuckle.
>
> Then came that sudden "Thank you, Mr. President," after a lull, and their Washington correspondents took them by the arms and presented them to Mr. Roosevelt. . . . He shook their hands with tremendous vigor—this Tired Old Man. He thanked them for their gladly given support of the bond drive. He rejoiced to hear they were feeling well and he told them that, given time (laughter), he'd make good reporters of their Washington men (laughter).
>
> Presently they were plodding across the White House park toward Pennsylvania Avenue. For a few moments they were silent. Then one of them observed that he'd be damned. Another said that in his opinion the President was a wonder. The third said that, anyway, Mr. Harold Ickes [FDR's secretary of interior and outspoken press critic] was an old fool. And then with one accord, they began tearing Mr. Ickes apart.[51]

Roosevelt also strengthened the press conference by relying upon it almost exclusively. With but one exception, he did not give private interviews. That exception is significant, however, because it reveals the entrenched character of the normative system prevailing in the palmy days of institutionalized pluralism. On February 27, 1937, the *New York Times* published a private interview with Roosevelt by Arthur Krock, perhaps Washington's most carefully read columnist. According to Krock's account of the incident, the next press conference was an angry one. The reporters accused Roosevelt of favoritism, which he had made all the more unacceptable by extending to a bureau chief rather than to a member of the working press. J. Frederick Essary, by then a senior Washington correspondent, asked the president pointedly whether he planned to repeat such favoritism. Roosevelt promptly confessed his blame. "My head is on the block. Steve's [press secretary Early] head is on the block. I promise to never do it again." [52] During the next eight years he kept his word.

Elevating the press conference to a place of primacy, Roosevelt offered the Washington press corps all that its profession required in its relations with the White House. As the Krock incident shows, however, this arrangement was not without cost. It ceded to the press corps control over the relationship to a degree that no president had done in the past or would do in the future. A few years later when Harry Truman was similarly cross-examined at a news conference about an exclusive interview, again with Krock, he retorted, "I'll give interviews to anybody I damn please." [53]

That the profession got its hard news, openly conveyed, is apparent. To appreciate what Roosevelt gained in return, one must largely trust the compliments of correspondents and the testimonials of disgruntled conservative editors. What they indicate is that Roosevelt succeeded in splitting off Washington correspondents from the editorial stance of their papers.

Evidence of this phenomenon is readily available in the election preferences of these two groups in 1936. In the spring of that year, Leo Rosten conducted an informal survey of Washington correspondents to determine their preferences. Of the 84 he questioned, 54 named Roosevelt as their first choice. Tying for second with 8 votes each were Republican preconvention front-runners Arthur Vandenberg and Alfred Landon. Altogether the Republican candidates had the support of 31 percent of the correspondents against Roosevelt's 65 percent.[54] By contrast, during the fall campaign 61 percent of the nation's major newspapers endorsed Republican opponent Landon.[55] Throughout his twelve years in office Franklin Roosevelt lived with a hostile newspaper industry and a friendly press corps.

Transition from the FDR System

The popular thesis that FDR's sympathetic treatment was a result of the times was presented earlier in this chapter. The Great Depression and the New Deal created a moment in history when the natural inclination of the government to retain information and of the press to extract it gave way to reciprocity. As never before, the president and the press needed each other to accomplish their respective tasks. Daniel Boorstin observed that Roosevelt's frequent conferences "bred intimacy, informality, and a set of institutionalized procedures; before long the spirit of those press conferences became on both sides much like that of any other responsible deliberative body." [56]

Figure 3-1 Growth of Washington Press Corps, 1864-1987

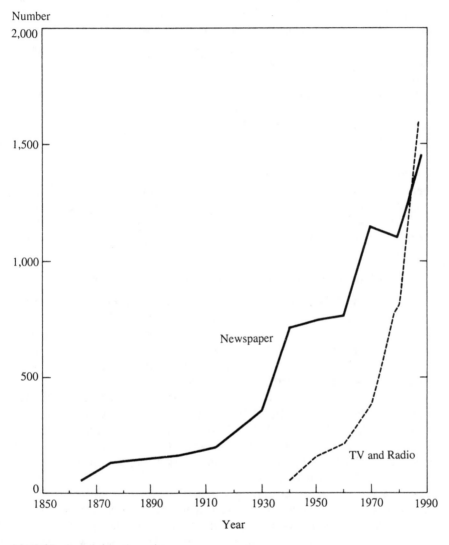

Number

SOURCE: Compiled by the author

The professional development of the Washington correspondent and the press practices Roosevelt established suggest, however, that systemic forces, unlike the crash of 1929, were also at work. Franklin Roosevelt succeeded with the press in the same way he succeeded with other Washingtonians. He founded a stable exchange relationship on the mutual professional needs of the participants.[57]

Given that the FDR system was rooted in the professional development of the Washington press, it seems ironic that these arrangements turned out to be fragile. Deterioration set in shortly after his departure not simply because Roosevelt's successors did not have his political acumen. The press conference declined because the needs of the participants changed. In different ways, advances in communications and transportation undermined the value of the FDR system for both the president and the press.

Radio, television, and air travel introduced the opportunity for presidents to engage in frequent, direct communication with the American public. No longer were they dependent upon the Washington press corps to convey their views to Washington and to the country. Going public would become a routine matter.

For the new breed of broadcast journalists who, as shown in Figure 3-1, grew rapidly in number and share of the press corps from 1940 on, Roosevelt's intimate family conferences held little attraction. As technology transformed the "press" into the "media," the press corps lost its corporate identity. "Hard news, openly conveyed" connoted something entirely different to broadcast journalists.

Press Relations under Truman and Eisenhower

For Harry S Truman (1945-1953) and Dwight D. Eisenhower (1953-1961), their styles and the needs of the press continued to shape presidential-press relations. Despite the manifold personal differences between Truman and Eisenhower, relations with the press retained a measure of continuity during the 16 years after Roosevelt largely because of the professional correspondents' attachment to the FDR system.

When Truman came into office he promptly announced that he would continue FDR's ground rules. Although Eisenhower during the transition period considered dropping scheduled press conferences altogether, he, too, ultimately made few changes in the Roosevelt format. Truman's directness and occasional irascibility at times reduced the news conference to verbal sparring matches; Eisenhower's famous syntactical convolutions left reporters scratching their heads and conferring among themselves after a conference to determine what the president had said. Under both presidents, news conferences displayed the structure if not the substance of the Roosevelt press conference. Moreover, neither Truman nor Eisenhower regularly went beyond the news conference to woo reporters with private interviews or with other practices that would become commonplace in the 1960s.

What these presidents did do during their combined 16-year tenure was to take small steps, more as concessions to the broadcast industry than as political strategies, that would make the dismantling of the FDR system under John Kennedy appear to be little more than the next step in an incremental progression. Midway through his second term, Truman permitted radio broadcasts of recorded excerpts of his news conferences. This meant that the president would normally be speaking for the record.[58] Transcription had begun earlier as a convenience to the press, but now with his comments being heard nationally, it was of little consequence when he permitted the press to publish a paraphrased transcript of his remarks. In 1950, with international events bringing the press to the president's door in greater numbers, the conference was moved from the Oval Office to a larger room in the State Department, then across the street from the White House. Added to the fact that Truman reduced the number of meetings from two to one a week, many reporters unhappily came to feel that the press conference had become a more formal affair. To them it lacked the spontaneity, and ultimately the newsworthiness, of the Roosevelt news conference with which it was invariably compared.

Eisenhower further eroded the intimacy of press conferences by holding them less frequently—only twice a month on average (see Table 3-2)—and by admitting television film crews in 1955. Neither practice was, it turned out, as disruptive as it might have been. When the president sought to gain the attention of the American public, he did so directly in a prepared address. Moreover, Eisenhower's press conference sputterings were hardly telegenic. After the novelty wore off, the networks rarely broadcast the entire conference.[59]

Robert Pierpoint, a veteran White House correspondent for CBS television, suggests also that in the 1950s television was not yet ready to make full use of presidential coverage. The news divisions of the networks were small, and until the middle of the next decade each network's evening news ran for only fifteen minutes.[60] Eisenhower's admission of filmed television altered presidential-press relations mostly by creating a precedent.

The Kennedy System: Press Relations in an Era of Direct Communication

The real break with the Roosevelt system came with John Kennedy. Everyone in Washington recognized the new president's rhetorical talents and expected him to use them. They had first been surprised when he won over Protestant voters in the West Virginia primary; they next had witnessed the way his addresses on college campuses ignited enthusiasm among students for the New Frontier; and they had judged his television performance favorably in the debates with Richard Nixon. Everyone, including the television networks, was primed for a publicly active president. They were not disappointed. Kennedy's innovations in presidential-press relations departed radically from the past and formed what may be called the Kennedy system. It remains in place today.

The Kennedy Press Conference

In early December 1960, at the behest of President-elect Kennedy, press secretary Pierre Salinger privately solicited reporters' views on the possibility of having live, nationwide televising of press conferences. We do not know their initial responses, but later in the month when Salinger announced the new policy to the regular White House correspondents, the reaction was clear. Salinger described the scene:

> I shall never forget this press conference. I went right into the live TV decision. . . . As I explained the ground rules, a storm of protest came from the assembled reporters. . . . I heard the gravelly voice of Bill Lawrence, then the White House correspondent of the *New York Times.* I do not remember his questions but the introductory phrase is sufficient: "Mr. Salinger, as you plunge deeper and deeper into matters about which you know absolutely nothing. . . ." That did it. I didn't wait for the rest of the sentence. Now I was shouting back. It was the President's press conference—not theirs—and he would run it his own way. The decision was final. They could take it or leave it.[61]

New York Times correspondent James Reston called Salinger's plan for live television "the goofiest idea since the hoola hoop." [62] The president's transition team clearly had a different view. Kennedy aide Theodore Sorensen displayed a conveniently poor sense of history when he asserted that the press conference was a forum "to inform and impress the public more than the press." And television, he added, "provided a direct communication with the voters which no newspaper could alter by interpretation or omission." During the next several years, "direct communication" would become the leitmotif of those in the White House concerned with such matters.[63]

A significant factor motivating "direct communication" was Kennedy's awareness of its value in the event he were to lose favor with the press. This better explains the urge to go public, however, than the specific form adopted. He could have instituted, as James Hagerty proposed nearly a decade earlier, regularly scheduled television addresses or fireside chats from the Oval Office. Such a format would have provided this highly telegenic president with control over the program's message and exposed him to none of the vagaries of reporters' questions or his own misstatements. But such an innovation was unprecedented; there is no evidence that it or any similar alternative was ever seriously contemplated by Kennedy's transition team. The reason Pierre Salinger and others probably thought only in terms of the televised conference is that it required so little innovation. The precedent for television cameras was already well established by 1960; all that had to be done was substitute the networks' film cameras with live ones. In seeking to extricate himself from the confining Roosevelt system, Kennedy adapted existing arrangements to new purposes. The innovative use of live television in this important instance was as much a political adaptation as a technological one.

The first live telecast of a presidential press conference, in late January 1961, drew 418 correspondents to the new State Department auditorium and an estimated prime-time audience of 65 million viewers. Virtually everyone who expressed an opinion agreed that the new president had done well. There was little doubt that live television would be a fixture in Kennedy's press conferences. The networks' news offices were happy. Even some of the newspaper correspondents extolled this innovation. Lester Markel in a *New York Times Magazine* article advocated more public activities by the president and the creation of a Department of Public Opinion within the White House.[64]

By summer, however, many newspaper reporters began to complain on grounds readily understandable to those who appreciate the virtues of the "private" press conference of an earlier era. Peter Lisagor of the *Chicago Daily News* compared the Kennedy press conference to "making love in Carnegie Hall." "A mess ... disorderly, disorganized, almost chaotic" is the way he summed up the new press conference.[65] Others, like Clark Mollenhoff of the Des Moines *Register,* complained about the declining quality of the questions: "Too many of the questions are lobbed setups, and blooper balls, and there is too little effort to obtain any more than generalized information. I don't blame the President for knocking them out of the lot." He added, "Unless I have a specific question to ask, I rarely go any more." [66] A third correspondent offered the following summary assessment.

> In its new setting, blindingly lighted and amphitheatrical, ... each reporter [tries] unvaliantly to capture the eye of the President.
> Random, inevitably, is the selection of questioners and even more random is the nature of the questions. Few significant queries are put and when one is posed, a follow-through is almost impossible.[67]

According to print journalists, television reporters "hammed it up" with long-winded questions, "thus cheapening the conference." [68]

Almost a decade later newspaper reporters would still be voicing many of the same complaints. A survey of prominent Washington journalists found most of them dissatisfied with the modern press conference, and television received much of the blame.[69] The complaints were chronic because the problem is structural. As background briefings and sustained questioning on issues gave way to presidential position-taking and evasion, the print journalists lost their hard news. With television providing instantaneous transmission to the country, whatever fresh news came out of a press conference was stale by the time their stories were printed.

The press conference consequently matured into something quite different from the biweekly gatherings of Roosevelt. Robert Pierpoint's description of his preparation for the modern televised conference makes this clear:

> The presence of a vast audience magnifies the significance of any possible errors in questioning or in commentary afterward, and I always feel a slight sickness in the stomach and a sweatiness of the palms and forehead.
> After more than twenty years, I still go through a "psyching up" period, similar to that of a professional athlete before the big game. I read the morning newspapers and follow the news on radio and television, concentrating on the questions I will ask and the issues that could

Table 3-2 Presidential News Conferences with White House
Correspondents, 1929-1984

President	Average per Month	Total Number
Hoover (1929-1933)	5.6	268
Roosevelt (1933-1945)	6.9	998
Truman (1945-1953)	3.4	334
Eisenhower (1953-1961)	2.0	193
Kennedy (1961-1963)	1.9	64
Johnson (1963-1969)	2.2	135
Nixon (1969-1974)	0.5	37
Ford (1974-1977)	1.3	39
Carter (1977-1981)	1.2	59
Reagan (1981-1984)	0.5	26

SOURCES: Data for Hoover, Carter, and Reagan are from *Public Papers of the President*
series. Data for the others were taken from Michael Baruch Grossman and Martha Joynt Kumar,
Portraying the President (Baltimore: Johns Hopkins University Press, 1981), 245.

emerge at that day's conference. This means writing down a half dozen
questions which the President should answer that day. I try to anticipate
how each might be answered, phrasing the question carefully so the
President cannot evade it. At the same time, questions must be designed to
elicit genuine information or reactions of national importance. And finally,
the questions cannot be so obscure or so simple as to risk making me look
foolish or to waste my colleagues' and the public's limited press-conference
time.[70]

Expanded television coverage of the presidency has made celebrities of
those who cover the White House for the networks. Many of these men and
women come to Washington after being newscasters for local television. On
arrival they commonly draw six-figure salaries. To them "professionalism" is
as likely to mean free agency as any collective interests of correspondents. The
advent of live television brought into the press conference new participants
who promptly became stars.[71] They assumed front-rank positions at the
conference and vied aggressively with one another as well as with the
newspaper correspondents for recognition from the president. And since they
were the conduit through which he gained a spot on the evening news, they
generally got it.

Another change, which makes the modern press conference more eventful, is its relative infrequency. Since Roosevelt, presidents have wondered how often they could go before the public and retain its attention. This consideration led Salinger to move Kennedy's press conferences off prime time to a normal midafternoon schedule. More generally, it has meant that they are conducted less frequently. Table 3-2 shows that in employing the conference to speak directly to the American people, Kennedy conducted fewer conferences on average per month than Eisenhower, and, more to the point, less than a third as many as Roosevelt. Since Kennedy, the average number of conferences per month has further declined. Full realization of the diminished status of the press conference had occurred during the Nixon presidency. Initially, his failure to meet with the press on average no more than once every two months was widely viewed as being a result of the particular circumstances of his administration—an early, muted suspicion that matured into an ardent hostility between the president and the press. But the similarly low frequency rates of press conferences for Ford, Carter, and Reagan suggest that the reduced status of the press conference has resulted more from changes in the system of presidential-press relations than from personal styles or transient political conditions.

Once the news conference failed to provide a steady diet of hard news, it quickly lost standing among print correspondents. Over the years journalists have offered numerous proposals to resurrect aspects of the FDR system.[72] For their daily stories, however, they began to look elsewhere in the White House and in the agencies for presidential stories. Consequently, when the press conference became moribund for long stretches under Nixon and Reagan, who preferred political travel and nationally televised addresses, the complaints came most heavily from among network correspondents rather than print journalists.

The Local Press and the Private Interview

As the press conference became yet more formal under the glare of studio lights, Kennedy introduced other avenues of access to the press. For the most part, these innovations gave the president greater control over the content of information the press received. One such innovation was special, informal news conferences with publishers and reporters of papers from a particular state or region. With Kennedy these generally took the form of White House luncheons. Every subsequent president has adopted some variant of Kennedy's innovation.

Another innovation, if it may be called that, was the frequent use of the private interview. As senator, Kennedy was reputed to have had more friends in the press than in the Senate. As president, he continued his close personal associations with Charles Bartlett of the *Chattanooga Times* and Ben Bradlee, then with *Newsweek*. He also conducted private interviews with such notables as James Reston of the *New York Times* and columnist Joseph Alsop. A perquisite of friendship with Kennedy was special access to stories. According to one source, "Any of a dozen Washington hands have access to the President's Oval Office. . . . where, in the old days, an [Ernest K.] Lindley or an Arthur Krock could count on guidance 'at the highest level' only on the rarest occasions, the newsmen count on it almost weekly." [73] Network correspondents were not to be excluded. Before long, Kennedy opened the Oval Office to television crews for taped interviews.

Initially, this practice—a single instance of which had put FDR's "head on the block"—raised the ire of many members of the writing press more than did the televised press conference. Reston had personally warned the president-elect that private interviews might generate too much ill will. (Later, after becoming a favored insider, he recanted.)[74] Lisagor, whose distaste for the Kennedy system has already been recorded, called it "a baneful thing—a reporter ought to keep a public official at an arm's length." [75]

As Kennedy's sessions with the press neared the end of the first year, the expected question finally surfaced. Did not the president think it unfair to feed stories to the favored few? Obviously groping, Kennedy replied: "I think—yes, I will let them [his staff] know, and I think I ought to. I don't think there should be discrimination because of size or sex or another reason." [76] Spoken like lip service.

Routine use of the exclusive interview, cultivation of the press outside Washington, and live telecasts of news conferences constitute the Kennedy system. Each feature violates some ground rule of institutionalized pluralism upon which its predecessor, the FDR system, had been founded. Exclusive interviews with correspondents frustrate the profession's collective interests, at least as the Washington press corps was formerly constituted. Special attention to publishers and reporters from outside Washington denies the insularity of community relations and may arouse suspicion that the president is trying to replace negotiation with public pressure. From the perspective of institutionalized pluralism, the live telecast of news conferences is the most objectionable of all. Its antithetical nature was summed up earlier in Sorensen's naive remark that the forum was intended more to inform the public than the press. With television, the Kennedy system corrupted this centerpiece of the FDR system. And by introducing new—and, from the perspective of the White House, more manageable—avenues of contact with the press, the Kennedy system depreciated the status of the news conference.

The Kennedy System as a Model for Presidents Who Go Public

During the past quarter century, encompassing five presidents, the Kennedy system has remained the working model of presidential-press relations. To the degree it has changed at all, the system reflects more the forces it set in motion than any new ideas of Kennedy's successors. As the formal press conference has withered, Kennedy's alternative forms of press relations have thrived. Precise numbers for each administration are difficult to come by, but Ronald Reagan's 194 press interviews and 150 special White House briefings of the press from outside Washington during his first three years indicate sharply increased growth in the use of this news outlet since the Johnson administration.[77]

The development of satellite communications permitting instantaneous transmissions from the White House to local news stations around the country has created a booming market for White House communications beyond Washington. From 1981 to 1984, the number of local news stations with Washington bureaus grew from 15 to more than 50.[78] The business between local Washington television producers and stations throughout the country has been burgeoning as well. Local television news coverage offers several advantages over presidents' traditional news outlets. First, it allows the White House to segment the market—"to narrowcast its message to a very specific audience," in the words of one Reagan staffer.[79] Second, these newscasters are interested in presidential activities that the networks and even local press pay little attention to. The presidency is a ceremonial office. From it flows an endless stream of medals, commendations, and sometimes just salutations. Private citizens from all over the country come to the White House daily to receive the president's congratulations. For local television bureaus, these happy, often sentimental ceremonies offer wonderful local color. Of importance to the White House, the president is invariably cast as a sympathetic figure. The third advantage of local television coverage over traditional news outlets is that journalists for these bureaus, as recent arrivals with few prerogatives and an uncertain mandate, abide by White House instructions. The head of one of the largest local bureaus observed:

> The regular White House press corps is adversarial with the President in ways the locals are not. If the President is giving an award to a kid from Michigan for starting a community library, that is a good human-interest story for us. But if you get Sam Donaldson of ABC in on one of these things, he's going to ask the President . . . something. It becomes difficult for the President, and the White House doesn't like that.[80]

Many of the local bureaus began setting up shop during Jimmy Carter's administration. Given their special attraction, Carter was understandably quick to invite them to the White House. It was left to the Reagan administration, however, to incorporate local television reporters fully into the ongoing routines of White House media relations. This innovation, wholly consistent with the premises of the Kennedy system, has become one of the established routines of presidential-press relations under President Bush.

Presidents have adapted the Kennedy system to their personal styles in other ways as well, but none has altered the system's basic structure. As noted earlier, Lyndon Johnson constructed a television studio in the White House and obliged the networks to outfit it with cameras ready to broadcast on a moment's notice. Richard Nixon dismantled the studio, but to offset his numerous, rough dealings with the television networks and particularly the *Washington Post,* he dramatically expanded press relations outside Washington.[81] Jimmy Carter went to the public in his own way, with informal but well-orchestrated town meetings. Ronald Reagan showed a special fondness for the radio. His Saturday afternoon broadcasts from the Oval Office were frequently compared with Roosevelt's famous fireside chats. As important as these and other practices have been to a given president's overall public relations program, they amount to little more than personal and ultimately transient enhancements of the Kennedy system.

What was lost to the press when the news conference became a forum for the president's direct communications to the country was not fully realized as gains to the White House. With the adoption of the Kennedy system, presidents took more away from the traditional relationship than they contributed. It was up to the correspondents to establish a new equilibrium by withdrawing deference to the president's representation of events and policies. While the emergence of an adversarial press can be attributed in part to President Johnson's Vietnam "credibility gap" and Nixon's Watergate cover-up, it is important to understand that it inheres in presidents' strategic reformulation of press relations, and thus will not disappear as memories of these events fade into history. As late as the Eisenhower era, the president and the White House press corps generally followed the rule of institutionalized pluralism; each party sought reciprocity with the other to reduce uncertainty and to advance its own goals. Under the Kennedy system, however, this relationship broke down. Peter Lisagor hit upon this fundamental shift when he complained that the press was merely "one of the props" of the Kennedy press conference.[82]

Live television requires the president to be ever mindful of the public audience, and this setting necessarily gives rise to posturing. The correspondent's job consequently becomes one of "isolating fact from propaganda when a president seeks to use the press as a springboard to public opinion, as he does in a televised press conference.[83] Journalists no longer pay homage to unobtrusive, objective journalism. Instead, they speak of getting at the facts behind the president's statement or press release. Senior Washington correspondent James Deakin remarked: "The White House reporter has one accepted role—to report the news—and several self-appointed roles. . . . I feel I'm there, in part, to compel the government to explain and justify what it's doing. A lot of people don't like that, but I feel we're the permanent in-house critics of government."[84]

The adversarial aspect of presidential-press relations is an elusive quality, difficult to quantify, and the systematic evidence on the subject is inconclusive.[85] From the testimonials of the sparring partners, however, the adversarial relationship appears to be a well-established fact of life. The arrival of less deferential correspondents, some of whom were media stars in their own right, frequently has turned the conference into an occasion of irritation and embarrassment for the White House. Although no president has yet been willing to excuse himself altogether from these encounters, none has been reluctant to tamper with its format and schedule in an effort to produce more favorable results. Johnson, Nixon, and Reagan provide examples. As the Vietnam War heated up at home, Johnson sensed that reporters were lying in wait for him at press conferences with loaded questions. To throw them off balance, he switched to impromptu and short-notice press conferences that gave reporters little time to arm themselves. To stave off embarrassing issues, Nixon occasionally limited questions to specified policy areas. (This change, however, was generally well received by many newspaper correspondents because it gave them the opportunity to pursue newsworthy issues in depth.) In early 1982 some of Reagan's aides believed that their president was suffering from unflattering network "take-outs" of his noontime press conferences. They therefore rescheduled these conferences to later in the day, nearly doubling the television audience and reducing the time available to networks to edit the president's remarks. However the president's aides tweaked the schedule and format, it still failed to provide Reagan with a satisfactory arrangement. He conducted three such sessions in 1987 and four in 1988. By the end of his second term, the formal news conference had become an endangered species.

George Bush's Adaptation of the Kennedy System

Threatened with extinction, preservation of the press conference became a *cause célèbre* during Bush's first campaign for the presidency, if not with voters, certainly with the reporters and a number of organizations that study these matters. In response, Bush announced soon after his election that he would sharply increase the frequency of news conferences.

Frequency may "depressurize" the relationship, as one White House aide put it, but for Bush it introduced another problem. The president and those who work with him agree that he does not perform well on television. (Reflecting our media age, the disjointed phrases that constitute his rhetoric are commonly referred to as "sentence segments.") The White House solved the dilemma by giving the press conference its greatest overhauling since Kennedy's innovations. Instead of prearranged, frequently prime-time sessions, Bush called brief, impromptu morning sessions in which the networks were allowed a few minutes to assemble the cameras if they were interested in covering the conference. Frequently they were not; Cable News Network was the only network to broadcast many of these sessions. As no advance notice was given for these conferences, many correspondents were absent, but this in itself did not prove controversial, probably because the president rarely used the occasion to make newsworthy remarks. By the end of his first year in office, President Bush had conducted 38 such mini-conferences compared with only one that followed the formal, prime-time format. The consensus among Bush's aides that the latter was a "disaster" reinforced the administration's enthusiasm for this new approach to the press. So, up until the reelection campaign, he held only one more formal news conference.

The revamped format should be viewed not so much as a restoration of the press conference but rather as simply a strategy for pacifying the press. The conferences were scheduled at the president's convenience; correspondents had little time to prepare difficult questions, yet they could not complain that the president was inaccessible.[86] While these sessions may have satisfied White House correspondents accustomed to Reagan's sparse offerings, they provided little opportunity for the president to advance his policies. In assessing Bush's damage-control approach to the press conference, Reagan's media adviser, Michael Deaver, cautioned that the downside of this strategy would come when the president "will have to go over the heads of this town and go directly to the American people." [87]

The Modern Trajectory of Presidential-Press Relations

Whether by cutting back the number of Washington press conferences or minimizing their importance, modern presidents are clearly opting for more controllable means to communicate their views to the American public. Kennedy's innovations, private interviews and news conferences outside of Washington, remain prominent features of contemporary presidential media strategies. Presidents are also enlisting techniques that do not require the direct participation of reporters. Through television and speeches to gatherings of special constituencies, presidents can attract favorable news stories and direct press attention to particular issues and policies. These are venerable practices, of course, but whereas in the past they seemed to be desultorily planned outings from the White House, prompted as much by an invitation from some group as any tactic initiated by the president, they are now part of the chief executive's weekly, almost daily, routine. In the next chapter we shall document the extraordinary growth in these news-generating activities over the past 30 years.

Presidents and reporters still jointly produce news, but it is no longer a collaborative undertaking. Bush's frequent mini-conferences aside, the modern relationship is one in which each side anticipates and responds to distant actions of the other. The president's staff plans events and writes speeches with an eye to shaping the evening news story. Getting out "the line for the day" is, in fact, one of the principal activities of the contemporary White House staff; by one estimate more than a quarter of the staff is dedicated in some way to producing the president's public activities. Network news bureaus resist influence by aggressively editing presidential rhetoric and editorializing about its purposes. Reflecting this strategy is the amount of time allotted to the president on the evening network news. As late as 1968, he spoke on camera without interruption for an average of about 40 seconds. Over the years this figure has dwindled to about 9 seconds.[88]

At a recent conference of former presidential press secretaries I had occasion to raise the issue of the president's shrinking sound bite.[89] This led to an exchange between NBC Nightly News anchor John Chancellor and President Carter's press secretary, Jody Powell, which accurately characterizes the tension between modern presidents and the press. Compare the tenor of their remarks with that of Roosevelt's "family conference" with which we began our discussion:

Chancellor: The fact is—I think television reporters out in the field, when presented with pre-packaged, pre-digested, plastic coated phrases and with no opportunity to question a president, want to get something that isn't just pre-packaged and pre-digested, and that's why you are getting a more contentious kind of reporting in the twenty seconds at the end of the spot. I had an argument with Tom Pettit during the 1988 election, and I said, "Why is it that all of our correspondents end their pieces with some little snippy, nasty saying? Why don't they just say, 'And tomorrow the president goes to Cleveland.'" And Pettit says, "It wouldn't come out that way. They would say, 'Tomorrow the president goes to Cleveland and no one knows why.'"

So that you set up a kind of contest of who controls and all of this is done in a piece of television that runs about a minute-and-a-half. So you compress the political propaganda on the one hand, you increase the reactive hostility on the other hand, and that's what a minute-and-a-half television spot is today. I think both sides are probably equally responsible for it, but I think that the politicians started it.

Powell: I will just raise a logical question. Assuming that there are other things to do in a White House and now and then something else comes along that might keep you busy, why would you go to all of the trouble to do all of these things that we are talking about [in packaging the president's message] if you did not find yourself faced with a situation in which it's the way to deal with it? Why would you go to all of this trouble?

Are we supposed to believe that one morning ten, fifteen years ago somebody in the Johnson White House or the Nixon White House or whatever woke up and said, "We don't need to do this, but just for the hell of it, why don't we create this whole structure here about going out on the road and doing that sort of thing," or rather perhaps it was a reaction—maybe intelligent, maybe unwise, maybe in the public interest, maybe not. It was a reaction to a set of circumstances which they saw and said, "We've got to do something."

With presidents increasingly going public and with a more assertive press, contention over control will remain a fixture of the modern system. Infrequent press conferences, cultivation of the press outside Washington, extensive private interviews, and adversarial relations are the new order. It is one in which pressure and competition have replaced professional reciprocity as the fabric of community relations.

Notes

1. Cited in Chalmers Roberts, "Franklin Delano Roosevelt," in *Ten Presidents and the Press,* ed. Kenneth W. Thompson (Washington, D.C.: University Press of America, 1983), 21.
2. Ibid. This incident is also reported in Olive Ewing Clapper, *Washington Tapestry* (New York: McGraw-Hill, 1946), 179-180.
3. Waldo continued as head of McClure until his death in 1943. "R. H. Waldo, Head of News Syndicate," *New York Times,* June 12, 1943, 13.
4. Roberts, "Franklin Delano Roosevelt," 22-23.
5. Clapper, *Washington Tapestry,* 180.
6. Roosevelt's relations with the press were not 12 years of uninterrupted bliss, however. Both the president and the press at times felt abused by the other. On one occasion, for example, the president went so far as to award an absent reporter the iron cross for a derogatory story on the newly formed Women's Army Corps.
7. It has been suggested that Roosevelt used his press conferences at times to complement his public strategies. Graham J. White notes that initiatives announced during Roosevelt's fireside chats were followed by background briefings for the press to sustain public interest and to prepare the ground for a formal message to Congress. See *FDR and the Press* (Chicago: University of Chicago Press, 1979), 20-22. Wilfred E. Binkley argues against the perception that all Roosevelt had to do was "glance toward a microphone" and a "congressional delegation would surrender." Instead, he credits much of Roosevelt's early success with Congress to the way he worked the Washington press corps. See *President and Congress,* 3rd ed. (New York: Vintage, 1962), 305.
8. Cited in James Sterling Young, *The Washington Community: 1800-1828* (New York: Columbia University Press, 1966), 6.
9. Douglass Cater, *Power in Washington* (New York: Vintage, 1964), 224.
10. Ibid., 226.
11. Typical is Daniel J. Boorstin's, "Selling the President to the People," *Commentary* (July 1955): 427.
12. See Philip Selznick, *TVA and the Grassroots* (Berkeley: University of California Press, 1948).
13. See Peter Irons, *The New Deal Lawyers* (Princeton, N.J.: Princeton University Press, 1982).
14. In 1918 the editors of *The Nation* used the obituary of a prominent correspondent as occasion to criticize this practice of political jobbing. "The pernicious habit of appointing Washington correspondents to political office has also had a good deal to do with the loss of prestige of the correspondents' corps" ("Washington Correspondents," *The Nation,* November 30, 1918, 638).
15. Nelson W. Polsby, "The Institutionalization of the U.S. House of Representatives," *American Political Science Review* 62 (March 1968): 144-168; and H. Douglas Price, "The Congressional Career—Then and Now," in *Congressional Behavior,* ed. Nelson W. Polsby (New York: Random House, 1971), 14-27.
16. *The Education of Henry Adams: An Autobiography* (Boston: Massachusetts Historical Society, 1918), 253.
17. For the modern era, see Alan P. Balutis, "The Presidency and the Press: The Expanding Presidential Image," *Presidential Studies Quarterly* 7 (1977): 244-251. The findings for the nineteenth century are reported in Samuel Kernell and Gary C. Jacobson, "Congress and the Presidency as News in the Nineteenth Century," *Journal of Politics* 49 (November 1987): 1016-1035.
18. Before 1880 well over half of the papers represented by correspondents listed in

the *Congressional Directory* closed their Washington offices within two years. Less than 10 percent did so in 1930.

19. By the 1930s when Franklin Roosevelt arrived on the scene, government contacts had become a critical underpinning of the correspondent's professional stature. Raymond P. Brandt noted,

> The good Washington reporter has news sources which he does not discuss by name, even with his own colleagues. They are the key men in the various departments who can be called on by telephone or met at lunch or on the golf course. They are the officials who give the real "off the record" information. They know the existence of a little known public document, or what their chief is about to do. They are the men who stay on in Washington regardless of whether the Democrats or Republicans are in power. Their cultivation is a matter of years. They must know their trust will not be betrayed.

"The Washington Correspondent," *Journalism Quarterly* 13 (June 1936): 176.

20. These generalizations come from the brief biographical sketches of members of the 1903 House gallery compiled by the Gridiron Club. Ralph M. McKenzie, *Washington Correspondents Past and Present* (New York: Newspaperdom, 1903).

21. Silas Bent, *Ballyhoo* (New York: Boni and Liveright, 1927), 85.

22. The trend toward multiple paper clients appears in Table 3-1 to have been arrested by the early 1930s. Although increased numbers of correspondents were writing simultaneously for two or more papers, they constituted a smaller share of the press corps. Two trends—one demographic, the other political—were at work. First, as America's cities continued to grow, more papers developed the circulation necessary to underwrite individual representatives in Washington. According to one study, the critical city size for Washington coverage during this era was 50,000 to 100,000. The number of cities in this population range increased sharply from the 1910 to the 1930 census. Second, with the nation's attention shifting to Washington in the late 1920s, more urban papers in all population classes began supplementing wire service news with individual coverage. Hence, over time the need for multiple clients to ensure job stability declined as well. On both points, see Malcolm M. Willey and Stuart A. Rice, *Communication Agencies and Social Life* (New York: McGraw-Hill, 1933), 168-170.

23. Bent, *Ballyhoo*, 87.

24. J. Frederick Essary, "President, Congress, and Press Correspondents," *American Political Science Review* 22 (November 1928): 903.

25. Walter Lippmann, "The Job of the Washington Correspondent," *Atlantic*, January 1960, 47-49. An excellent treatment of objective reporting as an ideology can be found in Michael Schudson, *Discovering the News* (Chicago: University of Chicago Press, 1978), 121-159.

26. The modern variant of this time-honored practice is described vividly by James Deakin in *Straight Stuff* (New York: William Morrow, 1983), 131-132.

27. One president who refused to submit to press interviews was Grover Cleveland (1885-1889, 1893-1897). Instead, he communicated to the press, and through it to the public, with routine Sunday evening press releases. James E. Pollard describes how awkward exclusive reliance on this form could at times be in *The Presidents and the Press* (New York: Macmillan, 1947), 528.

28. Ibid., 558.

29. David S. Barry, *Forty Years in Washington* (Boston: Little, Brown, 1924), 270.

30. George Juergens, *News from the White House* (Chicago: University of Chicago Press, 1981), 17.

31. Ibid.

32. George H. Manning, "Liberalizing of President's Contacts with Press Hoped for from Hoover," *Editor and Publisher*, January 12, 1929, 6.

33. Juergens offers individual accounts of this requirement in operation in *News from the White House*, 23.

34. This account of Wilson's presidency relies heavily on Juergens, *News from the White House*, 126-166; and Pollard, *Presidents and the Press*, 630-696.

35. Juergens, *News from the White House*, 151.

36. Willis Sharp, "President and Press," *Atlantic Monthly*, July 1927, 240.

37. Clapper, *Washington Tapestry*, 14-15.

38. See "Editor's Ire at Coolidge Innuendo," *Literary Digest* 96 (November 12, 1927): 12; "Covering Washington," *The Nation*, June 27, 1928, 714; David Lawrence, "President and the Press," *Saturday Evening Post*, August 27, 1927, 27; O. G. Villard, "Press and the President," *Century*, December 1925, 193-200; and S. Moley, "Trials of the White House Spokesman," *Illustrated Independent Weekly*, September 19, 1925, 317-319.

39. Pollard, *Presidents and the Press*, 743.

40. Ibid.

41. Anthony Smith, *Goodbye Gutenberg* (New York: Oxford University Press, 1980), 173.

42. Leo Rosten, *The Washington Correspondents* (New York: Harcourt, Brace, 1937), 4.

43. Journalist Walter Davenport wrote in "The President and the Press," *Colliers*, January 27, 1945, 12: "A most important contributing factor to the grip that Mr. Roosevelt has on the imaginations of the Washington correspondent corps and consequently on the quality of his press [is] the enthusiasm he generated in the beginning—in 1933—[that] is still visible and still vocal."

44. Roberts, "Franklin Delano Roosevelt," 24. He adds that they applauded "because the reporters knew they were going to have access to news, the meat and potatoes of their profession."

45. The reporter quoted here is Henry M. Hyde of the *Baltimore Evening Sun*. Cited in Rosten, *The Washington Correspondents*, 50.

46. Marlan E. Pew, "Shop Talk at Thirty," *Editor and Publisher*, April 8, 1933, 36.

47. Pollard, *Presidents and the Press*, 775.

48. Rosten, *The Washington Correspondents*, 50. Arthur Krock once remarked, "He [Roosevelt] could qualify as the chief of a great copy desk" (in Rosten, *The Washington Correspondents*, 53). Heywood Broun complimented Roosevelt as "the best newspaper man who has ever been President" (in Pollard, *Presidents and the Press*, 781).

49. Raymond Clapper is cited in Pollard, *Presidents and the Press*, 780, stating, "The President and his most indefatigable critic, Mark Sullivan, still exchange pleasantries at press conferences."

50. Ibid., 776.

51. Davenport, "The President and the Press," 11-12.

52. Arthur Krock, *The Consent of the Governed* (Boston: Little, Brown, 1971), 242.

53. Ibid., 243.

54. Rosten, *The Washington Correspondents*, 58-61.

55. Walter Davenport reported in *Editor and Publisher* that 45 percent of the nation's major newspapers supported Roosevelt in 1932, 34 percent in 1940, and 60 percent in 1944. "The President and the Press," *Collier's*, February 3, 1945, 16. White's *FDR and the Press* takes a revisionist stance, arguing that Roosevelt was far more hostile to the nation's publishers than to them. See especially chaps. 3, 4, 5.

56. Boorstin, "Selling the President to the People," 425.

57. For another example of FDR striking a bargain by creating a relationship, see Richard Fenno's study of the appointment of Jesse Jones as Roosevelt's secretary of commerce in *The President's Cabinet* (New York: Vintage, 1959), 234-247.
58. A. L. Lorenz, Jr., "Truman and the Press Conference," *Journalism Quarterly* 43 (Winter 1966): 671-679, 708.
59. The standard procedure was for press secretary James Hagerty to give permission to the network for use of a given excerpt. This gave the White House the prerogative of censoring parts of the press conference. Reportedly, it was an option rarely invoked.
60. Robert Pierpoint, *At the White House* (New York: G. P. Putnam's Sons, 1981), 155-156.
61. Pierre Salinger, *With Kennedy* (New York: Doubleday, 1966), 57. In a conversation with James Rowe, President Kennedy said, "I am convinced that the press will turn against me sooner or later while I am President, and I must have a way to get to the American people. So, therefore, I have to use television to get there, to speak directly to them when the press is so hostile" (cited in Blaire Atherton French, *The Presidential Press Conference* [Washington, D.C.: University Press of America, 1982], 13).
62. Cited in Harry Sharp, Jr., "Live From Washington: The Telecasting of President Kennedy's News Conferences," *Journal of Broadcasting* 13 (Winter 1968-69): 25.
63. Cited in Newton N. Minow, John Bartlow Martin, and Lee M. Mitchell, *Presidential Television* (New York: Basic Books, 1973), 39. Similarly, Nixon remarked at a press conference, "I consider a press conference as going to the people" (*Public Papers of the Presidents of the United States, Richard Nixon, 1969* [Washington, D.C.: Government Printing Office, 1971], 301). And early in the Reagan administration, NBC executive Richard S. Salant sounded the same theme: "Presidents over the past 20 years have discovered that television provides them the means to go around and over print to talk directly and simultaneously to all the people, with no reporting filter in between" ("When the White House Cozies up to the Home Screen," *New York Times,* August 23, 1981, sec. 2, 25).
64. Lester Markel, "What We Don't Know *Will* Hurt Us," *New York Times Magazine,* April 9, 1961, 116-117.
65. Cited in Worth Bingham and Ward S. Just, "The President and the Press," *Reporter* 26 (April 12, 1962): 20.
66. Ibid.
67. Markel, "What We Don't Know," 116.
68. James E. Pollard, "The Kennedy Administration and the Press," *Journalism Quarterly* 41 (Winter 1964): 7. See also Alan L. Otten, "Whose Conference?" *Wall Street Journal,* August 5, 1970, 44.
69. Jules Witcover, "Salvaging the Presidential Press Conference," *Columbia Journalism Review* 9 (Fall 1970): 33.
70. Pierpoint, *At the White House,* 70-71. A similar account is offered by Alan L. Otten ("Whose Conference?" 44):

> With televised press conferences, every reporter sees himself as a television personality. Since he doesn't want to boot his moment in the camera's eye by stumbling over a spontaneously phrased question, he usually has his query prepared long in advance—often not so much a question as a long speech—and he asks it even if it is completely irrelevant to everything that's gone before and even if some earlier answer is crying for clarification.

71. Journalists writing about their profession appear compelled to mention the discrepancy in the salaries between broadcast and print correspondents. See, for

example, James Deakin on the "star system" of broadcast journalists, *Straight Stuff,* 107-109; and Stewart Alsop, *The Center* (New York: Harper and Row, 1968), 176-177.

72. Examples are Hedrick Smith, "When the President Meets the Press," *Atlantic,* August 1970, 65-67; and Witcover, "Salvaging the Presidential Press Conference," 28.

73. Bingham and Just, "The President and the Press," 18-20. In a blistering attack on the administration's press relations, Arthur Krock charged that Kennedy had done more to "manage the news" than any president in history. Krock, who was on the "outside," took special exception to the exclusive interview, though he had taken full advantage of this practice under both Roosevelt and Truman. "Mr. Kennedy's Management of the News," *Fortune,* March 1963, 82, 199-202.

74. Bingham and Just, "The President and the Press," 18.

75. Ibid., 20.

76. Pollard, "The Kennedy Administration," 6.

77. The figures for personal interviews come from Lou Cannon, "Phantom of the White House," *Washington Post,* December 24, 1984, 25. In Mark Hertsgaard, "How Reagan Seduced Us," *Village Voice,* September 18, 1984, 12, a White House aide offered the following description of a typical briefing:

> You'd bring in 80 or 90 [journalists], maybe from a certain part of the country . . . and invite anchormen or news directors from major markets and the editors of major newspapers. And this is how some press people from a little town in North Dakota or somewhere like that come to see things. And they're thrilled to come. We take them up to our main briefing room and have maybe 25 camera crews from local stations and then put on a real good program for them. . . . Then we take them over to the State Dining Room for a real good lunch with the president, and they are all very pleased to come to the White House, it's a nice trick.

78. Thomas B. Rosenstiel, " 'Local' News Bureaus Polish Reagan's Image," *Los Angeles Times,* July 14, 1984, 1.

79. Ibid., 18. In early 1985 the Reagan administration announced plans for a facility to allow direct television hookups from the White House to local stations around the country. Gerald M. Boyd, "White House Plans Direct TV Links," *New York Times,* January 8, 1985, 9.

80. Rosenstiel, " 'Local' News Bureaus," 18.

81. Richard Nixon's confrontations with the press have been amply documented in William E. Porter, *Assault on the Media: The Nixon Years* (Ann Arbor: University of Michigan Press, 1976); James Keogh, *President Nixon and the Press* (New York: Funk and Wagnalls, 1972); and George C. Edwards III, *The Public Presidency* (New York: St. Martin's Press, 1983), 104-133.

82. Pollard, "The Kennedy Administration," 7.

83. Witcover, "Salvaging the Presidential Press Conference," 28.

84. Cited in J. Anthony Lukas, "The White House Press 'Club,' " *New York Times Magazine,* May 15, 1977, 67. Fred Barnes, a senior editor of *The New Republic,* has described one of the "operating assumptions of the press" as being the view of many Washington reporters that "their job . . . [is] one of attacking, and if a president, say, retains high popularity, they take it as an affront" (cited in "Calling the Press on the Carpet," *Wall Street Journal,* August 21, 1985, 22).

85. Two studies that fail to find negative stories or hostile news conference questions are Michael Baruch Grossman and Martha Joynt Kumar, *Portraying the President* (Baltimore: Johns Hopkins University Press, 1981), chap. 10; and Jarol B. Mannheim, "The Honeymoon's Over: The News Conference and the Development

of Presidential Style," *Journal of Politics* 41 (February 1979): 55-74. Dan Hallin takes exception to the notion of an adversarial press in "The Myth of the Adversary Press," *Quill* 71 (November 1983): 31-36.

86. An incident occurred in early 1990 that reveals this purpose of the new-style press conference. After reading a spate of articles on White House secrecy and deception, President Bush lashed out at the small pool of reporters traveling with him on Air Force 1. "We've got a whole new relationship," he announced. Then he added, "I think we have had too many press conferences." Although the events resulting in critical reportage were completely unrelated to the format or to statements made at one of the president's press conferences, it was the conference that the president threatened to cut off. After all, his exceptional availability to White House correspondents was designed to shield him from this kind of press carping. Nonetheless, for the next two years the president continued to rely on these informal sessions. Andrew Rosenthal, "Bush's In-Flight Show: Pique, and a Bumpy Ride for the Press," *New York Times*, February 16, 1990.

87. Instead, Bush appears to have thought he could return to the golden years of Roosevelt's press relations. One morning he sought to enlist the help of White House correspondents in propelling his legislative program through the Democratic Congress. "I urge you people to join me in calling out for congressional action," he said, adding that the Democrats deserved an "editorial pounding . . . to support the President as he tries to move this country forward." Thomas B. Rosenstiel, "The Media: Bush Plays It Cozy," *Los Angeles Times*, December 9, 1989, 1.

88. Daniel C. Hallin, "Sound Bite News: Television Coverage of Elections, 1968-1988," Occasional Paper, Media Studies Project, Woodrow Wilson International Center for Scholars, Washington, D.C., 1991.

89. "The Presidency, the Press and the People," University of California, San Diego, January 5-6, 1990. Transcript reprinted in *APIP Report* 1 (January 1991): 4-5. John Anthony Maltese provides a history of the development of White House staffing for presidential communications in *Spin Control: The White House Office of Communications and the Management of Presidential News* (Chapel Hill: University of North Carolina Press, 1992).

The Growth of Going Public 4

The preceding chapters have presented the reasons modern presidents go public. Modern technology makes it possible. Outsiders in the White House find it attractive. And the many centrifugal forces at work in Washington frequently require it. The frequency with which presidents in the past half century have communicated directly with the American public shows that the more recent the president, the more often he goes public.

The most memorable such occasions occur when the president goes on national radio or television to solicit public support for his legislative program stalled in Congress or to define the U.S. position in an international crisis. Although these dramatic forms of going public have become more commonplace in recent years, they still constitute only a small share of the many kinds of public activities in which modern presidents daily engage. Going public usually involves quieter overtures to more select audiences. Just as bargaining presidents must continually nurture the good will of their trading partners, so, too, must public-styled presidents diligently cultivate public opinion. We commonly call the routines by which presidents do this "public relations." [1]

Like advertising generally, public relations perform the homeostatic function of maintaining public support of the president. Whenever the president's popularity begins to wane or press coverage appears unduly critical, the White House compensates with increased public relations. As much as the occasional dramatic moment when the president rallies the country behind his policies, these routines define the style of modern leadership from the White House.

The following two episodes illustrate the variety of resources available to the modern president seeking to promote himself and his policies with the American public. In February and March of 1971, Richard Nixon faced widespread criticism and protest of the U.S. invasion of Laos. To offset this opposition, the president took his case to the public. Biographers Rowland

Evans and Robert Novak leave little doubt that Nixon's public relations campaign was precipitated by a five-point drop in his popularity rating.

> Shortly after that Gallup finding, it was decided by Nixon's public relations experts to give the American people the largest concentrated dose of this president on television and in interviews with journalists. The purpose was to stimulate an immediate upward movement in the polls and thus prevent further deterioration of the president's position on Capitol Hill and in the nation.
>
> In quick succession, in the six weeks ending March 22, Nixon made these appearances: an interview on February 9 with conservative Peregrine Worsthorne of *the London Sunday Telegraph;* a non-televised press conference on February 17; a special televised press conference on March 4 limited to foreign policy questions; an interview on March 11 by Barbara Walters of NBC's Today show for broadcast on March 15; an interview on March 11 by nine women reporters for publication on March 13; a one-hour live televised interview on March 22 by ABC's Howard K. Smith—a rate of exposure to major media outlets of more than one a week.[2]

Ronald Reagan faced somewhat different circumstances in the spring of 1982. Falling as unemployment rose, his popularity had begun a gradual but cumulatively greater overall descent than Nixon's in 1971. Whereas Nixon could try to convince the public of the merits of his policy, there was little President Reagan could do to sell the country on unemployment. He could, however, shore up his softening support with appeals on other issues. After learning from in-house polls that he was losing the approval of blue-collar workers at an alarming rate—many of whom were Democrats who had crossed over to vote for him in 1980—Reagan decided to target special appeals to them.[3]

Along with other public activities directed to this constituency, President Reagan addressed a conference of Catholic lay organizations in Chicago in behalf of a proposal to have the federal government subsidize private school tuition. For the Catholic church, financially strapped by rising costs and declining enrollments in many communities, and for parents who send their children to these schools (or would like to), enactment of the president's proposal would be a godsend. Because of Reagan's penurious domestic budget and his heavy cutbacks in funds for education, the trip to Chicago was widely interpreted to have been inspired more by an immediate political need to shore up support with this constituency than by any expectation that this might give his stalled legislation on this issue a boost in Congress. It also promised an enthusiastic reception before a traditionally Democratic audience, one that would ensure prominent coverage on the networks' evening news programs.

Though the reasons for Nixon's and Reagan's difficulties in the polls were quite different, both men sought remedy in rhetoric. In neither instance did the loss of popular support prompt the president to reconsider those policies that displeased the public. The loss was sufficient in each case, however, to trigger concerted public relations. These cases also illustrate how public speaking, political travel, and appearances before special constituencies outside Washington constitute the repertoire of modern leadership.

Trends in Going Public

Going public can take a variety of forms. The most conspicuous is the formal, often ceremonial occasion, such as an inaugural address or a State of the Union message, when official duty places the president prominently before the nation. Going public may, however, involve no more than a pregnant aside to a news reporter. This sort of casual, impromptu activity eludes systematic analysis, but speeches, travel, and appearances—all of which take place in public view and therefore can be easily counted—form a good record of significant events with which to measure the rise of going public. Each of these nonexclusive activities can be further divided according to its locale or prominence.[4] (More detailed definitions of these categories can be found in the Appendix.)

Public Addresses

Appeals for support to constituencies outside Washington are the core activities of going public. Form, audience, and content make each appeal unique. Kennedy's October 1962 address to the nation, in which he announced a quarantine of Soviet ships laden with surface-to-surface missiles en route to Cuba, is different in each respect from Carter's trip to Iowa in 1977 to sell his agricultural policies before a gathering of farmers. With such diversity, one may reasonably wonder what any trends discerned from a large volume of public addresses could mean.

Without delving too deeply into form, audience, and content, I shall offer a general distinction by classifying public addresses as major and minor. Major addresses are those in which the president speaks directly to a national audience over radio or television. Minor addresses, by comparison, are those the president delivers to a special audience either in person or via some broadcast medium. By these definitions, Kennedy's statement on the Cuban missile crisis qualifies as a major address and Carter's farm speech as a minor address.[5]

The average yearly numbers of major and minor addresses for each elected president since Herbert Hoover are displayed in Figure 4-1.[6] Both forms of going public have been on the rise, although to far different degrees. Given the opportunity costs, as well as network resistance to presidents commandeering prime time television, it is not surprising that the use of major addresses has increased only slightly.

Ronald Reagan's major addresses in Figure 4-1 include only television broadcasts. In 1982 after becoming unhappy with press representation of his policies, he initiated a lengthy series of Saturday afternoon radio broadcasts. To include these addresses, which attracted small audiences, would misrepresent the frequency with which he issued dramatic national appeals. Nonethe-

Figure 4-1 Presidential Addresses, 1929-1990 (Yearly Averages for First Three Years of First Term)

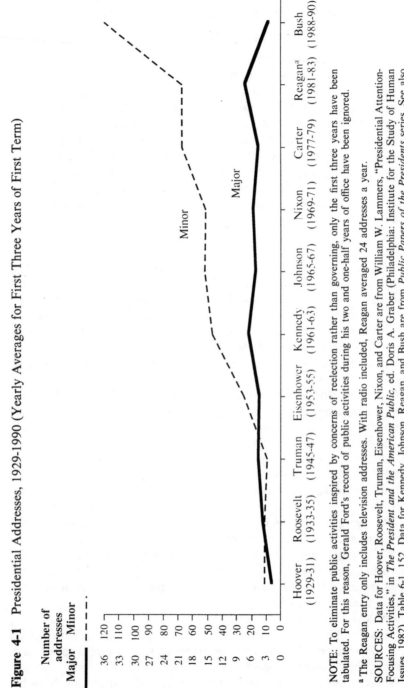

NOTE: To eliminate public activities inspired by concerns of reelection rather than governing, only the first three years have been tabulated. For this reason, Gerald Ford's record of public activities during his two and one-half years of office have been ignored.

[a] The Reagan entry only includes television addresses. With radio included, Reagan averaged 24 addresses a year.

SOURCES: Data for Hoover, Roosevelt, Truman, Eisenhower, Nixon, and Carter are from William W. Lammers, "Presidential Attention-Focusing Activities," in *The President and the American Public*, ed. Doris A. Graber (Philadelphia: Institute for the Study of Human Issues, 1982), Table 6-1, 152. Data for Kennedy, Johnson, Reagan, and Bush are from *Public Papers of the Presidents* series. See also Kernell, "Presidency and the People," 242.

less, the eight major televised addresses by President Reagan in 1981 (a month of which was spent convalescing from an assassination attempt) is a first-year record for any president. President Bush's major addresses, by contrast, have returned to the level of Reagan's predecessors.

Of the major addresses, the most dramatic and potentially the most effective are the special reports presented by the president on prime-time television to the nation. The subjects of these television talks, listed in Table 4-1, provide a calendar of the crises and national exigencies that have preoccupied presidents since 1953. Carter's appeals for energy conservation and for support of his legislative program and Reagan's regular appeals for support of his economic policies suggest that domestic issues are replacing international crises as the main occasion for prime-time addresses.[7]

Although major addresses may be the most dramatic and most effective approach for influencing public opinion, they also can be the most taxing. The public's attentiveness corresponds to the number of such appeals. If every presidential tribulation were taken to the country on prime-time television, people would soon lose interest. In private correspondence with a friend, Franklin Roosevelt said as much: "The public psychology ... [cannot] be attuned for long periods of time to the highest note on the scale ... people tire of seeing the same name, day after day, in the important headlines of the papers and the same voice, night after night, over the radio." [8] As noted earlier, John Kennedy and members of his staff had the same misgivings after his first, prime-time news conference and scheduled subsequent conferences for daytime television.[9] During the Carter presidency, Gerald Rafshoon, upon assuming his duties in the rejuvenated White House Office of Communications in the summer of 1978, sent a memorandum to the president that established his media strategy for the rest of his tenure. Rafshoon cautioned, "The power of presidential communication is great, but not unlimited. You may be able to talk to the people all day ... but the people can handle so much. *Investment of that power in too wide a range of issues will dissipate it. This has happened over the last eighteen months.*" After elaborating this theme, Rafshoon concluded, "Your involvement should always be weighed with an eye towards preventing the devaluation of presidential currency." [10] By potentially reducing the size and responsiveness of the audience for his next appeal, each prime-time address entails opportunity costs for the president.[11]

Although these concerns are still pondered in the White House, presidents in the past 25 years have continued to expand their prime-time exposure. Table 4-2 shows that Kennedy appeared on national television more frequently than did any president elected after him, but, with four exceptions, he limited himself to daytime exposure. By holding his press conferences in the early afternoon and delivering few direct television addresses—surprisingly few given the unsettled state of international affairs—Kennedy accumulated fewer than two hours of prime-time television during his first 19 months in office.

Table 4-1 Calendar of Presidential "Reports to the Nation" on National Television, Jan. 1953-Dec. 1991

	Jan.	Feb.	Mar.	Apr.	May	June	July	Aug.	Sept.	Oct.	Nov.	Dec.
Eisenhower 1953												
1954	Review			World affairs		Review		Congress				
1955							Geneva conference					
1956		Reelection announcement		Veto-agriculture						Middle East		
1957		Middle East			Mutual aid				Little Rock		Science, security	
1958												
1959			Berlin					Labor reform	Europe			International peace
Kennedy 1960		National defense	Latin America		Paris summit	Far East Europe meetings						
1961							Berlin					
1962			Nuclear tests					Taxes		Cuba	Cuba	
1963				Railroad labor dispute (2)		Civil rights		Test ban	Tax cut	Cuba		
Johnson 1964								Tonkin Gulf		International affairs		

1965				Dominican Rep.	Dominican Rep.							
1966	Bombing North Vietnam		Vietnam; non-candidacy					Steel strike	Steel strike			
1967	Pueblo			Martin Luther King		Violence	Riots					
1968					S.E. Asia					Halt of bombing		
Nixon 1969	Veto-H.E.W.			Vietnam (2)				Welfare		Peace initiative	Vietnamization	S.E. Asia
1970			Postal strike		SALT	Cambodia (2); Economy						
1971	S.E. Asia		Busing	Vietnam	Vietnam		China trip			Economy		
1972	Vietnam		Economy	Vietnam		Economy		Economy				
1973	Vietnam			Watergate				Watergate			Energy crisis (2)	
Ford 1974	Egypt-Israel			Watergate	Middle East crisis		USSR trip (2); economy		Pardon of Nixon			
1975	National issues		Tax cut		Mayaguez (2); energy					Tax cut		
1976												
Carter 1977		Fireside chat; Panama Canal Treaty		Energy							Energy	
1978										Inflation		China

Table 4-1 (Cont.)

	Jan.	Feb.	Mar.	Apr.	May	June	July	Aug.	Sept.	Oct.	Nov.	Dec.
1979	Farewell (Carter)	Economy		Energy		SALT II	Crisis of confidence		Soviet troops in Cuba			
1980			Economy									Poland
Reagan 1981		Economy										
1982				Budget					Economy; budget	Economy	Arms control	
1983			Defense-national security	Central America					Middle East (2) Korean airliner	Lebanon, Grenada		
1984				Budget	Central America Tax reform							
1985		State of the Union; National security									Soviet-U.S. Summit	
1986	Space Shuttle explosion		Nicaragua				Independence Day		Drug abuse	Meetings with Gorbachev	Elections Iran and Contra aid	Iran arms and Contra aid
1987	State of the Union		Iran arms and Contra aid			Economic summit		Iran arms and Contra aid				Soviet-U.S. Summit
1988	State of the Union											
1989	Farewell to the nation											Panama

Bush									
1989	Inauguration	Administration goals					Thanksgiving		
1990	State of the Union			Kuwait invasion	Persian Gulf; budget deficit	Budget agreement		Thanksgiving	
1991	Desert Storm; State of the Union	Persian Gulf; Iraqi withdrawal	Persian Gulf		Drug control strategy / Nuclear weapons reduction				Christmas

SOURCES: The entries from 1953 through November 1963 are from "Presidents on TV: Their Live Records," *Broadcasting*, November 8, 1965, 55-58; those from December 1963 through December 1975 are from Denis S. Rutkus, "A Report on Simultaneous Television Network Coverage of Presidential Addresses to the Nation" (Congressional Research Service, Washington, D.C., 1976, Mimeographed), appendix; entries since 1976 are from the *Public Papers of the Presidents* series and a tentative compilation by Denis Rutkus.

Table 4-2 Presidential Television from Kennedy to Bush, First 19 Months
in Office

President	Number of Appearances in Prime Time	Time on Air in Prime Time (hours)	Total Number of Appearances	Total Time on Air (hours)
Kennedy	4	1.9	50	30.4
Johnson	7	3.3	33	12.5
Nixon	14	7.1	37	13.5
Carter	8	5.1	45	32.2
Reagan	12	8.9	39	26.5
Bush	7	3.7	56	22.3

NOTE: Gerald Ford has been omitted from analysis since his first 19 months in office cross into the reelection period.

SOURCES: For Kennedy, Johnson, and Nixon, data were supplied by the White House Press Office, quoted in *New York Times,* August 3, 1970, 16. For Carter, Reagan, and Bush, data are from program logs at CBS News, New York. Data are for speeches (including inauguration) and press conferences broadcast live on national television.

Richard Nixon surpassed this figure by nearly fourfold and in doing so raised the ire of network executives and their news departments. His mix of daytime and evening television was the reverse of Kennedy's. While holding fewer news conferences (hence, his low total number of hours), Nixon delivered more direct, prime-time addresses to the nation. With barely a third of Kennedy's overall television exposure, Nixon dominated the medium in a way none of his predecessors had come close to doing. He paved the way for Carter and Reagan, who relied upon equally heavy television schedules, but with a greater share of it during non-prime-time hours. Surprisingly, President Bush eclipsed all of his predecessors in the number of television appearances during his first nineteen months in office, but comparatively little of his network exposure occurred during prime time.

Going public is neither premised on nor does it promote a perception of America as a homogeneous society. Nor does it reduce politics to a plebiscite in which the president seeks continually to bring the weight of national opinion to bear in the resolution of policy questions.[12] Governance under individualized pluralism remains largely a process of assembling temporary coalitions from among diverse constituencies. For this purpose, minor presidential addresses directed toward special constituencies are particularly well suited. Not only are they less taxing on some future opportunity to gain the nation's attention, they may succeed where an undifferentiated national appeal may not. President Reagan's Chicago speech before Catholic organizations is a good illustration of why and how presidents cast appeals to particular publics.

Aside from being more focused and less obtrusive than major addresses (and therefore less taxing on future public appeals), minor addresses are attractive to presidents because the opportunities to give them are plentiful. The president is importuned daily to appear before graduation exercises, union conferences, and the conventions of trade and professional associations. With such advantages, minor addresses are understandably an integral component of a more general strategy of going public.

President Bush's calendar of speaking engagements for September 1991, presented in Table 4-3, illustrates how heavily presidents sometimes engage in these kinds of activities. During that month he delivered remarks and formal addresses on 19 occasions in 11 cities throughout the country. What makes this schedule even more impressive is that he also found time to deliver four national television and radio addresses, far exceeding any previous month of his tenure.

The real explosion in presidential talk has occurred in the class of minor addresses. Reagan, Carter, and Nixon on average surpassed Truman, Roosevelt, and Hoover by nearly fivefold in the use of such rhetoric. And President Bush managed to double these already high levels of targeted addresses. During his first three years in office he averaged a minor address nearly every other day. While this heavy schedule involved an unprecedented amount of travel to his audiences, he also addressed distant gatherings from the Oval Office by means of teleconferencing technology, which had been less available to his predecessors.[13]

If asked to name a president who could speak skillfully, one probably would think first of Franklin Roosevelt or perhaps John Kennedy, two men whose speeches have weathered time and relistening well. Nixon's pronouncements—such as his pre-presidential "Checkers" speech and later the Watergate denials—will be remembered mostly as objects of ridicule and, ultimately, of historical curiosity. Carter's and Bush's addresses will be recalled, if at all, as instructive examples of poor elocution and syntax. Of the recent class of presidents going public, only Ronald Reagan scores well as a thespian. The trends reported here reveal that it is not success but the type of politician recruited to the office and the strategic environment within which he operates that determine the volume of presidential rhetoric.

Public Appearances

Visual images can at times convey messages more effectively than talk. The audience to whom the president speaks and the location and circumstances of the event may contribute as much to his message's effectiveness as what he has to say. Jimmy Carter's inaugural stroll down Pennsylvania Avenue and the cardigan he wore at his first fireside chat on national television were gestures calculated to set the tenor of his administration in the

Table 4-3 President Bush's "Minor" Addresses, September, 1991

Date	Location	Audience	Subject
Sept. 3	Lewiston, Maine	High school faculty/students	Improvement of schools, education
Sept. 12	Philadelphia, Pennsylvania	Veterans' Hospital	Drug abuse
Sept. 17	Teleconference	School children	Education, NASA
Sept. 18	Grand Canyon, Arizona	Environmental-agreement signing ceremony	Environment policy
Sept. 18	Salt Lake City, Utah	Upon arrival	Education, volunteerism
Sept. 18	Salt Lake City, Utah	Children's Hospital staff	Infant mortality, Healthy Start
Sept. 18	Salt Lake City, Utah	Republican Party dinner	Choice in family affairs and education
Sept. 19	Portland, Oregon	Fundraising breakfast	Education, domestic policy
Sept. 19	Los Angeles, California	Construction workers	Transportation issues
Sept. 19	Los Angeles, California	Fundraising dinner	America 2000 (education), crime bill
Sept. 20	Chicago, Illinois	National convention of U.S. Hispanic Chamber of Commerce	North American free trade agreement, America 2000
Sept. 23	United Nations	General Assembly	Free trade, coup in U.S.S.R., Saddam Hussein, Zionism
Sept. 24	East Brunswick, New Jersey	Republican Party dinner	Energy, education, transportation
Sept. 25	Washington, D.C.	Blue Ribbon schools	Education reform, America 2000
Sept. 30	Orlando, Florida	575 Points of Light	Volunteering in community to help others
Sept. 30	Miami, Florida	Beacon Council annual meeting	Crime package, free trade agreement, education
Sept. 30	New Orleans, Louisiana	Fundraising dinner	Child care, civil rights, crime, transportation, capital gains, America 2000

SOURCES: Weekly Compilation of Presidential Documents, Office of the Federal Register, vol. 27, nos. 36-40, (Washington D.C.: Government Printing Office).

public's mind. Similarly, the image of President Nixon donning a hard hat and waving to cheering construction workers on the scaffolding above him made a strong pitch for support among his "silent majority."

Appearances are usually accompanied by public speaking, although, as in the Nixon example above, they need not be. Like minor addresses, appearances before select audiences offer the president an opportunity to target his appeals. In a preinaugural memo, Carter's pollster Patrick Caddell urged the president-elect to use "his personal leadership—through visits and political contacts—to maintain his base in the South." [14] As another example, President Reagan made some 25 appearances around the country in 1983 promoting his views on "excellence in education" (principally, merit pay for teachers and classroom discipline) after polls indicated a two-to-one public disapproval of his budget cutbacks in education. [15]

Appearances are distinguished in Figure 4-2 by locale, those in Washington from those throughout the rest of the United States. The number of public appearances outside the city generally reflects the president's non-Washington origins and divided party control of government. [16]

Political Travel

Generally, presidents travel in order to appear before particular constituencies or to find locations suitable for sounding a particular theme. Ronald Reagan kicked off his tax reform proposal in 1985 in Williamsburg, Virginia, to play up the plan's theme as "the new American Revolution." Days logged in domestic travel have no importance beyond the appearances or addresses before non-Washington audiences they reflect and the telegenic evening news spots they attract. As such, they offer another useful measure of the president's public activity.

When presidents travel abroad, however, they frequently do so in search of special opportunities to appear presidential. Meetings abroad with other heads of state are especially valuable in reminding the electorate of the weighty responsibilities of office and of the president's diligence in attending to them. Could future incumbents fail to notice the salutary effects of Kennedy's confrontation with Nikita Khrushchev in Vienna in 1961 and of Nixon's celebrated trip to China in 1972 on these presidents' images as national leaders? One may reasonably argue that affairs of state rather than voracious demands for publicity were the real reasons for these trips. Kennedy's biographers make clear his strongly felt need to impress the Soviet leader with America's commitments to its allies. And without the dramatic expression of national good will that Nixon's trip conveyed, the thaw in relations between the United States and China might not have been so complete. The considerable diplomatic merits of these trips notwithstanding, the fact is that both presidents thoroughly exploited their opportunities for publicity at home.

Kennedy's staff rushed film of the president with the Soviet leader to the Paris airport to give it the earliest possible airing on the networks' evening news.

Figure 4-2 Public Appearances by Presidents, 1929-1990 (Yearly Averages for First Three Years of First Term)

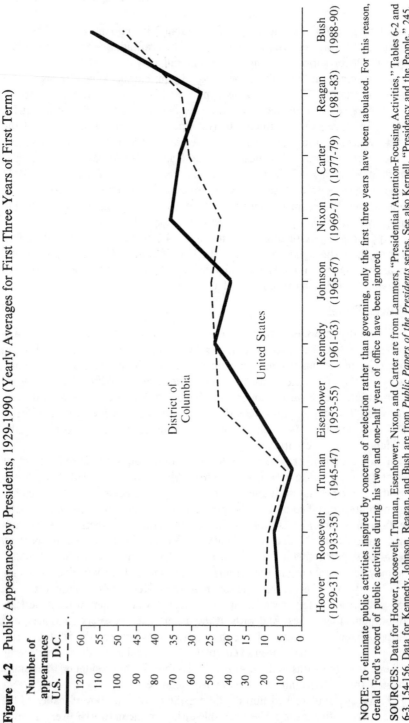

NOTE: To eliminate public activities inspired by concerns of reelection rather than governing, only the first three years have been tabulated. For this reason, Gerald Ford's record of public activities during his two and one-half years of office have been ignored.

SOURCES: Data for Hoover, Roosevelt, Truman, Eisenhower, Nixon, and Carter are from Lammers, "Presidential Attention-Focusing Activities," Tables 6-2 and 6-3, 154-156. Data for Kennedy, Johnson, Reagan, and Bush are from *Public Papers of the Presidents* series. See also Kernell, "Presidency and the People," 245.

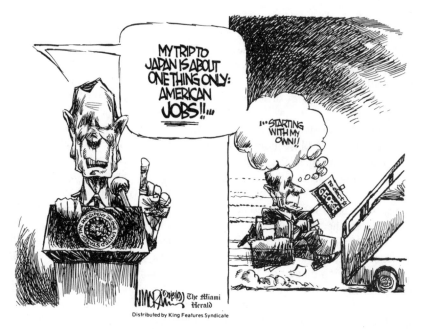

Reprinted with special permission of King Features Syndicate, Inc.

By the time Nixon visited China, 11 years later, new technology had greatly expanded the opportunities for public relations. Hours of President Nixon's tour of famous sites and formal expressions of mutual friendship with China's leaders were televised by satellite. Air Force One landed in Peking during prime time at home; the president's tour of the Great Wall and ancient palaces and the state banquet in the Great Hall were broadcast live back to the United States; and for a finale, after a timely nine-hour layover in Anchorage, Air Force One touched down in Washington just in time to make the evening network news. All in all, the networks broadcast more than 41 hours of the seven-day trip. Afterwards, syndicated columnist Art Buchwald satirized the whole affair by reporting his wife's assumption that the television set must be broken because Nixon's program was not available on any channel.[17]

The logistical planning of the China trip remains an impressive example of making the most of the opportunities for favorable publicity at home. Advances in transportation and communications, of which the China trip took full advantage, have so reduced travel time and so enhanced its public relations value that modern presidents might contemplate trips abroad solely for this purpose. Insiders increasingly voice suspicion that, in fact, they already do.

In 1973, President Nixon went to Iceland for a special meeting with France's President Georges Pompidou. No major policy decisions were made, as those privy to the trip's preparations had predicted. The *New York Times* reported the comments of one foreign service officer: "All they cared about was how things would look on television. White House aides fussed about the lighting, about who would stand where, what the background would be, and the furniture. The entire time I was assigned to the detail, no one asked me a substantive question. I'm sure they didn't care. All they seemed to care about was television." [18]

Since Nixon's world travels during the Watergate investigation, in what turned out to be the last months of his presidency, White House correspondents have been especially mindful of the public relations value of trips abroad. During Reagan's first presidential trip to Europe, it was not surprising that network correspondents pointed out the publicity purposes of the visual images so carefully produced by Reagan's aides. What is remarkable, however, was the willingness of White House staffers to discuss openly the trip's value in just these terms. Taken together, their comments reveal the motive of the trip. Because the polls were showing a drop in the president's popularity—which made him vulnerable in Washington—his advisers decided that conferring on location with European heads of state would be good for his image as a leader. After assessing the poll results that shortly followed the trip, White House aides voiced delight that their goal had been achieved. [19]

In the age of television, every president may be suspected of, and perhaps forgiven for, engaging in strategic travel and posing for the continuous "photo opportunities." The president who rests his leadership on going public will be tempted to travel frequently, in search of sympathetic audiences and "presidential images."

Because foreign and domestic travel often have different political purposes, they are measured separately in Figure 4-3. Each increased significantly in the past half century. Domestic air travel for presidents began with Truman, but aside from brief vacation trips to his home in Independence, Missouri, he seldom took advantage of this new opportunity. Eisenhower was the first president to travel extensively around the country. [20] Not until Reagan and Bush, however, did presidents spend a total of a month away from Washington each year. Bush even challenged the two-month marker every year, and in 1991 he broke it, despite getting off to a late start because of the outbreak of the Gulf War in January of that year.

International political travel by presidents increased most sharply during the late 1960s. Eisenhower's 1959 "good-will" tour around the world is generally recognized as the first international presidential travel where favorable publicity appeared to all to be the primary consideration. As the figures for subsequent presidents suggest, it was an idea whose time had come. Both Presidents Carter and Bush, who enjoyed their major policy successes in foreign affairs, traveled extensively. By the close of his third year in office, Bush's overseas travels had become so conspicuous that his critics found a large segment of the public agreeing with them that the president wasn't

Figure 4-3 Days of Political Travel by Presidents, 1929-1990 (Yearly Averages for First Three Years of First Term)

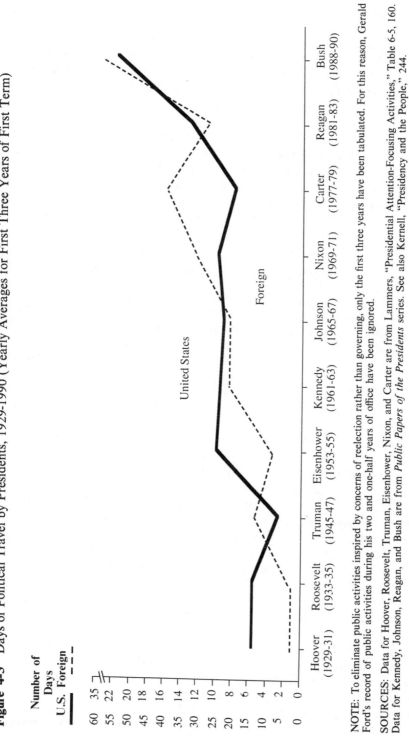

NOTE: To eliminate public activities inspired by concerns of reelection rather than governing, only the first three years have been tabulated. For this reason, Gerald Ford's record of public activities during his two and one-half years of office have been ignored.

SOURCES: Data for Hoover, Roosevelt, Truman, Eisenhower, Nixon, and Carter are from Lammers, "Presidential Attention-Focusing Activities," Table 6-5, 160. Data for Kennedy, Johnson, Reagan, and Bush are from *Public Papers of the Presidents* series. See also Kernell, "Presidency and the People," 244.

paying enough attention to the nation's troubles. Under pressure to focus more on domestic issues, Bush announced in November 1991 that he was postponing an Asian trip late that year, ostensibly to keep tabs on the Democratic Congress. Whatever the Bush presidency lacked in vision during its first three years, it certainly made up in motion.

During the past half century, trends in presidents going public—from political travel to public addresses and appearances—have moved steadily upward. There are some differences among them, however, in both the overall rate of growth and the timing of the sharpest increases. The number of minor public addresses, for example, has increased dramatically, even leaving aside Bush's exceptional level of activity. Political travel and public appearances also show differences in pace and timing. Cumulatively, these trends point toward a president today who is far more personally involved in public relations than were his predecessors 30 and 40 years ago.[21]

The Incremental Growth of Going Public

The rise of going public has proceeded more or less incrementally with each president taking advantage of the precedents and extensions of public activity offered by his predecessors. For the purpose of discussion, the various reasons for gradual change can be classified broadly as technological and political. The former have to do with opportunity, the latter with inspiration.

Incrementalism as a Function of Technology

Any explanation of the emergence of public strategies in the standard repertoire of presidents must take into account the continuous technological advances in transportation and mass communications during the past half century. Consider the difficulty a president 50 years ago would have encountered had he sought to rally the country behind his policies. By today's standards, the national transportation and communications systems of the early 1930s were primitive; barely 40 percent of all households owned radios. The president's potential audience was not only relatively small, one may assume that during the Great Depression it was also heavily skewed toward more affluent citizens. When Herbert Hoover defended his depression policies on national radio—and he did so regularly—he preached mainly to the converted.[22]

Transportation in the 1930s posed even greater difficulties. Air travel for presidents would not come for another two decades, and rail transportation was so slow and arduous that one did not undertake it casually. In the early 1920s, President Wilson suffered a stroke and President Harding a fatal heart attack during long political trips. Anxious to gain the legitimacy and the audience shares regular presidential appearances would provide, radio executives commonly cited these instances in promoting heavier presidential use of the new medium.[23] A decade later, a round trip from the east to the west coast still took about a week.[24] Obviously, slow transportation limited a president's appearances before and appeals to select audiences around the country.

International travel was even more time consuming and therefore infrequent. Woodrow Wilson's trip to Europe in 1919 to make the peace was a rare gesture befitting the historic moment. The first international flight by a president came in 1943 when Franklin Roosevelt secretly traveled to North Africa to meet with Winston Churchill. Compare the logistics of this trip with those described on page 101 for Nixon's trip to China 29 years later.

> The straight-line distance from Washington to Casablanca is 3,875 miles. A modern jet transport could have made the trip comfortably and without stopovers, in seven hours. But in 1943, the limited range, slower speeds, and lack of sophisticated navigational aids in the Boeing 314 and Douglas C-54 had required four legs of flying, three stopovers, a change of planes, and more than three days' travel time for the President—in each direction. The circuitous route required the President to touch three continents, cross the Equator four times, and spend approximately ninety hours in the air. When his train travel between Washington and Miami was included, Roosevelt had covered more than 17,000 miles before he was once more back home in the White House.[25]

The growth in presidential travel occurred piecemeal, with each new opportunity made possible by an advance in transportation technology. The 55 years shown in Figure 4-3 span the period in which travel shifted from rail to air and from prop to jet.

Technological breakthroughs in broadcast communications have had an even more profound effect on the opportunities for presidents to go public. Radio and television are, of course, the major developments, but smaller technological advances also had their effects. In 1955, for example, Kodak introduced its Tri-X film, which reduced the lighting requirements of television cameras; shortly thereafter Eisenhower admitted film crews into his news conferences.[26] The subsequent development of live satellite communications created a variety of new opportunities for live presidential television. Nixon's prime-time trip to China, Carter's town meetings at home and abroad, and Bush's teleconferences with national conventions in distant locales illustrate the kinds of public activities modern satellite communications make possible. The steady growth of going public during the past half century follows the sequence of technological advances in communication as well as transportation.

Going public increased incrementally not only with the introduction of new means of communication, but also with their dissemination. One may assume that the appeal to presidents of communicating via radio and television relates to the size of the audience. President Roosevelt's participation in an experimental television broadcast at the 1939 World's Fair had no real political significance if for no other reason than that only a minuscule audience could view the broadcast.[27] Figure 4-4 displays the rate with which

Figure 4-4 Households with Radios and Televisions, Cable TV and VCRs, 1930-1990 (Percent)

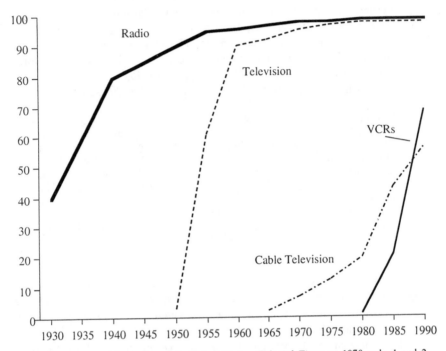

SOURCES: *Historical Statistics of the United States: Colonial Times to 1970,* vols. 1 and 2 (Washington, D.C.: Government Printing Office, 1975), series R104, R105, and A335. Data for 1975 through 1990 are from *Statistical Abstract of the United States* (Washington, D.C.: Government Printing Office, 1991), 556.

radio and television entered America's homes. By the early 1960s, the market was virtually saturated: more than 90 percent of households owned these appliances. During that decade presidents began more actively devising new ways to gain access to the nation's airwaves.

Although trends in going public follow the stepwise introduction and dissemination of technology, the correlation is not perfect. Presidents have adopted new technology cautiously.[28] In some instances this caution has resulted in a substantial time lag between a technology's availability and its political use. Harry Truman was the first president to go to the country on national television, but by modern standards he did so sparingly. Truman generally reserved television for moments of crisis, such as his announcement of the Korean War and seizure of the steel mills. On many pressing domestic issues of the day, he spoke to the country exclusively over radio and via newsreels. In the judgment of one observer, Truman failed "to use broadcasting consciously as a lever for increasing his influence on the Congress."[29]

Presidential television came of age in the 1952 election when Dwight Eisenhower became the first candidate for president to use television commercials heavily in his campaign.[30] In the postelection euphoria, press secretary James Hagerty referred to the advent of presidential television as a "new age" and raised the prospect of a regularly scheduled, monthly television program from the White House. Nothing came of this idea, however. During his eight years in office, Eisenhower instead continued Truman's practice of reserving television addresses mainly for international crises. Not until Lyndon Johnson and Richard Nixon did routine affairs of state become the subjects of presidential, prime-time television.

There is a similar time lag between technology and practice in presidential travel. Harry Truman valued the mobility offered by a plane designated for presidential use, but more for personal reasons (returning home to Missouri) than for possible political advantage. One might think that Truman, having assumed office on the death of FDR, would also have found good reason to travel around the country to gain national exposure and build support among local party organizations. But, as shown in Figure 4-3, Truman took few political trips. Eisenhower in turn was tardy in using jet transportation to travel abroad. It was left to his successors, principally Nixon, to make foreign travel a standard feature of the president's public repertoire and to discover, notably in the case of Bush, that the political limitations of extensive travel are more severe than the physical. These instances of a time lag between the availability of an innovation and its use suggest that something other than availability enters a president's decision to exploit new technology in going public.

Incrementalism as a Function of Politics

Going public is a strategic choice grounded as much in contemporary political relations as in available technology. The decline of party and institutional leadership in Congress and the rise of divided government have made the Washington community progressively more susceptible to public opinion throughout the past several decades. At the same time, the decay of protocoalitions has made bargaining at once both more difficult and less likely to suffice. Moreover, presidential selection reforms are sending people to the White House who are neither trained nor interested in learning the "ways" of Washington. These outsiders frequently prefer to go public rather than engage in quiet diplomacy. Technology has offered ever expanding opportunities, but changes within the political environment have provided the inspiration.

The decision to bargain or to go public is based upon a comparison of the relative costs and benefits of each strategy in a particular setting. Technology and evolving political relations have made the public approach increasingly attractive. But there are also costs that attend innovation and going public, which at times have applied a brake on the rapid expansion of public strategies. During an era of entrenched leaders, going public would generally be construed as an exercise in pressure politics and unless practiced delicately could easily backfire. Any public activity—but especially innovation—runs this risk of violating established expectations and triggering hostile reactions from other political elites in Washington.

Franklin Roosevelt's court-packing campaign illustrates this well. Fresh from a landslide reelection victory and perhaps suffering from euphoria, Roosevelt early in 1937 unveiled at a press conference his proposal for legislation to increase the number of Supreme Court justices and thereby gain more sympathetic treatment of New Deal programs.[31] In doing so, he broke with existing protocol by failing to brief key members of Congress before making a public announcement of a legislative initiative. In the opinion of many participants and commentators, this early mistake contributed to the proposal's eventual defeat. Even Roosevelt's staunchest supporters in Congress were taken aback; his detractors, predictably outraged. The court packing proposal was FDR's most stunning legislative failure in his 12 years in office. It was also the only time he used one of his famous fireside chats to ask the public to pressure Congress in behalf of his policies.[32] From the Senate, Harry Truman witnessed firsthand the ill will sowed by Roosevelt's innovative use of the press conference. Citing it a decade later, Truman as president would refuse to use the press conference for unveiling congressional initiatives.[33]

The court-packing episode is instructive in two ways. First, it shows that in the realm of public opinion, where politicians will understandably be quite sensitive, departures from established practices can easily backfire, even for someone as popular as Franklin Roosevelt. Second, Truman's response reveals how the experiences of one president become lessons for the next. Whether learned firsthand or observed from the sidelines, the negative reactions of other politicians serve to bring presidential strategy into conformity with expectations founded upon established practice. To the degree these forces impress themselves on political behavior, one president's activity will not much differ from that of his predecessor. Innovation occurs "at the margin." The results can be seen in the aggregate trends—both in the steady growth of direct communication and, as shown in Chapter 3, in the gradual decline of the traditional press conference.

Resistance to Innovation in Going Public

A president's decision to go public by enlisting a new technology or by employing an old one in a novel fashion brings forces of change into conflict with those of stability. New opportunities made possible by advances in technology and rising incentives brought on by changing political circumstances run up against the established prerogatives of other politicians. When the choice favors innovation, the president can try to minimize the political costs by having it conform to, or at least resemble, existing practices as much as possible. Two strategic devices are available to the president. First, he can summon precedents in introducing a new form of public activity. Second, he can expand a base by simply doing more of a familiar public activity. Both are venerable strategies of incremental politics.

In Chapter 3 we encountered an instance of the former in President Kennedy's introduction of the televised news conference. He adapted existing arrangements to a new purpose—direct communication with the public—and thereby managed to undo the old order even as he conformed to its expectations.

Examples of an incremental expanding of the base can be found in the gradually rising trends in going public presented in this chapter. Presidents have tended to increase their public activities only marginally beyond a base of accepted practice. As long as a president can credibly argue that his activity does not much differ from that of his predecessor, he should be able to blunt criticism from those who are adversely affected by his public activities. The greater the departure of current from past practice, of course, the less credible the president's claim becomes and the greater the likelihood of a negative response. This is precisely what happened after Nixon's first year in office when he began appearing on evening network television to an unprecedented degree. By one count Nixon appeared on national television 17 times within nine months beginning in late 1969. On 11 of these occasions, he preempted evening commercial television.[34]

The sudden surge in presidential television appearances generated complaints from various quarters and assumed the status of a prominent news story in its own right. During the summer of 1970, Washington correspondents began pressing Nixon at news conferences with pointed questions about his television strategy. The White House responded by arguing that the president was simply subscribing to the practices of past presidents. Aide John Ehrlichman compiled figures on the television appearances of Presidents Kennedy and Johnson, as well as Nixon, arguing that his president had been on television less than Kennedy and about as often as Johnson.

Ehrlichman's argument did little to allay criticism, however. A group of antiwar activists, citing repeated instances of Nixon's use of television to promote his Vietnam policies, had petitioned the Federal Communications Commission (FCC) for network time to respond to the president's remarks under the fairness doctrine. The Democratic National Committee appealed directly to the networks for a similar opportunity to rebut the president. In midsummer the FCC ruled for the first time that a president's repeated addresses on a subject had produced an imbalance in public debate and that those holding opposing views should be given network air time to respond.[35] Independent of the FCC ruling, the networks liberalized access of Democrats to answer the president's remarks.

The idea of granting air time to the president's opponents was not new. After Harry Truman blasted "greedy" steel company executives in announcing his seizure of the mills in 1951, the networks gave rebuttal time to the president of Inland Steel Company. During the mid-1960s, networks began the practice of granting air time to congressional opponents to answer the president's annual State of the Union message. According to archival research performed by the Library of Congress, opposition spokespersons—whether individuals, congressional leaders, or representatives of the opposition party— were allotted free response time on national television on only 4 occasions from 1961 to 1964. But from 1970 to 1974, during Nixon's administration, there were 14 such occasions; from 1975 to 1984, there were 34.[36]

Today, the right of opposition parties and congressional spokespersons to respond to presidential addresses remains a subject of some dispute and negotiation between politicians and network executives. Chief among the many issues yet to be resolved are which presidential statements warrant equal time, who is to respond, and when opposition responses will be aired.[37] Congressional and party opponents assert their right for equal time, the networks their prerogative to judge each request on its merits, and the FCC its intention to remain uninvolved. What is clear from the record, however, is that Nixon's heavy use of television helped establish strong precedents that will ensure opposition parties in the future their time on television.[38]

Opposition groups are not alone in complaining about the frequency of presidential rhetoric. After the heavy dose of prime-time television during President Nixon's first year, CBS head Frank Stanton publicly began to characterize the White House strategy as an attempt to monopolize the airwaves.[39] Given that a prime-time, thirty-second commercial can cost $200,000 or more, it is understandable why network executives might be concerned that the president was enjoying undue political advantage through his special access to national television. Granting the opposition party response time would seem to restore political parity, but this would, of course, result in an additional lost opportunity for the network to sell products.

In October 1975, the networks hit upon a less expensive way to rein in presidential television. Although the next election was over a year away, CBS and NBC refused to carry President Ford's address on tax reform on the dubious grounds that they would have to provide equal time to other announced candidates. (At that early date, there was apparently only one—an obscure, perennial candidate in Massachusetts.) Not until Reagan's second term did the networks enlist their prerogative to turn down a presidential request, but it is apparent that this first instance made gaining access to the airwaves an important factor as presidents and their aides considered their options. In late 1978, President Carter's communications director planned a media strategy involving unprecedented levels of national television. He advised the president to cultivate warm relations with the network heads, so that they would be less likely to balk at complying with his subsequent request for air time.[40]

From mid-1986 through the fall of 1987, one or more of the networks refused to give President Reagan air time on at least three occasions. Two of these involved appeals for public support for aid to the Nicaraguan *contras*;

the third concerned support for Judge Robert Bork, Reagan's nominee to the Supreme Court. During this nonelection period, the networks could not fall back on equal time for opponents as their rationale for denying the president's request. Instead, they used the criterion of newsworthiness, which would appear difficult to apply since little more than the topic of the address would have been known to those making the decision. One network comment struck directly at the strategy of going public: "Tonight's address is really directed at a small group of people on Capitol Hill, so my recommendation is not to interrupt our prime-time broadcast to carry that." [41]

The adverse reaction to presidential television from the opposition party in Congress and network executives pales in comparison to that from a third class of participants—the viewing public. Broadcast technology enabled the president to enter the homes of citizens, and the development of VCRs and cable technology, shown in Figure 4-4, is allowing these same citizens to usher him out.

In the 1960s and 1970s, when the three networks controlled 90 percent of the audience share in most markets, the president enjoyed a seemingly captive audience for his addresses to the nation. There is no evidence, based on audience size, that an appreciable number of viewers chose to turn off their televisions.[42] But with the rise of new technology providing alternative programming and tape formats, people have proven nimble at changing channels. However well they may be doing in the Gallup polls, recent presidents are clearly slipping in A. C. Nielsen's audience ratings. Figure 4-5 depicts a point-a-year decline on average in percentages of households with televisions that have tuned in to presidential addresses during the past five administrations. The high point is the first observation available in this series: President Nixon's statement of the Vietnam War in November 1969. Presidents Carter and Reagan nearly matched him once, in their first addresses to the nation, but Bush has not come close. His first address to the nation garnered only 38 percent of the households with televisions.[43] Despite a brief war and dramatic world events in which President Bush played a significant role, he managed no better than a 43 percent audience rating—that after the Gulf War in 1991.

Undoubtedly, many citizens who were unenthusiastic and hence inattentive viewers when they had few choices have now abandoned the president's audience. But since these were probably the least responsive members of the audience, their departure will not greatly affect the president's capacity to generate vocal support for his policies. Of greater strategic concern to a president is the fact that other viewers, as a result of the new technology, can now decide on each occasion whether to watch the president or turn their attention elsewhere. Their choice will rest on the comparative appeal of the president's message. In March 1986 when President Reagan spoke to the nation on increased U.S. support for the *contra* rebels in Nicaragua, an estimated 16 million households switched to alternative programming. Eight

Figure 4-5 The Declining Presidential Audience: 1969-1992

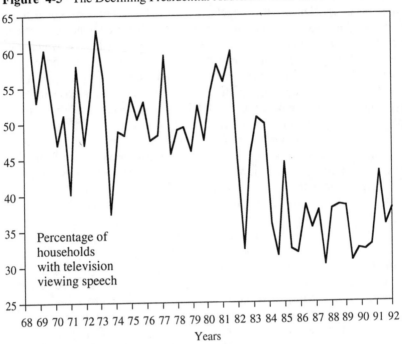

Percentage of
households
with television
viewing speech

Years

SOURCE: Nielsen Media Research. Reprinted with permission.

months later during the Irangate scandal, the president defended himself at a nationally televised press conference. This time only 4 million households defected.[44] Today, with uncertainty about whether the networks will decide to broadcast the president's message and about whether viewers will opt to receive it, the availability of the audience becomes a serious consideration in planning the president's public strategies.

Conclusion

A proposition of this book is that the degree to which a president goes public determines the kind of leader he will be. With it I have argued that the style of leadership in the White House is changing. Modern presidents rely upon public opinion for their leadership in Washington to an extent unknown when Dahl and Lindblom in the early 1950s described the president as "an embodiment of a bargaining society," or later when Neustadt predicated presidential power on bargaining.[45]

The above proposition, claiming a change in the degree of going public and inferring a change in the character of leadership, is subject to rejoinder on two fronts. Because every president since Theodore Roosevelt has sought at some moment to rally public opinion to his side, and each in his public activity has drawn on the precedents and departed only marginally from the base lines of his immediate predecessor, one can easily miss the striking degree to which presidents today go public compared with the presidents of the 1930s, the 1940s, or even the 1950s.

Moreover, I suspect that the increasing quantity of public activity has tended to be obscured by the varying quality of public rhetoric, which is always more memorable than the quantity. To those who compared Ronald Reagan's rhetorical talents with those of Franklin Roosevelt, little appears to have changed in the past 50 years.

One misconception that results from incremental change is that in retrospect the past resembles the present. This, after all, is the purpose of the incremental strategy. A case in point is the story Arthur Schlesinger recounts of a phone call he received one morning from President Kennedy. The president asked how frequently FDR had held fireside chats. He said that *New York Times* correspondent Lester Markel was with him complaining that he ought to go before the American people more often. "Lester ... seems to think that Roosevelt gave a fireside chat once a week." Schlesinger subsequently reported to Kennedy that before the war, Roosevelt averaged no more than two of these now famous radio addresses a year.[46] A couple of years later the issue was still current when Schlesinger passed along to Kennedy a letter from Samuel Beer, a prominent political scientist and former national chair of the Americans for Democratic Action, which said:

> I certainly do not agree, let alone sympathize, with my liberal friends who say that it is all the fault of the President; that if he would only resort to the magic of the "fire-side chat" he would create great waves of public opinion which would wash away Congressional obstruction. They simply don't remember the way FDR actually worked—e.g. the prolonged and tortured operation by which he got the Wage-Hour bill—and totally forget the political situation that gave him leverage.[47]

When it comes to collective memory of presidential performance, one seems as inclined to impose the present on the past as vice versa. Either way, the result is that nothing much *appears* to have happened.

Another counter-argument accepts the trends examined in this chapter but holds that they have little bearing on the character of presidential leadership. The president may be a more familiar face on television, and he may spend more time on the road, but his public relations have not reduced the role of bargaining in presidential leadership. Against this argument, quantitative indexes of public activity, no matter how dramatic the changes they depict, stand mute.

To conclude that the multitudinous public activities of modern presidents do matter—that they have altered the character of leadership in Washington—one needs to consider more qualitative evidence, such as the transactions between the president and those whom he seeks to influence. The next chapter examines the ways Ronald Reagan promoted his budget with Congress during his first three years in office. The budgetary politics of these years show how a president, who took pride in his skills as a communicator, enlisted public support in his dealings with congressional leaders and how these activities substituted for and at times interfered with bargaining.

Notes

1. In an early study of what has only recently become a prominent fact of presidential governance, Stanley Kelley, Jr., described the linkages between presidential activities (including campaigning) and professional public relations in *Professional Public Relations and Political Power* (Baltimore: Johns Hopkins University Press, 1956).
2. Rowland Evans and Robert Novak, *Nixon in the White House* (New York: Random House, 1971), 388-389.
3. Since fall 1981, Reagan's pollster, Richard Wirthlin, had been advising the president of his slipping popularity among blue-collar Democrats—many of whom are Catholic—who had supported him against Carter in 1980. See B. Drummond Ayres, Jr., "G.O.P. Keeps Tabs on Nation's Mood," *New York Times*, November 16, 1981, A20; and Howell Raines, "Reagan's Gamble: Bid for Popularity," *New York Times*, March 30, 1982, A27. Similar evidence of Reagan's decline in the polls is reported by Hedrick Smith in the CBS-*New York Times* survey in "Blue-Collar Workers' Support for Reagan Declines," *New York Times*, March 8, 1982, 1. The association between the president's decline in the polls and his tuition tax credit proposal is made by Dennis Williams, Lucy Howard, and Frank Marer, "Tax Credits for Tuition?" *Newsweek*, April 26, 1982, 86. See also Seymour Sudman, "The President and the Polls," *Public Opinion Quarterly* 46 (Fall 1982): 301-310; and Harrison Donnelly, "Little Hope Seen for Tuition Tax Credit Plan," *Congressional Quarterly Weekly Report*, April 24, 1982, 911-913.
4. These categories of going public correspond to those developed by William Lammers, who was the first to examine systematically trends in presidents' public activities. William W. Lammers, "Presidential Attention-Focusing Activities," in *The President and the American Public,* ed. Doris A. Graber (Philadelphia: Institute for the Study of Human Issues, 1982), 145-171.
5. Omitted from major addresses are presidential press conferences and purely ceremonial functions (for example, calls to astronauts and Christmas tree lighting ceremonies). See Table 3-2 for the decline in the use of press conferences. Lammers provides evidence that presidents adapt conference schedules to their strategic goals and to more direct means of communication in "Presidential Press Conference Schedules: Who Hides and When?" *Political Science Quarterly* 96 (Summer 1981): 261-267.
6. In Figures 4-1, 4-2, and 4-3, only the first three years have been tabulated in order to eliminate activities inspired by concerns for reelection rather than governing.

Since Gerald Ford's tenure does not include three nonelection years, his record of public activities has been ignored.

7. As a cautionary note, the sources used to compile this list of television addresses appear to provide a more inclusive definition in recent years.

8. Roosevelt continued, "If I had tried [in 1935] to keep up the pace of 1933 and 1934, the inevitable histrionics of the new actors, Long and Coughlin and Johnson, would have turned the eyes of the audience away from the main drama itself." Cited in Douglass Cater, "How a President Helps Form Public Opinion," *New York Times Magazine*, February 26, 1961, 12.

9. Pierre Salinger, *With Kennedy* (New York: Doubleday, 1966), 138-144. For a discussion of other presidents' concerns with overexposure, see Godfrey Hodgson, *All Things to All Men* (New York: Simon and Schuster, 1980), 188-189.

10. From a memorandum to President Carter, June 30, 1978, personal papers of Gerald Rafshoon.

11. Although systematic evidence on the size of the president's audience as a function of the number or recency of previous addresses is not now available, a cursory inspection of scattered audience rating data does not suggest a strong relationship. The series of Nielsen ratings below do show that the two largest television audiences came for Presidents Carter and Reagan in their first national address within weeks of their inauguration. Audience share and size have not otherwise varied significantly in the past 15 years.

        Figure 4-1   Yearly Average
                        Major Addresses: 9
                        Minor Addresses: 120

        Figure 4-2   Yearly Averages
                        Washington D.C. Appearances: 49
                        U.S. Appearances: 114

        Figure 4-3   Yearly Averages
                        U.S. Travel: 54 days
                        Foreign Travel: 33 days

12. Examples of such statements are Hodgson, *All Things to All Men*, and Arthur Schlesinger, Jr., *The Imperial Presidency* (Boston: Houghton Mifflin, 1973).

13. Enlisting a new technology and enlisting it well are, of course, different matters. On the problems Bush experienced in adapting to the teleconferencing format, see Michael Wines, "In Scripts for Bush, Questions on Images," *New York Times*, November 28, 1991.

14. James T. Wooten, "Pre-Inaugural Memo Urged Carter to Emphasize Style Over Substance," *New York Times*, May 4, 1977, 1.

15. Mark Hertsgaard adds that these efforts turned public opinion around on Reagan's education policies to a 2:1 favorable ratio. "How Reagan Seduced Us," *Village Voice*, September 18, 1984, 12.

16. An example of this genre is President Reagan's warm-up routine at a Jaycees convention in San Antonio the summer of 1981 while pressuring Democrats in Washington to accept his budget. To a roaring audience Reagan intoned, "Where on earth has he [Tip O'Neill] been for the last few years?" After a pause he continued, "The answer is, right in Washington, D.C." See "Reagan's Sweet Triumph," *Newsweek*, July 6, 1981, 18.

17. Newton N. Minow, John Bartlow Martin, and Lee M. Mitchell, *Presidential Television* (New York: Basic Books, 1973), 65-68.

18. Cited in George C. Edwards III, *The Public Presidency* (New York: St. Martin's Press, 1983), 75.

19. Another example of modern press treatment of presidential travel is Hedrick Smith's observation that Reagan's trip to China in the spring of 1984 was intended in part to "enhance his bid for reelection by casting himself as a negotiator for peace" ("The Road to Peking," *New York Times*, April 25, 1984, 6).
20. J. F. terHorst and Col. Ralph Albertazzie provide a lively chronology of presidential air travel in *The Flying White House* (New York: Coward, McCann, and Geoghegan, 1979).
21. Because the categories of public activity are not mutually exclusive, it is not possible to obtain comparable averages for other presidents by simply adding their appearances, travel days, and speeches.
22. "Hoover, with 37 Radio Talks in Past Year, Made a Record," *New York Times,* December 28, 1930, 1.
23. "Health of President Coolidge Conserved by Broadcasting," *New York Times,* February 24, 1924, 15.
24. Travel time during this era is nicely displayed in the isochronic map "Rates of Travel, 1930" in Charles O. Paullin, *Atlas of the Historical Geography of the United States* (Washington, D.C.: Carnegie Institution, 1932), plate 138D.
25. terHorst and Albertazzie, *Flying White House,* 33.
26. Douglass Cater, *The Fourth Branch of Government* (Boston: Houghton Mifflin, 1959), 40-42.
27. Roosevelt reportedly expressed to a friend his wish that the development of television would speed up. See Hodgson, *All Things to All Men,* 186.
28. See Samuel L. Becker, "Presidential Power: The Influence of Broadcasting," *Quarterly Journal of Speech* 47 (October 1961): 17.
29. Ibid.
30. Eisenhower spent $800,000 on television time compared with $77,000 spent by the Democratic candidate, Adlai Stevenson. See Kathleen Hall Jamieson, *Packaging the Presidency* (New York: Oxford University Press, 1984), 43.
31. Joseph Alsop and Turner Catledge, *The 168 Days* (New York: Doubleday and Co., 1938), 13-79.
32. Although as a *New York Times* commentary on earlier fireside addresses pointed out, the implications of the direct public approach in motivating Congress were clear. "His use of this new instrument of political discussion is a plain hint to Congress of a recourse which the president may employ if it proves necessary to rally support for legislation which he asks and which legislators might be reluctant to give him." Cited in Becker, "Presidential Power," 15.
33. *Memoirs by Harry S Truman: Years of Trial and Hope,* vol. 2 (Garden City, N.Y.: Doubleday and Co., 1956; reprint New York: New American Library, 1965).
34. Minow, Martin, and Mitchell, *Presidential Television,* 69-72.
35. Denis Steven Rutkus, "President Reagan, the Opposition and Access to Network Airtime" (Congressional Research Service, Washington, D.C., 1984, Mimeographed), 69-71.
36. The figures for the years 1961-1966 come from Robert Lee Baily, *An Examination of Prime Time Network Television Special Programs, 1948-1966* (New York: Arno Press, 1979), Appendix A; for the years 1967 and 1968, network program logs and secondary sources were used, and for the years 1969-1984, Denis Steven Rutkus, "President Reagan, the Opposition and Access to Network Airtime," Congressional Research Service, August 1984, Appendix C.
37. Rutkus, "President Reagan," 36-59.
38. More recently, Republicans claimed that President Jimmy Carter similarly violated established protocol. In an article in 1978, Ronald Reagan cited

Republican National Committee figures in calling for greater opportunities for opposition spokespersons. See Ronald Reagan, "Do the Networks Always Short-change the 'Loyal Opposition?' " *T.V. Guide*, March 11, 1978, 4-5.

39. Robert B. Semple, Jr., "Nixon Eludes Newsmen on Coast Trip," *New York Times*, August 3, 1970, 16.
40. Rafshoon to Carter, June 30, 1978.
41. Peter J. Boyer, "Networks Refuse to Broadcast Reagan's Plea," *New York Times*, February 3, 1988.
42. Nielsen estimates comparing audience size during presidential addresses and normal programming have found no significant differences. One study actually found that during President Ford's tenure, the audience grew slightly when he was on television. These findings are reported in Newton N. Minow and Lee M. Mitchell, "Incumbent Television: A Case of Indecent Exposure," *Annals of the American Academy of Political and Social Science* 425 (May 1976): 74-77.
43. While the 54 ratings graphed in Figure 4-5 do not represent all presidential prime-time addresses, they come close. I wish to thank Professor Joe Foote and Diane Buono at A.C. Nielsen for making available the data reported here. Various statistical tests of the change in the way Nielsen monitors viewers in the fall of 1987 did not turn up a significant effect on declining presidential audience shares.
44. This discussion is based on information provided in Joe S. Foote, *Television Access and Political Power* (New York: Praeger, 1990), 152-156.
45. See Robert A. Dahl and Charles E. Lindblom, *Politics, Economics, and Welfare* (New York: Harper and Row, 1960); and Richard E. Neustadt, *Presidential Power* (New York: John Wiley and Sons, 1980).
46. Arthur M. Schlesinger, Jr., *A Thousand Days* (Boston: Houghton Mifflin, 1965), 715. The following memorandum from Schlesinger to Kennedy, dated March 16, 1961, indicates that other members of the press were already forming similar expectations of the president.

    There is increasing concern among friends in the press about the alleged failure of the Administration to do as effective a job of public information and instruction as it should and must. Lippmann had a column about this last week. Joe Alsop has been haranguing me about this over the telephone and plans to do some columns about it soon. Lester Markel is going to do a long piece about it in the *Times Magazine*.

47. Cited in William E. Leuchtenburg, *In the Shadow of FDR* (Ithaca, N.Y.: Cornell University Press, 1985), 114.

President Reagan and His First Three Budgets   5

Try to imagine an individual better suited by experience, temperament, and ideology to lead by going public than Ronald Reagan. It is difficult to do so. Certainly not President Bush, who served eight years as his understudy but in office proved long on motion and short on vision. Reagan brought to the presidency ideal qualities for this new strategy of leadership, and his performance was not disappointing. When presented at critical moments with the choice to deal or to go public, he preferred to go public—sometimes exclusively, other times in combination with bargaining. The trends in direct public appeals surveyed in Chapter 4 culminated in Reagan's distinctive style of leadership, unimagined 30 years ago.

Contrary to some predictions, this outsider, this public president did not fall on his face. While his legacy is already being measured in terms of the volume of red ink it incurred, judged politically—that is, according to the accomplishment of his own programmatic goals—Reagan's record of going public proved fruitful. Political elites in Washington initially expressed surprise at the president's maneuvers—during the 97th Congress the words "shock" and "bewilderment" were recurrently attributed to Democrats in Congress—but more so at their profound effects on the behavior of fellow politicians than at the acts themselves. Nearly five years later, after the president had accumulated some political bruises that invariably come with time and his approach to leadership was no longer novel to Washington politicians, they were still paying him grudging respect. One Democratic member summed up congressional sentiment toward Reagan after five years in office: "He's still formidable, no question about that. We're still a bit afraid of him." [1]

Ronald Reagan's first three years contained all the variation in prestige and legislative accomplishment necessary to study the downside as well as the upside of public leadership. Success came early and in heaping portions, but it did not last. By the beginning of his third year, with his popularity spent, the president struggled to preserve the earlier budgetary achievements of real growth in defense expenditures, reductions in social programs, and a 25 percent cut in income taxes. Although the dollar amounts varied marginally from one budget to the next, President Reagan remained consistent, both in the substance of policies as well as the strategies he employed in their behalf. The politics that ensued in each of his first three budget seasons differed greatly, however. And yet they did so in a manner altogether consistent with the theory of individualized pluralism.

Not unlike various fairy tales with famous threesomes, "President Reagan and His First Three Budgets" is a didactic story, each episode instructive in itself as well as in its overall moral. It is worth telling here, for it fleshes out the emerging features of the modern office in a way that charts and tables cannot, however steep the trends they may depict. Before beginning, however, I need to introduce the main character.

Reagan as an Outsider

Ronald Reagan's previous career in movies, television, and public affairs groomed him well for the role of a president who goes public routinely. Movies brought him fame, a considerable resource employed by military heroes of earlier eras in transferring laterally to a public career. Reagan's early years in Hollywood contributed incidentally to his political maturation as he waged ideological war with liberals during his tenure as president of the Screen Actors Guild.[2] Later, a decade of television spent largely as spokesman first for Borax and then for General Electric gave him mastery of the requisite techniques. In his autobiography, *Where's the Rest of Me?*, Reagan described his duties for General Electric. "I know statistics are boring, but reducing eight years of tours, in which I reached all the 135 plants and personally met with 250,000 employees down to numbers, it turns out something like this: two of the years were spent traveling and with speeches sometimes running at 14 a day, I was on my feet in front of a 'mike' for about 250,000 minutes."[3] These ancillary public relations activities had him in training for the 32-round presidential primary campaign long before the reforms had been instituted. And they gave him ample opportunity to perfect his familiar criticisms of big government and his encomiums to private enterprise.[4]

In 1967, at the age of 55, Ronald Reagan embarked on a career in politics when he defeated Pat Brown for the governorship of California. Entering the public arena comparatively late in life and high on the rung of public offices also contributed to his style of leadership in the White House. If one considers a political career as a learning or developmental process where lower office not only promotes but also prepares a politician for higher office, Reagan's path to the presidency is clearly deficient. He skipped those formative experiences that take place mainly in legislatures—city councils, state assemblies, and Congress—and that expose a politician to bargaining and to compromise. Instead, as governor of California, Reagan's political tutelage occurred in peculiarly solitary yet visible environs for socialization. His tenure during years of campus unrest and Democratic legislatures gave him ample opportunity to hone his considerable rhetorical talents for the political arena. After eight years Reagan retired from office "to speak out on the issues," which meant to campaign full time for the presidency. Being a nationally syndicated columnist and radio commentator and one of the most sought-after speakers on the Republican circuit, Reagan was better positioned than anyone else to do so.

Finally, one must consider the extensive campaign experience any candidate for the presidency invariably accumulates. Ronald Reagan may have begun a public career late and held only one office before the presidency, but he nonetheless managed to contest more than 61 primary and general elections, amassing a record of 44 victories against 17 defeats. All of them were in the national limelight.[5]

Such experience prepared Reagan to be a public president as much by what it omitted as by what it included. Other twentieth-century presidents had won the office with the thinnest of claims of insight into the ways of Washington, much less of the presidency. But with the exception of Jimmy Carter, none was so bereft of such experience as Reagan. Eisenhower, avowedly apolitical, could and did point to his "invaluable," albeit brief, service in the War Department under George Marshall and subsequently as army chief of staff.[6] That Carter and Reagan should be so inexperienced is not, of course, mere coincidence. The reformed presidential nomination system coupled with lingering public memory of corruption and scandal in Washington allowed each man to convert his deprived political upbringing into a campaign asset.

Political ideology further distanced Ronald Reagan from Washington. Since his early and ardent conversion from the New Deal, Reagan has been an aggressive exponent of a traditional strain of Republican conservatism.[7] A favorite rhetorical device of his over the years was to decorate his attack of whatever Democratic policies were emanating from Washington at the moment with a simple, often folksy, statement of his own values and a caricature of Washington officials as "bureaucrats" and "spendthrift politicians." Reagan's insistent rhetoric helps to explain why on entering the White House he had accumulated an unusually large number of both intense followers and detractors.[8] As a conservative outsider moving to a city he perceived to be dominated by liberal insiders, Reagan was unsuited to be a pluralist president. Lou Cannon, a White House reporter and longtime Reagan watcher, attributes to him before he entered office a concept of the presidency that is consistent with his outsider status.

> Reagan is a modest man, but he did not object to the frequent descriptions of him as "the Great Communicator." He approvingly cited Theodore Roosevelt's description of the presidency as "a bully pulpit." With the forum of national television available to the President, Reagan was certain

that his own communicative skills were sufficient to persuade Congress and the country to do whatever it was that was asked of them.[9]

As president, a politician is subjected to a brief and intense stint of decision making. Little time is available for leisurely learning. Absent is any semblance of apprenticeship, a norm that pervades virtually all other work settings including those in Washington. Rather, the president enters office with great latitude to be the kind of politician he wants to be. His definition of the presidency derives from preconceptions grounded in experience, temperament, and ideology. In Franklin Roosevelt, a man who groomed himself to serve in the office, these qualities were so configured as to present a consummate bargainer. Roosevelt's self-concept was so pure that presidential scholars have been able to glean from his performance insights into this style of pluralist leadership. So it was with Ronald Reagan. His personal qualities combined to provide similarly pristine material for the study of going public as a strategy of leadership. What other president, can one imagine, would repeatedly insist to his Soviet counterpart that he be given television time to address the Russian people?[10]

Reagan's Three Budgets

Doonesbury's barbs about the president's laziness notwithstanding, Ronald Reagan's first three years in office were full ones. Contradicting skeptical predictions, he extracted from a Democratic House of Representatives and a narrowly Republican Senate the three major planks of his campaign platform: unprecedented budget reductions, increased military spending, and a massive three-year tax cut.[11] At the end of the first summer many observers were favorably comparing his legislative accomplishments with those of Franklin Roosevelt and the first New Deal and of Lyndon Johnson and the Great Society. The legacy of a massive national debt that this combination of policies would create was not yet fully realized.

As he accumulated an impressive string of victories during the summer of 1981, President Reagan increasingly appeared unbeatable. Liberal Democrats, at first stunned, gradually became more stoic. Many took solace in the rarely heard notion of letting the president have anything he wanted so he would be held responsible in the next election if the promised cornucopia of economic benefits failed to materialize.[12] Not until September 1981 when he proposed changes in social security benefits—which he quickly retracted—did the president's fortunes begin to turn. Even so, at the close of 1981, not even the most optimistic Democratic prognosis foresaw his political discomfiture the next year.

The second session of the 97th Congress, in 1982, gave President Reagan some legislative victories, but these pale against the triumphs of the preceding year. Real growth in military spending continued despite a swelling budget deficit and louder rumblings from Democrats.[13] Congress agreed to another round of budget reductions, but this time the administration was forced to make numerous concessions after its initial budget reconciliation resolution was defeated in the House (along with every Democratic alternative). The greatest alteration of the Reagan blueprint was the tax increase of $99 billion drafted not by House Democrats but by the Republican Senate Finance Committee. This, the largest election-year tax hike in history, triggered a curious coalitional realignment in Congress.

Because midterm elections were approaching and the economy was souring quickly, the president's control over political affairs began to slip badly. A balanced budget became an increasingly distant goal; only record deficits and double-digit unemployment were in immediate sight. The economy manifested itself politically in the president's steady decline in the polls and, in turn, in the diminished support of politicians about to stand for election. The president was no pariah, but he was no longer the local hero.

Democratic hopes and Republican fears about the changing fortunes were confirmed in the November 1982 elections; 26 House seats switched over to the Democratic column, about the margin of the president's recent floor victories. From the election until the president's State of the Union message in January 1983, the foremost question among Washington politicians and bureaucrats, including many of the White House staff, was, could the president adapt to the new, harsher political realities? The answer was no. Unwilling to compromise with the Republican Senate Budget Committee, President Reagan gave up on the budget resolution and announced his intention to veto any appropriations bills that violated his budget recommendations. The story of Reagan's first three budgets spans the peaks and valleys of leadership based on going public.

Budget Politics in 1981

The early history of President Reagan's budget and tax cuts largely comprises televised presidential addresses to the nation. The first occurred on February 5 when he announced that the country faced "the worst economic mess since the Great Depression" and presented the broad contours of an economic program that resembled the tax and budget cuts on which he had campaigned. On February 18, the president returned to prime-time television to fill in the details. Addressing a televised joint session of Congress, he unveiled a package of tax cuts totaling $53.9 billion for individuals and businesses and spending reductions of $41.4 billion for fiscal year 1982. The initial response was muted, and the popular wisdom in Washington was that success would be neither quick nor easy because of the many organized constituencies opposed to reduced spending.[14] Ten days later the White House announced that an additional $13 billion cut in expenditures would be necessary to keep the budget within the targeted deficit ceiling.

As the president's economic program began wending its way through Congress's budget labyrinth, it received critical scrutiny by the press and interested constituencies. By mid-March the president's rating in the Gallup Poll stood at 59 percent approving and 24 percent disapproving, the poorest approve-to-disapprove ratio the Gallup Poll has ever recorded for a president in his second month of office. Press Secretary James Brady explained, "The fat's gotten into the fire more quickly with this [economic] proposal than in normal administrations because of [its] comprehensive nature . . . and the fact it's changing the direction of government. There's resistance to change." [15] An independent pollster concurred: "He's spending his savings [in popularity] and he has less in the bank now, that's all." [16]

The assassination attempt in late March erased his early decline in the polls. In typical fashion the public immediately rallied to his side; Reagan's approval rating went up by 10 points or more in every national survey taken shortly after he was shot. More important, according to White House poll-watcher Richard Beal, the shooting and the president's unaided, almost nonchalant entry into the hospital, both of which were videotaped and reshown repeatedly on national television, "focussed uniquely on the President. It did a lot to endear the President to the people. . . . His personal attributes might never have come across without the assassination attempt." [17]

When Richard Wirthlin, the president's pollster, reported that the "resistance ratio" (a figure constructed from a battery of survey questions on the president's performance) to Reagan had improved from 2:1 to 3:1, presidential assistant Michael Deaver convened a strategy meeting to evaluate how this new "political capital" should be spent. Various options were aired, ranging from a radio address to a trip to Capitol Hill. Sensing the opportunity for high drama, they agreed on the latter course, a speech before a joint session of Congress. Journalist Sidney Blumenthal notes, "This decision was in keeping with overall strategy. To a greater extent than any other policy initiative, the President's economic program was being conducted as a national political campaign." [18]

To soften up potential allies before the president's appearance, Lyn Nofziger, the president's chief political aide, arranged for the Republican National Committee (RNC) to send party officials to the South over the Easter recess to stimulate grass-roots pressure on those Democratic representatives whose districts had gone heavily for Reagan in the November election. [19] By the time of his address to Congress on April 28, Reagan's surging popularity and the grass-roots campaign had created a vote deficit for the Democratic opposition. Democratic Whip Thomas Foley informed Speaker Thomas P. O'Neill, Jr., on his return from an Easter trip abroad that they were already down 50 to 60 votes. Then came the president's speech.

All news accounts depict President Reagan's reception from Congress as a love feast, which is ironic given that the audience was mostly Democrats who were well aware the president had come to advocate a starvation diet for many of the programs they had proudly enacted during the preceding decade. *Newsweek* reported, "His performance was a smash from the moment he entered the soaring House chamber, smiling and waving, to a three-minute thunderburst of whistles, huzzahs, and hand-clapping." [20] In the speech the president endorsed the Gramm-Latta budget reconciliation resolution (named for sponsors Phil Gramm and Delbert Latta), which carried the administration's proposals. He then attacked the Democratic alternative, calling it the "old and comfortable way." In closing his comments on the budget, President Reagan reminded the assembled legislators,

> When I took the oath of office, I pledged loyalty to only one special interest group—"We the people." Those people—neighbors and friends, shopkeepers and laborers, farmers and craftsmen—do not have infinite patience. As a matter of fact, some 80 years ago Teddy Roosevelt wrote these instructive words in his first message to the Congress: "The American people are slow to wrath, but when their wrath is once kindled, it burns like a consuming flame." [21]

A week after the speech and shortly before the budget's first major floor test, Speaker O'Neill could round up no more than 175 votes in opposition. A heated Democratic caucus followed in which O'Neill pleaded with fellow Democrats not to abandon the party and warned them: "The opinions of the man in the street change faster than anything in this world. Today, he does not know what is in this program, and he is influenced by a President with charisma and class [who] is a national hero. . . . But a year from now he will be saying, 'You shouldn't have voted that way.'" [22] For all his effort, O'Neill made but a single convert. Two days later, the House voted 253 to 176 to substitute Gramm-Latta for the Democratic bill and then promptly passed it by a wider margin. Fully a quarter of the House Democrats supported Reagan. "They say they're voting for it," reported Rep. Toby Moffett, a Connecticut liberal, "because they're afraid." [23]

It is one thing to support a general resolution that contains broad policy targets, and quite another to vote for the individual program cuts required to implement them. In mid-June, as the various House committees reported legislation implementing Gramm-Latta, the Reagan administration faced a difficult decision. With many of the spending measures departing sharply from the spending cuts mandated by the budget guidelines, should the president try to preserve his earlier victory through bargaining or going public? Each position was supported by a senior White House aide. Budget Director David Stockman urged the president to renew his public campaign to keep up the pressure on Democrats who had broken ranks with their party's leadership a month earlier. Chief of Staff James Baker and Communications Director David Gergen disagreed. Fearful of overtaxing public support, they advised the president to save his public strategy for his major tax initiative, Kemp-Roth, which was to come to a vote the next month. Stockman reports the argument this way: " 'We have to understand,' Baker warned Reagan, 'that we're running a very great risk here. If we throw down the challenge and lose, it'll sap our momentum.' " [24] The president was persuaded and instructed his aides to cut whatever deals were necessary to solidify his position with the boll weevils (southern Democrats) and gypsy moths (northern Republicans who did not favor cuts in social spending). Stockman recalls these transactions with disgust, blaming this decision for the failure of the Reagan revolution to cut back government while avoiding deficits: "[House Minority Leader Robert] Michel and I went straight from lunch to his office to preside over one of the most expensive sessions I have ever attended on Capitol Hill. I lost $20 billion in proposed three year budget savings in four hours. . . . Michel and I crammed . . . some of the worst features on the committee bills. Hour by hour I backpedaled." [25]

With mainstream House Democrats left out of the compromises, the party leadership and the House Rules Committee decided to induce second thoughts among the wayward Democrats by having the appropriations for individual programs voted on separately. By making their colleagues face up to these tough decisions, the Democratic leaders still appeared to have a chance to win.

On June 24, two days before the floor vote, President Reagan learned of this legislative maneuver while en route to San Antonio to deliver a speech. He responded with two quick public statements that made the networks' evening news on consecutive days, many phone calls to persuadable representatives, and private appeals for assistance from his business allies. According to one Reagan aide, the White House was amazed by the effectiveness of these lobbies. "Within 24 hours," he said, "one congressman had between 75 and 100 phone calls from businessmen in his district." [26] Again the president prevailed. This time by a narrow margin of 217 to 211, the full House overturned the Rules Committee's partitioning of the budget and substituted a single "up or down" vote. The House then promptly passed the president's budget by a comfortable margin of 232 to 193.

Understandably, the Democratic leaders who had just lost control over the chamber's procedures were shellshocked. Rules Committee chair Richard Bolling added Reagan to his list of "imperial presidents" along with Johnson and Nixon. Majority Leader James Wright complained bitterly that the administration was trying to "dictate every last scintilla, every last phrase" of legislation. Summing up the Democratic glum, Speaker O'Neill said, "I hope someday, this day is forgotten." [27]

Since early May, the taxation parts of the president's program had proceeded down a different institutional path. In late July, closely following his budget victory, President Reagan won his three-year, 25 percent income tax cut with the same coalition of Republicans and southern Democrats. His *modus operandi* was much the same and included a dramatic public appeal within a week of the House vote.

There were, however, some important differences in the budget and tax issues that made the president's task on the latter more difficult and, consequently, the need for a successful public strategy crucial. One problem clear to everyone was that the massive tax reductions contained in the Kemp-Roth bill (named for sponsors Jack Kemp and William Roth) would produce a huge shortfall in government revenues. Many of the southern Democrats who had favored reduced government expenditures were also committed to a balanced budget. Yet the president's plan moved the deficit in the opposite direction. Another difficulty was that as revenue legislation the tax bill had to pass through the House Ways and Means Committee chaired by Illinois Democrat Daniel Rostenkowski. Although this committee was no longer as formidable as it had once been under Wilbur Mills's leadership, it remained the chief fount of revenue legislation. Standing in the president's way was a committee run by northern Democrats who were unsympathetic to his economic philosophy and bent on protecting their prerogative to legislate tax policy.

In working with legislative sponsors to draft the Kemp-Roth bill, President Reagan agreed to the only compromise he would make during this budget session. He allowed the first-year tax cut to be reduced from 10 to 5 percent and to begin in October 1981 rather than to be retroactive to January. Both changes would reduce the growing deficit and in doing so would improve the bill's acceptability among the president's earlier congressional supporters. Unveiling the new tax package, the president announced that he would "compromise" no further.

His steadfastness was amply demonstrated in early June when he met at the White House with Democratic leaders who were clearly looking for a deal.[28] Rostenkowski began the meeting by offering Reagan the Democrats' support for a two-year tax cut. Reagan rejected it immediately stating that three years were "a matter of principle." Senate Minority Leader Robert Byrd then tried to sweeten the proposal with a full 10 percent cut the first year and a trigger clause allowing additional reductions later if economic conditions permitted. At this point the president reportedly glanced over to his counsel Edwin Meese, who shook his head, before replying with a simple "no." Next came House Majority Leader James Wright's turn. He tried a guaranteed three-year program of 5 percent tax cuts each year, but it drew hardly a response. Recognizing that a battle with the president was inevitable, Speaker O'Neill concluded the one-way negotiating session by telling him, "When you offer us a bill, we'll have an alternative. If you roll us, you roll us." [29]

The bravado with which the president rejected the Democrats' overtures is all the more impressive when one recognizes that all who attended the meeting knew that the administration did not then have sufficient votes to pass the Kemp-Roth bill. Confronted with this by a reporter after the meeting, Reagan responded, "If we don't have enough votes, we'll get them." Speaker O'Neill described the situation candidly in a nationally televised interview: "If the vote were tomorrow we could win it. Right now we have the votes. Can [Reagan] take them away from us? Let's wait and see." [30]

After the bargaining session with Reagan failed, the Democratic leadership tried to woo northern Republicans and southern Democrats with special tax concessions for constituencies in their districts. This approach, it was soon discovered, had two serious limitations. First, Rostenkowski was constrained by liberal Democrats on Ways and Means who preferred to let the president win and be held responsible. The second drawback, even more serious, was the president's willingness to match everything Rostenkowski offered. By the time the bidding ended, one embarrassed White House aide joked, "There's a good argument that we gave away the store." [31]

Advised by Wirthlin that "if push comes to shove" the public would easily side with him over Congress, President Reagan also embarked on a public strategy with several objectives. [32] Early in June, he played an important card when he told a group of southern Democrats, "I could not in good conscience campaign against any of you Democrats who have helped me." [33] This pledge quickly circulated on Capitol Hill, and within days it had received prominent press notice. With the president fully recuperated and able to be involved more personally in the campaign to pass the Kemp-Roth bill, the White House decided against another raid on southern districts. Besides, conceded a liberal Democrat, "They don't need to do it again. The point was made." [34]

In late June, Reagan traveled to Texas (the home state of a large Democratic House delegation whose support would be necessary for victory), Colorado, and California to speak for the Kemp-Roth bill and against the Democratic alternative. But these efforts proved to be only warm-up exercises. On July 27, two days before the floor vote in the House and the administration still short of victory, Reagan returned to national television. At first the network executives balked, arguing that the speech was too patently partisan, but after the Republican National Committee threatened to purchase air time, they relented and reserved rebuttal time for Democratic leaders O'Neill and Rostenkowski. With visual displays that represented the administration's savings in green and the Democrats' deficit in red, the president accused the Democrats of "sleight of hand." He conceded mockingly that a working person would fare better under the opposition's legislation but "if you're only planning to live two more years." Reagan then urged the American public to join him in lobbying Congress:

> I ask you now to put aside any feelings of frustration or helplessness about our political institutions and join me in this dramatic but responsible plan to reduce the enormous burden of federal taxation on you and your family.
>
> During recent months many of you have asked what can you do to help make America strong again. I urge you again to contact your senators and congressmen. Tell them of your support for this bipartisan proposal. Tell them you believe this is an unequaled opportunity to help return America to prosperity and make government again the servant of the people. [35]

Everyone in Washington who saw the speech knew that it was a blockbuster. Celebrating that evening, Treasury Secretary Donald Regan proclaimed it "a home run with the bases loaded." The only recorded reaction to be found from the normally garrulous O'Neill was one rueful word, "Devastating." These early reviews were correct; the public's reaction was swift and overwhelming. Ways and Means Democrat Richard Gephardt remarked, "The dam broke. . . . It fell apart." [36]

House Democrats who, before the president's speech, were either undecided or had announced support of the Democratic bill came under enormous pressure from constituents moved by Reagan's entreaty. The day after the speech, Caroll Hubbard of Kentucky received 516 calls from his district, and Norman Dicks of Washington received 400; each then changed his position and voted for the Kemp-Roth bill. Bo Ginn of Georgia was encouraged to maintain his support of the Democratic bill by Jimmy Carter, Andrew Young, and Coretta Scott King, but 600 appeals from "less famous constituents" swept him over to the president's side. Ralph Hall of Texas had made a deal with House Democratic leaders—a tax break for his district's oil industry in exchange for his support of their bill. But even Hall's pro-Reagan constituents held sway in the end, and he, too, voted in support of the president.[37]

The experiences of these Democrats appear typical. Within hours the issue was decided, as wavering representatives played it safe and went with the president. When the waters receded, Reagan had moved from an apparent defeat to a sizable victory. The closest of the key votes was 238-195. Forty-eight defections by Democrats made the difference.

Reviewing this extraordinary first session of the 97th Congress, reporter Steven V. Roberts found two basic reasons for Reagan's success: "Lawmakers believed their constituents supported that program and they were afraid that Mr. Reagan could galvanize that support through an adroit use of television and punish any dissidents at the polls." [38] Not without reason. The national polls showed strong support for Reagan as president, for increased defense spending, for elimination of waste, and for lower taxes. Supplementing these poll data in forms more compelling to representatives with close ties to their home district were the waves of mail, telegrams, and phone calls that overwhelmed Congress after each presidential address. Reagan's public appeals generated about 15 million more letters than normally flowed into congressional mailrooms each session.[39] What better testimony to the prowess of the president skilled at going public?

By the next budget season, in 1982, President Reagan's standing in Washington and the country had weakened considerably. His problems began in the fall of 1981 with a proposal to trim social security benefits that made even his own party's congressional leadership wince and stirred up an outpouring of protest from elderly voters. *Newsweek* announced in headlines, "The Runner Stumbles." [40] Quickly, President Reagan backtracked and agreed to await a report from a bipartisan commission reviewing social security. Shortly thereafter, in late September, he returned to the airwaves, this time calling for $24 billion in additional spending cuts. Sensing the president's vulnerability, Democrats were unsparing in their criticism. Many House Republicans were also annoyed—especially those who had reluctantly gone along with the deep reductions in domestic spending just two months earlier with the understanding that additional cuts would not be requested. Beyond Washington, the early responses were equally chilly. Bond prices fell sharply, and the Dow Jones industrial average plummeted 11 points to the lowest level since spring. Nor did representatives report a surge in their mail. On notice from his party's congressional leaders, the president quietly agreed to postpone the issue and reintroduce the cuts in his next year's budget.[41]

For many observers of the Reagan presidency, the social security and budget-cutting proposals of fall 1981 were the turning point. From then until after the Grenada invasion in late 1983, the president found himself dealing with Congress on its terms. An in-depth Gallup survey reveals, however, that Reagan retained much of his influence with the American public, who had served him so well in the summer.[42] Two weeks after Reagan's television address, a national survey asked, "In general are you in favor of budget cuts in addition to those approved earlier this year or are you opposed to more cuts?" More said they opposed (46 percent) further cuts than favored them (42 percent), an apparently unfavorable climate for the president's new initiative. Yet when asked specifically about the Reagan proposal three questions later, 74 percent answered that they approved the program, and only 20 percent expressed disapproval. Those who identified themselves as Democrats, a majority of whom by now were disapproving of his "job performance," gave his budget package an endorsement of 71 percent![43] Clearly, the president remained a persuasive force with a broad cross section of the American public.

There were other irritants for Congress as well. Late in the legislative year the president had surprised the leadership of both parties in Congress with a veto of a continuing appropriations bill that maintained current expenditures until the normal appropriations bills could be enacted. Of all the administration's pratfalls to occur in a season full of them, the most extraordinary was a long interview published in the *Atlantic* with David Stockman, director of the Office of Management and Budget. In it the president's chief architect of the budget laid bare and even caricatured the haphazard way the budget had been assembled.[44] Many within Congress felt betrayed; it seemed that they had been subjected to an ordeal for what appeared to be little more than a sham.

How much these incidents hurt the president and his policies in the polls is difficult to say.[45] In the fall his popularity began a descent that would continue through 1982. As for Reaganomics, Figure 5-1 shows that this neologism began to lose much of its appeal during this time. The index displayed in the figure registers the intensity as well as the direction of opinion by weighing emphatic responses twice as much. The mostly negative scores indicate that the public was never very optimistic about the personal financial rewards of Reaganomics, and by the close of 1981 was decidedly pessimistic.

Figure 5-1 Public Opinion on the Effects of Reaganomics on Personal Finances, March 1981-March 1983

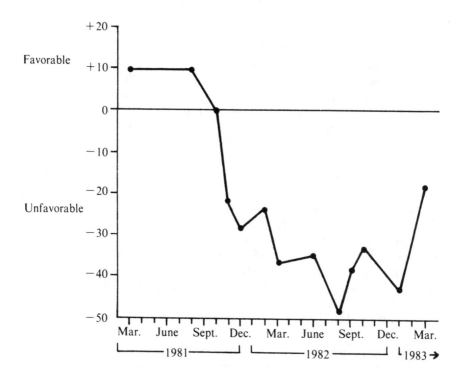

NOTE: Question: "Do you feel your financial situation will be much better, somewhat better, somewhat worse, or much worse as a result of Reagan's economic policies?" Responses are scored +2 for "much better," +1 for "somewhat better," 0 for no opinion or unsure, −1 for "somewhat worse," and −2 for "much worse." Polls were taken in March, August, October, and early and late November 1981; in February, March, June, August, September, and October 1982; and in January and March 1983.

SOURCE: *Gallup Report* 211 (April 1983): 14.

Whatever the cumulative effects of presidential retractions and subordinates' confessions, one need look no further than the economy to explain the beginning of the public's loss of confidence in Reagan and his policies. During the summer and fall of 1981 unemployment rose steadily. The projected budget deficits grew apace, in part because more unemployed workers were claiming benefits. The swelling deficits meant heavy federal borrowing in the financial markets, which contributed to historically high "real" interest rates. Completing what seemed to be a self-fueling spiral of economic deterioration, high interest rates prevented recovery in the credit-sensitive auto and construction industries, which were experiencing unemployment of nearly 20 percent. Even conservative economists joined in the growing speculation that a full-fledged depression was no longer unthinkable.[46]

Budget Politics in 1982

When the president unveiled his economic program in the spring of 1982 before the same lawmakers who had the previous year given him a rousing greeting, it was clear to everyone in the audience—if perhaps not to the man at the podium—that contrary forces of political economy were at work. All of the representatives and a third of the senators would have to stand for reelection in November; this made the president's audience all the more uneasy as he called for additional domestic spending cuts, continued growth in the defense budget, and reduced outlays for social security. Moreover, his proposal for a three-year, $55 billion increase in taxes seemed modest given the size of the deficit.

The president's budget found few takers. Republican Senator William Armstrong, a member of the Budget Committee and a Reagan supporter, declared unequivocally, "There is no chance that Reagan's budget will pass. Very few Republicans would vote for it. I know of no one." Senate Republican Whip Ted Stevens described himself in "sort of a state of shock" from the president's proposal. House Minority Leader Robert H. Michel, who would face the toughest reelection campaign of his career within six months, agreed that the proposed deficit was "mind boggling." [47] Democrats, needless to say, were just as critical and not nearly so restrained.

Because Republican unity was disintegrating, Reagan's parliamentary-like victories of the preceding session would not be repeated. As one representative said, "If anyone thinks that this is going to be a nice, neat package, with everyone jumping up and down and passing it in a few hours, well, that's not going to happen." [48] Whether President Reagan recognized this is unclear. Press reports of anxious hand wringing by the president's advisers over his blasé intransigence were mixed with those of kudos from among this same group for the astute manner with which he was preparing for future compromise.

The latter proved to be wishful thinking, for Reagan began the task of assembling a congressional coalition by following the straitlaced, strategic prescriptions of going public. In February he toured the Midwest where he employed tough language: "The budget we propose is a line drawn in dirt"; and he challenged "paid political complainers ... to put up or shut up." According to White House sources, these speeches were intended to shore up his crumbling congressional base.[49]

Although by early April several of his advisers were engaged in budget talks with party leaders of the House and Senate, the president continued to work Congress by going public. "He very much wants to regain the initiative," said a staffer. "The best way to do that in his estimation is to have him come directly to the people." [50] Accordingly, in mid-March the president planned two major television addresses for April; a switch from afternoon to evening press conferences, which he reasoned would double his television audience and prevent network newscasters from unfairly filtering his message; a series of live radio broadcasts on Saturdays in the vein of Franklin Roosevelt's fireside chats; and, finally, a heavy schedule of political travel.[51]

To White House political adviser Edward Rollins, the new offensive was necessary to get Republicans "back in line." He added, "It is imperative we put discipline back in this town." With the apparent blessing of the White House, Rollins initiated his own educational campaign. For those Republicans who expected difficulty in the fall elections and had begun "carping" at the president's policies, his message was simple: undermine the president and you will hurt yourself because "his strength and popularity will be a factor in [your] own elections." He went further. To make sure the association was appreciated, Rollins announced that neither President Reagan nor Vice-President Bush would assist any Republican who had been "blasting the hell out of the president." [52] Little did he realize that by fall, few Republican incumbents would be soliciting help from these men.

While Reagan was busy in public posturing, his lieutenants were quietly engaged in budget negotiations with the House Democratic and Senate Republican leadership. Whether the participation of the White House in the bargaining sessions indicated genuine flexibility on Reagan's part or simply reflected the stark certainty that his initial proposal did not stand a chance in Congress is difficult to say. Two conclusions, however, may be drawn from these negotiations. First, at risk of being wholly excluded from drafting the budget, the president did finally shift from his original hard-line stance. He agreed to smaller growth in defense spending, increases for social programs, and, most significant, a near doubling of new tax receipts from $55 billion to $99 billion during the next three years.

Second, though the extensive bargaining sessions failed to yield a compromise bill, they succeeded, according to White House estimates, as a public relations coup. On April 28 with reporters trailing behind, the president traveled down Pennsylvania Avenue for a summit meeting with Speaker O'Neill. As a bargaining session it went nowhere, but it did allow President Reagan to claim in an address on prime-time television the following evening that he had "gone the extra mile."

The president's speech followed a format by now familiar: black-white presentation of the issues, visual props, and an appeal for public support. Arguing that his and not the Democrats' budget was the one of moderation, Reagan departed from the standard script to describe in detail his efforts to reach a compromise.

> In yesterday afternoon's meeting on Capitol Hill, Speaker O'Neill, Senator Howard Baker, myself, and five of the Gang of 17 participated. As I say, the figures on which the group had found some agreement were far from those

we'd proposed in February. But I decided against trying to start the negotiations on the basis of that original budget.

Our original cuts totaled $101 billion. They—I can't make a big enough mark to show you [referring to a chart]—but they were rejected, believe me. Our own representatives from the Congress proposed compromising at $60 billion. Their counterparts from the Democratic side of the aisle proposed 35. In our meeting yesterday, which went on for more than 3 hours, our compromise of $60 billion was rejected—now my pen is working. And then I swallowed and had volunteered to split the difference between our 60 and their 35 and settle for 48, and that was rejected. The meeting was over.[53]

After viewing the president's address, Speaker O'Neill voiced suspicion that once again he had been set up in a public relations ploy. For a president who goes public, failure at the bargaining table may be rewarded with success in the public arena.

Once again, President Reagan closed his speech by exhorting the public to "make your voice heard." [54] Unlike the previous summer, however, this appeal was not followed by major tremors on Capitol Hill. Instead, a complex sequence of legislative maneuvers ensued over which few participants— foremost among them the president—appeared to exert much control. The Republican Senate proceeded to pass its own budget containing provisions substantially different from those Reagan had originally submitted. The president promptly endorsed it; he had little choice.[55]

In the House, Minority Leader Michel rejected the Senate version as unsalable to his Republican colleagues, many of whom were facing difficult reelections. Instead, he created a special panel to formulate a Republican alternative to the budget expected from the Budget Committee, which was controlled by Democrats. Again the president endorsed the Republican product, although this one differed significantly from the Senate version. By the time of the House floor vote, there were seven different budget proposals, none of them able to muster a majority. Two weeks later, with both parties agreeing that any budget resolution was better than none, the Republican proposal, more popular than any of the others, was passed without Democratic resistance; shortly thereafter it was reconciled with the Senate version in conference committee.

Through much of the remainder of the session, as the various committees in both chambers drafted appropriations and revenue legislation in rough accord with the provisions of the budget resolution, President Reagan kept a low profile. He traveled to Europe, vacationed on his Santa Barbara ranch, and spoke to Republican gatherings.[56] Only in late August, when it became apparent that his help would be required to line up reluctant House Republicans for a $99 billion tax hike, did President Reagan return to active duty.

By that time the tax provisions of the budget differed considerably from the president's February proposals, but Reagan embraced them as if they were his own. And well he should have. They raised substantial new revenues to close a yawning deficit while preserving his three-year, 25 percent tax cut.

Congress approached the largest election-year tax increase in history with caution befitting politicians whose jobs were in jeopardy. The posturing that resulted from calculations of political survival gave rise to an interesting configuration of alliances. Three blocs of representatives and senators were decisive to the outcome: loyal House Democrats, Senate Republicans, and House Republicans. The peculiar way in which political considerations aligned these groups in support for or in opposition to the tax increase gave President Reagan one last chance to win Congress by going public.

The Democratic leaders did not want their party blamed by the electorate for the tax hike, nor, having conceded so much to the president in the preceding 18 months, did they wish to leave themselves open for future accusations of undermining his policies. Consequently, they agreed to provide the administration the margin of victory on three conditions: (1) the legislation raising taxes would be drafted by the Republican-controlled Senate Finance Committee, and House Democrats would participate only at the conference stage; (2) a majority of House Republicans (about 100) would vote for it; and (3) indicative of the Democrats' queasiness, the president would write personal letters of appreciation to supportive Democrats, which could be used in the fall election to stave off criticism from Republican challengers.

As a group, Senate Republicans were unenthusiastic about the bill, but because of the swelling deficit, most realized they had little choice. They could vote higher taxes at that time—a year in which only 12 of their number were standing for reelection—or they could do so later, when more would be facing their constituents. Given the electoral calendar and the demand of House Democrats, the Republican Senate Finance Committee wrote the bill that the Republican Senate passed intact by a narrow margin.[57]

The political needs of the president, of Senate Republicans, and especially of House Democrats combined to create a serious dilemma for House Republicans. Because the Democrats were insisting that the Republicans be responsible for the tax increase, and because their Republican colleagues in the Senate and White House were willing to go along, many election-bound House Republicans felt they were being sacrificed to the deficit. Moreover, some of Washington's most fervent supply-siders came from the ranks of House Republicans. One was Rep. Jack Kemp, cosponsor of the Kemp-Roth bill, who immediately began to line up opposition to the unholy alliance. By late August, when the conference report was awaiting House ratification, Kemp could count on more Republican votes than could the White House. As the president began a public offensive to rally House Republicans, he had fewer than half the number of votes necessary to fulfill his end of the bargain with the Democrats. At this point Reagan's close friend Senator Paul Laxalt publicly observed, "This is the most difficult legislative challenge this President has had to face. It's tight as hell."[58]

One indicator of the difficulty facing a president who seeks to lead by going public is his popular standing across the country. Perhaps Laxalt had this fact in mind, for in mid-August a Gallup survey reported that the president's latest job performance rating stood at only 41 percent approving against 47 percent disapproving. Moreover, when questioned further about the president's economic performance, respondents were even more critical. Only 31 percent approved his handling of the economy overall, and because the unemployment rate was into double digits, only 23 percent were willing to endorse his handling of the unemployment problem.[59]

From such figures one might conclude that President Reagan's ratings were too thin to give him much chance of success. Had he been required to win substantial Democratic defections, as in the past session, such an assessment would be correct. In this instance, however, the political circumstances were tailored for victory. The president was simply trying to bring along fellow Republicans whose districts were generally believed to remain more favorably disposed to him and his policies than was the country overall. More important, because the Democrats had agreed to supply the rest, he had to pull only 100 Republican votes. The peculiar coalitional requirements of the tax bill gave the increasingly unpopular Reagan a last crack at success.

As the White House cranked up its public campaign to work its magic on the 97th Congress for the fourth time, the standard operating procedures were followed. Only the target differed. Once again the president embarked on political travel in search of telegenic and sympathetic audiences. Once again the numerous White House staffers assigned to public and congressional relations got busy. Speech writers prepared another national television address and a series of presidential commercials to be broadcast in select markets across the country by the Republican National Committee; Richard Wirthlin conducted briefings for Republican House members, explaining to them that the president's leadership image would be critical to their own success in November; and other staffers busied themselves contacting more than 5,000 business leaders across the country to stimulate yet another grass-roots campaign.[60] (More than 30,000 similar appeals were sent to local party leaders by the RNC.) To top it off, Rollins, posing threats as he had in the spring, spread the word that party campaign funds might be withheld from Republican representatives who bucked the president. After a congressional outcry, however, the White House retracted this form of coercion. By the time of the floor vote, more than 150 Republican House members had been escorted into the Oval Office or to Camp David for a friendly chat. All of these activities culminated with the president's prime-time address on August 16, in which he once again called on citizens to lobby Congress. Three days later the tax bill passed the House by a vote of 226 to 207. President Reagan had fulfilled his end of the bargain by bringing along 103 reluctant Republicans.

President Reagan exerted far less influence over the budget in 1982—both its substance and politics—than over the one in the preceding year. He gave concessions on taxes and expenditures, and by the end of the session he was championing a tax increase others had written that was nearly twice the figure he had proposed in February. In large part this change in fortune must be credited to his reduced political capital with Congress. The further he cut domestic spending, the fewer the number of natural allies that remained. Budget politics in 1982 reflected the president's decline in public opinion. High interest and unemployment rates and swelling projected deficits had sapped his popularity. All of these weaknesses were compounded in the minds of Washington politicians by the fall elections.

Still, the budgetary season was not as disastrous as these political conditions suggest. Reagan's fundamental economic policies survived. Real growth in the military budget continued, domestic spending was reduced further, and the tax increase did not touch his 25 percent cut in income taxes. In 1982 Ronald Reagan relinquished control of the legislative process to those with whom it properly belongs, but he was still able to set the agenda of Congress's budget deliberations. Although Reagan's weak popularity prevented him from producing the groundswells he had generated a year earlier, he did not shy away from publicly promoting his policies. The addition of his Saturday radio broadcasts gave him even greater occasion to go public than in 1981. On a more limited scale he continued to summon public support in his dealings with Congress. Judged by the budget politics of the next year, 1982 would appear successful indeed.

Budget Politics in 1983

The political context of any presidential action is defined by two realities: objective conditions and politicians' responses to those conditions. By the time President Reagan introduced his next budget, in 1983, both realities had become distinctly unfavorable for him. The reasons were that fewer Republicans would be returning to the 98th Congress, and the president's popularity was at a historic low.

Although the Democrats narrowly failed to improve their party's share of Senate seats, they gained a net of 26 seats in the House of Representatives, which exceeded preelection estimates of the number required to undo Reagan's coalition of Republicans and southern Democrats. A *New York Times* survey of newly elected members, including Republicans, confirmed the widespread suspicion that the new class would be decidedly less sympathetic to the president's economic policies than the members they had replaced.[61]

President Reagan's nearly continuous decline in the polls during the campaign season further aggravated the unfavorable election results. As shown in Table 5-1, Reagan had begun 1982 with almost a majority of respondents to a Gallup Poll approving his overall performance. Even then, however, there was the prospect of subsequent decline if the economy worsened. In the same survey only 41 percent endorsed Reagan's "handling of

Table 5-1　Performance Ratings of President Reagan, 1982-1983 (Percent)

Question	Jan. 1982		Aug. 1982		Nov. 1982		Dec. 1982		Jan. 1983	
	App.	Dis.	App.	Dis.	App.	Dis.	App.	Dis.	App.	Dis.
Do you approve of the way President Reagan is handling economic conditions in the country?	41	51	31	59	—	—	36	56	29	64
Do you approve or disapprove of the way Ronald Reagan is handling his job as president?										
National	49	40	41	47	43	47	41	50	37	54
East	43	46	40	49	42	51	36	57	35	55
Midwest	51	38	45	45	42	47	46	44	41	50
South	50	38	38	46	41	46	38	52	35	57
West	54	36	40	48	49	43	46	48	35	55

NOTE: App. = approve; Dis. = disapprove.

SOURCES: All data are from the Gallup Poll. Responses to the economic performance question as reported in *National Journal,* March 5, 1983, 524. Evaluations of President Reagan's overall job performance are from various issues of the *Gallup Report.*

economic conditions." During the year, unemployment climbed to a record post-depression high. Responses from a concerned public to Gallup's "most-important-problem" question shifted dramatically from inflation to unemployment.[62] At the opening of the 98th Congress, only 37 percent of the respondents registered overall approval, a figure lower than for any previous president at this stage of his first term.

Given the regional character of the president's Republican-southern Democrat coalition in the preceding Congress, the regional breakdown of his growing unpopularity is revealing. At the beginning of 1982, a majority of southerners and westerners approved his job performance; by the next year, respondents from these regions were no more supportive than respondents elsewhere. A national consensus appeared to be forming against the president.[63]

In a variety of ways, these harsh objective conditions were accentuated by politicians' strategic responses to them. During the fall congressional campaigns, Republican incumbents discovered on their own what can be seen in Figure 5-1; their association with Reaganomics was a political liability. With Democratic challengers everywhere taking up the issue, the president's Republican and boll weevil supporters found themselves forced to explain, excuse, apologize for, and in a few instances even recant their past association with these once popular policies.[64] Speaker O'Neill's prophecy of a year earlier about the fickleness of the typical voter had come to pass.

By Election Day 1982, so many Republican incumbents had become preoccupied with distancing themselves from Reagan and his economic policies that it was apparent before the first ballot was cast that the president's position in the next Congress would be weaker. Instead of the most active midterm campaign in recent history, as promised by political affairs aide Rollins in the spring of 1982, President Reagan stayed in Washington or on his Santa Barbara ranch as if sequestered there by Republican candidates. Mutual advantage dictated that he make cameo appearances in only the safest Republican districts.[65] Two weeks before the election, Rep. Guy Vander Jagt, the party's official booster and chair of the Republican National Campaign Committee, was steadfastly forecasting Republican gains in the House. Other more sober members, like House Republican Whip Trent Lott, had arrived at a different judgment. "Obviously, we won't have the same euphoria after this election we had two years ago," he told a reporter.[66]

Unfortunately, the press offers little insight into the all-important expectations of rank-and-file Republicans at the beginning of the 98th Congress. Rather, press accounts include only the comments of their leaders and of White House spokesmen about the administration's landslide victory, the better-than-expected victory, and the "moral" victory that had just occurred. Cutting through these traditional, self-serving post mortems, one may assume that instead of elation, those Republicans who were victorious sensed only relief. The 1982 midterm ended the 1980 mandate.

After the election, the boll weevils were on the move. These conservative southern Democrats who had provided President Reagan with the critical margin of victory began ambling back to the Democratic camp.[67] Rep. Buddy Roemer of Louisiana, a leader of the group and a former Reagan enthusiast, had a quick change of heart: "I don't think we need the President to write a budget," he told a reporter. Why the sudden turnaround? According to Rep. G. V. (Sonny) Montgomery of Mississippi, it was simply that the thrill of running around with the fast crowd uptown had faded.

> "There was a fascination about going to the White House," Mr. Montgomery recalled. "I was down there more in two years than in the whole 14 years I've been up here. But maybe the glamour and glitter has worn off a bit.
> "I think we might have gotten carried away with the White House," the Mississippian continued. "We weren't working enough with the Democratic leadership. That's the big change. We're trying to implement our philosophy through our party, not join somebody else." [68]

Although Montgomery's explanation reads more like a rationalization than a reason, it reveals that this boll weevil had returned to the ranks of his party.

The real reason, one suspects, these members gave up their apostasy can be found in the altered political circumstances. With the addition of 26 loyal Democratic members after the election, the conservative southerners no longer provided a swing vote. Even if this group voted solidly against their party, the Democratic leaders with their new 103-seat majority were generally assured victory. Consequently, confessed Representative Montgomery, "Nobody much talks to us." Another added, "Why get out there and take a bullet when you can't win anyway." [69]

Supporting the president not only was futile, and possibly injurious to their standing in the congressional party, it also had become risky at home. The midterm campaign appears to have conveyed the same messages to the boll weevils as it did to other politicians around the country. Rep. Charles Stenholm of Texas, a spokesman of the southern defectors, confessed, "We're having difficulty. There's a large amount of concern on the fairness question. The perception in the 17th District of Texas is that Reagan's program is basically unfair." [70] Testimony taken from these politicians led one reporter to conclude that the main reason for their return was "the declining support for President Reagan and his policies." [71]

It was evident early on to knowledgeable political elites in Washington that the election and the posturings of politicians had weakened President Reagan's hand with the 98th Congress. Whether it was as equally clear to the president, however, was anything but certain. As at the opening of the previous session Washington politicians were asking, did this outsider know the score? Could he adapt to the new political realities by becoming more flexible and more conciliatory toward the Democratic leadership? Such questions are appropriately asked about any president after his party has just suffered a setback; but with an outsider in the White House, especially one whose propensity to go public had been rewarded so handsomely during his first two years, these questions assumed a special poignancy.

Between the closing of the 97th Congress and the convening of the 98th, these questions were foremost among the concerns of the Washington press corps. Articles with such titles as "Midterm Malaise," "In the Event of a Presidential Power Vacuum...," "The MX and Reagan's Receptivity to Compromise," and "At the Brink" proliferated in the news publications favored by those in power in Washington.[72] Nearly everyone was consulted on the matter, but nowhere did the press pry for answers more earnestly than at the White House.

The responses they received from White House insiders were as tentative and contradictory as elsewhere. No one knew how this president facing a novel situation would behave. One early prognosis, offered anonymously by a Reagan staffer, came as close to the mark as any: "He will submit a budget completely consistent with his program and philosophy, and it will probably get shot down pretty quickly." [73] Another gave a more moderate forecast that Reagan would happily agree to 75 percent of his request. A few were even more optimistic. Arguing that Reagan "has been willing to listen to people around him when they told him something would not work," one presidential adviser predicted that compromise would follow the tough proposals.[74]

With the exception of a conciliatory State of the Union address, the early signals were those of an uncompromising president who planned to spend more time in the country than at the bargaining table. The president's third budget was designed to "stay the course." Savings from additional reductions in domestic spending were to finance a 10 percent real growth in the Pentagon's budget. No major new taxes were called for, but if large deficits persisted beyond the 1985 fiscal year—and not coincidentally beyond the next election—contingency taxes were proposed.

Consistent with hanging tough on the budget, Reagan began a series of public relations maneuvers to enhance his public standing. John Herrington, an ardent Reaganite and assistant secretary of the Navy, was brought into the White House office to improve that organization's efforts in communicating his chief's positions to the American public. The president's travel budget was increased to permit more frequent trips to blue-collar constituencies with whom, his pollsters were telling him, he had experienced the greatest loss of support. Shorter, more narrowly focused news conferences were planned to give the press less opportunity to fish for negative stories.[75] A few of the president's strategists even urged him to declare his candidacy for renomination in January. This maneuver would put him on a campaign footing and "buttress his standing in current political struggles," they reasoned, adding that he could always choose not to run later.[76]

The Democratic response to the president's budget was swift and unequivocal. On March 15 after a single day of discussion, the House Budget Committee passed the Democratic leadership's budget without changing a cent. This plan differed from the president's in limiting growth of defense spending to 4 percent rather than the president's 10 percent figure, in mandating $30 billion in additional taxes during the next fiscal year, and in restoring many of the 1981-1982 cuts in social programs. Republican leader Michel labeled the Democratic bill the "Revenge on Ronald Reagan Act of 1983."[77]

With a 103-seat majority, the Democratic leadership was again firmly in control of procedures, and it exploited its prerogatives to the fullest. The Rules Committee refused a request from southern Democrats to allow amendments to the budget resolution on the floor. Rather, the House would be permitted a vote for a single Republican alternative—presumably the president's—if one were offered. Moreover, in an effort to head off intense lobbying from the White House that had preceded floor votes in the past, the leadership scheduled the vote within the week.

The president and his staff were given little time, but by all accounts they made the most of it. On March 19 at a televised, impromptu press briefing, Reagan denounced the Democratic resolution as a "dagger aimed straight at the heart of America's rebuilding program." Of the reduced growth in the Pentagon's budget, he added, "Nothing could bring greater joy to the Kremlin." He went on to characterize Democrats' domestic spending proposals as "a reckless return to the failed policies of the past." [78] And as for the resolution's provision for increased revenue, the president declared his readiness to veto any legislation that rescinded the third installment of his tax cut. The president served as the point man, while his staff got busy organizing constituent drives by the Chamber of Commerce and other business groups against targeted representatives. Though short on time, "our troops are fired up" and confident they could win, reported one White House staffer.[79]

The next day Speaker O'Neill fell under the grip of déjà vu. He told the press, "We thought we were in pretty good shape last week. Until this morning everybody was in accord." However, he continued, suddenly because the president and the Chamber of Commerce are out there beating the bushes, "the Democratic fissures were reopening." [80]

The Democratic majority, however, proved too great a hurdle for the administration. Three days later the House adopted the Budget Committee's resolution by a vote of 229 to 196. With Republicans in open disagreement among themselves over what an alternative budget should look like, none was offered. Despite a public invitation from the Rules Committee, the president's budget, remarkably, was never formally introduced in the House either in committee or in floor proceedings. Twenty-two of the conservative southern Democrats voted against the Democratic proposal, but this vote showed that their ranks had been thinned, and four northern Republicans further eroded their leverage by crossing over to support the Democratic resolution. For the first time since Ronald Reagan had entered office, the Democrats would take to conference a budget of their own making.

Undaunted, President Reagan returned to television within hours of the floor defeat. A national address had been scheduled to announce research into new forms of strategic weaponry. As forecast by aides, however, the president twice digressed from that subject to blast the Democratic budget. With an eye toward the Senate's upcoming markup of the legislation, he once again appealed to the public to demonstrate its continued support for his policies. "The choice is up to the men and women you have elected to Congress—and that means the choice is up to you." And later, "This is why I am speaking to you tonight—to urge you to tell your Senators and Congressmen that you know we must continue to restore our military strength." [81]

Indicative perhaps of the president's reduced status, the most noticeable response to the speech came not from the public but from congressional leaders. Even House Minority Leader Michel delivered a mild rebuke. Too much "overkill" and "macho image," he termed the performance. He further complained that since it deflected public attention away from House Republicans' criticisms of the Democratic budget, the speech "couldn't have come at a worse time." [82]

If the president expected more favorable treatment in the Senate, he was to be greatly disappointed. In a meeting with the Senate Budget Committee in early April, he was told by fellow Republicans that the projected deficit and continued military buildup were unacceptable. Reportedly, even the president's staff joined in urging him to compromise. He refused.

To give Reagan an opportunity to reconsider, Budget Committee chair Pete Domenici postponed his committee's markup for a week; and offering his president plenty of leeway, he told reporters that the president was simply assuming a "negotiation stance." [83] Meanwhile, Defense Secretary Caspar Weinberger was openly campaigning with President Reagan to ignore the budget process. In mid-April with no movement from the president, the Senate Budget Committee began the business of writing its own budget. What came out of markup was distinctly unfavorable to the White House: $30 billion in new taxes, an $11 billion increase in domestic spending over the president's figure, and a modest 5 percent growth in the defense budget.

As this resolution was presented on the floor, it remained unclear whether it or any budget bill could pass. In the absence of strong leadership from the White House, the Senate was divided into three distinct camps. On one side there were the Democrats who by and large were supporting the House bill; on the other side were the conservative Republicans who were prepared to stick with the uncompromising president. In the middle were the Republican moderates, including Majority Leader Howard Baker and most of the Republican members of the committee. Because the president was unable to unify his party "by rallying public support for his program . . . the factions have grown bolder," reported one correspondent.[84] Pessimistic forecasts were fulfilled as the Senate rejected the committee's budget. A week later, Domenici returned with a fatter military budget and a substantial tax increase. Although Reagan was hardly enthusiastic and the Democrats were calling the new budget "rinky-dink," it passed by a single vote after 11 ballots.

As the conference committee negotiations were reported daily in the press, Reagan distanced himself ever farther from the budgetary process. When the brokered budget finally passed Congress in late June, the president had retreated to threats of a veto of any appropriations bills that violated his own earlier proposal. When questioned by a reporter on the wisdom of such a course, one senior White House official replied, "I just don't know what we have to gain from playing the budget game with Congress this year." He continued saying that having shown he could work with Congress over the past two years, President Reagan could now "afford to be more confrontational." Pressed further, the official conceded that the administration would likely get the "short end of the stick" on defense spending because opinion polls were not supportive. But on social spending and taxes, he insisted, "Those are the issues he [the President] can go to the people on every time." [85]

With the tax cut in place and the budget growing now from a smaller base, the president stepped back from the budget process. By the close of the 1983 budget season, President Reagan had assumed a defensive posture, threatening vetoes and promising public appeals at least on those issues where even an unpopular president might be able to elicit a favorable public response.

Going Public and Leadership: The Lessons of Reagan's Budgets

President Reagan may have radically altered the strategic routines of presidential leadership, but initially these changes did not disturb the routines of the Washington press in reporting on his performance. Accustomed to explaining presidential success by digging beneath the surface and ferreting out quiet compromises and discrete logrolling, the press was especially diligent in these activities in 1981. After all, a great deal needed to be explained. For their efforts they uncovered a few truffles. A story on Rep. Lawrence DeNardis's swap of budget support for renovation of the New Haven train depot was typical. Other commodities traded during the session included sugar price supports, restoration of some energy subsidies for the poor, more funds than originally budgeted for Medicaid, and a slowdown of the conversion of industrial boilers to coal in oil-producing states.[86] Even more heavily reported were various photo sessions at the White House and the liberal distribution of such patronage as theater tickets and special $4.40 cufflinks to representatives who voted with the president.[87] As indications of President Reagan's leadership strategy, however, all of these minor deals and presidential gifts pale in significance when placed next to the meeting in 1981 with Democratic leaders when he rejected their entreaties to compromise even while he was still short of votes.

Reagan's record as a president who preferred going public to bargaining remained virtually unblemished. On a few occasions, however, a public appeal would be accompanied with minor, face-saving concessions or side payments to fence-sitters. The bidding war with Rostenkowski for stray votes on the tax cut in 1981 offers the most prominent and substantial examples of such payments. When one considers that it was a game initiated by the Democrats and, as far as one can tell, was unanticipated by the White House, the bidding war appears more an unhappy outcome of failure to accept the generous overtures of the Democratic leaders than a planned strategy of coalition building.

One might even be tempted to find pluralist flexibility in Reagan's acceptance of the $99 billion tax hike the next year. However, the summer's sharply rising deficit projections that had so altered the fiscal environment and the public enthusiasm with which he ultimately embraced this legislation rather than try to split the difference with his original proposal suggest that the president's change of position was more a conversion than a political compromise. In accepting higher new taxes, more social spending, and less for defense than he had originally sought, President Reagan conducted himself less as a skilled bargainer than as a president who, having lost his leverage, was forced to accept more or less what others served up. Even in these episodes, he demonstrated a greater flair for going public than for negotiation.

He would continue to do so in his second term. After his huge victory over Walter Mondale in November 1984, a Reagan aide announced that the president would "take advantage" of his mandate and soon tour the country "to sell this budget package.... We have to look at it, in many ways, like a campaign. He wants to take his case to the people." [88]

Dependence of Policy on Popularity

Undeniably, going public rewarded the president handsomely in his dealings with Congress while he remained popular. During the first session of the 97th Congress the president achieved rare mastery over both policy and the legislative process, the likes of which had not occurred since Lyndon Johnson had enjoyed a surfeit of liberal Democrats in both chambers nearly two decades earlier. True to his campaign pledge, Reagan managed to slash domestic spending, boost the Pentagon's budget, and cut taxes.

The second budget, which sought to continue or to preserve the gains of the first, was not nearly as successful. In the spring of 1982 with his popularity in steep descent and the deficit and unemployment increasing with each new report, President Reagan found his messages less inspiring to Congress and the country. His leadership style precluded resorting to pluralist methods to continue his mastery of Congress; instead, he left Washington and budget policies to others. When called upon to cast a public appeal for a tax increase—one not of his making—President Reagan still managed to provide the margin of difference at a key moment.

Largely as a consequence of his diminished popularity, Reagan's majority coalition departed in the fall 1982 election. By the beginning of the third budget season, his popularity was still down. White House staffers were wondering aloud whether the president would even be allowed to participate in the game. His budget was delivered stillborn, never to be introduced on the floor of either chamber. When the Republican Senate insisted on reduced military spending and new taxes, Reagan gave up the budget fight and announced repeatedly that he would veto appropriations bills to defeat the "credit card Congress." Fearing a street fight with the president before public opinion, the House leadership reduced its spending bills to bring them more in line with the president's initial requests. Yet in 1983, the budget was made by Congress.

From late 1982 on, the White House gradually redirected its campaign from generating public support for the president's policies to support for the president himself. By the summer of 1983, many political elites subscribed to the view that Reagan was prepared to sacrifice his budget to gain an issue for the next election a full year and a half away.[89] The polls show little evidence that the concerted efforts to alter public evaluations of the president's performance met with much success. A resurgence in the polls did finally occur, but only after the economy began to rebound in the fall of 1983—too late to help him with the budget.

One lesson of Reagan's record, therefore, is that the public president may perform better in the "expenditure," or transference, of popular support than in its resupply. Individualized pluralism helps to explain why he performs well in using his public support, but as a model of Washington politics, it is silent on the subject of what an unpopular president should do to restore the public's confidence. The supply of popular support rests on opinion dynamics over which the president may exercise little direct control. This is not to say that the president will not try to improve the public's estimate of him. Given who public presidents are, one suspects the temptation for self-promotion will be irresistible.

Governing as Campaigning

Whether in exploiting favorable conditions to advance policy goals or in attempting to improve the incumbent's prestige, the strategic prescriptions of going public put the office on a campaign footing. Governing, according to a Reagan staffer, amounts to little more than an extension of the campaign that brought him into office. In early 1983 aides were urging him to announce his candidacy for reelection to strengthen his hand in Congress.

President Reagan's conduct of office closely resembled his campaign for it. Both entailed heavy political travel, numerous appearances before organized constituencies, and extensive use of television—even paid commercials during nonelection periods. Moreover, both campaigning and governing required systematic planning and extensive organizational coordination. Each major television appeal by President Reagan on the eve of a critical budget vote in Congress was preceded by weeks of preparatory work. Polls were taken; speeches incorporating the resulting insights were drafted; the press was briefed, either directly or via leaks. Meanwhile in the field, the ultimate recipients of the president's message, members of Congress, were softened up by presidential travel into their states and districts and by grass-roots lobbying campaigns, initiated and orchestrated by the White House but including the RNC and sympathetic business organizations. After describing some of these routines of Reagan's staff, Sidney Blumenthal draws the parallel between campaigning and governing.

> Once elected, candidates have to deal with shaky coalitions held together by momentary moods, not stable party structures. They then must try to govern through permanent campaigns. This is something more than the selling of the President—even of a telegenic President able to project an attractive image. It has become an inescapable necessity for Reagan, and probably for his successors.
>
> The President's strategists are at the center of the new political age. At the end of the day, they become spectators, seeing their performance tested by the contents of the television news programs. For the Reagan White House, every night is election night on television.[90]

As presidential governance has assumed the form of a campaign, the White House office has added trappings of a campaign organization. The available evidence indicates that Reagan's transition advisers appreciated the organizational imperatives of the public president. Although their fees were to be paid by the Republican National Committee, pollsters Richard Wirthlin and Robert Teeter were made proximate and frequent counselors to the president. Initially, the position of press secretary was downgraded to make room for an expanded Office of Communications, which was given a broad mandate to plan and coordinate all public affairs activities for the White House and executive agencies.[91]

With this office taking care of public relations, a smaller political affairs office transacted more partisan business. In addition to traditional White House political activities, such as monitoring gossip and polls and advising the president, its mandate was also to exercise the administration's political muscle. Patronage and campaign support from a variety of sources flowed to members of Congress through this office, headed for most of this period by Edward Rollins. Testimony to the office's integral role can be found in a comment by Rollins's deputy, Lee Atwater: "This shop is a new venture. I don't think the White House has ever had one before, but I think that every White House from now on will have one." [92]

Finally, as governing becomes campaigning, policy serves rhetoric. Rather than the substance of detailed scrutiny and negotiations, policy questions become overly simplified and stylized to satisfy the cognitive requirements of a largely inattentive national audience. Positions, publicly proclaimed, become fixed; intransigence among elites sets in. President Reagan's declaration before a midwestern audience that his 1982 budget was "a line drawn in dirt" is typical of what happens when partisan discussion flows through public channels.[93]

By any standard, Ronald Reagan and his three budgets constitute an extraordinary story. Extraordinary because no president in recent memory established such a presence as did Reagan vis-à-vis the 97th Congress. Extraordinary, moreover, because no president managed to exhaust his popular support so thoroughly by his first midterm election as did Reagan. And finally, extraordinary in retrospect because within a year of the budget vote in 1983, the president entered his reelection campaign generally conceded to be unbeatable and went on to amass one of the greatest landslides of this century.

These extraordinary swings in policy success and popularity reflect the volatility of a marketplace whose currency of exchange increasingly is public opinion. As exceptional as the Great Communicator's record appears today, there is good reason to suspect that it harbingers things to come. If individualized pluralism is indeed ascendant, an era of presidents who routinely go public is at hand. President Reagan's "peculiar" performance will cast a long shadow, not unlike that of Franklin Roosevelt's, against which the performance of future presidents will be judged.

Notes

1. Steven V. Roberts, "Reagan and Congress: Key Tests Ahead," *New York Times*, June 16, 1985. 14.
2. Lou Cannon, *Reagan* (New York: G. P. Putnam's Sons, 1982), 319.
3. Ronald Reagan, with Richard G. Hubler, *Where's the Rest of Me?* (New York: Duell, Sloan, and Pearce, 1965), 257.
4. Leslie H. Gelb, "The Mind of the President," *New York Times Magazine*, October 6, 1985, 4-5.
5. Reagan contested 4 gubernatorial primary and general elections and 57 presidential primaries in the 1976 and 1980 presidential elections. Richard M. Scammon and Alice V. McGillivray, *America Votes 14: A Handbook of Contemporary American Election Statistics* (Washington, D.C.: Congressional Quarterly Inc., 1980), 27-37.
6. Fred I. Greenstein attaches great significance to Eisenhower's Washington experience in arguing that his style in office, including his image among Washingtonians as a "bumbler," was actually an adroit strategic device to disarm potential adversaries and deflect responsibility. *The Hidden-Hand Presidency* (New York: Basic Books, 1982), chaps. 2, 3.
7. Reagan's rhetoric over the years portrays such consistency, as well as conviction, that his record refutes the "selling of the president" myth, which holds that television packaging requires plastic candidates whose issue positions can be molded by advertising executives guided by marketing surveys. A best-selling example of this genre is Joe McGinnis, *The Selling of the President* (New York: Trident Press, 1969).
8. "Reagan Popularity below Predecessors'," *Gallup Report* 186 (March 1981): 2-9.
9. Cannon, *Reagan*, 319.
10. Bernard Weinraub, "Reagan Wants to Voice Views on Russian TV," *New York Times*, September 4, 1985, A1.
11. There were other, equally impressive victories as well. When Reagan learned that a resolution vetoing the administration's planned sale of AWACS planes to Saudi Arabia had garnered a majority of the Senate as cosponsors, he went into action. In a brief flurry of phone calls, meetings in the Oval Office, and public pronouncements, he unraveled the coalition and salvaged the sale.
12. Peter Goldman, "The Reagan Steamroller," *Newsweek*, May 18, 1981, 40. Some became downright monastic. By summer, Mondale had publicly embarked on a retreat to contemplate the country's needs.
13. Notable among defense issues was the MX missile program, which was greatly scaled down yet spared from what at moments appeared to be its certain demise.
14. Lynn Rosellini, "Lobbyists' Row All Alert for Chance at the Budget," *New York Times*, February 26, 1981, 9.
15. George Skelton, "Reagan Dip in Poll Tied to Spending Cuts," *Los Angeles Times*, March 19, 1981, 6.
16. Ibid.
17. Sidney Blumenthal, "Marketing the President," *New York Times Magazine*, September 13, 1981, 111. Much of the subsequent material on the budget cut comes from Blumenthal and from Elizabeth Drew, "A Reporter in Washington," *New Yorker*, June 8, 1981, 138-142.
18. Blumenthal, "Marketing the President," 112.
19. Party officials were also sent to Ohio where Republican representatives were reportedly wavering. Drew, "Reporter in Washington," 138-142.
20. David M. Alpern, "The Second Hundred Days," *Newsweek*, May 11, 1981, 23.

Time reported that on "only a few occasions had a President enjoyed such a shouting, clapping, emotional reception from the assembled law-makers" (Ed Magnuson, "Reagan's Budget Battle," *Time,* May 11, 1981, 16).

21. "President Reagan's April Address on Economy," in *Reagan's First Year* (Washington, D.C.: Congressional Quarterly Inc., 1982), 118-119.
22. Goldman, "The Reagan Steamroller," 39.
23. Ibid. In an effort to downplay Reagan's public leadership, some scholars have searched for evidence of bargaining. And in fairness they have found important instances that went undetected in this book's first edition. However, on the passage of the Gramm-Latta budget resolution, signs of bargaining are quite thin. Some have said that agreeing to allow Phil Gramm, Democratic representative (soon to be Republican senator), to be the chief sponsor of the administration budget proposal was a major concession—a bargain if you will. But citing decisions that will give members of Congress credit for "carrying the president's water" strike me as dubious evidence of bargaining. The second "bargain" takes the form of President Reagan's assurances to individual members of Congress that some of the proposed cuts would later be reopened for discussion, and implicitly negotiation, if they supported the president's targets in the Gramm-Latta guidelines. Here, too, the president made no substantive concessions in return for a budget resolution vote. Such claims of bargaining demeans the concept. Marc A. Bodnick overstates the significance of these transactions in " 'Going Public' Reconsidered: Reagan's 1981 Tax and Budget Cuts, and Revisionist Theories of Presidential Power," *Congress and the Presidency* 17 (Spring 1990), 13-28.
24. David Stockman, *The Triumph of Politics* (New York: Avon, 1986), 211-212.
25. Ibid., 214.
26. Blumenthal, "Marketing the President," 112.
27. Peter Goldman, "Reagan's Sweet Triumph," *Newsweek,* July 6, 1981, 20.
28. This meeting between Reagan and five Democratic leaders is described in Peter Goldman, "Tax Cuts: Reagan Digs In," *Newsweek,* June 15, 1981, 26-27; and George J. Church, "He'll Do It His Way," *Time,* June 15, 1981, 10-12.
29. Goldman, "Tax Cuts," 25. Because reporters had gathered outside to receive the visibly glum Democrats, O'Neill may have been justified in his suspicions that they had been set up by the president for a media event.
30. Irwin B. Arieff, "Conservative Southerners Are Enjoying Their Wooing as Key to Tax Bill Success," *Congressional Quarterly Weekly Report,* June 13, 1981, 1024.
31. Peter Goldman, "Rest in Peace, New Deal," *Newsweek,* August 10, 1981, 17.
32. Wirthlin likely based such an assessment on poll results that gave the GOP almost as many identifiers as Democrats and that showed more than two-thirds of the respondents approving of Congress's earlier vote on the Gramm-Latta budget resolution. Elizabeth Wehr, "Reagan May Try to Block August Recess ... If Work Unfinished on Tax Cut Measure," *Congressional Quarterly Weekly Report,* June 27, 1981, 1134-1135.
33. Goldman, "Tax Cuts," 27.
34. Wehr, "Reagan May Try," 1135.
35. "Reagan's TV Address on Tax Bill," in *Reagan's First Year,* 122-124.
36. Goldman, "Rest in Peace," 16-20.
37. Ibid.
38. Steven V. Roberts, "President's Coalition," *New York Times,* October 27, 1982, 13. For another case study of the politics of the 1981 budget, see Allen Schick, "How the Budget Was Won and Lost," in *President and Congress,* ed. Norman J. Ornstein (Washington, D.C.: American Enterprise Institute, 1982), 14-43.
39. The 15 million figure was calculated by subtracting the total mailings (letter-sized

and larger envelopes) in 1980 from those in 1981. The source for these figures is Norman J. Ornstein et al., *Vital Statistics on Congress, 1982* (Washington, D.C.: American Enterprise Institute, 1982), 141. The 1984-1985 edition of *Vital Statistics* notes that mailings the next year returned to the 1980 levels, but fails to provide the data. Norman J. Ornstein et al., *Vital Statistics on Congress, 1984-1985 Edition* (Washington, D.C.: American Enterprise Institute, 1984), 142.

40. David M. Alpern, "The Runner Stumbles," *Newsweek*, September 28, 1982, 26-27.

41. For the standard journalistic treatment of this event, see Tom Morganthau, "Running to Stay in Place," *Newsweek*, October 5, 1981, 24; and Walter Isaacson, "Rough Waters Ahead," *Time*, October 5, 1981, 8-11.

42. The data used in the following analysis came from the American Institute of Public Opinion, Survey No. 183-G, October 2-5, 1981. The overall results are described in the *Gallup Opinion Index* (November 1981): 3-8. For a more detailed examination of this survey, see Samuel Kernell, "The Presidency and the People: The Modern Paradox," in *The Presidency and the Political System*, ed. Michael Nelson (Washington, D.C.: CQ Press, 1984), 250-253.

43. The question was worded: "To reduce the size of the 1982 budget deficiency, President Reagan has proposed cutting $13 billion in addition to the $35 billion in cuts approved earlier this year. About $11 billion of the new cuts would come from social programs and about $2 billion from defense programs. In general, would you say you approve or disapprove of the President's proposal?" (*Gallup Opinion Index*, 6).

44. William Greider, "The Education of David Stockman," *Atlantic*, December 1981, 32-43.

45. When a Gallup Poll in mid-November asked respondents if they had heard or read "about the situation in Washington involving David Stockman," 66 percent answered affirmatively. When these informed respondents were asked if it made them more or less confident in Reaganomics, 34 percent said less confident, 9 percent said more confident, and 53 percent said it had not changed their opinion. *Gallup Report* 194 (November 1981): 15.

46. Alan Greenspan, who chaired the Council of Economic Advisers under President Gerald Ford, was quoted as saying, "This scenario [of depression] still has a low probability, but it should no longer be put into the bizarre or kooky category" (George J. Church, "A Season of Scare Talk," *Time*, March 15, 1982, 12).

47. Ed Magnuson, "A Line Drawn in Dirt," *Time*, February 22, 1982, 12.

48. Ed Magnuson, "Stumbling to a Showdown," *Time*, April 26, 1982, 12.

49. Magnuson, "A Line Drawn in Dirt," 12.

50. Howell Raines, "Reagan's Gamble: Bid for Popularity," *New York Times*, March 31, 1982, A27.

51. Ibid.

52. Jack Nelson, "Administration Seeks to Stem GOP 'Potshots' against Reagan," *Los Angeles Times*, April 14, 1982, 14. Shortly thereafter, Rollins retracted the threat, but said such members of Congress would have low priority for White House assistance. Lee Atwater, Rollins's assistant, pedaled a softer line. "We'll never ask a member to vote against his own political interest, but we sure will . . . try to show them that it may be in their interest to support the President," he told reporter Dick Kirschten. See "Reagan's Political Chief Rollins," *National Journal*, June 12, 1982, 1054-1057. For congressional testimony to threats, see Jack Nelson, "President's 'Bad-Boy' List Aims for Republican Unity," *Los Angeles Times*, May 23, 1982, 11.

53. "Fiscal Year 1983 Federal Budget," *Weekly Compilation of Presidential Docu-*

ments 18 (May 3, 1982): 545-549. Speaker O'Neill and Rules Committee chair Richard Bolling disputed the president's rendition of the negotiating sessions; they claimed instead that both sets of figures used by the president were Republican in origin. "They rigged the sheet of paper we were working from," said Bolling. "This is a case where they split the difference between their figure and their figure" (Dale Tate, "Budget Battle Erupts on Hill as Compromise Talks Fizzle," *Congressional Quarterly Weekly Report,* May 1, 1982, 967-969).

54. He continued, "Let your representatives know that you support the kind of fair, effective approach I have outlined for you tonight. Let them know you stand behind our recovery program. You did it once, you can do it again. Thank you, and God bless you" ("Fiscal Year 1983 Federal Budget," 549).

55. Sen. Ernest Hollings and Sen. Daniel P. Moynihan, both Budget Committee Democrats, pressed Republican chair Pete Domenici for a vote on the president's original budget. He refused, responding, "We don't have to be subtle. The President's budget will not pass" (Tate, "Budget Battle Erupts on Hill," 968).

56. Shortly before the president's trip to Europe, two White House aides confided their anticipation to Elizabeth Drew. They "talked openly about the political fruits of the television spectacular, and the picture of the President as a leader." One said, "It's going to be great theater" (Elizabeth Drew, "A Reporter in Washington, D.C." *New Yorker,* June 21, 1982, 97). See also Karen Elliot House and Alan L. Otten, "White House Hopes Summit Will Enhance the President's Stature," *Wall Street Journal,* May 28, 1982, 1. Wirthlin would later claim that the trip improved Reagan's job performance rating the next month. "Pollster Finds a 'Pool of Patience' with Reagan Economics Program," *New York Times,* July 31, 1982, 8. See also Jack Nelson, "Public Still Patient with Reaganomics, Poll Finds," *Los Angeles Times,* July 31, 1982, 1.

57. Martin Tolchin anticipated the inherently conflicting budget considerations six months earlier in "G.O.P. Clocks Differ on Timing of Budget Moves," *New York Times,* November 12, 1981, 26.

58 Ed Magnuson, "Reagan Says All Aboard," *Time,* August 23, 1982, 7.

59. "Gallup Survey Finds Approval of Reagan at Its Lowest Point," *New York Times,* August 19, 1982, 14.

60. A defeat on the tax bill, he told them, "would make the President look weak and damage the party's candidates across the board." The record is unclear on the success of this argument with the House Republicans, but it certainly caught the attention of the press, which depicted Reagan's "leadership" on the line with this vote. For examples of the press buildup, see Howell Raines, "Leadership Image Risked," *New York Times,* August 17, 1982, 1; and Hedrick Smith, "Reagan's Big Victory," *New York Times,* August 20, 1982, D14. In an earlier article Howell Raines reported Wirthlin's lobbying activities, "Reagan Runs a Reverse, Collides with Right Wing," *New York Times,* August 15, 1982, E4.

61. Hedrick Smith, "New House to Back Reagan Less, Poll Shows," *New York Times,* November 4, 1982, E4.

62. The relative importance of unemployment and inflation as "the most important problem" is charted for the years 1977-1983 in *National Journal,* February 19, 1983, 401.

63. The CBS News/*New York Times* survey revealed an equally sharp decline in Reagan's support at the close of 1982. See Howell Raines, "Reagan's Policies Lose Favor in Poll," *New York Times,* January 25, 1983, 1.

64. Hedrick Smith, "Now Democrats Attacking President," *New York Times,* September 18, 1982; David S. Broder, "GOP Will Be Hurt, Both Parties Agree," *Washington Post,* October 19, 1982, A1.

65. This did not keep the president off national television, however. On October 14, 1982, he rejected Democratic criticisms and appealed to the American public to stay the course.

66. Roberts, "President's Coalition," 13. Even in the Senate where the Republicans staved off strong Democratic challenges, the message of the elections was clear. Because 19 Republican incumbents were facing reelection in 1984, Republican senator William Cohen of Maine predicted, "The Senate is going to be more independent next year" (Walter Isaacson, "Trimming the Sails," *Time*, November 15, 1982, 16). For an assessment of the reasons Republicans lost fewer House seats than widely predicted by various statistical models of the relation between economic conditions and the congressional vote, see Gary C. Jacobson and Samuel Kernell, *Strategy and Choice in Congressional Elections*, 2d ed. (New Haven: Yale University Press, 1983), 94-110.

67. All except one. The former head of the boll weevils, Rep. Phil Gramm of Texas, lost his committee assignment because of his collusion with Republicans and shortly thereafter changed parties.

68. Steven V. Roberts, "The Eclipse of the Boll Weevils," *New York Times*, March 26, 1983, 10.

69. Ibid.

70. Ibid. Montgomery's message from his Mississippi constituents parallels that of Stenholm: "People in my district used to say, 'support the President.' Now I'm not hearing that much."

71. Roberts, "President's Coalition," 13.

72. Rich Jaroslovsky, "Reagan's 'Revolution' Stalls as Policies Falter Both Here and Abroad," *Wall Street Journal*, December 23, 1983, 1; Leslie Gelb, "In the Event of a Power Vacuum . . . ," *New York Times*, February 23, 1983, 12; Hedrick Smith, "The MX and Reagan's Receptivity to Compromise," *New York Times*, December 16, 1982, B16; "At the Brink" is the front cover title of the *National Journal*, March 5, 1983.

73. Isaacson, "Trimming the Sails," 16.

74. Hedrick Smith, "Reagan at Midterm," *New York Times*, December 29, 1982, 1; and Smith, "The MX," B16.

75. Francis X. Clines, "An Outsider (Soon to Be an Insider) Stirs Concern," *New York Times*, February 4, 1983, 8; and Juan Williams, "Presidential Newsmaking," *Washington Post*, February 13, 1983, A18. Another tactic was to have President Reagan tape a brief statement for the nightly news whenever some economic index became favorable. See Jonathan Fuerbringer, "Good News Often Brings More News," *New York Times*, February 21, 1983, 10. See also Dick Kirschten, "Distributing Poll Data Prompting White House to Woo Alienated Voting Blocs," *National Journal*, March 5, 1983, 488-492.

76. *Wall Street Journal*, January 14, 1983, 1.

77. Edward Cowan, "Democratic Budget Is Adopted by House, 229-196," *New York Times*, March 24, 1983, 1. For a detailed breakdown of the differences between Reagan's and the Democrats' budgets, see "Two Budget Plans with Little in Common," *National Journal*, March 26, 1983, 670.

78. Juan Williams and Helen Dewar, "President Assails House Democrats' '84 Budget Plan," *Washington Post*, March 19, 1983, A1.

79. Ibid.

80. Dennis Farney, "House Democrats Waver on 1984 Budget, Leaders Concede, after Reagan Criticisms," *Wall Street Journal*, March 22, 1983, 2.

81. "President's Speech," *New York Times*, March 24, 1983, 8.

82. Steven V. Roberts, "Bill to Make Jobs Gets Final Assent," *New York Times,* March 25, 1983, 9.
83. Martin Tolchin, "Budget Process in Peril?" *New York Times,* April 16, 1983, 5.
84. Steven V. Roberts, "The Budget Victim: G.O.P. Senate Coalition Unravels," *New York Times,* May 7, 1983, 7.
85. Steven R. Weisman, "Turning Point on Budget," *New York Times,* June 22, 1983, D23.
86. In another instance cited in the press, some Florida lawmakers, disturbed by the rising crime rate in their state, sought and won an exemption of the 4 percent cut in federal law enforcement funds. Steven V. Roberts, "How Reagan Won in Congress," *New York Times,* December 30, 1982, 11; Hedrick Smith, "Taking Charge of Congress," *New York Times Magazine,* August 9, 1981, 17.
87. Taking a broader view of the marketplace, Alistair Cooke inferred meaning from the two-way traffic along Pennsylvania Avenue. By his counting, the president conducted 69 meetings with more than 400 members of Congress, which Cooke cites as indicative of a president who shed the uncompromising campaign rhetoric and quickly learned to behave like a "political veteran" reminiscent of Lyndon Johnson. Cooke even discerned parliamentary-like relations in these traffic patterns. "Getting the Hang of It," *New Yorker,* March 14, 1983, 148-153.
88. Bernard Weinraub, "Reagan Sets Tone of Nation to Seek Economic Victory," *New York Times,* January 25, 1985, 1. President Reagan hinted that he would pursue such a course the day after the election when he told reporters in Los Angeles that he would take his case "to the people" to force congressional cooperation. Jack Nelson, "Reagan Vows to Extend Conservative Agenda," *Los Angeles Times,* November 8, 1984, 1.
89. Hedrick Smith, "Budget Maneuvers: Prime Concern Is '84 Election," *New York Times,* May 11, 1983, 9; Steven R. Weisman, "Budget Tie-Up: Reagan at the Crossroads," *New York Times,* April 20, 1983, A21; and Steven V. Roberts, "Conferees and the Budget," *New York Times,* June 20, 1983, 9.
90. Blumenthal, "Marketing the President," 114.
91. Dick Kirschten, "Life in the White House Fish Bowl—Brady Takes Charge as Press Chief," *National Journal,* January 31, 1981, 180-183.
92. Dick Kirschten, "Reagan's Political Chief Rollins: 'We Will Help Our Friends First,'" *National Journal,* June 12, 1982, 1057. See also Francis X. Clines, "Propaganda, Propagation or Just Prop," *New York Times,* June 15, 1984, A16.
93. Magnuson, "A Line Drawn in Dirt." In early April 1984, President Reagan's difficulties with Congress reached a breaking point. At a nationally televised news conference the president attacked Congress on many fronts—from aid to El Salvador to Congressional Budget Office figures. With the exception of House Republican Whip Trent Lott, Democratic and Republican leaders of both chambers took umbrage. "I want to help him," House Minority Leader Michel said of the president, "but if in the process you get torpedoed without warning, I don't appreciate that. It's always one step forward and two steps backward." A Republican Senate aide summed up the common assessment: "The President is banking on the fact that the support he needs is there in the boonies. He ran against Congress in 1980, and I assume he'll run against this body again" (Steven V. Roberts, "Pointing Fingers: Lawmakers Reply to Reagan," *New York Times,* April 11, 1984, 10). For a report of President Reagan's speech, see Francis X. Clines, "Reagan Attacks Congress' Role on Many Fronts," *New York Times,* April 5, 1984, 1.

Opinion Leadership and Foreign Affairs ═══════════ 6

On the evening of September 17, 1991, a discouraged Secretary of State James Baker boarded a flight from Jerusalem to Cairo, the next leg of what was then his latest effort at shuttle diplomacy. Unusually blunt statements had been issued at the close of his meeting with Prime Minister Yitzhak Shamir. Baker had not only failed to alter Israel's program of new settlements in the disputed occupied territories but had also come under renewed pressure to provide Israel with $10 billion in U.S. loan guarantees for housing recent Soviet emigrants.

Shamir believed his position was just on both issues, as did the majority of Israeli citizens, who consistently endorsed his stance in national opinion polls. His bluntness with the American emissary was probably inspired to a greater extent by his similarly strong support in the United States. Close to a majority of members of Congress were committed to sponsoring the enabling legislation for the loan guarantees when President Bush announced that, despite the "1,000 lobbyists" supporting the guarantees on Capitol Hill, he would veto any such legislation so long as Israel refused to freeze new settlements.

No president since Eisenhower had publicly issued such an indelicate rebuke to Israel. Supporters of the aid package claimed that the intemperate character of the president's rhetoric alarmed them as much as the veto threat. Politicians everywhere started making political calculations. Jewish groups were quick to express outrage. California Senate candidate Diane Feinstein represented the class of 1992 Democratic hopefuls when she called a press conference to label the president's position "reprehensible." Republicans made a similar political assessment. "I'm catching hell from the party," President Bush told a friend. "They're afraid we could lose some Senate seats out of this." [1]

Next came the Israelis. Foreign Minister David Levy's remarks seemed more threatening than reassuring to Bush: "Israel would never want to defeat the president of the United States.... But we also don't want to be humiliated." Then it was Shamir's turn. He could hardly have been more direct in mobilizing the formidable pro-Israeli faction when he stated that Jews in America "have learned a lesson from the Holocaust" and are therefore "now united and very active, to the surprise of political circles in their country." [2] Although several key members of the House and Senate expressed some appreciation of the president's position, and viewed the outcome of a fight with Bush as uncertain, "an early count suggest[ed] they may win." [3] Secretary Baker departed Israel empty-handed because Prime Minister Shamir appeared to hold the strongest hand.

During the flight to Cairo, Baker vented his frustration to the traveling reporters. Whether by inadvertence or stratagem, he played what proved to be the administration's trump card. Baker told them he would recommend that the president go to the American people to make the administration's case, including a national television address "if that is what it takes." [4] As soon as reports of his comments filtered back to Washington, the political winds appeared to shift. The next day various unnamed aides informed correspondents that the White House staff was preparing for a national campaign that would include television. As one aide explained, "As long as this is an 'Inside-the-Beltway' issue, it plays to our disadvantage. 'Outside the Beltway,' the position that the president, not the Congress and not Israel, determines foreign policy seems eminently reasonable." [5]

During the next week, as President Bush defended his position and appeared to stiffen his resolve to use the veto, public opinion polls began recording strong support for his position. In an ABC News survey, 86 percent backed the president's position on loan guarantees, while another poll found 69 percent agreeing with the president that the decision should be postponed for six months. As shown in Figure 6-1, these same surveys reported strong approval for the president lingering nine months after the war with Iraq. The public's approbation had begun descending from the stratosphere, as it was bound to, but 70 percent of the American public still approved Bush's performance—well enough to make him look unbeatable in the next election a year away.

These impressive numbers spawned doubts among Israel's supporters in Congress. One Democratic senator remarked, "No one wants to belly up to this buzz saw," and a House member observed in a similar metaphoric vein, "There is very little stomach to confront the President on this." Even the normally resourceful lobbyists became stoic. "If the President of the United States goes to the American people and says 'Enough already,' the Israeli lobby can't counteract that," explained a senior pro-Israel lobbyist. A week after Baker's conversation with reporters, the Associated Press distributed a photograph of a smiling Baker shaking hands with Israel's foreign minister to symbolize their agreement to postpone the loan-guarantee issue as the White House desired.[6] The benign ripples of Desert Storm continued to benefit the administration's foreign policy.

Figure 6-1   President Bush's Popular Support As A Product of Rally Events

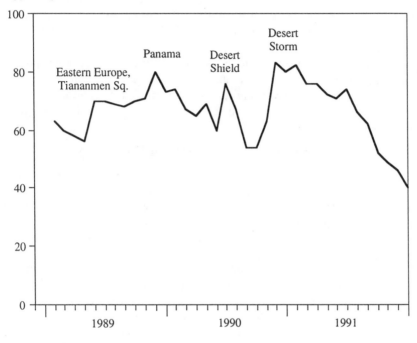

Percent
approving

SOURCE: Various issues of *Gallup Opinion Report*

By any measure, Desert Storm was an extraordinary political event. The loan-guarantee case is but one instance of the great political leverage it gave President Bush as he formulated U.S. foreign policy at home and conducted it abroad. But it was extraordinary only in degree, as international crisis is normally associated with leadership. The Cold War era provided numerous instances of crisis leadership. One inventory recorded 65 rally events during the 40-year period from the Truman through the Reagan presidencies, or about one every eight months.[7] The job performance ratings of some presidents—Kennedy and Bush come to mind—appear to reflect little more than the accumulated surges and declines accompanying a succession of rally events that dominated their tenure.

Scholars sympathetic to the presidency have applauded this phenomenon. Just when the country most requires leadership, they assert, the public gives the president free, or at least a looser, rein to act. Others, however, regard it as an opportunity for perniciousness. In retrospect, the Tonkin Gulf incident appears far too ambiguous an event to have impelled Congress to officially launch the Vietnam War with a joint resolution supporting whatever actions

President Johnson deemed necessary. Storytellers with a conspiratorial bent find presidents going beyond opportunism to the actual manufacture of crises. A classic Oliver Stone-like tale, which refuses to die, has Franklin Roosevelt exposing our defenses to the attack on Pearl Harbor in 1941 because it was the only way he could persuade the country to declare an all-out war on the Axis powers.

Whatever one's view about the wisdom of the rally phenomenon, it is widely recognized that a president made suddenly popular by an international crisis enjoys improved prospects for going public.[8] This assumption of the literature will be tested later, but first we need to review what is known about why citizens rally.

Rally Events and Presidential Popularity

Most rally events arise as crises, although other dramatic and sharply focused foreign policy developments, such as treaties consummated at heads-of-state summits, may also trigger a rally response. The launching of the Soviet satellite Sputnik in 1957, the atmospheric test ban treaty in 1961, President Nixon's 1972 trip to China, and the 1991 war with Iraq were all attended by an upsurge in approval of the president.

Many occurrences that would appear to satisfy the necessary conditions for a rally response fail to do so. When the reconnaissance ship *Pueblo* was seized by North Korea in 1968, the American public, which had grown increasingly weary of the Vietnam War, was not distracted from its steady withdrawal of approval for Lyndon Johnson. Seven years later, however, in a strikingly similar incident, when the Cambodians seized another reconnaissance ship, the *Mayaguez,* President Ford's popular support shot up 11 percentage points.

Moreover, the success or wisdom of the president's action apparently has little bearing on the public's response. President Carter's failed attempt to rescue American hostages in Iran was greeted by a 4-percentage-point rise in his popularity. After the U.S.-sponsored invasion of Cuba ended disastrously at the Bay of Pigs in April 1961, President Kennedy's already high approval rating rose another 5 percentage points. This occasioned the bemused president's observation, "The worse I do, the more popular I get."

These and other peculiarities make generalizations about the rally events hazardous. Clearly, the specific details, context, and symbols enveloping these events greatly shape the public's response. If the particular aspects of each event were all that mattered, we would be left simply reporting and describing their occurrence without much likelihood of understanding why they arise.

Rally events may be less idiosyncratic, however, than they sometimes appear. Consider why an individual might upgrade his or her evaluation of the president's job performance as a reaction to news of the bombing of Marine barracks in Lebanon or the downing of a U-2 flight over the Soviet Union. Perhaps these respondents were simply expressing their patriotic fervor in the face of an external threat. The president, after all, does stand for the nation in our foreign relations. Supporting him during a crisis could well reflect the venerable American creed that "politics stops at the water's edge." While this explanation would account for the failure of domestic crises, such as riots in the cities during the late 1960s, to generate the same surge in presidential approval, it does not take us very far toward understanding why rally events sometimes fail to materialize during international crises.

Citing the variety of public responses to crises, Richard A. Brody has looked elsewhere for an explanation—specifically, in other politicians' responses and journalistic coverage of potential rally events. Rather than a case of reflexive patriotism, the public's assessment of the president's job performance during crises may be formed no differently than in normal times. What changes is the informational environment upon which public opinion is based. Coding stories from leading newspapers during both normal times and international crises, Brody does indeed find a strong bias toward favorable presidential coverage during crises. But this finding gives rise to the next question: why would news critical of the president's performance be temporarily suspended? To answer this, we need to understand how politicians assess uncertain situations and how journalists alter the way they gather the news.

During crises (or "staged" international summits), the president will enjoy near-monopoly control over information. His authority to respond decisively during international crises is unmatched by that of anyone else in government. Others who might normally challenge his policy and interpretation of events lack the opportunity to formulate a position. For example, when presidents address the nation on television to report on a crisis, response time is not made available to opposition party congressional leaders. Partisan opponents will hesitate to step into a potential mine field of quickly unfolding events. Reporters also suspend the normal practice of seeking opposing points of view, which they follow for the more partisan domestic issues. Citizens, following their normal routine of sampling the news and responding to cues, arrive at more favorable assessments of the president's performance.

The easiest way to detect the subtle political dynamics that contribute to the formation of a rally event is to examine carefully the strategic behavior of the president and other Washingtonians who shape public opinion. Neither of the two case studies presented below shows the president dominating the other participants in the news-making process. In the first case, members of the press immediately challenge the president's interpretation of the event. In the second case, the president appears pivotal in framing the responses of other politicians and the public.

Case 1. On October 25, 1973, President Nixon summoned the network cameras to announce an alert of the armed forces for possible emergency action in the Middle East. With resolutions of impeachment referred to the House Judiciary Committee two days earlier and barely a third of the public endorsing his job performance, members of the press immediately began to suspect his motive. The next day they bluntly confronted Secretary of State Henry Kissinger at a news conference with the charge that the crisis had been fabricated to deflect public attention away from the president's Watergate troubles.[9]

Similarly, during the following June as President Nixon traveled abroad to meet with leaders from the Middle East and the Soviet Union, press suspicion followed him. One analysis of the stories about his diplomatic sojourns found half of them drawing an association between Nixon's travel and his domestic problems.[10] Modern White House correspondents, whose professional creed is to interpret as well as to report a president's actions, can more comfortably challenge an unpopular incumbent than one who enjoys the public's esteem.

Case 2.   Shortly after the U.S. invasion of Grenada in the fall of 1983, all opinion indicators pointed to a confused and ambivalent public. Politicians within both parties were uncertain what posture they should assume toward President Reagan's action. Some Democratic spokespersons, including House Speaker O'Neill, began lobbing salvos at the White House, describing the invasion as "gunboat diplomacy." [11] Democratic senator Daniel P. Moynihan publicly declared the invasion to be "an act of war," adding, "I don't know that you restore democracy at the point of a bayonet." [12] One Democratic representative went so far as to announce a petition drive calling for the president's impeachment. For the most part, however, Democrats—including, prominently, those seeking their party's presidential nomination—and Republicans temporized.

With the military operation concluded and public opinion appearing increasingly to echo the president's critics, Reagan went on national television to account for his actions. The poll takers were poised; when they revealed the public's early, highly favorable response, the critics hushed up, and Reagan's previously silent partners became vocal.[13] One Democratic senator remarked, "Most people, once they saw the polls come out, went underground." Within two weeks after his initial criticism, Senator Moynihan conceded, "The move is popular and therefore there's no disposition in the Senate to be opposed to it." [14]

Events as novel as this one pose a special problem for politicians. Preexisting cues in public opinion are unserviceable. When the political winds blow at crosscurrents, most politicians tread lightly, neither embracing nor scoffing the president. Once clear signals from the country begin arriving in Washington, however, they swiftly assume an appropriate posture.

Clearly, context is critical. The Nixon episode suggests that the president's ability to define a crisis event rests with his credibility with the public. This may well explain why President Johnson failed to win the public's support at the time of the *Pueblo* seizure. The second case indicates a more complex interaction between political leaders and followers than either explanation presented above allows. During Grenada the citizenry did not reflexively rally. Only when they saw images of rescued American medical students joyfully returning home did the president effectively make his case, leading a significant number of respondents to upgrade their evaluation of his performance. Other elected politicians who participated in shaping the domestic context of the event were clearly looking over their shoulders for guidance from voters.

Thus far we have considered as context only the reactions of presidents, other Washington politicians, and those who report on their activities. But the context includes another critical feature: the state of public opinion entering the crisis. Since a rally event is defined by a surge in presidential support and measured by its magnitude, other things being equal, a president who already enjoys a strong public endorsement should experience smaller rallies than will be the case for one who is less popular. In early December 1979, with barely a third of the public registering its approval of him, President Carter faced a stiff challenge from Senator Edward Kennedy. More attention was focused on whether he could again win the nomination rather than his chances in the fall general election. However, the seizure of the hostages in Tehran changed his fortunes. Reinforced by the Soviet Union's invasion of Afghanistan in January, Carter's job performance ratings rose 23 points—the largest such surge ever—and it stayed high throughout the spring primary season.

Statistical evidence based on 25 rally events during the post-World War II era supports the conjecture that the level of prior approval predictably conditions the rally response. This relationship is not strong, however, which is not too surprising given the handicap of an unpopular president trying to frame an event.[15] Still, the statistical relationship is suggestive.

During normal times the public's evaluation of the president follows partisan lines. Democrats are consistently the least approving of President Bush, Republicans the most so, with independents somewhere in the middle. As a consequence, there were many more Democrats than Republicans available to rally during Desert Storm, and more in fact did so. Nearly a quarter of the Democrats switched from disapproval to approval compared with only 10 percent of the Republicans. Over half of all the changes to approval during the brief war with Iraq occurred among Democrats.[16] The partisan response during Desert Storm follows a more general pattern. For the rally events reported above, 8.5 percent of the opposition party's identifiers on average upgraded their evaluations of the president compared with 6 percent of those who identified with the president's party.

Ironically, the net result of these different partisan propensities is the emergence of a nonpartisan consensus in support of the president.[17] This introduces a distinctly different political setting for the exercise of presidential leadership. A compilation of approval ratings for Franklin Roosevelt before and after the bombing of Pearl Harbor illustrates this point (see Figure 6-2).

In those days party identification was not a well-recognized concept, so that the best available means for measuring the partisan composition of FDR's coalition was income. Prior to the attack on Pearl Harbor, evaluation of the president adhered to class lines. After the president's detractors massively rallied, his popular support was pervasive. Acutely sensitive to the mood of the public, and armed with reports of these approval ratings (which after U.S. entry into the war were not published but privately given to him), President Roosevelt restyled his leadership, in his own words, from "Dr. New Deal" to "Dr. Win the War."[18]

Rally Events and Opinion Leadership

Politicians will occasionally have the firsthand evidence of a recent national appeal as they assess the president's ability to go public. More commonly, however, they must judge the president's potential prowess with the circumstantial evidence of his approval ratings in the polls. The president's popularity helps them gauge his ability to use public strategies. Politicians are not alone in drawing a close association between the president's popularity and his ability to influence public opinion. During the past 20 years, this relation has been a standard hypothesis of research on the subject.

Past research has approached the relation between support for the president and support for his policies in a number of ways. One survey study, performed during the time of a popular incumbent, found that respondents were significantly more likely to endorse a hypothetical policy when they were told that it represented the president's position.[18] Another approach has been to examine public support for policies on which the president had actually staked out a clear position. The studies have generally found that respondents who approved of the president's performance were more enthusiastic about the policy than were those who disapproved.[19] Finally, a few studies have sought to gauge changes in aggregate public opinion on policy questions as a function of a president's intervention. They similarly report a relation between the president's popularity at the time of a public appeal and the magnitude of opinion change that followed.[20] Although alternative explanations to the transference of support from the president to his policies are available to explain each of these findings, the similar results generated by these different research designs present compelling circumstantial support for the importance of a president's prestige on his opinion leadership.

Of course, all one is really saying is that people tend to evaluate a message according to its source. One can easily develop a rationale for such a transference from traditional consistency theory in social psychology. This theory is premised on the fundamental assumption that individuals generally prefer consistent to inconsistent beliefs and opinions. An individual seeking to incorporate new information in a consistent fashion has a number of mechanisms available for doing so. One of particular relevance here is the congruence between source and message.[21] Following this principle, citizens

Figure 6-2 Support for FDR among Income Subgroups: 1937-1942

Percent Approving

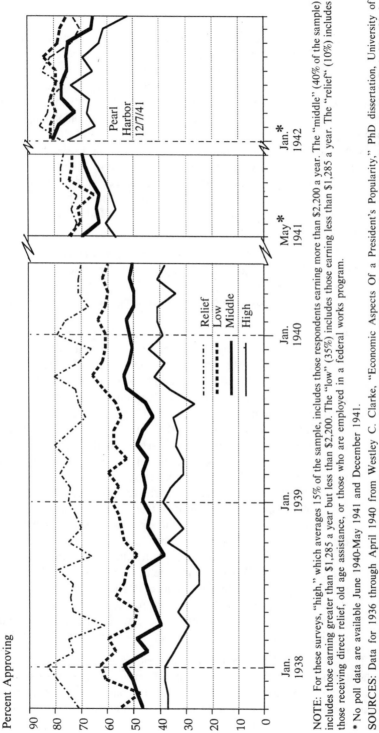

NOTE: For these surveys, "high," which averages 15% of the sample, includes those respondents earning more than $2,200 a year. The "middle" (40% of the sample) includes those earning greater than $1,285 a year but less than $2,200. The "low" (35%) includes those earning less than $1,285 a year. The "relief" (10%) includes those receiving direct relief, old age assistance, or those who are employed in a federal works program.

* No poll data are available June 1940-May 1941 and December 1941.

SOURCES: Data for 1936 through April 1940 from Westley C. Clarke, "Economic Aspects Of a President's Popularity," PhD dissertation, University of Pennsylvania, 1943. Figures for subsequent months obtained from the President's Personal Files at the Franklin Delano Roosevelt Library, Hyde Park, New York.

who are otherwise indifferent on a president's proposed policy will be inclined to adopt a position consistent with their evaluation of him as president. Approval inspires trust; disapproval, suspicion.

If going public is to succeed as a leadership strategy, presidential appeals must activate as well as persuade. Large numbers of citizens must be moved to contact their representatives. If the collective demonstration of support for the president's program impresses politicians, they will strategically align their public position on the policy in a way that is favorable to the president. The opinion dynamics required of going public, therefore, extend beyond mass persuasion, for which consistency between source and message is most appropriate. According to these dynamics, a national appeal will alter the preferences of sufficient numbers of politicians if the following four conditions are satisfied.

1. The president accurately communicates his preferences to the citizenry. The public recognizes the president's endorsement of a particular policy position. Past research on the public's familiarity with presidential appeals indicates that this is probably the least demanding condition.[22]
2. Citizens register favorable or unfavorable responses to a policy initiative according to their evaluation of the president. Moreover, the intensity as well as the direction of preference will be affected by the strength of the individual's position on an issue and of his or her evaluation of the president before learning of his position.
3. Citizens communicate support for the president's position to those politicians whom he hopes to influence. Ongoing communication is a commonly stipulated feature of representative democracy. Here, however, the principle takes on special emphasis, since the president will typically be trying to alter some specific behavior of politicians over a short time. For such a result, the more casual and leisurely forms of communication that arise from the representative's continuing contact with constituents will have to be supplemented by the direct effort of many citizens to contact their representatives.
4. To secure their own welfare, politicians strategically align their preferences with those of the president. Representatives do not have to decide that the president's position commands majority support among their constituents for such a posture to make political sense. A presidential appeal may succeed in creating a vocal, intense minority in support that will prevail over an indifferent or passive majority.

Facing these stringent conditions, a president might conclude that going public will not be worth the effort. Citing them, some observers have argued, in fact, that presidents should spurn going public as a substitute for bargaining. Here is what Nelson W. Polsby, a leading student of contemporary American politics, has said on the subject:

Efforts to ignore, bypass, or run roughshod over [national interest] groups by appealing over their heads to the people are doomed on at least two counts. First, the appeal to public opinion itself is likely to fail because of the ephemerality of mass public attitudes on most issues and because of the non-transferability of a president's popularity (when the president is popular) to the objects of a president's desires. Second, even if by some unusual combination of circumstances public opinion does for once yield to a president's entreaties, the effects may or may not reach Congress or influence congressional disposition of an issue.[23]

There are a number of ways to relax the four formal conditions above and to make the transference less dependent upon Polsby's "unusual combination of circumstances." First, the position of the president in the policy-making process allows him to choose from a large menu of policy proposals circulating around Washington at any moment. For those issues that are sufficiently advanced to merit the president's attention, much of the preparatory, coalition-building work will have been completed. Rather than being truly innovative and building winning coalitions from the ground up, presidents typically take up others' ideas and work at the margin of support that will make the difference in victory or defeat. An example of this tactic is President Reagan's use of national television and other public activities to swing 30 to 50 Republican House votes in the 1982 tax increase.

Further reducing the demands on the president's rhetoric, representatives also work at the margin of support within their constituencies. Even if a representative suspects that no more than 4 or 5 percent of the electorate will base its vote in the next election on his or her support of the president's program, it might still decisively alter his or her position on the issue.

The fact that marginal shifts of preferences, whether in Washington or in the rest of the country, often have major political consequences is what makes going public a viable strategy. The president makes an appeal; most citizens do not respond, but some do. A few of this latter group express their support actively. Most of the politicians who oppose the president's position will resist constituent pressure. A few whose positions are less fixed or who are electorally vulnerable will be persuaded that the president's course offers the least resistance. Frequently, this is all that is required for the president to appear to have worked his magic.

Moreover, the president possesses unusual institutional assets that may enhance his influence over public opinion well beyond that provided by his current popularity. The presidency's singular visibility allows its occupant to command the nation's attention; the office's broad constitutional mandate bestows upon him the authority to speak on any policy matter; and his acknowledged institutional expertise requires that his arguments be weighed and, even if opposed, dealt with.[24] In foreign policy, particularly, these resources will stand him in good stead.[25]

No president will ever persuade all of his admirers to support his cause. To the extent he fails, performance on condition 2 (transference of prestige to policy support) is weakened. But with the office's exceptional public standing, the incumbent president can also appeal to his detractors. His failure to persuade some of his admirers may be partly compensated by citizens who, while disapproving his current performance, nonetheless defer to his judgment. At times, consistency theory will be violated in ways that favor the president's efforts.

The remainder of this chapter tests the consistency model of opinion leadership on the Truman Doctrine speech of March 12, 1947. It is a single case, but a remarkable one. In the opinion of contemporaries and historians alike, President Truman faced a formidable task in preventing the country from settling comfortably into postwar isolationism and from failing to recognize the Soviet challenge. He certainly thought so. Some historians have argued that to achieve his goals Truman resorted to extraordinary rhetoric and other public activities that secured his program but also eventually unleashed an anticommunist phobia throughout the country. In this case, then, a president who set out to reshape public opinion on foreign affairs stands accused by some of having kicked off the Cold War at home.

The Truman Doctrine Speech: A Case Study

Delivered to Congress and broadcast across the nation on radio, this historic address has been widely credited not only with gaining the president his policy objectives but also with establishing the temper of U.S. foreign policy during the post-World War II era. Whether sympathetic to or critical of the Truman administration, historians agree that this speech more than any other single event marks the beginning of the Cold War between the United States and the Soviet Union. Moreover, its implications for the future did not require hindsight. Contemporaries in Washington and abroad grasped immediately that President Truman was advocating a fundamental change in the U.S. responsibility and posture toward the world. As Joseph Jones, a State Department participant in the formulation of the Truman Doctrine, recalled, "All who participated in the extraordinary developments of the period were aware that a major turning in American history was taking place." [26]

The Speech

Truman's speech to the country called for congressional authorization of $400 million in economic and military assistance to Greece and Turkey. Describing the deterioration of the Greek economy and the inability of its military to cope with Communist guerrilla activities, Truman starkly predicted that if the United States did not shortly replace the evacuating British forces, Greece would fall to the Communists. Turkey and the rest of the Middle East would succumb in turn. But he went beyond a simple request for aid. He described a bipolar world of democracy versus totalitarianism and called for the United States to assist "free people who are resisting attempted subjugation." Two major sections of the speech depicted the Communist threat and the American challenge. Midway through he turned his discussion from Greece and Turkey and spoke more generally:

> The peoples of a number of countries of the world have recently had totalitarian regimes forced upon them against their will. The Government of the United States has made frequent protests against coercion and intimidation, in violation of the Yalta agreement, in Poland, Rumania, and Bulgaria. I must also state that in a number of other countries there have been similar developments.
>
> At the present moment in world history nearly every nation must choose between alternative ways of life. The choice is too often not a free one.
>
> One way of life is based upon the will of the majority, and is distinguished by free institutions, representative government, free elections, guarantees of individual liberty, freedom of speech and religion, and freedom from political oppression.
>
> The second way of life is based upon the will of a minority forcibly imposed upon the majority. It relies upon terror and oppression, a controlled press and radio, fixed elections, and the suppression of personal freedoms.
>
> I believe that we must assist free people to work out their own destinies in their own way.
>
> I believe that our help should be primarily through economic and financial aid which is essential to economic stability and orderly political processes.

His peroration was even more graphic:

> The seeds of totalitarian regimes are nurtured by misery and want. They spread and grow in the evil soil of poverty and strife. They reach their full growth when the hope of a people for a better life has died.
>
> We must keep that hope alive.
>
> The free peoples of the world look to us for support in maintaining their freedoms.
>
> If we falter in our leadership, we may endanger the peace of the world and we shall surely endanger the welfare of our own nation.
>
> Greater responsibilities have been placed upon us by the swift movements of events.
>
> I am confident that the Congress will face these responsibilities squarely.[27]

At the close of the speech the assembled joint session responded with a standing ovation, and the immediate response of most columnists and editors around the country was favorable. There was some opposition, however, and it would be months before the aid authorization would pass Congress. Henry Wallace, who the next year would run for president against Truman as a third-party candidate, went on nationwide radio to lambast the speech and to characterize Truman, for his depiction of the gravity of the Soviet threat, "as the best salesman Communism ever had." [28] A number of prominent senators spanning the ideological spectrum from Robert Taft on the right to Claude Pepper on the left publicly expressed reservations.

After having experienced the Cold War rhetoric of the 1950s, one may not find much in Truman's statements that is particularly arousing or inflammatory. But it must be remembered that this was the first time a president had publicly identified the Soviet Union as an enemy and depicted so starkly the struggle between democracy and totalitarianism. Despite the disappointments after Yalta, Truman had repeatedly resisted making such public statements. Even now some of his closest advisers were disturbed by the speech's tenor. Secretary of State George C. Marshall en route to a Moscow conference was "somewhat startled to see the extent to which the anti-communist element . . . was stressed." [29] James Byrnes, who had recently resigned as secretary of state, complained that the speech was too general in tone and commitment.[30] George Kennan, shortly to be head of the State Department's policy-planning staff, also objected to the "sweeping nature of the commitments." [31]

It is obvious from reading the memoirs of those who participated in drafting the speech that President Truman had intended it to be hortatory. Several days earlier at a White House briefing for a number of important senators and representatives, he had viewed the chilly response accorded Secretary Marshall's humanitarian reasons for giving assistance to Greece and Turkey. Only after Dean Acheson's presentation of the issue in strong anticommunist terms did the lawmakers warm to the proposal.[32] And as noted in Chapter 2, this is when Senator Arthur Vandenberg, the respected foreign policy expert, is reported to have advised the president that he would have to "scare hell out of the country" if he wanted to get authorization through Congress.[33] Moreover, other recent reconstruction programs proposed by the administration had received hostile responses from Congress and clearly would never be reported out of committee. Finally, Truman's vivid account of the speech writing reveals the dramatic rhetorical style he wanted infused into the text.

> The drafting of the actual message which I would deliver to the Congress had meanwhile been started in the State Department. The first version was not at all to my liking. The writers had filled the speech with all sorts of background data and statistical figures about Greece and made the whole thing sound like an investment prospectus. I returned this draft to Acheson with a note asking for more emphasis on a declaration of general policy. The department's draftsmen then rewrote the speech to include a general policy statement, but it seemed to me half-hearted. The key sentence, for instance, read, "I believe that it should be the policy of the United States. . . ." I took my pencil, scratched out "should" and wrote in "must." . . . I wanted no hedging in this speech. This was America's answer to the surge of expansion of Communist tyranny. It had to be clear and free of hesitation or double talk.[34]

As Richard M. Freeland has summed up the speech, President Truman committed himself and the nation to a "broad interpretative framework" of a "global assault of the 'totalitarian' forces against the forces of 'freedom'— calculated to command immediately the maximum public support." [35] When Marshall complained to the president that he had "overstated it a bit,"

Truman quickly replied that it had been necessary to receive favorable congressional treatment.[36]

After past wars the United States had withdrawn at least temporarily into an isolationist mood and policy. Despite the U.S. role in creating the United Nations, every indication from the recently elected Republican Congress was that U.S. economic and military commitments around the world would be sharply curtailed. Yet here was the president, only a year after the peace, attempting to commit a hostile Congress and an unconcerned nation to an activist, international posture.

Unlike President Reagan's use of national appeals as a bludgeon against his adversaries in Congress, President Truman's enterprise was more subtle. Working in an era where such force would have in all likelihood redoubled resistance, Truman sought to create an opinion climate that would make going along with his aid program for Greece and Turkey easier for members of Congress who might otherwise discern only the political costs to supporting such a policy. In going public, Truman sought not to circumvent bargaining. Indeed, by following Vandenberg's advice he tacitly agreed to shoulder responsibility for the policy and thereby remove a formidable obstacle to negotiation.[37] Truman's success, consequently, should be measured by the degree to which the speech generated a favorable opinion climate rather than by the volume of congressional mail it inspired. As such, it is an ideal case for testing at least the first two formal conditions of opinion leadership listed above.

I have hinted at another reason why the Truman Doctrine speech is of interest here. Since the late 1960s, a number of historians (whom I shall call revisionists) have been reevaluating the Truman presidency and concluding that the United States fomented the Cold War abroad and at home. Among them, Freeland identifies Truman's March 12 speech, as well as subsequent propaganda and "police" activities against subversion, as creating an opinion climate of anticommunism that made the McCarthyism of the early 1950s unavoidable.[38] Freeland's depiction of events, like that of other revisionist historians, is simple. He contends that President Truman raised the specter of Communist subversion to prompt Congress and the nation to embrace his foreign policy. Having succeeded in linking foreign and domestic threats and getting his program enacted, Truman found himself unable to turn off the pathological fear of Communism he promulgated. It is a parsimonious theory. It dismisses eventual passage of the Greco-Turkish aid program as well as the Marshall Plan; it explains away the president's pro-civil libertarian resistance to congressional investigations in the late 1940s and the early 1950s; and it accounts for the rise of McCarthyism. And finally there is a moral: we reap what we sow. During the 1952 presidential campaign, Truman and the Democrats were roasted for being soft on Communism.

This reinterpretation of foreign affairs in the late 1940s covers a broad range of occurrences in and out of government, and findings on the effect of a

Table 6-1 Public Concern over Foreign Policy before and after
Truman Doctrine Speech

Date	Percent Naming Foreign Problems as Most Important
Before Truman Doctrine Speech	
October 1945	7
February 1946	23
June 1946	11
September 1946	23
December 1946	22
After Truman Doctrine Speech	
March 1947	54
July 1947	47
September 1947	28
December 1947	30
February 1948	33

SOURCES: Gabriel Almond, *The American People and Foreign Policy* (New York: Praeger, 1960), 73; Samuel Kernell, "The Truman Doctrine Speech: A Case Study of the Dynamics of Presidential Opinion Leadership," *Social Science History* 1 (Fall 1976): 28.

single event no matter how dramatic can neither confirm nor deny revisionist history. Yet this history relies heavily upon the assumption that elites could easily manipulate public opinion. The Truman Doctrine speech is commonly regarded in revisionist statements as one of Truman's most prominent and successful efforts.[39] In investigating the public's response to Truman's address in a realm beyond policy support, one can test, in part, these revisionist claims and explore the limits of presidential opinion leadership.

Public Familiarity with the Speech

During the two-week interval between the March 12 address and the Gallup survey that queried the public about it, the president's remarks and proposal received continuous coverage in the nation's newspapers. As a result, an unusually large share of respondents, 84 percent, reported having heard or read about the speech. This compares with only 54 percent who would claim familiarity with the Marshall Plan in the summer at a later stage of that issue's development.[40]

Given the extent to which Truman's address reached its audience, it is not surprising that the speech coincided with heightened public awareness of international problems, as Table 6-1 shows. In March 1947 when a Gallup survey asked what was the nation's "most important problem," more than half of the respondents volunteered foreign affairs. Only three months earlier, barely a fifth had done so; and by late summer, pressing domestic issues would reemerge as the dominant public concerns. Although international events were

Table 6-2 Distribution of Public Support for Foreign Aid Requests in Truman Doctrine Speech (Percent)

	Aid for Greece	Aid for Turkey
Strongly oppose	20	22
Weakly oppose	18	23
Uncertain (don't know)	14	16
Weakly favor	29	22
Strongly favor	20	17

NOTE: Percentages may not total 100 because of rounding.

SOURCES: American Institute of Public Opinion, Survey No. 393, March 26-27, 1947; Kernell, "Truman Doctrine Speech," 34.

occurring quickly during this period, the Truman Doctrine speech appears to have been the most prominent one between the December and March surveys and probably accounts for the brief ascent of foreign affairs as the nation's "most important problem." Because the president's address to the joint session of Congress was an important event not only in Washington but in the rest of the country, one may consider the answers to the survey questions to be real opinions rather than merely obligatory responses.

Effects of the Speech on Public Opinion

Two aspects of the March 1947 survey indicate the success of the speech in achieving its primary goal, support for the administration's foreign aid package. First, respondents were asked whether they would like to see their representatives vote for or against Truman's aid requests of $250 million for Greece and $150 million for Turkey.[41] The distribution of opinions is displayed in Table 6-2. Given the novelty of the issue, it is somewhat surprising that 85 percent of the sample expressed a preference, and nearly half felt strongly either for or against the president's proposals. Aid for Greece was the more popular of the two requests. Among those registering an opinion, 57 percent favored aid for Greece compared with only 46 percent for Turkey. The president's speech, as well as subsequent daily news reports, clearly identified Greece as being in the more precarious position; Turkey was described as having a relatively healthy economy and being in no immediate danger unless Greece were to collapse. Although perhaps short of a mandate, Truman succeeded in quickly generating substantial public enthusiasm for his internationalist policy. If contemporaneous informal readings of public opinion were correct in portraying a pervasive isolationist mood throughout the country, these percentages represent a sizable turnaround in public opinion.

The second aspect of the March 1947 survey that reflects on the success of Truman's speech is the relation between source and message. Table 6-3 shows that the president's approvers were more supportive than his detractors

Table 6-3   Relationship between Approval of President Truman and Support for His Foreign Aid Requests (Percent)

	Aid for Greece		Aid for Turkey	
	Disapprove of Truman	Approve of Truman	Disapprove of Truman	Approve of Truman
Strongly oppose	38	13	41	16
Weakly oppose	21	16	26	21
Uncertain (don't know)	9	14	9	17
Weakly favor	24	32	14	26
Strongly favor	9	25	10	20

SOURCES: American Institute of Public Opinion, Survey No. 393; Kernell, "Truman Doctrine Speech," 38.

on both policy questions but that his opinion leadership was not limited to his admirers. A third of those respondents who disapproved of Truman's job performance nonetheless agreed to his aid program for Greece, and a fourth to his aid for Turkey. Because of the president's special credibility in foreign affairs, this finding is not unusual. Overall, approximately two-thirds of the respondents in Table 6-3 held opinions of the requests consistent with their evaluations of Truman's performance in office.

I enlisted consistency theory above to create a model of presidential opinion leadership that had the citizens' evaluations of Truman shaping their preferences about the president's policies. Of course, there is no intrinsic reason why consistent opinions could not arise from a reverse causal flow— that is, responses to the speech could have altered evaluations of the president. Causation is always a slippery problem in nonexperimental settings, and with a single survey, it is impossible to pin down the degree to which the president was leading public opinion or simply espousing what proved to be a popular policy. One must make educated guesses about the direction of causality from more circumstantial evidence. Since few citizens could have been so prescient as to have formed opinions on this issue before the speech, when even the State Department several weeks earlier had been caught unaware, one suspects that evaluations of the president's job performance probably heavily influenced opinions about his proposal.[42]

Although it is impossible to shed more light on the causal direction of opinion change with these data, one can tease out some of the probable dynamics of opinion change by learning more about who responded favorably to the president's appeal. Table 6-4 partitions respondents according to their 1944 presidential vote and their education. (Because the aid questions for Greece and Turkey yield highly similar relationships, I shall limit the remainder of the analysis to opinion on aid for Greece.) For only one subgroup—poorly educated Dewey voters—does the overall positive relationship between evaluations of Truman's job performance and support for military aid to Greece fail to turn up.

Within each educational class, the greatest support for Truman's proposal came from respondents who had both voted for Franklin Roosevelt in 1944 and approved of Truman's job performance at the time of the survey. The percentage endorsing aid to Greece varied from 60 to 86 percent depending upon educational class. The reinforcement of partisanship and approval contributes to this high approval rating.

The straightforward consistency model fails, however, to explain why Roosevelt voters who disapproved of Truman's performance consistently volunteered the least support for Truman's aid program. According to the consistency rationale, this distinction should belong to disapproving Dewey voters who had both partisanship and current opinions of Truman's performance to buttress a negative opinion. Yet controlling for education, these voters are consistently more supportive of Truman's policy than are their disapproving Democratic counterparts.

In the absence of better data, one can only speculate on the reason. Perhaps Truman's Democratic-voting detractors disproportionately belonged to some constituency for whom military aid to Greece and Turkey was objectionable. There are two difficulties with this argument, however. First, past research has identified no major segment of the Democratic constituency that was so positioned on these issues. Former Democratic vice-president Henry Wallace soon became an outspoken critic of the speech, but as he would demonstrate in garnering about 3 percent of the national vote as a third-party candidate in the next year's presidential election, the Wallace faction was too small—especially among voters with the least education—to produce the low support from Truman's detractors shown in Table 6-4. During these years, Republicans throughout the country as well as in Congress have been generally portrayed as more disposed to isolationism. Presumably, if any constituency's prior opinions would have led them to reject Truman's appeal, it should have been Republican voters. And yet roughly half of the Dewey voters who disapproved of Truman's job performance supported him on this issue.

Another possible explanation is the relative intensity with which Dewey and Roosevelt voters may have disapproved of Truman's performance. Many Dewey voters who disapproved of Truman may simply have been responding to partisan cues, and therefore their opinions had little intellectual basis or emotional investment. This cannot be said, however, of many Roosevelt voters who found reason to disapprove of Truman's job performance despite their shared partisanship.[43] Consequently, disapproving Dewey voters, on the whole, may have found it less disruptive to their prior opinions to go along with President Truman's foreign policy recommendations than would those Democratic voters who had a stronger, more substantive basis for their opinion.

Table 6-4 Relationship between Approval of President Truman and Support for Aid to Greece, Controlling for Education and Presidential Vote (Percent and Number Who Favor Aid to Greece Among Respondents Who Heard or Read about the President's Speech)

Evaluation of Truman	Low Education (0-8)				Moderate Education (9-12)				High Education (Some College +)			
	Voted for Dewey		Voted for FDR		Voted for Dewey		Voted for FDR		Voted for Dewey		Voted for FDR	
	%	(N)	%	(N)	%	(N)	%	(N)	%	(N)	%	(N)
Disapprove	48.1	(27)	23.9	(46)	46.2	(80)	33.8	(74)	57.7	(71)	35.3	(51)
Approve	47.8	(69)	59.9	(187)	64.4	(146)	64.9	(259)	74.7	(150)	86.0	(150)
Difference[1]	−0.3		+36.0		+18.2		+31.1		+17.0		+50.7	

[1] Positive percentage point differences indicate the beneficial effect of approval on favoring aid to Greece.

SOURCES: American Institute of Public Opinion, Survey No. 393; Kernell, "Truman Doctrine Speech," 39.

Table 6-5   Educational Differences in Support for the Truman Doctrine
(Percentage Points)

1944 Vote	Truman Evaluation	Difference between Respondents with Moderate and Low Education[1]	Differences between Respondents with High and Moderate Education[1]
Dewey	Disapprove	−1.9	+11.5
Dewey	Approve	+16.6	+10.3
FDR	Disapprove	+9.9	+1.5
FDR	Approve	+5.0	+21.1

[1] Based on responses in Table 6-4. Positive signs indicate that the higher educational category was more supportive of aid to Greece.

SOURCES: American Institute of Public Opinion, Survey No. 393; Kernell, "Truman Doctrine Speech," 40.

Such an explanation is rooted in the intensity of presidential performance evaluations rather than in the substance of the particular appeal. If correct, it should reappear in other issues with different presidents. Until such confirmation is available, however, only two general conclusions from the relationships in Table 6-4 are possible. First, the president's opinion leadership is associated with evaluations of his performance. Second, at least in the realm of foreign policy, the president may find a receptive audience among those citizens who would normally not number among his political allies. The findings offer empirical evidence of the familiar creed "Partisanship stops at the water's edge."

Another politically relevant finding is embedded in these relationships, namely, the effect of education on the public's receptivity to Truman's appeal. The subgroup differences in Table 6-4 have been rearranged in Table 6-5 to show the differences in support for aid to Greece according to education among groups who are otherwise similar. For example, where in Table 6-4, 46.2 percent of moderately well-educated and disapproving Dewey voters supported Truman's policy compared with 57.7 percent of their highly educated counterparts, in Table 6-5, this difference reappears as a difference of 11.5 percentage points in support. The positive signs indicate that in seven of the eight pairings, respondents in the higher educational category were more supportive.[44]

One might have supposed that education would have been correlated in the opposite direction, with poorly educated citizens being more susceptible to presidential appeals. Yet the finding shown here agrees with the results from other research. John E. Mueller, for example, discovered that public support for U.S. conduct of the Korean and Vietnam wars also came more heavily from the well-educated segments of the population.[45] In a somewhat different vein, another study found that politically attentive citizens, who also tend to be better educated, are the main source of shifts in American public opinion on emergent issues.[46]

Another basis of opinion leadership suggested earlier is that the president won support for his foreign policy by scaring the hell out of the country. In doing so, the argument continues, Truman nurtured an anticommunist phobia at home. Fortunately, questions in the Gallup survey of March 26-27, 1947, make it possible to test this claim.

Anticommunism as a Basis of Truman's Opinion Leadership

Revisionist historians emphasize the fear arousal aspects of Truman's rhetoric. They maintain that the president consciously sought to frighten the nation with the threat of Communist aggression and to mobilize this fear into public support for his policy. According to Walter LaFeber, "Insofar as public opinion was concerned this tactic worked well for the Administration." Arthur Theoharis argues that it "heightened public fears" and "contributed to a parochial, self-righteous nationalism." [47] But did it really have these effects? Could it account for the widespread endorsement of aid to Greece, especially among the president's detractors? To answer these questions, one must examine the anticommunist sentiment after the speech and the relation between these opinions and support for the Truman Doctrine program.

Although the Gallup survey did not query respondents directly about their fear of an external Communist threat, several questions did measure their concerns about domestic Communism. One can therefore test during this early period the presumed ultimate effects proposed by the "seeds of McCarthyism" thesis. Each survey item on the issue contains a prominent civil liberties component, and most of these items gained such a strong anticommunist endorsement, they contain too little variation with which to test the effect of Truman's message on opinion.[48] One item that did escape overendorsement asked the respondent simply, "Do you think the Communist Party in this country should be forbidden by law?" (I shall call this the "forbid-Communist-party" question.) Sixty percent agreed, 30 percent disagreed, and 10 percent held no opinion. Later this question would become a standard item of Gallup and the other national opinion surveys, but the March 26-27, 1947, survey appears to have been its first employment in a national poll.

Did the speech arouse anticommunism on the domestic front? The figures in Table 6-6 suggest not. Of all respondents, a slightly greater share of those who had heard or read about the Truman Doctrine speech did indeed register an anticommunist opinion. At the same time more of them also gave a pro-civil liberties response. These answers indicate only that citizens who are attentive to public affairs tend also to be more opinionated on political issues

Table 6-6 Relationship between Familiarity with Truman Doctrine Speech and Response to Forbid-Communist-Party Question (Percent and Number of Respondents)

Heard about Truman's Speech?	Forbid Communist Party?			
	Don't know	No	Yes	(N)
All responses				
No	24.8	18.3	56.8	(387)
Yes	8.3	31.4	60.4	(2,205)
Difference	−16.5	+13.1	+3.6	
Opinionated responses only				
No		24.4	75.6	(291)
Yes		34.2	65.8	(2,023)
Difference		+9.8	−9.8	

SOURCES: American Institute of Public Opinion, Survey No. 393; Kernell, "Truman Doctrine Speech," 35.

of the day. The direct effect of the speech is indicated by removing the replies of respondents who failed to offer an opinion to the forbid-Communist-party question. Table 6-6 shows that, contrary to the revisionist hypothesis, a greater percentage of those who were familiar with the speech opposed banning the Communist party than those who were not familiar with the speech.

The reason for this result again probably has more to do with a self-selection bias in respondents' exposure to the address than with any independent effects of the speech itself. This bias suggests the need for control variables to measure the direct effect of the speech. In an analysis of these data reported elsewhere, responses to both the forbid-Communist-party and "heard or read about the speech" questions were associated with education and past voting participation.[49] In Table 6-7, these variables are introduced as controls, but once again the predicted relationship between exposure to Truman's address and an anticommunist opinion fails to appear. For all but one instance (those with low education who did not vote in 1944), there was either no relationship or one opposite that predicted.[50]

Presidents, as well as scholars, should recognize that all segments of the public are not equally attentive to presidential messages. This may at times have important implications for the president's ability to rally public support. Before casually deriving or concluding mass attitude change from a president's appeal, one first needs to identify his audience. This should provide a clue as to how generally effective his message will be. There is some evidence in Table 6-3 that the effects suggested by revisionist

Table 6-7 Relationship between Familiarity with Truman Doctrine Speech and Anticommunist Opinion, Controlling for Education and Participation (Percent Who Favor Forbidding Communist Party)

Familiarity with Speech	Low Education (0-8)				Moderate Education (9-12)				High Education (Some College +)			
	Did not vote in 1944		Voted in 1944		Did not vote in 1944		Voted in 1944		Did not vote in 1944		Voted in 1944	
	%	(N)	%	(N)	%	(N)	%	(N)	%	(N)	%	(N)
No	80.0	(60)	76.6	(94)	69.4	(36)	78.0	(82)	—[1]		53.8	(13)
Yes	85.0	(113)	76.5	(433)	68.5	(178)	69.8	(738)	41.5	(53)	48.2	(508)
Difference[2]	+5.0		−0.1		−0.9		−7.8		—[1]		−5.6	

NOTE: Percentaging based only on responses holding an opinion.

[1] Insufficient N for percentaging.

[2] Positive percentage point difference indicates that effects of hearing about speech are in the predicted direction.

SOURCES: American Institute of Public Opinion, Survey No. 393; Kernell, "Truman Doctrine Speech," 32.

historians may have been produced for the least-educated and nonparticipating segment of society. Familiarity with a speech depicting an external threat may have decreased this group's support of civil liberties for Communists. The president was talking disproportionately to other segments of the population, however, who were better equipped to differentiate their environment and therefore less likely to generalize in this fashion. Moreover, for highly educated and participating respondents, virtually all of whom said they were familiar with the president's address, to assume an antilibertarian stance would have probably required a significantly greater attitude change. Ample evidence has accumulated from past research to show that support for civil liberties in America is greatest among those citizens who, as found in these tables, were the most likely to have heard the speech and who offered the strongest endorsement of President Truman's proposal.[51]

There is some evidence and much argument that the public became less supportive of civil liberties from the late 1940s through the mid-1950s.[52] Although with these limited data one cannot wholly dismiss charges of Truman's culpability, one can conclude that his most forceful public expression of an anti-Soviet theme had little apparent effect on anticommunist sentiment in the country. To the extent that critics have employed this speech to indict Truman for the McCarthy era, the evidence presented here weakens the charge.

A second prediction of the revisionist model is that Truman traded upon anticommunism in mobilizing support for his foreign aid package. Although the Truman Doctrine speech does not appear to have stirred up greater anticommunist sentiment, it remains possible that such opinions could, nonetheless, have served as a useful resource. If Truman's support were found to have rested in large part on anticommunist sentiment, this finding would offer at least a partial confirmation of the revisionist's depiction of events. In Table 6-8 support for aid to Greece and Turkey turns out to be weakly associated with anticommunist opinion and quite possibly the result of measurement error.

This absence of a stronger relationship between these variables may strike some readers as surprising, but it corresponds well with the results of Mueller's analysis of public support for the Korean War. Examining responses to a Gallup survey of October 1950, he also found that opinions on the same forbid-Communist-party question were unrelated to support for the Korean War.[53] Although some attitude research during the mid-1950s found an empirical association in the public's perception of internal and external Communist threats on diffuse, generalized variables, the evidence reported here should caution one against imposing a simple opinion structure on the mass public.[54] Anticommunist sentiment at home did not necessarily strengthen the president's hand in fighting Communism abroad.

Table 6-8 Relationship between Response to Forbid-Communist-Party Question and Support for Aid to Greece and Turkey (Percent and Number of Respondents)

Truman's Foreign Aid Requests	Forbid Communist Party		
	No	Yes	Difference[1]
For Greece			
For	55.6	57.6	+2.0
Against	44.4	42.4	
(N)	(753)	(1,280)	
For Turkey			
For	44.5	48.1	+3.6
Against	55.5	51.9	
(N)	(730)	(1,249)	

[1] Neither percentage point difference is statistically significant. Positive differences are in the predicted direction.

SOURCES: American Institute of Public Opinion, Survey No. 393; Kernell, "Truman Doctrine Speech," 35.

Conclusion

The Truman Doctrine speech is an exceptional historic event, yet it has proved to be ordinary as an exercise of opinion leadership. It is historically exceptional because it has come to be widely viewed as ushering in the Cold War. It is exceptional also because contemporaries—at least those in Washington—sensed its profound significance. Finally, it is exceptional as a test case for studying opinion leadership because President Truman was so intent on reconstructing the nation's world view.

The Truman Doctrine speech has been found here to be typical, however, in the way it influenced public opinion. Although the overall extent of exposure to his declaration was indeed high, the president's message did not equally penetrate all segments of the citizenry. Better-educated citizens were on average both more familiar with the speech and, controlling the partisanship, more receptive to its content. And despite the highly charged rhetoric, President Truman's influence on public opinion remained specific to the issue.

Large numbers of citizens rallied behind the president's legislative proposals, but there is little evidence that the speech triggered a massive, domestic anticommunist phobia or exploited anticommunism already prevalent in the country at the time. Instead, opinion formation seems to have followed a normal pattern characterized by consistency in evaluations of source and message. The appeal of Truman's programs varied with respondents according to their evaluations of him as president. Also, approval of aid to Greece and Turkey came disproportionately from among the well-educated segments of the public, which perhaps helps to explain why anticommunism failed to materialize as an important factor.

The effects of President Truman's speech on public opinion are, therefore, consonant with the conventional wisdom of politicians rather than with history. Although the information on which these conclusions are based is, as noted, less than ideal, it is probably the best that will ever be available. Taken together, the findings portray a consistent and reasonable image of opinion leadership. Dramatic events may be able to generate a national phobia, but presidential rhetoric cannot. Instead, President Truman's capacity to lead the nation into a new, foreboding era of foreign affairs reflected in large part the citizenry's trust of him as its leader. How presidents go about maintaining this trust—their popular support—so that their public appeals will be received favorably is the subject of Chapter 7.

Notes

1. Doyle McManus, "Bush Prevailing in Battle With Israeli Lobby," *Los Angeles Times*, September 30, 1991, A16.
2. Jackson Diehl, "Israeli Minister Bars Concessions," *Washington Post*, September 20, 1991, A24; and Clyde Haberman, "Shamir Unmoved by Bush's Threat," *New York Times*, September 14, 1991.
3. Christopher Madison, "A Not-So-Sure Thing," *National Journal*, September 14, 1991, 2200.
4. Thomas L. Friedman, "U.S. Links Loan Guarantees to Freeze on Settlements as Baker's Israel Trip Fails," *New York Times*, September 18, 1991, 1.
5. John E. Yang, "Bush Tries to Ease Loan Crisis," *Washington Post*, September 20, 1991, A24.
6. Ibid., and McManus, A16.
7. Richard A. Brody, *Assessing the President* (Stanford, Calif.: Stanford University Press, 1991), 57-58.
8. The strongest case that presidents sometimes strategically confront crises is made by Ronald H. Hinckley, who documents instances of presidents consulting public opinion polls before deciding on a course of action. See *People, Polls, and Policy-Makers* (New York: Lexington Books, 1992).
9. This incident is described in Henry Kissinger, *Years of Upheaval* (Boston: Little, Brown, 1982), 587-589, 591. See also John Hebers, "Nixon's Motives in Alert Questioned and Defended," *New York Times,* October 26, 1973, 20; "Was the Alert Scare Necessary?" *Time,* November 5, 1973, 15; and "Transcript of Kissinger's News Conference on the Crisis in the Middle East," *New York Times,* October 26, 1973, 18-19.
10. Michael Baruch Grossman and Martha Joynt Kumar, *Portraying the President* (Baltimore: Johns Hopkins University Press, 1981), 237.
11. Hedrick Smith, "O'Neill Now Calls Grenada Invasion 'Justified' Action," *New York Times,* November 9, 1983, 1.
12. Stuart Taylor, Jr., "Experts Question the Legality of the Invasion of Grenada," *New York Times,* October 26, 1983, 7.

13. Barry Sussman reported that a *Washington Post*/ABC News survey the day after the speech showed a sharp rise in Reagan's support. The article provided figures from a November 3-7 survey, roughly a week after the speech. They show that from late September, approval of President Reagan's handling of foreign affairs increased from 42 to 55 percent, and during the same period he passed Mondale on a presidential preference question. "Reagan's Broad Gains in the Wake of Grenada," *Washington Post*, November 21, 1983, 10. See also James M. Perry, "Voters Strongly Back Invasion of Grenada but Waffle on Lebanon," *Wall Street Journal*, November 11, 1983, 1.

14. Republican senator Charles McC. Mathias also commented, "There's no question the President is on a high with Grenada" (Hedrick Smith, "Capitol Hill Clamor Softens as Public's Support Swells," *New York Times*, November 4, 1983, 11). See also Francis X. Clines, "The View from a Capitol Colored by Grenada," *New York Times*, November 4, 1983, 14; and Rudy Abramson, "Democrats Wary of Using Lebanon against Reagan," *Los Angeles Times*, December 10, 1983, 1.

15. The regression slope for the president's popularity in the month preceding the rally event is -.11 and not significant. The change score and prior approval are correlated at -.26.

16. Warren E. Miller, Donald R. Kinder, Steven J. Rosenstone, and the National Election Studies. AMERICAN NATIONAL ELECTION STUDY: 1990-1991 PANEL STUDY OF THE POLITICAL CONSEQUENCES OF WAR/1991 PILOT STUDY [computer file]. Ann Arbor, MI; University of Michigan, Center for Political Studies [producer], 1991. Ann Arbor, MI: Inter-University Consortium for Political and Social Research [distributor], 1991.

17. Brody, *Assessing the President*, pp. 70-71; and Lee Sigelman and Paula J. Conover, "The Dynamics of Presidential Support During International Conflict Situations," *Political Behavior* 3 (1981): 303-318.

18. Carey Rosen, "A Test of Presidential Leadership of Public Opinion: The Split Ballot Technique," *Polity* 6 (Winter 1973): 282-290. For a survey of this literature, see George C. Edwards III, *The Public Presidency* (New York: St. Martin's Press, 1983), 39-46. One experimental study in which the president's job performance is included in the analysis is Lee Sigelman and Carol K. Sigelman, "Presidential Leadership of Public Opinion: From 'Opinion Leader' to 'Kiss of Death'?" *Experimental Study of Politics* 7 (1981): 1022.

19. For analysis of the relation between performance evaluations and support for President Reagan's second round of budget cuts, see Samuel Kernell, "The Presidency and the People: The Modern Paradox," in *The Presidency and the Political System*, ed. Michael Nelson (Washington, D.C.: CQ Press, 1984), 250-253. See also Lee Sigelman, "The Commander in Chief and the Public: Mass Response to Johnson's March 31, 1968 Bombing Halt Speech," *Journal of Political and Military Sociology* 8 (Spring 1980): 1-14.

20. Examples of this research are Eugene J. Rossi, "Mass and Attentive Opinions on Nuclear Weapons Tests and Fallout, 1954-1963," *Public Opinion Quarterly* 29 (Summer 1965): 280-297; and John E. Mueller, *War, Presidents and Public Opinion* (New York: John Wiley and Sons, 1973). The most systematic and comprehensive study of this type to date is Benjamin I. Page and Robert Y. Shapiro, "Presidents as Opinion Leaders: Some New Evidence," *Policy Studies Journal* 12 (June 1984): 647-662.

21. An early exploration of the source-message relation in social psychology is C. I. Hovland and W. Weiss, "The Influence of Source Credibility on Communication Effectiveness," *Public Opinion Quarterly* 15 (1951): 635-650. An outstanding collection of conceptual and research articles on consistency theory is available in

Robert P. Abelson et al., *Theories of Cognitive Consistency: A Sourcebook* (Chicago: Rand McNally, 1968).
22. In a survey of the literature Donald R. Kinder and Susan T. Fiske conclude that for public opinion about the president, "Consistency appears to be a rather unimportant determinant of information-seeking." See "Presidents in the Public Mind," in *Handbook of Political Psychology*, vol. 2, ed. M. G. Hermann (San Francisco: Jossey-Bass, forthcoming).
23. Nelson W. Polsby, "Interest Groups and the Presidency: Trends in Political Intermediation in America," in *American Politics and Public Policy*, ed. Walter Dean Burnham and Martha Wagner Weinberg (Cambridge: MIT Press, 1978), 51.
24. In an earlier study on diffuse support for the presidency, my colleagues and I found strong endorsement for the president as the nation's leader. See Samuel Kernell, Peter W. Sperlich, and Aaron Wildavsky, "Public Support for Presidents," in *Perspectives on the Presidency*, ed. Aaron Wildavsky (Boston: Little, Brown, 1975), 148-183. See also Fred I. Greenstein, "Popular Images of the President," *American Journal of Psychiatry* 122 (November 1965): 523-529; Roberta S. Sigel, "Image of the American Presidency: Part II of an Exploration into Popular Views of Presidential Power," *Midwest Journal of Political Science* 10 (February 1966): 123-137. For a more recent and richly analytic statement, see Kinder and Fiske, "Presidents and the Public Mind."
25. Opinion leadership in foreign policy has long been acknowledged. As examples, see Aaron Wildavsky, "The Two Presidencies," in *The Presidency*, ed. Aaron Wildavsky (Boston: Little, Brown, 1969), 230-243; and Elmer E. Cornwell, Jr., *Presidential Leadership of Public Opinion* (Bloomington: Indiana University Press, 1965).
26. Joseph Jones, *The Fifteen Weeks* (New York: Vintage, 1955; reprint Corte Madera, Calif.: Harbinger, 1964), vii. Much of the subsequent account of political conditions in Washington at the time of the Truman Doctrine speech will be drawn from Jones.
27. *Public Papers of the Presidents of the United States, Harry S Truman, 1947* (Washington, D.C.: Government Printing Office, 1963), 176.
28. Jones, *The Fifteen Weeks*, 178.
29. Charles Bohlen, *The Transformation of American Foreign Policy* (New York: Norton, 1969), 86-87.
30. Richard M. Freeland, *The Truman Doctrine and the Origins of McCarthyism* (New York: Knopf, 1972), 100-101.
31. George F. Kennan, *Memoirs: 1925-1950* (Boston: Little, Brown, 1967), 319-322.
32. Dean Acheson, *Present at the Creation* (New York: Norton, 1969), 292-294.
33. Cited in David S. McLellan and John W. Reuss, "Foreign and Military Policies," in *The Truman Period as a Research Field*, ed. Richard S. Kirkendall (Columbia: University of Missouri Press, 1967), 55-57; and in Freeland, *The Truman Doctrine*, 89.
34. *Memoirs by Harry S Truman: Years of Trial and Hope*, vol. 2 (Garden City, N.Y.: Doubleday, 1956), 105-109.
35. Freeland, *The Truman Doctrine*, 114-118.
36. Bohlen, *Transformation of American Foreign Policy*, 87. This comment has received widespread circulation in revisionist accounts; see Joyce Kolko and Gabriel Kolko, *The Limits of Power* (New York: Harper and Row, 1972), 342; and Herbert Feis, *From Trust to Terror* (New York: Norton, 1970), 193.
37. Neustadt, *Presidential Power*, 39.
38. Three daily newspapers during the period were examined, and subsequent references to the news media reflect their coverage. These are the *New York*

Times, Chicago Daily Tribune, and the *San Francisco Chronicle.* There are as many revisionist interpretations as there are scholars writing on the subject. In some respects Freeland's thesis is among the bolder reinterpretations. All, however, tend to agree in emphasizing the effects of elite rhetoric on the formation of mass opinion.

39. Arthur G. Theoharis devotes five pages in his *Seeds of Repression* (Chicago: Quadrangle Books, 1971) to description of and excerpts from the speech. He concludes that the "oversimplified moralism of this [the speech's] rhetoric was to effectively reduce the administration's own political maneuverability" (56). See pages 47-49 and 51-53 for discussion of the speech. See also Theoharis's "The Rhetoric of Politics: Foreign Policy, Internal Security, and Domestic Politics in the Truman Era, 1945-1950," in *Politics and Policies of the Truman Administration,* ed. Barton Bernstein (Chicago: Quadrangle Books, 1970), 196-241. Walter LaFeber is more explicit in concluding the speech's effect on public opinion in *America, Russia, and the Cold War, 1945-1971,* 2d ed. (New York: John Wiley and Sons, 1972), 43-48. Kolko and Kolko give exhaustive attention to the speech's construction in *The Limits of Power,* 338-346. They suggest that the speech "manipulated" public opinion and "did not so much mirror the global facts as tend to transform and create them." Feis devotes two chapters (25 and 26) in *From Trust to Terror* to the Truman Doctrine speech and obliquely refers to its effect on public opinion in the following way: "Most Americans found temporary relief for their own exasperation and fears in Truman's blunt challenge to Communism and its agents in many lands" (198).

40. In May 1950, only 23 percent had heard of Truman's Point Four Program. Only 71 percent claimed familiarity with the Taft-Hartley legislation in mid-1948, although it was a major campaign issue. In 1963 the same percentage was familiar with the Peace Corps two years after it had been in operation. Only major international events and crises such as Sputnik, the U-2 incident, and the Berlin crisis in 1961 reached a higher plateau of public familiarity. David O. Sears, "Political Behavior," in *The Handbook of Social Psychology,* vol. 5, ed. Gardner Lindzey and Elliot Aronson, 2d ed. (Reading, Mass.: Addison-Wesley, 1969), 324-328.

41. LaFeber, *America, Russia,* 45; and Theoharis, "The Rhetoric of Politics," 206.

42. Another causal sequence might have individuals responding favorably or unfavorably to both the source and the message at the same time. Although such an occurrence poses no real problem for making a general case for presidential opinion leadership, it does describe a different process of opinion change that makes the policy or some other aspect of the appeal (such as acting presidential), rather than prior support, the primary basis of his success. If this is what explains the association of Truman's popularity with support for his aid program, it should show up in a surge of approval in the March 26-27, 1947, survey. From late January until this survey, Truman's job performance rating rose by 11 percentage points. This was part of a trend that had begun in October 1946 and would continue into the fall of 1947. It is impossible to know whether or how much the Truman Doctrine speech boosted the president's standing in the polls.

43. One can also argue that nonsupport among Democratic disapprovers reflected dissonance reduction. Because they had *decided* against the president earlier, opposition to President Truman's policies offered confirmation of their prior choice. See Leon Festinger, *A Theory of Cognitive Dissonance* (Stanford, Calif.: Stanford University Press, 1962).

44. The reason for this support could not have been the topic of the president's appeal; otherwise, Dewey voters would show similar levels of nonsupport. Note that the

exception is for a category that includes few members and is particularly susceptible to sampling error.

45. John E. Mueller, *War, Presidents and Public Opinion* (New York: John Wiley and Sons, 1983), 122-136.
46. Johannes Pederson, "Sources of Change in Public Opinion: A Probability Model with Application to Repeated Cross-sectional Surveys" (Paper delivered at the Annual Meeting of the American Political Science Association, Washington, D.C., September 5-9, 1972), 17-21.
47. LaFeber, *America, Russia,* 45; and Theoharis, "The Rhetoric of Politics," 206.
48. Although it is possible that President Truman's speech increased anticommunist sentiment on domestic affairs, the skewed responses are consistent with previously recorded anticommunism and may be in large part an artifact of question wording.
49. See Samuel Kernell, "The Truman Doctrine Speech: A Case Study of the Dynamics of Presidential Opinion Leadership," *Social Science History* 1 (Fall 1976): 20-45.
50. One might argue familiarity in itself is insufficient, and more direct exposure, such as having heard the address live over radio or having read the text in the newspaper, would have differentiated the public opinion on the civil liberties question in the predicted direction. Given the present findings, this appears unlikely. The 15 percent who claimed unfamiliarity represent a rather pure category, and the 85 percent who said they had heard or read about the speech include respondents who were directly exposed to the stimuli. Therefore, if there is an underlying relationship in the predicted direction, it may be weaker with the cruder operational measures, but there still should be some relationship. Yet there is none. Only if respondents in the middle range of familiarity are assumed to have responded in the opposite direction—which seems implausible—could this argument be maintained in the face of the slight inverse relationship for most of the subsamples.
51. Samuel Stouffer, *Communism, Conformity, and Civil Liberties: A Cross Section of the Nation Speaks Its Mind* (Gloucester, Mass.: P. Smith, 1955).
52. Herbert H. Hyman, "England and America: Climates of Tolerance and Intolerance," in *The Radical Right,* ed. Daniel Bell (Garden City, N.Y.: Doubleday, 1963), 268-306.
53. Mueller, *War, Presidents,* 161-163.
54. Daniel J. Levinson, "Authoritarian Personality and Foreign Policy," *Journal of Conflict Resolution* 1 (March 1957): 37-47. The scale is described and evaluated in *Measures of Political Attitudes,* eds. John P. Robinson, Jerrold G. Rusk, and Kendra B. Head (Ann Arbor: Michigan Survey Research for Social Research, 1968), 306-308.

The Politics of Popularity —————— 7

So long as the citizenry remains attentive to matters of peace and prosperity, so must the president. Otherwise, his popular support will suffer and with it his ability to govern. In this chapter I shall marshal evidence that confirms this relationship between national conditions and evaluations of the president.[1] In our fragmented political system, holding the president accountable has the potential for injustice. The public will occasionally punish a hardworking president who is doing as good a job as one can reasonably expect under unfavorable circumstances, while on another occasion it will reward an underachiever who is blessed by good times.

So be it. Fairness to presidents is less important than motivating them to deal with the country's problems. The public must hold them responsible, even if at times it does so naively. To do less would encourage presidents to shirk their duties. A good example of the functional value of naive judgment by the public can be seen in the aggressive way recent presidents dealt with the energy crisis. No one would deny that events beyond their control caused the steep increases in energy prices during Nixon's and Carter's years in office. Nonetheless, rather than seek refuge behind the truth that the problem was not their fault, both presidents, to their credit, actively sought a solution even at the risk of promoting unpopular policies. The fact that energy-induced inflation ultimately took a heavy toll on the prestige of both men will undoubtedly provide future historians a basis for sympathetic revisions of their performance. But for the citizenry, such sentiments have little value.

One might expect that modern presidents, heavily dependent on popularity for their leadership, would be especially attuned to matters of peace and prosperity. If so, the emergence of such presidents would assure the public of politicians in the White House who will aggressively tackle the country's problems. Before resting easy, however, one must face two possible flaws in this conclusion. First, presidents who routinely go public might misinterpret weak approval ratings. Second, they might undertake activities other than problem solving to improve their standing in the polls. Either way they would be less than full-fledged problem solvers.

No matter how motivated they may be to satisfy the public, if presidents fail to appreciate the real sources of the nation's distress and their low ratings, their actions will probably miss the mark. Politicians who routinely engage in public relations to promote themselves and their policies may be especially prone to misperception. They must have abiding faith in the power of rhetoric. The way these politicians approach the electorate may well shape how they come to view it. Preceding chapters have recounted numerous instances of a modest downturn in a president's poll rating triggering a flurry of public relations activities from the White House. Moreover, the efficacy modern presidents assign to their own rhetoric they do not deny to others, especially members of the press. The readiness with which recent presidents have enlisted television and their attention to the nuance of public relations gives one cause to wonder whether they might fail to comprehend that the citizenry will ultimately judge them not on their rhetoric (or that of anyone else) but on their performance.

Even if a new-styled president realizes that his unpopularity is rooted in something more substantial than the rhetoric of others and that more is required of him than better public relations, the second flaw may come into play: what he is likely to do about it. How will he equate his unpopularity with the nation's problems? Strategic responsiveness and democratic responsibility can yield quite different outcomes, at moments at sharp odds with each other. The American system aspires toward the latter but is guaranteed only the former. A president whose leadership is heavily invested in public opinion offers no assurances. His preoccupation with public opinion guarantees no more than that as he pursues policies he will be acutely sensitive to his popularity ratings.

This condition may pose a problem akin to one raised by Henry Kissinger during the OPEC-induced inflation of the mid-1970s. Because industrial economies and, in turn, incumbent governments were suddenly becoming shaky, Kissinger voiced concern that public policy might become perversely driven by the requirements of political survival.

> There is the problem that as the pressures of their electoral process have increased, governments have become more and more tactically oriented. The more tactically oriented they are, the more short-term their policies. The more short-term their policies, the less successful they are. So we have the paradox that governments following public opinion polls begin to look more and more incompetent. As they look incompetent, confidence in government begins to disintegrate.[2]

The specific historical cause of Kissinger's pathology was a rapid and severe downturn in national economies. The cause of the myopia posed here is more endemic; it is the installation of politicians in the White House who soar or fall in Washington according to their popularity in the country. How to induce self-interested politicians to recognize the citizenry's concerns and to structure their incentives so that self-interest leads them to act in ways that promote the general welfare are related issues that have challenged political theory since the founding of the republic. They are no less relevant today as one ponders the emergence of presidents whose leadership rests heavily on the moods of the American public.

Popularity and Public Relations

If one could have asked Richard Nixon to assess the relative importance of rhetoric and performance as he orchestrated a multifaceted public relations campaign to offset his rising unpopularity after the Laos invasion, or similarly, if one could have posed the issue to Jimmy Carter when he hired public relations consultant Gerald Rafshoon to beef up the White House's media relations, both men, if candid, probably would have admitted they believed that rhetoric—public and press relations—was important in deflecting the full impact of unfavorable political circumstances. Moreover, they could have staked high ground by asserting that their official responsibilities included informing the public about national problems and the administration's policies. Does not the Constitution, after all, require the president to report to Congress on the state of the nation? They could also have argued that any marginal support for themselves generated by these activities would do no one any harm.[3] Public relations purchased for them the time necessary to solve tough problems, thereby allowing them to escape Kissinger's dilemma of strategic myopia. Finally, both men might have added as an afterthought that whatever the effect, it was far easier to turn on a media campaign than to turn off a war or inflation.

Public Relations as a Convenient and Satisfying Activity

The relative ease of public relations is no trivial matter. Without making any special claims for its efficacy, modern presidents may be tempted to resort to public relations for the simple reason that it is manageable. Chapter 4 showed that Presidents Nixon, Carter, and Reagan were preoccupied in their prime-time addresses with the Vietnam War, historically high inflation, and double-digit unemployment, respectively. None of these was in any way a trivial issue that rhetoric could gloss over. In going to the airwaves, these presidents sought the public's patience. However much they hoped to gain politically in their television addresses, their activities had the piquant quality of being doable.

Convenience alone is insufficient to explain the dedicated way in which presidents and many of their staff pursue public and press relations. Presidents do it because they believe it wins the public's sympathy. One need not make presidents into Frank Capra's arrogant manipulators of public opinion in his film *Meet John Doe* to have them believe that they can talk their way into the hearts of the citizenry. Well before they had the wherewithal to do so, presidents must have felt this way. Recall FDR's 1939 lament on the slow development of television.

The desire to explain one's actions and to respond to criticism springs from human nature. Probably every occupant of the White House has at some point blamed press treatment for his troubles in the country.[4] Probably each has also depreciated the public's current disfavor by stressing the proverbial "burdens of office" and "complexity of problems," neither of which the average citizen can appreciate. In the face of tough problems and a "bad press," presidents want to tell their side of the story. Books on the subject with such sinister titles as *The Selling of the President* and *On Bended Knee* miss the point.[5]

However phrased, the public's lack of expertise offers a comforting rationalization to a president who must otherwise confront the stark reality that he has failed. As self-serving as these sentiments are, one may assume they are sincere. The fine line between "bad news" and a "bad press" gives presidents ample opportunity to think this way. That these feelings are genuine helps to explain why modern presidents are quick to go public to defend their actions. Rationalizations that offered presidents of an earlier era a measure of solace today prescribe a course of action.

How Public Relations Matter

Thus far in this analysis I have treated going public to counter falling popular support as a form of therapy and the product of an interaction between human nature and advanced technology. There is, however, another reason, peculiar to the modern setting, why presidents will be especially inclined to resort to public relations to offset a decline in the polls. What fellow Washingtonians say publicly about the president's performance will, in fact, significantly influence the way people in the country judge him. What makes this explanation peculiar to the modern era is the extraordinary volume of messages transmitted from Washington to the country. One of the ways in which individualized pluralism is distinguished from institutionalized pluralism is precisely this attribute. Because present-day Washington is less insulated from outside pressures, politicians are both more sensitive to public opinion and more inclined to try to shape it as a way of controlling their own destiny and of influencing that of other politicians. One member of Congress, Senator Jesse Helms, went so far as to try to gain control of a major network for the stated purpose of altering its putative political slant in reporting public affairs.

An important result of the increased two-way communications is that the ordinary citizen has gained more information about the president and more varied opinions about his performance. Veteran Washington correspondent James Deakin concurs:

> The relationship between the president of the United States and the nation's news media is a subject of endless fascination. It exerts an irresistible attraction for presidents, members of the White House staff, reporters,

© 1991 by Herblock in The Washington Post

editors and broadcasters, politicians, bureaucrats, political scientists, historians and an increasing number of ordinary citizens. For a long time, it was a local cottage industry in Washington, of no great interest to the rest of the country. Now it is a vast national enterprise whose tentacles spread into every village and shire.

How is the president getting along with the news media? Are they treating him well or badly? Is he a master of communications or an ineffective performer on the tube? Is he accessible to reporters and candid with them? Or is he secretive, misleading the press. . . ? Why doesn't he have more press conferences? Why have his press conferences become such increasingly meaningless spectacles? Why does he manipulate the press so brazenly to achieve his purposes? Why doesn't he use the press more effectively to achieve his purpose? Why is the press so subservient to the president? Why is the press so hostile to the president? The relationship between the president and the news media is a long-running soap. Drama. Suspense. Conflict. And a large, rapt audience.[6]

The recency with which the American public has become privy to political relations in Washington probably accounts for why presidential scholars have traditionally paid little attention to these events, compared, say, with the presidential pundits who look for great consequence from the most trivial pursuits. Conventional scholarship insists that presidents stand or fall on their performance in providing satisfactory conditions for the ordinary citizen. Richard E. Neustadt writes, "What a president should be is something most men see by light of what is happening to *them*. Their notions of the part a president should play, their satisfaction with the way he plays it, are affected by their private hopes and fears. Behind their judgments of performance lie the consequences in their lives. What threatens his prestige is their frustration." [7] Whatever slant the press may take, bad news will represent objectively unfavorable conditions and events—that is, poor performance. Stacked against paychecks and prices, a "bad press" and criticism from other politicians are inconsequential. So the argument goes. Maligned presidents may respond to the rhetoric of others, but they are just making noise as far as public opinion is concerned. Their performance is all that really matters.

With this in mind, Neustadt speculated that press revelations that Eisenhower's chief of staff, Sherman Adams, had improperly accepted gifts from an individual who transacted business with the government probably caused the White House more consternation than it should have.[8] President Eisenhower's approval rating remained stable as long as national conditions were static. It surged temporarily with the peace in Korea and briefly dipped below 50 percent approving during the recession of late 1957. President Johnson's popularity declined as U.S. casualties in Vietnam mounted; Nixon's and Carter's tracked inflation; Reagan's fell sharply in 1982 as unemployment skyrocketed. And the cushion of support provided President Bush in early 1991 by Desert Storm did not prevent his popularity ratings from dropping below 50 percent later in the year as the recession deepened. These are the kinds of experiences conventionally enlisted to explain past presidents' declining popular support.[9] They make eminent sense. If such experiences are *all* that matter, however, presidential self-promotion through intensive public relations makes no sense at all.

The public's reliance upon experience rather than news about Washington politics is consonant with the kind of political setting for which a bargaining president is ideally suited. Discounting the significance of public relations means all the more that presidents will succeed in the country only as they successfully negotiate coalitions that implement policies that work. Having the public monitor the outcomes of policies rather than the politics involved in their creation contributes to Washington's insularity and in large measure shields the bargaining society from intensive public posturing.

The analysis in preceding chapters provides reason to suspect that this traditional, exclusively experiential view of public opinion is deficient and that modern presidents may be smart in going public to check their adversaries and counter bad news. In Chapter 6, for example, presidents were found to be communicators whose messages are endorsed or rejected largely according to the citizen's regard for them as a source. In Chapter 5, strong circumstantial evidence of this appeared in the testimonies and behavior of other politicians in response to President Reagan's efforts at opinion leadership. Moreover, when the president's public standing changes from, say, 50 to 45 percent approving, relatively few citizens need to be monitoring politics in Washington for events there to generate prominent feedback in the monthly poll reports.

Recent survey and experimental research in public opinion also raises questions about the adequacy of relying exclusively upon direct, personal experiences to explain political judgments. Consider, for example, how the economy as an issue has been recently discovered to influence voting in congressional elections.[10] When survey respondents are asked general questions such as, "Do you think economic conditions in the country are getting better or worse?" their answers tend to be more closely aligned with their voting preferences than are their answers to other questions that deal exclusively with the respondent's personal financial well-being. Responses to "Are you personally better or worse off financially today than a year ago?" are at best only weakly related to voting preferences. Employing multivariate statistical procedures, researchers have found that these personal experiences influence political behavior largely to the degree that they filter into the more general sentiments, but there is no certainty that they will be so elevated.[11] This helps to explain why over the years polls have repeatedly found unemployed respondents holding political evaluations of the current president's performance similar to those of their employed counterparts.[12] "In evaluating the president," concluded Donald R. Kinder, "citizens seem to pay principal attention to the nation's economic predicament, and comparatively little to their own."[13]

Generalized evaluations of the current state of the economy and other politically relevant conditions reflect precisely the kinds of civic information citizens are likely to obtain in watching evening news programs and in reading their local newspapers. More direct evidence on the effect of news on presidential evaluations is available from an experimental study of opinions about then-president Jimmy Carter. Several groups of subjects attended six evening sessions in late 1980 and early 1981 in which they watched what was said to be a taped viewing of the previous evening's news broadcast. In fact, portions of each newscast had been altered to present a series of stories on one of several topics—American defense preparedness, inflation, or pollution of the environment. After viewing these messages over the course of a week, the subjects began assessing President Carter's overall performance by the issue to which they had been repeatedly exposed. The researchers concluded that "a president's overall reputation, and, to a lesser extent, his apparent competence, both depend upon the presentation of network news programs." [14]

The finding that generalized sentiments, based on the kind of civic data conveyed by news rather than personal experience, are consequential for political behavior is crucial to understanding how citizens in an information age evaluate their leaders. Later in this chapter I shall return to this finding in considering the kinds of policies for which the citizenry rewards and punishes the president in the polls. Here the implication for the effect of elite discourse on presidential approval is indirect but no less crucial. What the public learns from national news about the state of the country and from the president's competitors about his performance will frequently be more relevant than personal experience in their evaluations of him. If a president sometimes becomes exercised when the Commerce Department issues a high inflation rate, or when a commentator or another politician publicly questions the wisdom of his policy, or when members of the press appear to dwell upon his failures rather than his achievements, perhaps he is right to do so. Today, what others in Washington have to say about the president may shape what the rest of the country thinks of him.

Does this mean that the traditional observation that the president's standing in Washington bears little relation to his status in the country was wrong? Not at all. Washington has changed. What was true for Presidents Truman and Eisenhower may not be for Presidents Reagan and Bush. If the public now pays closer attention to politics in Washington than before, it is not because citizens today are somehow cognitively processing political informa- tion differently.[15] Nor has there been a national epidemic of "Potomac fever." Rather, the reason is simply that citizens are exposed to more—and more critical—information about the president than ever before. This is the argument. Now for some evidence.

News from the Capital: Then and Now

The record of White House coverage in the press during the past 30 years confirms the kind of change detected by Deakin and hypothesized here. One commonly employed indicator of the growing preponderance of presidential news is obtained by comparing it with news about Congress. Such comparisons are available for news coverage extending back to the mid-nineteenth century when, by one account, presidents received less press attention than congressional committees. During the twentieth century, the share of White House news has increased steadily to the point that today it attracts substantially more news stories than Congress.[16]

Behind the increased coverage of the presidency lie differences in how news was reported from one era to the next. Treatment by the Washington press of two presidential events 20 years apart illustrates this better. The first is a confrontation between President Eisenhower and the White House press corps; the second, the candid revelations of President Reagan's Budget Director David Stockman to a Washington journalist. Both events are purely political "news," generated by and about Washingtonians. To the extent they were communicated to the country, both stories were potentially damaging to the president's prestige. In the first instance, the message was not transmitted to the nation, the potential harm not realized. In the second instance, the story occupied front pages of the nation's newspapers and appeared prominently on the networks' evening news programs for nearly a week.

The first comes from an Eisenhower news conference in November 1953, shortly after Attorney General Herbert Brownell accused former president Truman of harboring a known "Communist spy" in his administration. As President Eisenhower responded to the regular assemblage of White House correspondents, he found himself quickly dogged with pointed questions about Brownell's statement.[17] When confronted with conflictual matters, especially those involving disagreement with other politicians, President Eisenhower typically obfuscated and temporized. He did so here, much to the chagrin of the correspondents. When challenged by a reporter's rhetorical question whether the Eisenhower administration had not, in fact, embraced McCarthyism, the president, stunned and flustered by the questioner's directness, replied that he would "take the verdict of the body on that." From the available accounts, it appears that at this point the president lost control of the conference. He stood watching, dumbfounded, as *New York Times* reporters Anthony H. Leviero and James Reston canvassed fellow correspondents. The verdict went against Eisenhower. That such an incident occurred is less remarkable today perhaps than that it failed to receive prominent coverage in the nation's press. Deakin relates this incident to illustrate the kinds of understandings that existed between the president and the press during this era.

> Very little of the atmosphere of Eisenhower's confrontations with reporters found its way into their stories. There was an occasional hint that the proceedings had been raucous, but overall the news accounts were bland. What had been a knock-down-drag-out at the press conference emerged in the news stories as a waltz-me-around-again-Willie. The press conferences

were essentially in-house encounters between the president and the reporters. The news, in the Eisenhower era, was objective. The flavor was lacking. So the public was not aroused. It slept easy.[18]

In vivid contrast, when David Stockman's book-length confessional was published in the September 1981 issue of the *Atlantic,* it was the gala political event of the season in Washington.[19] Everyone who had opposed President Reagan's budget program or whose clientele had suffered from it found in Stockman's "education" vindication for their differing view. And after months of imposed silence they now spoke up. Washingtonians had a field day predicting what President Reagan would do and, after he took Stockman "to the woodshed," forecasting when his by-now contrite young miscreant would reappear in public.

Unlike the preceding case, little about this incident was confidential, beginning with Stockman's ill-advised remarks and ending with his meeting with the president. To the contrary, much of what took place was designed to create publicity. The budget director lunched weekly with a well-known correspondent, revealing all kinds of damaging gossip with the full knowledge that by fall his comments would be published.

Dwight Eisenhower had a budget director, as had all of his predecessors back to President Harding; but unlike Reagan's and, before him, Carter's (Bert Lance), Eisenhower's assistant was a private officer whose sole mandate was to advise his president. Consequently, Joseph Dodge never became the "personality" outside Washington as did Stockman, who around the country became a favorite subject of political cartoonists and the object of such epithets as the "blow dried reaper." Had Dodge made similar observations about budget making under Eisenhower, they probably would not have attracted much press attention, much less become a major exposé.[20]

Eisenhower's run-in with the press corps did not alter public opinion because few, if any, of the participants in the news business reported it. This was certainly not the case with the Stockman story. Beyond the readership of the *Atlantic,* most of the country soon learned about the confessional from wire service and network news stories throughout the next week. The Gallup Poll felt it a public matter sufficiently familiar to warrant adding a battery of questions about the incident to one of its national surveys. Within two weeks of the appearance of the magazine article on newsstands, two-thirds of the respondents in a national survey reported "hearing or reading" about the "recent events of David Stockman." Among those familiar with the story, most felt that Budget Director Stockman's activities had hurt President Reagan's position politically and, by a narrow margin, that Stockman should leave office.[21] As discussed earlier, several unfavorable conditions were eroding the president's popular support in the fall of 1981—the most prominent among them, a rising unemployment rate. But the abundant adverse publicity Stockman generated hurt Reagan nationally in a fashion unknown to presidents of an earlier era.

Although both incidents were memorable in Washington, they differ in that the Eisenhower story was a nonevent in the country. Differences in the individual details of each story may have contributed to their dissimilar national coverage. Yet they illustrate in their respective extremes how differently present-day Washington elites conduct business from their not-so-distant predecessors and how these differences affect the way citizens judge their leaders.

These content analyses and case studies should be understood to offer no more than suggestive evidence of the hypothesis that presidents *must* pay closer attention to press and public relations today because they matter more. Rarely is the evidence of public opinion, such as that for Stockman, available for claiming more. The data necessary for citizens critically to judge the president's Washington performance is, however, increasingly easy to come by. It is safe, therefore, to assume that presidents will continue to engage in intensive public relations to counteract the probable effects of unfortunate news on public opinion.

Chapter 6 concluded that susceptibility of modern politicians to the president's public appeals is bringing the president's reputation in Washington and his prestige in the country into an alignment that did not exist in Truman's and Eisenhower's time. Another reason for this convergence is that events in Washington, which in an earlier era would have only pricked the attention of the small segment of the public who are politically attentive, today frequently hold the entire country enthralled. Peace and prosperity may remain the primary concerns of citizens as they judge the president, but president watchers both in Washington and throughout the country are sharing and comparing data as never before. The modern president who fails to rebut unfriendly remarks of Washington elites or to blunt criticism from the press may soon begin hearing echoes of these complaints emanating from the country.

The general strategy of going public, discussed in previous chapters, applies also to modern presidents who go public to help themselves. Technology makes it possible for them to satisfy the natural urge to answer their critics. Outsiders in the White House, who achieved their position by repeatedly winning presidential primaries, have a special faith in rhetoric. Channels of competing and at times unfavorable news from Washington have opened up as the president's adversaries also go public. And a less deferential news media more willingly transmit, if not actually stimulate, unfavorable stories about the White House. All this suggests that when a president goes public to counter his decline in the polls, he may be acting on more than rationalization. Indeed, he may be acting rationally.

Thinking Strategically about Popularity

Having considered the case for intensive public relations, one may have several questions about the modern president who often goes public. Does he recognize a world beyond communications and images? Will he retain the perspective that a bad press—even when it is that—feeds on bad news? Does he grasp that only by solving the nation's problems will he solve his own as president?

The anecdotal record for recent presidents cautions against alarmism. The convergent forces promoting public relations in the White House have not overwhelmed the capacity of presidents and their advisers to monitor accurately the concerns of the citizenry. Parts of the institutional apparatus that has grown up in the modern White House mitigate against such myopia. The president's pollsters and other staff who gather opinion data from a variety of sources continuously record the public's views on current issues. A president's heavy investment in public opinion should serve as a counterweight to whatever faith he places in rhetoric. Jimmy Carter's press secretary, Jody Powell, expressed a sentiment one commonly hears from the White House: "Communications and the management of them, the impact is marginal. The substance of what you do and what happens to you over the long haul is more important, particularly on the big things like the economy." [22]

Although presidents freely blame the news media for their difficulties in the polls, there is little evidence that they have lost sight of the real sources of the public's disillusionment with them. Lyndon Johnson and Jimmy Carter suffered both in the polls and with the press; against the latter, their spokesmen sometimes railed bitterly. Yet neither man had any difficulty appreciating the effects of major issues on his popular support. Johnson observed, "I think [my grandchildren] will be proud of two things. What I did for the Negro and seeing it through in Vietnam for all of Asia. The Negro cost me 15 points in the polls and Vietnam cost me 20." [23] Carter, too, was aware of the real reason for his low standing in the polls:

> I think the Roper poll shows that I was below 60 percent, the Gallup Poll about 60 percent. Of course, I would like to have higher than either one of those, but I think that the controversial nature of some of the things that we put forward inherently causes a concern about me and reduces my standing in the polls, although I didn't want the prediction to come true. When I announced that I would put forward an energy package, I predicted my poll rating would drop 15 percent. [24]

Reagan, despite his repeated complaints of unfair coverage throughout 1982, faced up to double-digit unemployment when he confided to a reporter in early 1983 that if his policies failed to produce a recovery it "obviously . . . would be a sign" that he should not seek reelection. [25] Meanwhile, White House Chief of Staff James Baker ranked for reporters the following reasons for President Reagan's decline in the polls: "the economy, the economy and the economy." [26] These are the kinds of excuses in which one should wish presidents to indulge.

The dependence of modern presidents on public support appears, therefore, to keep them attentive to "real world" problems, even as they engage in public relations. Because strict adherence to his fiduciary responsibility to promote the general welfare occasionally requires the president to adopt unpopular policies that undermine his public support, one may assume that he also behaves strategically. That is to say, as the president makes policy, his own political well-being will be a foremost concern.

A strategic president must answer for himself two kinds of questions. First, what does the public want? That is, what will it tolerate, and what will it not? A president may have hunches, but he can never be sure how the public will respond to an initiative. Those presidents who lead by going public will be especially dedicated to reducing uncertainty on this score. Staffed with professional pollsters, econometricians, and political analysts, modern presidents go to great lengths to improve their understanding of public opinion.[27]

The second question a strategic president must address is much like the first, except that he must ask it of himself. Having defined what he wants to accomplish, he must decide how much popular support he is willing to give up to secure his policy goals. This question arises because no president will be a strict popularity maximizer. Popularity is, after all, a resource that allows a president to go public, a means for achieving other ends. The decision to spend some of his support on a favored program, to husband what support remains, or to seek more is complex and fraught with risk. This introspective question is probably familiar to all twentieth-century presidents, but acutely so to those modern incumbents whose leadership is closely bound to their popularity. To appreciate better how presidents adapt policy to the requirements of popular support, one needs to understand how they go about answering these questions about the public and themselves. As E. E. Schattschneider exhorted the profession half a century ago, "What is now needed is a politician's theory of politics."[28]

Different presidents, similarly situated, may arrive at different answers. Strategic judgment will depend on the composition of the president's coalition of support, which is largely identified by his party label; on his own policy aspirations; on his view of the office and its responsibilities; and on his personal makeup, particularly his willingness to take risks. It is beyond the scope of this book to survey recent incumbents on these attributes, and to speculate on how they might be configured in some future president would be an exercise in fatuity. One can, however, learn more about how presidents think through the relation between their political options and their popular support by examining the common political circumstances that condition their choices.

How Much Popularity Is Enough?

Popularity is like ice cream in that the more of it one consumes, the less satisfying the next helping will be. Beyond some point, the value of additional increments of support will diminish sharply. The point at which diminishing return sets in will vary from one president to the next, depending on his leadership style and on his political circumstances in Washington. Harry

Truman disdained pandering to the polls (his euphemism for the public) and has been judged to have more freely spent his popular support than did others who have occupied the office since the time the president's popularity could be measured with any precision. Not surprisingly, Truman's tenure was marked by greater swings of popularity, an experience he once described as "like riding a tiger." [29]

His successor has often been depicted as a man who valued the public's approbation far more than most presidents. According to one recent portrait, President Eisenhower coveted the public's favor as if it were an end in itself. Fred I. Greenstein writes, "Eisenhower's seemingly effortless facility in weaning public confidence never stopped him from also working to find additional ways to enhance his support." [30] Eisenhower's failure to champion unpopular programs, his refusal to engage critics, incuding those within his administration, his pusillanimous defense of the State Department against McCarthy's witch hunt, and his willingness to delegate to subordinates responsibility for unhappy occurrences are all perfectly consistent with this view of a president intent on preserving his prestige as if it were an end rather than a means to other goals. Greenstein summarizes Eisenhower's style as "refusing to go public as a politician, looking carefully rather than leaping, and striving always to represent himself as President of all Americans." [31] In this both Eisenhower and Truman appear exceptional. For the others, the point at which a diminishing return in popularity sets in falls somewhere between the endpoints established by these two presidents.

Each president must answer for himself how much support is enough, but one may assume that none will have an insatiable appetite. Whatever equilibrium forces may be operating within the country to prevent the president from long remaining universally beloved, one such force operates within the White House itself—namely, that popular presidents will tend to spend surpluses of support. As discussed in Chapter 5, Reagan's polls began to show increasing public disapproval of his job performance before the attempted assassination in 1981. To a reporter's query about this early development, one Reagan aide observed matter-of-factly, "The job's gotten into the fire more quickly with this [budget] proposal than in normal administrations because of [its] comprehensive nature. There's resistance to change." A Republican pollster added, "He's spending his savings [popularity] and he has less in the bank now, that's all." [32]

Another principle governing the strategic expenditure of popular support is, the closer the next election, the farther away the point of diminishing return. Whatever the role going public plays in his leadership, every sitting president is aware that his popularity is critical to his reelection chances. Today, with party nomination decided by caucuses and primaries, unpopular incumbents are no longer even guaranteed renomination.

At what date on the electoral calendar presidents become transfixed on husbanding and where necessary rekindling the public's approbation depends upon how much of it they already have and how much of it they think they will require to win reelection. In the spring of 1983, with President Reagan the least popular of any president by the end of his first two years, many Republican senators who had been Reagan's cheerleaders just a year earlier began carping that the president was shying away from tough budget cuts in deference to an election nearly two years away. By summer, White House aides confirmed the president's election concerns while announcing an extensive itinerary of political travel that would include a visit to China. Reflecting his unprecedented weak popularity at midterm, President Reagan's fence-mending activities appropriately began earlier than most. Spring of the election year is the season one hears politicians voicing unfamiliar concerns, in some instances the same concerns they had turned a deaf ear to only a few months earlier.[33] Perhaps not coincidentally, presidents tend to become more popular during the six months preceding the beginning of the reelection campaign.[34]

In considering how much popularity is enough, Eisenhower's political adviser Bryce Harlow appeared conservative when he confided, "The trick is to get the president into the fourth year with an approval rating still over 50 percent." [35] In fact, his estimate accords well with the track record of the seven incumbents who have sought reelection since 1948. In Figure 7-1 each president's share of the vote is plotted against his job performance rating for the preceding June. The regression line crosses 50 percent of the vote precisely at 50 percent approving.[36] During the postwar era, no president lost who entered a reelection campaign with half or more of the public behind him. According to the estimate in Figure 7-1, any incumbent who fails to achieve this golden mean is destined to lose. Understandable was the panic that struck the Bush White House early in the 1992 election year when his approval rating dropped to 46 percent and failed to improve after his State of the Union address.

Strategic presidents balance their ongoing need for popular support against their desire to achieve policy goals important to them and to their party's core constituencies, and therefore they do not always automatically act to increase their popularity. When a president enjoys a surplus of popular support, he may be expected to try to convert some of it into support for his policy objectives. The pursuit of popularity will also be regulated by the proximity of the next election. As the election nears, a president will be tempted to husband even what he regards as surplus support. Accordingly, an unpopular president nearing reelection should come as close to resembling a single-minded popularity maximizer as one will find in the White House, and newly elected presidents basking in victory may be expected to be as programmatic as they will be for the remainder of their term. Franklin Roosevelt, Lyndon Johnson, and Ronald Reagan all exploited their early support to advance ideological policies dear to their core constituencies. Their failure to sustain their early accomplishments has frequently been blamed

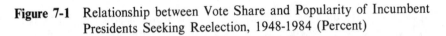

Figure 7-1 Relationship between Vote Share and Popularity of Incumbent Presidents Seeking Reelection, 1948-1984 (Percent)

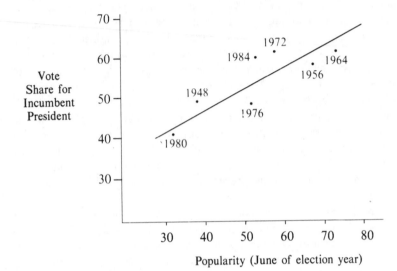

Popularity (June of election year)

NOTE: The estimated equation represented in the regression line in the figure is Vote = 30.4 + .44 × Popularity. This single variable explains 70 percent of the variance in the vote share of the incumbent president.

upon the intrusion of unfortunate events that made them lose their way, and the historical record provides numerous instances to support this argument. Fully cognizant of its potential damage for his domestic agenda, Lyndon Johnson initially resisted being sidetracked by Vietnam.[37] Even were no such events to intrude, the strategic considerations should, however, inspire presidents to pursue their preferred programs less and those that promise to enhance their popular support more. The advancing electoral calendar and the seemingly inexorable loss of their early support force them to respond to current events.[38]

Another more fundamental consideration is involved in weighing policy against popularity—the cost in public support of a particular policy venture. The severity of the trade-off will vary from one issue to the next. Some will impose little or no costs at all; a few may actually increase the president's popular base.[39] How presidents calculate this trade-off is the subject of the following sections.

Calculating Gains and Losses

This chapter so far has treated the president's approval rating as if it were a highly liquid commodity—something that can be spent and conserved in precise, calculated amounts. It is, of course, no such thing. Calling popular support a currency conveys its instrumental value, but once one tries to calculate the gains and losses resulting from a particular policy, the glint of this metaphor begins to fade. The exchange value of popularity will always be somewhat uncertain, depending upon the skill of the president in going public and upon only dimly understood dynamics of opinion change. At times a policy will provoke a particular constituency to withdraw its approval en masse—as in the farmers' reactions to President Carter's embargo of grain exports to the Soviet Union in 1980. At other times a policy will elicit no apparent response. There is perhaps no better example of the uncertain public reception to presidential actions than Gerald Ford's pardon of Richard Nixon. Could he, or for that matter could his pollsters, have foreseen that his brief televised announcement of the pardon would precipitate a 30-point drop in his approval rating or that nearly two years later voters would cite it as much as anything else as the reason for whatever unfavorable opinion they harbored toward him?[40] In a world where politicians strive for safe and certain outcomes, spending popularity can be a risky venture.

The downside risks and ease of miscalculation do not prevent presidents from entering the market, however. For presidents who are inclined to go public, popularity is, after all, their chief resource. Moreover, in that gains and losses of popular support inhere in presidential choice, strategic calculation is an activity that cannot be lightly ignored. President Reagan and his aides must have frequently pondered whether to fire James Watt, the controversial secretary of the interior. This issue arose recurrently because they knew that to do nothing might itself be costly. Strategic questions of this caliber confront every president. President Bush grappled with several issues. Should unemployment benefits be extended another 12 weeks? Should he sign or veto a new civil rights bill establishing new standards for combating discrimination in the workplace? How should the administration respond to the variety of health-care reform proposals circulating in Congress? These questions did not arise principally out of concern for Bush's popularity. They were policy matters that demanded a presidential position before other governmental actors would do their part. Yet they all contained important political stakes. One may assume that in none of these cases did the political ramifications escape President Bush or his staff. For a president to fail or to refuse to think about policy strategically is tantamount to a decision to spend his support inefficiently.

Presidents must associate policy with popularity. The reflections of Presidents Johnson and Carter show that they do, at least in retrospect. Although the question of how they calculate their gains and losses has no simple answer, presidents may be expected to consider the political consequences of their policy choices in one of two alternative ways.[41]

The first approach I shall call "general problem solving," or GPS. It offers a president a simple decision rule and promises not to lead him down too risky a path. In exchange, it limits the field of strategic policy choice and may require that the president produce outcomes that are beyond his capacity. The alternative approach can be stated largely as the converse of general problem solving. It requires the president to take a highly differentiated view of the public and to entertain a myriad of policy choices that would permit him to stitch together a national governing coalition from the particularistic and sometimes conflicting interests of diverse constituencies. This approach I shall call the "marginals" strategy.

These approaches will not always prescribe conflicting policies. In confronting a dominant national issue, the president may find that he is also making a strong bid to attract marginal constituencies into his coalition. Although the president's choice of strategies will depend in part on his own experiences as a politician, the approach he finds most attractive will sometimes have more to do with the character of the policy under consideration than with the character of the man making the choice.

To see how the substance of policy affects strategic considerations, it is helpful to classify the president's policy options. First, some policies will be national in scope, and their benefits broadly distributed. The most commonly cited example is national defense. Because of the president's national constituency, the visibility of his actions, and his position in national policy making, he more than anyone else will find his choices cloaked in a collective goods mantle. To continue the above example, as soon as the president's defense proposal reaches Congress and is parceled among the various committees and subcommittees, it will be disaggregated into a collection of decisions, each of which may have quite specific effects on particular constituencies. Which military installations and defense contractors should provide for the collective defense is historically how the president's defense proposals get restated. On its face, the general problem-solving strategy appears well suited to issues of this kind; for this reason it is a peculiarly presidential strategy.[42]

A second category of policies at the other extreme are those in which the president's choice will have highly specific, or particularistic, effects in the country. Here, specific localities and constituencies can be readily identified as the chief beneficiaries or victims of the president's policy. If there is a collective goods rationale for the policy, it will tend to be secondary to its particular effects in the way the public and Washington elites view the policy. Extension of unemployment benefits, an excise tax on the purchase of luxury yachts and expensive automobiles, start-up loans through the Small Business Administration, reregulation of the cable television industry, and duties on lumber imports from Canada are issues of this type that confronted Bush from 1989 through 1992. A policy's political ramifications may be assumed to be as specific as its effects on particular constituencies; consequently, policies of this kind invite presidents to take a highly differentiated view of the public in assessing potential gains and losses.

Sometimes a third kind of policy arises in which both its national and particular effects are prominent. The general welfare is at issue, but at the same time some constituencies will be asked to suffer more than others.[43] The most persistent policy question of this type is the economy. The general welfare component can be seen in widespread agreement over what an ideal economy should be, but since few ever expect this ideal to be fully realized, ample room remains for disagreement. Which economic problems of the moment should the White House address, and who should be asked to make the necessary sacrifice to correct the economy's course? Differing opinions arise in large part because economic conditions have disproportionate effects on the labor force. Blue-collar workers, for example, are hurt more by increases in unemployment than are white-collar workers. Conversely, some economists have argued that upper-income groups suffer relatively greater losses from inflation.

These economic effects take on special political significance because they correspond to the party cleavages of the electorate. Given their respective constituencies, Democrats and their core support group, organized labor, have emphasized employment policies, and Republicans and their allies in the business community have traditionally shown greater concern with inflation. Since the ideal economy is unrealizable, politicians as purveyors of their party's creed will frequently find cause to dispute the priorities contained in any administration's current economic program.

There is another aspect of economic relations that pushes policy discussion in this realm toward the particular distribution of benefits rather than the general welfare. "It turns out that good economic policies that bring you better growth, better employment, lower inflation and higher levels of prosperity usually have short-run cost," observed Beryl Sprinkel, who as chair of Reagan's Council of Economic Advisers was in a good position to appreciate the political dilemmas attending economic policy. He elaborated, "You go through the pain first, and get the goodies later. If I could change something, I would certainly get the goodies up front because it would solve a lot of political problems." [44] Fellow economist Lester Thurow similarly argues that these up-front costs to particular constituencies prevent good economic planning in the United States.[45] Economists may provide politicians with any number of economic proposals that would eventually move the economy to some better state for everyone, he argues, but because each imposes immediate cost to specific groups, presidents will be reluctant or unable to implement them.[46]

That the costs precede the gains is less significant in evaluating the relative attractiveness of GPS and the marginals strategies than that the short-run costs tend to be distributed unevenly. To improve one aspect of the economy, politicians must tamper with another; one group will be asked to pay for another's gain. The Phillips curve trade-off between inflation and unemployment is the most prominent example of the distributional consequences of alternative economic policies. The country is threatened with "runaway" inflation, and the administration responds by trying to reduce economic expansion by trimming federal spending and tightening credit to consumers and producers.[47] The predictable consequence is an increase in unemployment. When unemployment is high, conversely, presidents have typically sought to stimulate the economy by increasing government spending, cutting taxes, or lobbying the Federal Reserve to loosen credit. As presidents evaluate different doses of economic medicine, they must—to economists' lament—weigh the requirements of politics against those of economic theory.[48]

Within the past half century, managing the economy has joined "maintaining the peace" as one of the president's chief responsibilities. A president's success has been closely linked with his ability to maintain balanced growth. Because economic policy involves both the broad and the specific distribution of benefits, it affords an opportunity to study the implications for public support of these alternative approaches to calculating the political gains and losses embedded in policy alternatives.

General Problem Solving. Edward R. Tufte has offered a straightforward statement of the general problem-solving approach to popular support: "If there is a single, highly visible economic problem that is very important to the electorate, [the president should] seek preelection improvements on that problem regardless of the economic priorities of the party program." [49] Tufte's prescription applies to preelection economic policy, but one can readily extend it to other times and issues. Essentially, what GPS asks of the president is programmatic flexibility. The president who succeeds will be the one who neither slavishly serves the preferences of his political party and its core constituency nor panders to the special claims of narrow constituencies on the periphery of his coalition for maximum short-run payoff. Rather, he must address whatever economic problem threatens to throw the economy out of balance. If the unemployment rate had risen, say, by three percentage points in the past year, the president, regardless of his political party, should generate employment.

When more than one economic malady is present, especially when they appear to require contradictory policy responses as in the Phillips trade-off, Tufte has the president follow the preferences of his political party. Facing both high unemployment and inflation, a Republican in the White House would tackle inflation; a Democrat, unemployment. To be consistent with the spirit of GPS, however, the president would continue to address whichever problem appeared to be most severe. In the abstract, this kind of problem-solving politician cuts an attractive figure—a rare instance where the requirements of the general welfare are congruent with those of political ambition.

Immediately, however, GPS raises the question, could a president succeed by being seemingly indifferent to the particular distributional effects of his policy? Earlier I offered a rationale for an affirmative answer in the survey findings that individuals evaluate the president's performance more according to their assessment of general economic conditions than on the basis of their current financial well-being. This allows the distinct possibility that the president will not be exposed to the political costs—at least in public opinion—of policies that more greatly hurt some groups than others. That the public behaves this way is, of course, critical if GPS is to be a viable strategy. Otherwise, by failing to include the real costs of policy options in his deliberations, the president would probably choose a politically less attractive course.

More direct evidence of how the public assesses economic conditions is mixed. One study found that when survey respondents are presented with the Phillips curve trade-off between unemployment and inflation, those who by their occupation were more exposed to unemployment consistently selected it as the greater evil; those less threatened by unemployment chose inflation.[50] According to these findings, citizens do not appear to be indifferent to the particular effects of macroeconomic policy.

More consistent with the findings presented earlier in this chapter, however, is evidence showing that these occupational cleavages largely disappear when respondents are not presented with the stark choice between unemployment and inflation. When asked simply to identify the "most important problem facing the country today," Gallup Poll respondents over the years have typically named unemployment or inflation to about the same degree regardless of their positions in the labor force. These similarities are shown for manual and professional workers since 1974 in Table 7-1. Only during periods of high unemployment do the responses of these groups differ significantly; at these times, manual workers do become somewhat more sensitive to unemployment. With this occasional divergence, however, the occupational differences are neither statistically significant nor, one may assume, politically consequential. From this evidence, general problem solving does not appear to entail a sizable, hidden trade-off in the president's public support.[51]

Table 7-1 also presents answers to the most-important-problem question according to respondents' party identification. Consistent with the political parties' traditional constituencies, marginal differences in the preferences between Democrats and Republicans resemble those between the occupational classes. These preferences contribute to the political incentives facing Democratic and Republican presidents as they calculate the effects of alternative economic policies on their popularity.

Evidence of GPS in Presidential Economic Policy. Circumstantial evidence suggests that in setting overall economic policy, presidents have usually followed the dictates of general problem solving. For the period 1947 to 1976, Tufte found that when unemployment or inflation was a serious problem during the year preceding a presidential election, it tended to improve during the election year, regardless of which party controlled the White House.[52] Evidence that presidents routinely engaged in general problem solving during nonelection years can be found in another of Tufte's exercises. Using the number of mentions of "unemployment" and "inflation" in the annual

Table 7-1   Group Preferences in Selection of Unemployment and . . .

	Preferences by Working Group					
	Actual Rates		Manual		Professional	
Date	U	I	U	I	U	I
Oct. 1974	6.0	0.9	3	81	2	84
Mar. 1975	8.7	0.3	21	61	19	66
July 1975	8.4	1.0	22	51	20	52
Oct. 1975	8.6	0.6	23	56	21	60
Jan. 1976	7.8	0.4	25	45	20	54
Oct. 1976	7.9	0.3	35	45	26	54
Mar. 1977	7.3	0.6	43	58	36	60
Oct. 1977	6.8	0.3	23	35	24	33
Apr. 1978	6.0	0.9	23	50	10	62
Oct. 1978	5.8	0.8	11	76	5	76
May 1979	5.8	1.1	6	53	3	59
Oct. 1979	6.0	1.0	8	61	6	67
Jan. 1980	6.2	1.4	3	39	4	40
Mar. 1980	6.3	1.4	5	75	3	76
Nov. 1980	7.5	1.1	13	50	7	57
Feb. 1981	7.4	1.0	10	72	5	71
Jan. 1982	8.5	0.3	33	49	23	54
Aug. 1982	9.9	0.3	48	27	40	22
Oct. 1982	10.5	0.4	66	19	54	18
Apr. 1983	10.2	0.6	55	20	52	17
Nov. 1983	8.4	0.0	38	11	22	9
Feb. 1984	7.8	0.2	33	10	20	9
June 1984	7.1	0.3	33	13	23	14
Jan. 1985	7.3	2.4	28	12	15	8
Nov. 1985	7.1	2.4	30	7	17	5
July 1986	7.0	1.0	26	5	16	4
Apr. 1987	6.3	4.2	18	5	9	6

NOTE: Respondents were permitted more than one choice. U = Unemployment; I = Inflation.

Economic Report of the President from 1962 to 1977 to determine the president's priority, he tested the numbers against variations in economic conditions and the political party controlling the White House. Table 7-2 contains the data necessary to extend Tufte's original analysis through 1992. A casual inspection of these data reveals that mentions of unemployment (*UM*) and of inflation (*IM*) rise and fall with changes in the respective economic indexes and with the party in the White House.

To test these relationships more precisely, I shall follow Tufte's procedure of combining and converting the unemployment and inflation indexes into ratios. This results in two new variables: *UM/IM*, indicating the president's relative priority, and *U/I*, measuring the severity of unemployment relative to

... Inflation as the Most Important Problem, 1974-1987 (Percent)

	Preferences by Party Identification					
	Democrats		Independents		Republicans	
Date	U	I	U	I	U	I
Oct. 1974	2	81	3	78	3	82
Mar. 1975	23	63	19	61	17	60
July 1975	22	52	17	51	23	50
Oct. 1975	25	61	19	54	18	56
Jan. 1976	25	47	19	50	26	45
Oct. 1976	40	46	24	45	22	51
Mar. 1977	44	62	35	52	33	59
Oct. 1977	26	33	26	35	20	40
Apr. 1978	21	52	17	57	14	56
Oct. 1978	12	79	12	58	7	79
May 1979	7	58	4	52	3	62
Oct. 1979	8	62	5	63	6	65
Jan. 1980	5	43	3	37	2	38
Mar. 1980	5	71	3	78	3	75
Nov. 1980	12	51	10	56	6	54
Feb. 1981	11	68	8	77	3	76
Jan. 1982	31	46	29	50	21	56
Aug. 1982	55	22	40	22	36	25
Oct. 1982	68	15	58	19	54	19
Apr. 1983	57	19	49	16	49	16
Nov. 1983	39	11	28	10	22	10
Feb. 1984	36	10	25	11	22	7
June 1984	35	14	21	13	18	16
Jan. 1985	27	13	15	12	16	7
Nov. 1985	35	8	18	4	15	7
July 1986	30	3	18	4	20	3
Apr. 1987	16	7	12	4	8	4

SOURCE: Various issues of *Gallup Report*.

inflation. These indexes are correlated with each other at .61, and the ratios of mentions at .46 with a dummy variable for political party (*PP*, where 1 = Democratic president and 0 = Republican). The regression estimates presented in the following equation show the relative importance of these two variables on this measure of the president's economic priority.[53]

$$UM/IM = -.04 + .36\ U/I + .77\ PP$$
$$(4.2) + (3.3)$$

The *t*-statistic figures in parentheses indicate that both the ratio of the economic indicators and the party of the administration are significantly related to the ratio of presidential references to unemployment and inflation. The coefficients in the equation cannot be readily compared since they are based on variables with different metrics. One way to solve this problem is with the elasticity coefficient, which standardizes a regression coefficient against the mean values of the dependent and independent variables. A comparison of elasticities in the equation shows that the ratio of presidential references is roughly twice as sensitive to changes in the economic variable as to party turnover.[54]

The equation and Table 7-2 reveal a general agreement in the way the public and presidents assess economic priorities. While presidents are, by these indicators, more partisan than their followers, both place greater emphasis on those economic conditions that are widely recognized to be problems. These findings offer compelling circumstantial evidence on behalf of general problem solving as a representation of the way presidents make strategic presidential policy, at least in the realm of managing the economy.

The Marginals Strategy. "Support thy friends and woo thine enemies" is a long-practiced political maxim. It would appear as valid for a president seeking to improve his standing in the polls as it would for a local alderman trying to put together a victory on Election Day. At various points, this study has examined presidents putting this maxim into practice. President Reagan's school reform and tax credit proposals were designed more to strengthen wavering support among certain traditionally Democratic constituencies than to serve as blueprints for policy. If this simple maxim does not fully capture the range of alternatives offered by the marginals strategy, it does, nevertheless, establish the important analytic principle that politicians should differentiate their constituencies.

The maxim is too limited because frequently it will be contradictory. After all, one's friends and one's enemies have found some compelling reason for disagreeing with each other. Also, as discussed earlier, presidents might decide to pursue unpopular goals. Presidents enter office with policy objectives, which one may assume will generally be consistent with the traditional commitments of their political party. A popular president for whom additional increments of support will have little value may well prefer to forfeit these marginal gains in favor of his policy objectives. In effect, he would be practicing the less venerable but equally ancient strategy of "support thy friends and screw thine enemies," more commonly known as majority rule.[55] Although, as the initial maxim suggests, the pursuit of core objectives need not always jeopardize support from more distant constituencies, there are good structural reasons in the class composition of the parties and the economic trade-offs that confront policymakers for believing this will frequently, perhaps generally, be the case.

With the help of a class of citizens I shall call "captive approvers," the marginals approach of differentiating constituencies can even be found to

Table 7-2   Relative Importance of Unemployment and Inflation in the Annual *Economic Report of the President,* 1962-1992

Date of Report	President's Party (PP)[1]	Mentions in President's Report[2]		Economic Conditions[3] (percent)	
		Unemploy-ment (UM)	Inflation (IM)	Unemploy-ment (U)	Inflation (I)
1962	D	13.0	3.2	6.7	0.9
1963	D	9.2	3.6	5.5	1.8
1964	D	9.4	6.3	5.7	1.5
1965	D	4.8	5.4	5.2	1.6
1966	D	7.7	5.5	4.5	2.3
1967	D	6.0	3.0	3.8	3.3
1968	D	5.6	2.0	3.8	2.9
1969	D	5.7	3.8	3.6	4.5
1970	R	10.3	21.7	3.5	5.0
1971	R	20.0	38.5	4.9	5.4
1972	R	18.8	29.2	5.9	5.1
1973	R	12.8	34.0	5.6	4.1
1974	R	7.0	18.3	4.9	5.8
1975	R	9.3	16.7	5.6	10.0
1976	R	16.1	26.8	8.5	9.3
1977	R	4.9	23.2	7.7	5.1
1978	D	15.2	21.3	7.1	5.8
1979	D	5.3	32.0	6.1	7.4
1980	D	12.0	28.7	5.8	8.6
1981	D	3.7	22.1	7.1	9.2
1982	R	3.8	20.0	7.6	9.4
1983	R	12.5	10.0	9.7	6.0
1984	R	11.1	18.9	9.6	3.2
1985	R	8.6	18.5	7.4	4.3
1986	R	1.8	13.6	7.2	3.6
1987	R	1.25	13.75	7.0	2.8
1988	R	5.0	11.0	6.2	3.6
1989	R	2.7	6.4	5.5	4.1
1990	R	3.8	7.5	5.3	4.8
1991	R	1.0	7.0	5.5	5.4
1992	R	2.0	4.0	6.6	4.2

[1] Reports are filed in January and February. Note that after election years with party turnover, the former administration issues the first report of the new administration's term, as in 1969, 1977, and 1981.

[2] Number of mentions of root word per 10 pages of text.

[3] Unemployment and inflation rates during the preceding year.

SOURCES: The data for 1962 through 1977 are from Edward R. Tufte, *Political Control of the Economy* (Princeton: Princeton University Press, 1978), 79-81. The data for 1978 through 1992 are from yearly issues of the *Economic Report of the President.*

prescribe that rational presidents pursue the opposite strategy of "screw thy friends and woo thine enemies." If the president is so popular among his own party's identifiers that he believes an unpopular policy would not be greeted by a mass exodus, he might seek to expand his coalition by enticing marginal constituencies with policies they favor.[56]

Clearly this strategy appears too risky for the elected politician to be as commonly practiced as either of the above variants. One can, nevertheless, easily turn up instances of politicians putatively practicing it. Justifiably or not, black civil rights leaders have long complained that Democratic politicians have inadequately addressed their needs because they know that black voters are locked into the Democratic column on Election Day. More recently, the same theme was sounded by the conservative right under Bush. They have charged repeatedly that to maintain a broad popular base, President Bush has sacrificed his predecessor's supply-side economics and paid only lip service to the social agenda of his party's conservatives. Both of these charges became the bread-and-butter issues of his insurgent challenger, Patrick Buchanan, in the 1992 Republican presidential primaries. At least one study has investigated the possibility that presidents might strategically enlist economic policy in this manner. The results were mixed, but they do indicate that from 1947 to 1977, real income of major occupational groups tended to rise faster when the political party associated with a group's opposition (Republicans for blue-collar workers, for example) controlled the White House.[57]

This last variant of the marginals approach to strategic economic policy is most interesting here for two reasons. Since economic policies generally involve an unequal distribution of short-term costs and frequently entail trade-offs, the first maxim of taking care of everyone will generally be unavailable. (And when it is available, it will be so obvious as to be uninteresting for the study of strategic calculation.) The second maxim of playing a majority rule game is more strategic. In it, the president has consciously decided to spend his popular support, even at the risk of shortening his time in office. Only when a president is unpopular within his party will such a policy course also give him a chance to improve his standing in the polls. Since this circumstance rarely arises, the third strategic course of "woo thine enemies" will normally be the one that extends the greatest potential rewards to a president bent on improving his standing in the polls. For such a strategy to be attractive, the president must already enjoy strong support among his own party's identifiers. This situation both encourages him to look elsewhere for new supporters and frees him to pursue policies that are more attractive to marginal constituencies than to his core. As shown in the average popularity ratings of presidents by party in Table 7-3, this condition has frequently been satisfied. Only Jimmy Carter failed to average approval from two-thirds or more of his party's members. Considering that these figures include respondents who offered no opinion, Presidents

Table 7-3 Average Popularity Rating of Presidents by Partisan Group

President	President's Partisans		Independents		Opposition Partisans	
	Mean	S.D.	Mean	S.D.	Mean	S.D.
Eisenhower	87	4.0	67	7.4	49	8.3
Kennedy	84	5.4	66	7.5	49	10.3
Johnson	69	10.7	49	13.2	39	13.8
Nixon	76	12.4	50	13.6	35	12.5
Ford	66	6.0	46	7.5	35	6.5
Carter	57	12.2	44	11.7	32	10.4
Reagan	84	5.5	54	7.4	31	8.2
Bush (Jan. '89–Jan. '92)						
	85	7.1	64	10.9	52	12.1

NOTE: S.D. = standard deviation.

SOURCES: Various issues of *Gallup Report* and the International Survey Library Association.

Eisenhower, Kennedy, Reagan, and Nixon (until Watergate) found few within their ranks who needed conversion. The search for new support required them to look elsewhere.

Evidence of a Marginals Strategy under Reagan and Carter. Because of the way the public evaluates the economy, a marginals strategy may be less suited for macroeconomic policy than for issues less national in scope. Nonetheless, one can catch glimpses of it in the strategic planning of the Carter and Reagan administrations.

In late August 1981, with all of Reagan's major budget requests having sailed through Congress, the president's pollster and adviser, Richard Wirthlin, reflected on the future. Despite the president's continued strong popular support (about 60 percent approving) throughout the summer, Wirthlin's prognosis was guarded: "Political allegiances are deeply rooted. We are going to have to be very effective in order to keep the Reagan coalition together because the *natural tendency* will be for groups to go back to their original base" [emphasis added.][58] Among these groups, he singled out Catholics, certain blue-collar workers, and southern Protestants—all traditionally Democratic voters who had swung heavily to Reagan in 1980 and who were still behind him nearly a year later. Considering future developments, Wirthlin identified one potential problem area: blue-collar workers on the margin. "If unemployment increased to 10 percent next year that probably would have a more serious consequence on our new coalition than if inflation stayed at 15 percent." [59]

By the end of the next year, Wirthlin's dire scenario had come to pass. With it, Reagan's popular support plummeted to the 30 to 35 percent approval range, dropping even more sharply among Democrats and independents. Echoing his adviser's earlier prognosis, Reagan told a reporter that if he could not get unemployment down, it might indicate that he should not seek a second term.[60] When in late 1983 the economy turned up sharply and with it his popular support, this septuagenarian's talk of early retirement was replaced by renewed rhetoric about leading the way to an ascendant Republican party. In the 1984 presidential election, these marginal constituencies supported Reagan even more strongly than they had in 1980.

Jimmy Carter was not so fortunate at the marginals game. In the end, his failure to contain inflation may be judged to have cost him reelection. The irony is that throughout his term, this president, who came to the White House with weak ties to his party's core constituent groups, appears to have appreciated the political risks of inflation more than most Democrats in Washington. This can be seen in his posture toward the Humphrey-Hawkins full employment bill. Despite a ringing endorsement of this legislation early in his term, President Carter quietly insisted on an amendment that would allow him to suspend the program if inflation became a problem. And later, as increasing consumer prices, fed by spiraling energy prices, spread throughout the economy and Carter's popular support dissipated, there was little doubt that he preferred to deal with inflation rather than the by-now chronic 7 percent unemployment rate. By 1979, according to one White House planner, although the administration recognized that "the [unemployment/inflation] tradeoff is worse than it used to be," it would tackle inflation anyway, even at the risk of appearing "callous" to the unemployment problem. Another White House aide said candidly, "What Carter needs to get reelected is a policy that's pro-investment, maybe even pro-business." [61]

In this instance, inflation fighting conformed to the prescriptions of both the marginals and the GPS strategies, yet it remained highly risky. No president in Table 7-3 suffered weaker support among his own party's identifiers than did Carter. By turning away from the unemployment problem, Carter ran the risk of further alienating the party faithful, many of whom openly preferred Senator Edward Kennedy as their party's nominee in the next election.

Shortly after Carter's November defeat, former secretary of the Treasury Michael Blumenthal reflected upon the reasons for the failure of the administration's economic policies. In his opinion, failure resulted from "a basic schizophrenia within the Administration." The president was committed to an anti-inflation effort "if for no other reason than they know [inflation] is politically damaging." He then added, however, "the liberals [in the White House] believe that high interest rates are bad, that fighting inflation hurts poor people, and that we have to be very careful how we fight inflation in order not to hit 'the natural constituency of the Democratic Party.'" The net result was a policy of "fighting inflation but not too hard. It was tighten the belt, but don't cut out any important programs, cut down on government regulation but don't offend any special interest groups." [62]

The vacillation of the Carter administration reveals how presidents are sometimes pulled in opposite directions as they formulate economic policy. This is consistent with an earlier finding of independent effects of party and economic conditions on mentions of unemployment and inflation in the president's annual economic report. Although in the above cases the language of the marginals strategy appears to have dominated policy discussion, it remains unclear more generally whether presidents in deviating from their party's economic priorities are playing a marginals game at the expense of their supporters or are engaged in general problem solving. Under certain economic conditions each will yield similar results. In the absence of detailed, even intimate, information about the way individual presidents have examined their options, the question of which approach comes closest to representing strategic policy making must remain open.

Short of this, however, one can obtain from the study of public opinion suggestive information about incentives that inform the strategic thinking of presidents. If, for example, party groups similarly evaluated the president's performance as suggested by responses to Gallup's most-important-problem question, there would be little reason for presidents to calculate the relative gains and losses among different groups required by the marginals strategy. The following section presents direct evidence that the public judges the president as a national problem solver.

Presidential Popularity and Economic Performance

To assess their relative merits as strategies of presidential policy making, general problem solving and the marginals strategy need to be stated more precisely as predictions about public opinion, which one can then test. GPS holds that citizens, whatever their party or position in the labor force, will judge the economy on the basis of general conditions. Two specific predictions spin off from this statement. First, whatever economic condition is widely regarded to be a problem will be the one citizens will use to evaluate the president's performance. Second, Democrats, independents, and Republicans will not significantly differ in the relative importance they attach to this issue as they judge the president's performance. If these predictions are borne out in the public opinion data, it will mean that the president is on solid ground when he takes on national economic problems even when his policies impose costs on particular constituencies.

The marginals strategy views public opinion differently. Reflecting the class composition of the political parties, Democrats and Republicans will tend to pay greater attention to different features of the economy in evaluating the president's performance. The first prediction, therefore, is that Democrats' support of the president will be more closely associated with unemployment; and Republicans' support, with inflation. Under certain conditions, the marginals strategy also holds out the prospect that the president can gain new support among opposition identifiers. For this strategy to succeed, the president's identifiers would need to be less responsive to changes in the economy than independents or supporters of the opposition party.[63] Although this is not in itself a prediction that derives from the marginals strategy, it is a necessary condition for this strategy to be opportune. In sum, the marginals approach to strategic policy will be best suited for a setting in which party groups differ in their economic assessments and support among the president's partisans is less affected by changes in the economy.

To test these predictions on the monthly popularity ratings for each president beginning with Eisenhower, I have disaggregated the president's approval rating for the 368 national polls that make up the overall time series. Altogether, the hypothesized relationships require an examination of 24 different time series—the monthly ratings of Democrats, independents, and Republicans for eight presidents.

In estimating the effects of the economy on presidential popularity, one must address several critical methodological issues. These include identifying exogenous variables in addition to the economy so that the results for the economic conditions will not be biased; operationally measuring these variables in a way that makes good theoretical sense and allows their true effects to be best represented; and specifying the functional form of their relationship with presidential popularity. None of these issues has simple answers, a fact fully supported by the great variety of preferences on these matters that can be found in the burgeoning scholarship on presidential popularity.[64] These methodological issues are only tangentially related to the substantive questions here, and so I have reserved a full discussion of them for the Appendix. Because the way the analysis is performed greatly affects the results reported below, the reader is urged to consult this discussion.

In Table 7-4 the statistics necessary for testing the competing predictions have been collected from the analysis of the different time series. (See Tables A-1, A-2, A-3, and A-4 in the Appendix for a full presentation of the regression estimates.) The coefficients for unemployment and inflation have been adjusted by their variables' mean values so that their actual effects on popularity are broadly comparable. Because inflation failed to produce the correct sign for any of the partisan groups during the Kennedy or Reagan administrations, they were omitted from the analysis.[65] Only one other coefficient—that, ironically, for unemployment for Democrats under Carter—fails to show the correct negative sign, signifying an inverse relation between the economic indicator and the president's approval rating. Finally, the deleterious effects of rising unemployment on President Bush's public approval was delayed by Desert Storm. As a result, the unemployment rate rather than its change was used for this administration.

On the whole, the evidence presented in Table 7-4 offers impressive evidence on behalf of the general problem-solving approach to strategic

Table 7-4 Relative Effects of Unemployment and Inflation on Presidential Popularity among Party Groups

President	Unemployment			Inflation		
	Same party	Independents	Opposition party	Same party	Independents	Opposition party
Eisenhower (N=86)	−.67	−.53	−.70	−1.8	−2.8	−3.5
Kennedy (N=32)	−9.8	−16.7	−8.0	—	—	—
Johnson (N=50)	−6.8	−11.4	−5.6	−4.0	−9.1	−7.7
Nixon (N=61)	−1.74	−1.0	−5.5	−5.2	−3.8	−.1
Ford (N=21)	−.26	−2.4	−1.1	−6.9	−4.7	−6.3
Carter (N=40)	+1.34	−3.3	−4.4	−19.2	−18.3	−8.7
Reagan (first term) (N=41)	−3.1	−4.3	−2.8	—	—	—
Bush (N=36)	−22.4	−57.8	−61.4	−9.4	−6.0	−3.9

NOTE: Coefficients are the long-term, mean effects of variable on the president's monthly Gallup rating. Unemployment is the annualized percentage change in the unemployment rate during the preceding six months. For the Bush estimates, the unemployment rate is used. (See the Appendix for discussion and full specification of the model.)

SOURCE: From Tables A-3 and A-4.

economic policy. There are differences in the relative strengths of the relationships across partisan groups, reflecting for the most part the random error yielded by the generally small number of observations on which the calculations are based. Except for the rankings for Johnson and Nixon, the relationships thoroughly support the GPS predictions. Partisan groups similarly weigh unemployment and inflation in evaluating the president's job performance.

Although they are not nearly so impressive as to dissuade a strategic president from general problem solving, traces of support can also be found for the marginals strategy. Neither unemployment nor inflation had much effect on Eisenhower's popularity, which is appropriate given the general unimportance of these issues during the 1950s; but the relationships do satisfy the critical conditions of the marginals strategy in being stronger for opposition identifiers than for the president's partisans. Only on this occasion, however, does this ranking appear for both economic indexes. Stronger evidence of different economic priorities for Democrats and Republicans can be seen in the relationships during the Johnson and Nixon years. Consistent with the marginals prediction, in both instances, unemployment is a stronger determinant of approval for Democrats, and inflation is stronger for Republicans.[66]

Conclusion

This chapter opened by asking whether rhetoric or performance governs the president's standing with the American public. The testimony and behavior of presidents and their lieutenants suggest both do. The evidence assembled here agrees.

What presidents say to the public, and what others say to the public about them, matters more today than ever before in part because of the emerging political relations I have called individualized pluralism. These relations have created a community that inspires, as it facilitates, every member to go public.

The president, of course, enjoys special legitimacy as well as other, more tangible resources for engaging in such activities, but others in more modest ways do so as well. The circular letters of early nineteenth-century congressmen are today live satellite feeds to local news stations back in the district. Agency heads collaborate with clientele groups to campaign publicly for some policies and against others. From all accounts, interest groups, braced with well-heeled political action committees, are more dedicated and systematic in mobilizing constituent pressure on Congress than ever before. Cumulatively, these activities provide a significant counterbalance to the public relations that flow from the White House. News from Washington abounds, and it shapes opinions in the country more so today for the simple reason that there is more of it.

The role of the press in the politics of popularity has undergone a more subtle transformation than has the Washington political community as a whole. Its mission has always been to communicate news from Washington to the country, but for the effects of individualized pluralism to be fully realized, the Washington press has had to be willing to accommodate the increased efforts of politicians to go public. The evidence presented here indicates that the press has indeed opened itself as a conduit for the greater flow of news from and about Washington—particularly news of a critical tenor.

Whether one abhors or applauds these developments depends upon one's view of presidents as public men. They are either being saddled with certain criticism or being exposed to the sunlight of truth. The public's continuing expectations of the president's performance should prevent these changes from distracting the chief executive from his primary duties of the office. Quite simply, the American public holds the president responsible for promoting the general welfare. Although presidents may be expected to engage in public relations, and, depending upon one's disposition, even forgiven for doing so, they will succeed neither in the country nor in Washington if they pursue their public image to the neglect of active problem solving.

Notes

1. Further evidence that the public acts this way, and that this behavior is politically consequential, can be found in the significant relationship between the success of congressional candidates of the president's party and the current state of the economy. This relationship persists even when the president's party does not control Congress. Gerald H. Kramer, "Short-Term Fluctuations in U.S. Voting Behavior, 1896-1964," *American Political Science Review* 65 (March 1971): 131-143; Edward R. Tufte, *Political Control of the Economy* (Princeton, N.J.: Princeton University Press, 1978).
2. From interview in "Is There a Crisis of Spirit in the West?" *Public Opinion* 1 (May/June 1978): 3-8.
3. Jody Powell's characterization of presidential public relations is apt: it cannot "turn a sow's ear into a silk purse . . . but just a silkier sow's ear." Cited in Michael Baruch Grossman and Martha Joynt Kumar, "Carter, Reagan, and the Media: Have the Rules Changed on the Poles of the Spectrum of Success?" (Paper delivered at the Annual Meeting of the American Political Science Association, New York, September 1981), 18. On the marginal effects of presidential rhetoric, see Lyn Ragsdale, "The Politics of Presidential Speechmaking, 1949-1980," *American Political Science Review* 78 (December 1984): 971-984.
4. Harvy G. Zeidenstein, "White House Perceptions of News Media Bias," *Presidential Studies Quarterly* 13 (Summer 1983): 345-356.
5. Joe McGinnis, *The Selling of the President* (New York: Trident Press, 1969); and Mark Hertsgaard, *On Bended Knee* (New York: Farrar Straus Giroux, 1988).
6. James Deakin, *Straight Stuff* (New York: William Morrow, 1984), 44.
7. Richard E. Neustadt, *Presidential Power* (New York: John Wiley and Sons, 1980), 70.
8. Ibid., 22.
9. Lest the reader believe that I am chastising scholars for their work on the subject, I offer as an example of this literature my "Explaining Presidential Popularity," *American Political Science Review* 72 (June 1978): 506-522.
10. M. Stephen Weatherford, "Economic Conditions and Electoral Outcomes: Class Differences in the Political Response to Inflation," *American Journal of Political Science* 22 (November 1978): 917-938; D. Roderick Kiewiet, *Macroeconomics and Micropolitics* (Chicago: University of Chicago Press, 1985); Donald R. Kinder and Roderick Kiewiet, "Sociotropic Politics: The American Case," *British Journal of Political Science* 11 (April 1981): 129-161; Donald R. Kinder, "Presidents, Prosperity, and Public Opinion," *Public Opinion Quarterly* 45 (Spring 1981): 1-21; Richard Lau and David O. Sears, "Cognitive Links between Economic Grievances and Political Responses," *Political Behavior* 3, no. 4 (1981): 279-302.
11. M. Stephen Weatherford, "Evaluating Economic Policy: A Contextual Model of the Opinion Formation Process," *Journal of Politics* 45 (November 1983): 867-888.
12. Kay L. Schlozman and Sidney Verba, *Injury to Insult: Unemployment, Class and Political Response* (Cambridge: Harvard University Press, 1979).
13. Kinder, "Presidents, Prosperity," 17. See also Mark Peffley and J. T. Williams,

"Attributing Presidential Responsibility for National Economic Problems," *American Politics Quarterly* 13 (1985): 393-425.

14. Shanto Iyengar, Mark D. Peters, and Donald R. Kinder, "Experimental Demonstrations of the 'Not-So-Minimal' Consequences of Television News Programs," *American Political Science Review* 76 (December 1982): 853. This line of research is developed further in Shanto Iyengar, *Is Anyone Responsible? How Television Frames Political Issues* (University of Chicago Press, 1991). Using a less elaborate research design, Michael T. Robinson concluded that exposure to negatively biased stories led to more cynical views of politics. See his "Public Affairs Television and the Growth of Political Malaise: The Case of 'The Selling of the Pentagon,'" *American Political Science Review* 70 (June 1976): 409-432.

15. On this issue of how personal and interpersonal variables mediate the way citizens process mass communications, see Michael MacKuen, "Exposure to Information, Belief Integration and Individual Responsiveness to Agenda Change," *American Political Science Review* 78 (June 1984): 372-391; and Lutz Ebring, Edie N. Goldenberg, and Arthur H. Miller, "Front-Page News and Real-World Cues: A New Look at Agenda-Setting by the Media," *American Journal of Political Science* 24 (February 1980): 16-49.

16. Relative press attention to the president and Congress has been examined systematically for different historical eras. Findings showing the preponderance of congressional news during the middle half of the nineteenth century are reported in Samuel Kernell and Gary C. Jacobson, "Congress and the Presidency as News in the Nineteenth Century: The Cleveland Press, 1820-1876" (Paper delivered to the Annual Meeting of the Southern Political Science Association, Savannah, Ga., November 1-3, 1984). The rise of presidential news from 1885 to 1957 is recorded in Elmer E. Cornwell, Jr., "Presidential News: The Expanding Public Image," *Journalism Quarterly* 36 (Summer 1959): 175-283. Continued expansion of presidential news relative to that of Congress for the years 1958 to 1974 is presented in Alan P. Balutis, "The Presidency and the Press: The Expanding Presidential Image," *Presidential Studies Quarterly* 7 (Fall 1977): 244-251.

17. This case study draws heavily from an account by Deakin, *Straight Stuff*, 159-162.

18. Ibid., 161. A sample of newspaper reports on these press conferences confirms Deakin's recollection: James Reston, "Patriotism Backed," *New York Times*, November 12, 1953, 1; Robert W. Richards, "Velde to Press Quiz of Truman on Spies," *San Diego Union*, November 12, 1953, 1. Some reporters complained that their criticisms of Eisenhower were being muted by Republican editors and publishers. A year later, TRB (Richard Strout) offered the following instances of insufficient questioning of administration policies: "The Administration's security risk 'numbers game'; the phony unleashing of Chiang Kai-shek; the President's personal order directing the Atomic Energy Commission to write the Dixon-Yates contract" (TRB, "Washington Wire," *New Republic*, December 27, 1954, 2).

19. Republished in book form: William Greider, *The Education of David Stockman and Other Americans* (New York: E. P. Dutton, 1981).

20. Perhaps the closest thing to the Stockman episode during Eisenhower's tenure was the Treasury secretary's denunciation of the administration's annual budget as he unveiled it to the press. Though the event aroused much comment in Washington, there is little evidence it had much effect on public opinion. See Neustadt, *Presidential Power*, 80-84.

21. "Public Leans to View Stockman Should Remain As OMB Director," *Gallup Opinion Index* 194 (November 1981): 14-16.

22. Quoted in George C. Edwards III, *The Public Presidency* (New York: St. Martin's

Press, 1983), 88.
23. Quoted in Daniel Wise, "The Twilight of a President," *New York Times Magazine,* November 3, 1968, 131.
24. Jimmy Carter, "The President's News Conference of October 27, 1977," *Public Papers of the Presidents, Jimmy Carter, 1977* (Washington, D.C.: Government Printing Office, 1978), 1914.
25. Rich Jaroslovsky, "Economic Upturn Aids President's Popularity, but It Is Not Panacea," *Wall Street Journal,* April 28, 1983, 1.
26. Ibid.
27. Based on correspondence with one of Nixon's economic advisers, Edward R. Tufte relates the following story:

> Gearing up for the 1972 campaign, staff members of the Office of Management and Budget under the direction of the Assistant Director for Evaluation developed statistical models and ran multiple regressions assessing the influence of economic conditions on the outcomes of presidential elections. The OMB studies concluded that between-election increases in real net national product per capita had a strong impact on the electoral support won by the presidential candidate of the incumbent party. These findings were then reported to George Shultz and John Ehrlichman in the fall of 1971.

In *Political Control,* 136.
28. E. E. Schattschneider, *Party Government* (New York: Holt, Rinehart and Winston, 1942), 16.
29. Nelson Polsby offers such an assessment in Nelson W. Polsby, ed., *The Modern Presidency* (New York: Random House, 1973), 37-38.
30. Fred I. Greenstein, *The Hidden-Hand Presidency* (New York: Basic Books, 1982), 98-99.
31. Fred I. Greenstein, "Ike and Reagan," *New York Times,* January 29, 1983, 19.
32. George Skelton, "Reagan Dip in Poll Tied to Spending Cuts," *Los Angeles Times,* March 19, 1984, 6.
33. For examples of Reagan's efforts to restore lost support among women in preparation for the election, see Barbara Bosler, "G.O.P. Starting Campaign to Show 'Reagan Is Terrific on Women's Issues,'" *New York Times,* April 6, 1984, 11; and "Reagan on Women's Issues," *New York Times,* April 6, 1984, 11.
34. This was first examined systematically by James Stimson, "Public Support for American Presidents," *Public Opinion Quarterly* 40 (1976): 1-21.
35. Bryce Harlow, in a private interview with Professor John H. Kessel; Kessel, letter to author, October 16, 1985.
36. This analysis follows the procedures employed by Michael S. Lewis-Beck and Tom W. Rice, "Presidential Popularity and the Presidential Vote," *Public Opinion Quarterly* 46 (Winter 1982): 534-537.
37. The result in the view of many who have retraced U.S. steps into the Vietnam War was a "muddling through" policy that was incapable of achieving military victory and that virtually guaranteed the high costs of the protracted conflict. See David Halberstam, *The Making of a Quagmire* (New York: Random House, 1965). How Johnson's concern for his domestic programs contributed to an incrementalist strategy is well documented in Larry D. Berman, *Planning a Tragedy: The Americanization of the War in Vietnam.* (New York: Norton, 1983).
38. Elsewhere, I have systematically examined the tendency for presidents to lose support during their first 18 months in office. See "The Presidency and the People: The Modern Paradox," in *The Presidency and the Political System,* ed. Michael Nelson (Washington, D.C.: CQ Press, 1984), 253-256.

39. The reason the happy coincidence of popular and preferred policy infrequently occurs has to do with the inherently imbalanced distributional consequences of policies that serve the interests of core constituencies. This line of argument is developed more fully below.

40. The effects of the pardon on President Ford's defeat in 1976 is documented in Arthur H. Miller and Warren E. Miller, "Partisanship and Performance: 'Rational' Choice in the 1976 Presidential Election" (Paper delivered at the Annual Meeting of the American Political Science Association, Washington, D.C., September 1-4, 1977).

41. These alternative approaches to strategic calculation are not presented as exhaustive, but as elaborated versions of underlying notions about public opinion that will probably be found in other conceptualizations of the president's strategic calculus.

42. On the extraordinary ability of members of Congress to particularize policy, see David R. Mayhew, *Congress: The Electoral Connection* (New Haven: Yale University Press, 1974).

43. The critical distinction between policy issues in the second and third categories may be little more than that the distribution of costs in the third category are "apparent," and in the second they are not.

44. Peter T. Kilborn, "Alive and Thinking in Economic Advice," *New York Times,* August 9, 1985, A12.

45. Lester C. Thurow, *The Zero-Sum Society* (New York: Basic Books, 1980).

46. After briefly reviewing the pluralistic features of American politics that have long troubled reformers, Thurow finally gives up hope for economic reforms in the present system. The book ends with a proposal to reform the political order along the lines of British politics so that the executive could better withstand the unpopularity that often attends good economic policy.

47. For the purposes of this analysis, it is less important whether there is anything more than a short-term trade-off between unemployment and inflation than that most politicians and those who advise them on these matters act as though there is. Since the early 1960s, the Phillips trade-off has come in and out of vogue in policy discourse. For a review of its varying fashionableness, see Leonard Silk, "Phillips Curve Back in Business," *New York Times,* May 18, 1978. See also John M. Barry, "Inflation and Unemployment," *Washington Post,* August 27, 1984, 19.

48. Political considerations intrude when economists cannot agree what policy to prescribe. Moreover, presidents generally have little trouble finding the prescriptive economic advice to satisfy their political goals. Leonard S. Silk, "Truth vs. Partisan Political Purpose," *American Economic Review* 62 (May 1972): 376-378.

49. Tufte, *Political Control,* 101.

50. Douglas A. Hibbs, Jr., "The Mass Public and Macroeconomic Performance: The Dynamics of Public Opinion toward Unemployment and Inflation," *American Journal of Political Science* 23 (November 1979): 705-731.

51. For a thorough treatment of the perception of inflation as a problem for different economic groups, see Paul Peretz, *The Political Economy of Inflation in the United States* (Chicago: University of Chicago Press, 1983), 71-105.

52. Tufte, *Political Control,* 76-83.

53. The logarithms of the economic and mentions ratios are used so that changes in either the numerator or denominator receive equal weight. The estimation procedure differs from Tufte's analysis in using the previous year's unemployment and inflation figures rather than a three-year average. For this longer series the latter procedure proved unnecessary to avoid the serious collinearity problem he encountered.

54. An alternative interpretation arises when one examines these variables' "mean"

effects. Multiplying each by its mean value reveals that over the 24-year period, alternations of party control of the presidency had a slightly greater effect on presidential references than did changes in the economic ratios. This procedure is explained in Christopher H. Achen, *Interpreting and Using Regression* (Beverly Hills, Calif.: Sage Publications, 1982).

55. One strategic rationale for this approach is the dilution of rewards to the core necessary to maintain high popular support. It is a variant of William H. Riker's theory of minimum winning coalitions. See his *The Theory of Political Coalitions* (New Haven: Yale University Press, 1962).

56. One catches a glimpse of such regard for the core constituency in Richard Wirthlin's observation that during Reagan's first year the president's "governing" decisions had generally been accepted by "the political coalition that elected him" (Dick Kirschten, "The 'Revolution' at the White House: Have the People Caught Up with the Man?" *National Journal*, August 29, 1981, 1532). See also Robert Pear, "Making Old Constituency a New One for Reagan," *New York Times*, March 14, 1984, 12.

57. Paul Peretz, "Who Gets What, How and Why: The Economic Effects of Party Change" (Paper prepared for delivery to the Annual Meeting of the American Political Science Association, New York, September 1978).

58. Kirschten, "The 'Revolution,' " 1532.

59. Ibid., 1536.

60. Jaroslovsky, "Economic Upturn Aids President's Popularity," 1.

61. Edward Cowan, "Carter's Policy: Storm Clouds Grow," *New York Times*, June 7, 1979, D1. Referring to the captive voter concept introduced by Anthony Downs, one Carter adviser confided in the spring of 1980 that "Jimmy Carter has become a thoroughly Downsian president" (private conversation).

62. Hobart Rowen, "Blumenthal Tells Where Carter Erred," *Los Angeles Times*, October 10, 1979, 1, sec. 4.

63. This does not mean that if the president's remedy is so draconian as to replace one dominant problem with another the public will remain supportive. President Reagan's precipitous decline in the polls when his and the Federal Reserve's anti-inflation policies pushed the unemployment rate toward double digits attests to the public's willingness to switch problems. (Note the most-important-problem trends in Table 7-1.)

64. For samples of the variety of models developed to explain presidential popularity, see the following: John E. Mueller, "Presidential Popularity from Truman to Johnson," *American Political Science Review* 64 (1970): 18-34; Timothy Haight and Richard Brody, "The Mass Media and Presidential Popularity," *Communications Research* (January 1977): 41-60; Samuel Kernell, "Explaining Presidential Popularity," *American Political Science Review* 72 (1978): 506-522; Douglas A. Hibbs, Jr., "The Dynamics of Political Support for American Presidents among Occupational and Partisan Groups," *American Journal of Political Science* 26 (1982): 312-332; David G. Golden and James M. Poterba, "The Price of Popularity: The Political Business Cycle Reexamined," *American Journal of Political Science* 24 (November 1980): 696-714; Michael MacKuen, "Political Drama, Economic Conditions, and the Dynamics of Presidential Popularity," *American Journal of Political Science* 27 (1983): 165-192; and Charles W. Ostrom, Jr., and Dennis M. Simon, "Promise and Performance: A Dynamic Model of Presidential Popularity," *American Political Science Review* 79 (June 1985): 334-358.

65. Rao and Miller recommend that wrong-signed coefficients be left in the equation unless one can justify their exclusion. I have omitted these variables in Table 7-4 because the resulting equations behave better on a variety of criteria. Serial

correlation, according to Durbin's *h*-statistic, becomes less severe in each case. Moreover, the commentary of pollsters and White House advisers in these administrations fails to mention inflation—even the declining one for Reagan—as a major source of the president's public support. For a discussion of the risk of omitting theoretically indicated variables because of wrong signs, see Potluri Rao and Roger LeRoy Miller, *Applied Econometrics* (Belmont, Calif.: Wadsworth Publishing Co., 1971), 32-40.

66. This finding for Nixon corresponds to the unusually consistent ranking of the correlates of unemployment and inflation on Nixon's popularity by income classes reported by Friedrich Schneider. The exceptional character of this pattern presented here is consistent with the failure of Schneider's results to be repeated in subsequent research. See Friedrich Schneider, "Presidential Popularity Functions of Different Classes: A Theoretical and Empirical Approach" (1977, Mimeographed). See also Kristen R. Monroe, *Presidential Popularity and the Economy* (New York: Praeger, 1984).

Conclusion: The Prospects for Leadership 8

It is traditional, if not quite obligatory, for studies that argue change as their central thesis to conclude with a speculation about the future. What is in store? With events daily yielding new insights into going public as a strategy for presidential leadership, it is appropriate to entertain this question here. Before considering the future, however, one should be aware of the opportunities and pitfalls presented by the current vantage.

Perhaps the most conspicuous limitation to projecting the future is the recency of the developments I have described. Reading current events to theorize about even the present state of presidential leadership is like walking a tightrope; one's footing is still more unsure for predicting the behavior of presidents throughout the next decade. No matter whether one arbitrarily designates Richard Nixon or Jimmy Carter as the president who initiated the *routine* practice of going public for his leadership in Washington, data are still insufficient to delineate fully the implications of going public for future politics. And yet, since Nixon was in the White House, regularities in presidential behavior and in others' responses to it, which are at odds with past practices, have begun to reveal how the new order might look. These emerging patterns appear all the more indicative since they are consistent with the model of today's Washington, which has been described as individualized pluralism.

Aside from the caution that must attend instant history, the personal character of the office also limits speculation about the future. The presidency affords each occupant the latitude to define the job for himself. In the absence of apprenticeship, the incumbent must lean heavily upon his experience in public life. In important respects, then, presidential leadership will be as varied as the political careers and talents of the politicians who occupy the Oval Office. Ronald Reagan eclipsed all of his predecessors in the quantity of national appeals and outdid most of them as well in the quality of presentation. George Bush took his public leadership in a different direction. Spurning ambitious policy departures, he sought instead to shore up public support for himself and his party through unprecedented levels of travel and personal appearances.

One is not completely adrift, however, in trying to chart the future. Some presidents leave their mark on the office. Occasionally a figure enters the White House whose political intuition eclipses the perspicuity of those who are currently studying the office. His success educates scholars and future presidents alike. Franklin Roosevelt was just such a president. Within a short time after his departure, Roosevelt emerged a paragon, clarifying for many the techniques of bargaining, for others the exercise of charisma, and for still others the inner bearings necessary for success at the job. Because Roosevelt established new standards, his successors have been saddled with comparisons of their performance against his.[1]

Will Ronald Reagan cut such a figure? Will his shadow loom over the next generation of White House occupants? Quite possibly. This is more than idle speculation, for Ronald Reagan relied on going public for his influence in Washington more heavily and more profitably than did his predecessors. His success has forced others in Washington to reevaluate the way they assess the office. How they adapt to these new assessments will permit, and even encourage, future presidents similarly to go public.

As instructive as Reagan's example may have been for Bush and future presidents, the accuracy of the prognosis for future leadership does not depend wholly on the length of his shadow. Going public is a leadership style consistent with the requirements of a political community that is increasingly susceptible to the centrifugal forces of public opinion. The choice to go public will be inspired less by Reagan's example than by the circumstances of the moment encountered by future presidents. The evolving structure of political relations along the lines described by individualized pluralism will continue to make going public a favored approach to leadership.

Other tendencies are emerging in Washington relations that reflect but also complement, accentuate, and reinforce the strategy of going public. Together they may shortly move community politics to a state even less recognizable to those steeped in the traditions of institutionalized pluralism. Future evolution can be classified into two broad types: the behavior of politicians and the effects on policy.

Adaptive Responses to Presidents Going Public

Expectations of going public routinely become incorporated into relations between presidents and other politicians, especially in this era of divided party control of government. Politicians from the opposition party plan their strategies to minimize the president's potential damage to their designs, and they look for opportunities to exploit for their own purposes his capacity to go public. Adaptive responses occur at a variety of levels—from the competing parties posturing on issues to individuals planning their careers. Examples of each abound.

Issue Posturing

When a president goes to the country, he is counting on his prestige to persuade sufficient numbers of citizens to communicate their support of his position to their representatives. Success depends neither on building majority support in the country nor on buffaloing other politicians into believing that he has. All the president need do is convince a sufficient number of politicians that the political cost of resisting his policy is greater than any potential gain.

Intense minorities scare politicians more than inattentive majorities for the good reason that the former will act on their beliefs and the latter will not. Presidents who exhort viewers to contact their members of Congress are trading upon the caution with which politicians greet intense preferences. At times, even when representatives know that their position and not the president's represents majority opinion, they will shy away from openly breaking with him for fear that he may take his case to the people. Such an instance occurred in the spring of 1985 when many House and Senate Democrats expressed reluctance to legislate an end to the financial aid for rebel forces in Nicaragua on the suspicion, as one Democratic leader explained, that President Reagan might make it a major public issue later in the summer. Fearful of being caught on the wrong side of the issue, as they had with Reagan in the past on budget cuts and defense spending, the Democrats ceded to the president greater latitude than they otherwise might have. The ability to go public presents presidents with the opportunity to control policy discussion to an extent unavailable to those who would rely exclusively upon elite negotiation for their leadership.

Strategic Planning

At a more advanced level of strategic calculation, politicians anticipate the president's option to go public as they engage in coalition building. On no subject is this calculation more precise than on taxes. Increasing taxes is always painful for politicians, especially during an election year when they must ask for taxpayers' votes shortly after taking their money. This accounts for the unusual wariness with which President Bush and the Democratic congressional leadership approached one another on a tax increase during the summer of 1990, at a time when a ballooning deficit was about to cause severe and politically unacceptable reductions in federal programs. Members of Congress were, if anything, even more squeamish about an election-year tax increase. Unlike Bush, whose first term still had two years left, all of the members of the House and a substantial part of the Senate Democrats faced reelection in November. The Democrats had been evading any association with taxes ever since George Bush had trumped Democratic candidate Michael Dukakis in the 1986 presidential election with the words "Read my lips: 'No new taxes.' "

The Democratic solution to their dilemma was to turn the president's capacity to go public to their advantage. Bush and by association his party's congressional candidates would bear principal responsibility for justifying the tax increase to the public. (Speaker of the House O'Neill, as noted in Chapter 4, had followed much the same course in successfully negotiating an election-year tax increase in 1982.) First, the Democrats demanded a *mea culpa* from Bush for his "no new taxes" pledge before they would enter into serious negotiations. In early summer the president tried to avoid political fallout by burying in a press release, in a list of possible revisions of the tax code, the phrase "tax revenue increases." Despite his best effort, this reference, stripped of its circumlocution, won banner headlines in the nation's newspapers and was the lead story on each network's evening national news program. Second, at the conclusion of negotiations in early October, the president agreed to present the proposed tax increase to the American people in a national broadcast. One can sympathize with the president's predicament and explain his tepid performance as he unveiled a budget compromise at odds with his campaign pledge and outspokenly opposed by his party's members of Congress. In the end, the Democratic Congress got an even more attractive tax package; the president's job performance rating went into a nosedive, and the Democrats picked up nine House seats in the November election.

Redefining the Strategic Repertoire

A third level of strategic planning, which derives at least in part from the president's demonstrated ability to go public, is the way other Washington politicians view their own strategic opportunities at public relations. Increasingly, whether learned independently or from observing the president, politicians throughout Washington are coming to adopt aspects of going public as part of their own repertoire.

One of the most striking examples occurred in late May 1985 when House Ways and Means Committee Chair Daniel Rostenkowski followed President Reagan's prime-time appeal for public support for tax reform with a national television appeal of his own. What an incongruous sight it must have been for the men and women who served with former Ways and Means Chair Wilbur Mills to watch a successor telling the country that with its active support his committee would beat back the "special interests" that would be hard at work to frustrate tax reform.

In adopting much of Reagan's script, Rostenkowski sought to neutralize the president's mandate as well as siphon off a share of whatever credit might be forthcoming if a popular tax reform measure were to be enacted. Those close to Rostenkowski offered another reason for his rousing appeal. Speaker O'Neill had announced his retirement and sealed it with a million-dollar contract for his memoirs, and Rostenkowski was planning "an outside" bid for the post. To stand a chance against fellow Democrat James Wright, whose job as majority leader made him heir apparent to the speakership, Rostenkowski was building a record of his ability to represent Congress in its dealings with presidents who go public.[2] This quintessential institutional actor appealed to the country to "write Rosty" not only to promote the Democrats' commitment to tax reform but also to advance his own claim later for the highest leadership position within the House of Representatives.

Rostenkowski's insight was not altogether lost on the man he hoped to succeed. In 1981 Speaker O'Neill hired a new, more publicly active press secretary. Although public relations cut against O'Neill's grain, he faced the dilemma, as observed by one congressional reporter, that "if he had not gone public, there would have been nobody at all to tell the Democratic story." [3] Strategic adaptation of this kind is increasingly common on Capitol Hill. Though on most occasions it does not arise directly in response to the president's initiative, his example nonetheless inspires others to try their hand at going public. House leaders, for example, have complained that junior members no longer toe the party line in hope of favorable committee assignments that might help them get reelected. Instead, according to one of O'Neill's senior staffers, they "go directly to voters via television." [4] Senate Majority Leader Howard Baker agreed: "If you don't let them do anything on the floor, they do it on the steps [of the Capitol]. And somehow there's always a TV camera out there." [5]

As politicians at every level routinely go public, the president's public activities become normal behavior to which others respond when they must but to which they no longer take exception. Furthermore, as other politicians similarly engage in public relations to pursue their own political objectives, public posturing will tend to displace quiet diplomacy as the normal means by which fellow Washingtonians communicate with one another across the institutional boundaries that separate them.[6]

Career Adaptations: Washington Correspondents and Presidential Aspirants

The rise of this new style of presidential leadership appears to have profoundly altered the careers of two groups in Washington: correspondents and presidential aspirants. I examined both in earlier chapters; I return to them here to clarify the ways in which political careers adapt to the altered circumstances posed by going public as a routine of the modern White House.

During the 1960s and 1970s, the reporting style of Washington correspondents evolved from objective to interpretive journalism. Various reasons have been offered for this reorientation. Certainly, any reporter whose Washington career spanned Johnson's Vietnam credibility gap and Nixon's Watergate would likely say that these events conclusively exposed the deficiencies of objective journalism.

As significant as these events were, other, more structural features of political relations in Washington had begun reworking the professional creed of Washington correspondents by the onset of the Vietnam War. With growing opportunities for news analysis provided by increasing network coverage of the White House, longer evening news programs, and televised news conferences, objective journalism made a hasty retreat. Reporters found themselves describing events their readers had already viewed for themselves. For traditional correspondents whose job it was to report on events in Washington for the readers back home, expanded network television coverage of the White House threatened to leave them without a purpose.

As politicians increasingly employed national media to market policies as well as themselves, objective journalism encountered another problem. Because this creed offers the reporter little latitude for evaluation and interpretation, it is better suited for covering what politicians do than what they say. Reporters found themselves serving as vehicles for the propaganda activities of politicians. Even in reporting what they privately regarded to be partial truths and outright falsehoods, objective journalism required them to play the role of neutral scribes. For some, the credibility gap of Vietnam and the coverage of Watergate posed this dilemma.

Perhaps at no time, however, was the dilemma more sharply felt by the working press in Washington than during Senator Joseph McCarthy's witch hunt in the State Department and the Army in the early 1950s. However outlandish were McCarthy's charges in the opinion of many correspondents, they felt obliged to report them in a straightforward manner as news. When privately pressed by these reporters to substantiate his claims, McCarthy would dissimulate and at times as much as admit that he had no proof.[7] Yet because these encounters were "off the record," many correspondents were obliged not to report this information to their readers. Some reporters did over time switch to a more evaluative, critical reporting of McCarthy's shenanigans, but one study of press coverage found that efforts to rebut false statements rarely appeared in the wire services and that the other critical stories were significantly less likely to be picked up by other papers around the country.[8] During the early 1950s, various internal and external mechanisms of the newspaper business were enforcing objective journalism. In the judgment of historians and journalists looking back on the era, the result was that the practice of objective journalism served to broadcast McCarthy's campaign.[9]

In mobilizing public opinion to sway events in Washington, McCarthy along with Senator Estes Kefauver, who conducted televised hearings into wrong-doing within the drug industry, were precursors of the modern politician who goes public. Confronted with going public as a political strategy, objective journalism neither supplies reporters with good copy nor permits them to assess rhetoric against reality. The creed of analysis and interpretation solves both problems.

Because going public is only one part of a broader transformation of community relations, one cannot state precisely the degree to which trends in presidents' public activities, such as those presented in Chapter 4, contributed to the professional reorientation of Washington correspondents in the 1960s.

There is little doubt, however, that this new style of journalism has correspondents balancing presidential rhetoric with independent analysis. One sees it in the insistent questioning at news conferences, in the television and newspaper commentary that follows presidential addresses, and in the coverage of presidents on the evening news. On this last score, one study of network news found that by 1985 the average taped segment of the president speaking lasted only 9 seconds, compared with 44 seconds during the years 1965 to 1972.[10]

The other group whose careers are being redirected in ways that reflect and reinforce the prospects of going public as presidential strategy is the men and women who aspire to hold that office. Reflecting the rise of the national government in public life at home and abroad, during the early post-World War II era the U.S. Senate replaced the states' governorships as the chief source of presidential timber. Senators enjoy resources that few other officeholders can match. Unlike their House colleagues, who are forced to specialize by their districts' narrower concerns and their chamber's greater number, senators find that their varied committee responsibilities and the relaxed floor procedures permit them to be reputable and vocal dilettantes on any number of domestic and foreign issues that arise from day to day. The Senate serves as a megaphone with which its members champion policies before a national constituency. Moreover, the Senate is a school for the pluralist arts. When elected to the White House, Lyndon Johnson and John Kennedy—but not Richard Nixon, who served in the Senate only briefly before entering the isolation booth of the vice-presidency—were familiar with, if not expert in, the requirements of a bargaining president.[11]

Since the presidential selection reforms and the entry of strong "outsider" contenders for the nomination, the Senate has lost some of its standing as the home of future presidents. This does not mean that it will go the way of the cabinet, which served briefly as the presidency's penultimate office in the early nineteenth century, but it does mean that aspiring politicians will no longer need to find their way to the Senate—or for that matter to Washington—to make a serious run for the White House.

The strategic effects of the biases of the reformed selection system on the 1988 election were already apparent by 1985, winnowing and tailoring candidates to generate party nominees who if elected might well seek to emulate Ronald Reagan's style of leadership. Observers caught a glimpse of these processes in late 1984 when Howard Baker retired early from the Senate after finding his duties as majority leader, and perhaps the "insider" status that comes with it, an encumbrance during his brief and uneventful bid for the Republican presidential nomination in 1980.[12] For much of 1985, three years before the election, private citizen Baker could be found on the circuit of New Hampshire's civic lunches and coffee klatches, which quadrennially provide citizens of that state with their special form of entertainment. While Baker was laying the groundwork for a bid in New Hampshire's early primary, his former Senate Republican colleagues, some of whom also aspire to the presidency, were stuck in Washington grousing with their president and struggling with such unpleasant subjects as the budget deficit, import quotas, and the multiple problems of the American farmer. The same consideration can be seen in the decisions of Arizona Governor Bruce Babbitt and incumbent Colorado Senator Gary Hart to forego promising races for the Senate in 1986 in order to free themselves to seek the Democratic party's presidential nomination in 1988. Their strategic preference to make an office-less bid for the White House was repeated in 1992 when two of the five principal Democrats competing in the presidential primaries did so as former officeholders. By having voluntarily stepped off the political career ladder, former California Governor Jerry Brown and former Senator Paul Tsongas were able to stake out the moral high ground over their officeholding rivals.

Finally, individuals who have never held public office, but who do possess the requisite resources—ample television exposure, political action committees, and an established fundraising list—will in the future be considered serious contenders for this pinnacle office of the political career structure. When television evangelist Pat Robertson declared his presidential candidacy in 1987, his announcement was greeted in Washington not with derision but with an invitation to speak at the National Press Club. Four years later, another never-elected television personality, Patrick Buchanan, undertook the apparently quixotic task of winning the Republican party's nomination away from its sitting president. That he turned in a credible performance in the early presidential primaries strengthens the prospect of future candidacies from nonofficeholding politicians. Neither Robertson nor Buchanan, however, enjoyed the status of a serious contender that H. Ross Perot's vast personal fortune conferred on him.

Throughout this book going public has been presented as a product of the new Washington and its new breed of presidents. Because the political marketplace is regulated in no small part by anticipation of and adaptation to others' choices, going public has become incorporated generally into the expectations and behavior of Washingtonians. In this way it reinforces and accentuates the community's continued evolution.

Public Policy and Going Public

The implication of public strategies of leadership for policy has been a subject of recurrent interest in this study. Thus far I have concentrated mostly upon the deleterious side effects of public activity on bargaining to show that rather than complement, public strategies, when frequently engaged, damage and displace bargaining. Public discussion requires issues to be stylized in ways that frequently reduce choices to black-and-white alternatives and to principles that are difficult to modify. In part this reflects the rigidifying effect of declaring one's preferences publicly, but it also results from the stylization of issues required to accommodate the limited attention span of the public audience and the brief time spots available on national television.

Perhaps more damaging, public discussion tends to harden negotiating positions as both sides posture as much to rally support as to impress the other side. Bargaining and compromise suffer. Even when a stalemate is avoided, the adopted policy may not enjoy the same firm foundation of support had it been enacted by a negotiated consensus. These are some of the unfortunate consequences of making policy in the public arena. Other consequences strike more deeply to the foundation of democratic politics, if not shaking it, at least altering the structure of political relations it supports.

Supply-side Politics

At first glance the perforated borders of individualized pluralism would appear to bode well for democratic politics. After all, should the citzenry's demands not flow more freely into Washington? Weakened leadership and the deterioration of other mechanisms of conformity to the requirements of protocoalitions have made institutions more easily penetrable and have weakened their resistance to poaching by others who compete for the same jurisdiction. As a result, outsiders today are provided with a porous governmental apparatus that contains numerous access points for those who seek to influence policy. Moreover, the increased sensitivity of politicians to public pressure, which follows from these relaxed internal constraints, improves the chances that outsiders will find the necessary institutional sponsorship for their views. A fair reading of these developments might lead one to assume a closer alignment between policies favored in the country and those deliberated in Washington. If so, whatever its ill effects on partisan discussion, individualized pluralism's corruption of the traditionally insular political relations would be a boon to democracy.

The swiftness with which some new issues sweep into present-day Washington and traverse its policy course appears to confirm this assessment. The "flat tax" drive of the late 1970s found eager congressional sponsorship, and under Reagan it emerged in altered form as the core concept of the administration's comprehensive tax reform proposal. An even more impressive example is the alacrity with which Mothers Against Drunk Driving (MADD) won federal legislation in a policy realm that had traditionally been reserved to the states. In 1980, just two years before its legislative triumph, MADD was created by two mothers who had lost children in automobile accidents involving drunken drivers. Enjoying continuous television and press coverage, by 1982 MADD had formed 230 chapters in 42 states with a quarter of a million members. Because of its inspired grass-roots campaign, the federal government today insists that states have tough drunk driving laws on their books.[13]

In 1983 the savings and loan industry staved off an imminent Internal Revenue Service (IRS) regulation that would have required banks and savings associations to withhold a portion of depositors' interest for taxes. The similar quick success of these bankers is less impressive only because they needed a simple resolution of Congress and did not require the president's signature to accomplish their goal.[14]

These cases and others like them succeeded by short-circuiting the slow and arduous process by which policy issues have traditionally attracted majority coalitions in Washington. The traditional method consisted of continuous discussions with representatives of those constituencies who would be most affected by the policy and with key governmental participants—most frequently committee and subcommittee chairs and agency heads who would be chiefly responsible for enacting and implementing the program. This involved ongoing reformulation to broaden the policy's political support and to make it administratively feasible. Ultimately, if in this incubation phase the issue succeeded in attracting the right sponsors and sufficient support to give it a reasonable prospect of success (and few did), it would then typically wait in queue for a presidential endorsement, which might provide the necessary impetus to get it enacted.

What allowed the issues described above to circumvent the traditional process was the massive grass-roots campaign generated outside Washington; by the time representatives of these campaigns approached potential legislative sponsors, many politicians had already begun lining up to support the policy. The savings and loan industry's campaign quickly generated millions of letters and post cards. One senator alone counted 769,000 pieces of constituent mail—almost all of it supporting the industry.[15] By so thoroughly stirring the opinion that flows to members of Congress, many of those promoting special causes find that they can frequently prevail even when their efforts fail to win the endorsement of the president, the relevant agency heads, or committee chairs. The most senior Republican the savings and loan industry could recruit to sponsor its cause was first-term Senator Robert Kasten of Wisconsin. A generation earlier, this member's status would have earned him little more than an opportunity to be seen but not heard. By 1983, of course, the Senate had changed, and the opportunities available to a junior member had greatly expanded. Over the opposition of his party's committee and floor leaders, his president, and the Internal Revenue Service, Kasten promoted the cause of the savings and loan industry to a resounding victory on the Senate floor.[16]

Even in the altered circumstances of present-day Washington, Senator Kasten's feat surprised the local cognoscenti. It demonstrated that great external pressure can be sufficient to induce congressional compliance even without engaging traditional avenues of influence. This is a far cry from the lobbyist's code of "never pressure" under institutionalized pluralism.

Pressure is the essence of public strategies, whether they are engaged in by presidents or outside groups. Going public succeeds not by adjusting policy to the mix of preferences represented in Washington but rather by trading on the strategic concerns of elected politicians and, thereby, changing those preferences. When success or failure is decided in the country, institutional leaders are less necessary; even a junior senator can do a splendid job.

If by now the activities of the savings and loan industry and MADD look familiar, they should, because they follow much the same strategic formula President Reagan employed so successfully in 1981 to push massive tax and social spending cuts through Congress. The difference is one only of scale. Whether undertaken by a president seeking to redirect the priorities of the federal government or by two mothers wanting tougher drunk-driving laws, going public has become a frequently preferred approach to coalition building in Washington. On their face, these cases appear to support the improved responsiveness of national political institutions to the citizenry's demands under individualized pluralism.

But is this really what is going on? Are demands flowing more freely into Washington and shaping policy, or rather, are they being created by politicians through inspired mass advertising? One might argue that the distinction does not much matter because the appeals must still strike a responsive chord, or they will be quickly deflated by the public's inattention or even its antipathy. One can support this argument by pointing to the dismal performance of grass-roots lobbying by the Natural Gas Supply Association in 1983. Seeking to decontrol natural gas prices, this organization created a $1-million front called Alliance for Energy Security to drum up a national letter campaign to Congress. A consultant who specializes in targeted mail was retained to mount special pressure on 15 members of Congress whom the gas lobby had designated as vulnerable. Despite enlisting sophisticated technology and an appeal for energy security, the effort failed to generate the desired groundswell of support.[17]

The distinction between the citizenry's continuing demands rooted in life experiences and those of a more ephemeral quality generated by issue entrepreneurs is critical for appreciating the working of modern democracy in a communications age. Do the fixed preferences of the public motivate and direct the strategic activities of politicians, or, conversely, do politicians shape the preferences of the public, at least those that are effectively communicated to Washington? To use an analogy from economics, the distinction is between demand-side and supply-side politics. At one time, before the media had begun to replace work-related, ethnic, religious, and other voluntary associations as the chief source of civic information, and before political entrepreneurs had the technological wherewithal to mass market ideas through such diverse and specialized media as television and targeted mail, it would have been easy to say that the citizenry's demands are the autonomous force of American politics. Today, however, the answer is less clear. The emergence of mass communications technology gives voice to politicians and organizations who enjoy the financial resources to broadcast commercials to millions of citizens or who have the legitimacy to command similar access via the news media. The president has both.

Except perhaps for the concerted efforts of the Framers to draft a Constitution that would mitigate transient, "inflamed popular passions," one seldom finds American political thought directed to this matter of supply-side politics. In early democratic theory, representatives served as passive receptacles with whom the citizens could deposit their demands. Later, when under Edmund Burke's influence, students of politics began to view representatives less as delegates and more as fiduciary agents, or trustees, who were to exercise independent judgment, little attention was given to marketing, except as an officeholder defended his policies in a reelection campaign. Even in twentieth-century discussions of party democracy, political parties formulate their programs through close association with mediating organizations that articulate constituency demands, and they adjust their programs to match the preferences of as broad a cross section of the electorate as they can.[18] The idea of campaigning to mobilize public opinion for issues currently before Congress has not so much been condemned by theory as ignored. Such campaigns and the continuing public relations of modern presidents suggest that traditional thinking about the relationship between the representative and the represented needs revision.

Consider the evidence of supply-side politics available in the cases introduced above. Before the efforts of MADD, the savings and loan industry, or the Alliance for Energy Security, one would have had difficulty finding instances of ordinary citizens importuning members of Congress to do something about drunk drivers, to rescind the IRS's plan to withhold interest, or to decontrol natural gas prices. Similarly, recall from Figure 5-1 that President Reagan's budget cuts enjoyed majority endorsement only briefly, and that moment came well before he initiated the public campaign for the policy's enactment. On none of those subjects does the issue's sponsor appear to have merely given expression to pent-up or nascent demands. Instead, they (the president included) acted as entrepreneurs creating demands and channeling their expression to Washington. These instances lend support to the recent observation by one member of Congress that "grass-roots lobbying today is a highly sophisticated effort. Just by the sheer mechanics of modern technology, they can often generate what [appears to be] a groundswell of public opinion, when in fact that groundswell does not really exist." [19]

A Variable Agenda and Volatile Outcomes

Individualized pluralism liberates politicians from institutional and party bonds. This has two effects on policy: politicians are freer to choose which issues they wish to sponsor, and the success of those issues depends more heavily upon the talents and fortunes of their sponsors. The first means greater variability in the issues that rise, albeit perhaps temporarily, to the top of the agenda in Washington. The second means that coalition building will be subject to new, extraneous forces and, hence, will be more volatile.

As presidents and aspirants to the office have traditionally tried to expand their electoral support beyond their party's core constituency, a number of political forces have kept them tethered fairly near home. The large role of state parties and mediating organizations in selecting presidential candidates at the party convention meant that these politicians could ill afford to advocate policies too distant from the priorities of the party's base. In Congress, the party supplied institutional leadership, which meant that its legislative agenda already enjoyed substantial progress toward the development of a winning coalition. Consequently, policies associated with political parties and their core groups resided comfortably atop the national agenda. Since the early 1970s, however, presidential selection reforms and the reduced role of the party in coalition building have relaxed the parties' influence on presidential policy.

Today's presidents, more likely to be outsiders, are freer to choose their issues than typically were their predecessors. As a consequence, the policy agenda will vary with the incumbent and will do so in ways that cannot be easily predicted by the president's party affiliation.[20] This does not mean that presidents will sponsor issues randomly. As individualized pluralism has loosened bonds to party and institution, it has tightened others. Attentiveness to public opinion, of course, has always been a chief occupational requirement for those who serve in elective office, but today's politicians are displaying exceptional sensitivity to the breezes that blow into Washington. Sometimes it shows up in the president's conformity to the perceived moods of the public, but more often it manifests itself in White House behavior in the way presidents seek to influence other politicians who are equally subject to public opinion and who have fewer resources at hand with which to mold opinion to their liking.

There is a compelling rationale for suspecting that the more presidents rest their leadership on going public, the more volatile policy outcomes in Washington will be. The public can be assumed to be more fickle in its assessments of politicians and policies than will be a stable community of Washington elites, whose business it is to make informed judgments. As the former becomes more important and the latter less, political relations will be more easily disrupted. Moreover, the effect of the president's own public standing on his ability to rally public opinion behind his policies exposes policy to extraneous and wholly unrelated events. Whatever affects the president's standing with the public will alter the prospects for those policies he sponsors. Sometimes the result may be altogether salutary, as in the boost President Reagan's 1981 budget proposals received after the assassination attempt. But if the president falters, so, too, will those policies that depend upon him for their sustenance.[21]

A president who is unable to generate a groundswell of popular support for his program may soon find others sharply escalating their demands on him in return for their cooperation. Unlike bargaining, where failure at one negotiating session can be repaired at the next, going public does not appear to offer similarly easy avenues for remedying failure. Also, one may assume that public opinion will be more volatile than elites' expectations for exchange. So too, then, will be a style of leadership that relies more heavily upon popular support.[22]

By virtue of going public, a president may actually contribute to unfavorable swings of opinion in the country. Casting himself as the fount from which the answers to the nation's problems flow, such a president may raise public expectations to unrealistic heights.[23] If so, he will be setting himself up for a fall in the polls, which will be closely followed by a decline in his fortunes in Washington. No modern occupant of the White House may be able to repeat President Truman's performance in maintaining a large measure of his influence in Washington while barely a quarter of the country approved his job performance. Going public may allow a popular president to soar, but even as he does so, he creates the risk of an eventual collapse.

The volatility of modern politics is plainly conveyed in the interpretations Washington politicians and the press give to presidential events. Two occurrences within a six-week period during the summer of 1985 illustrate the heavy dependence of policy on the public fortunes of its sponsor. After recouping much of his sagging popularity during late spring with a forceful national appeal for tax reform, President Reagan entered June with tax reform the number one issue on Congress's agenda. Other less politically favorable developments during these weeks, such as the controversial U.S. support for the contras in Nicaragua, had failed to register in the news and the public utterances of politicians to the same degree they might have had tax reform not grabbed the headlines. On June 14, however, terrorists hijacked an international airliner and took more than 50 American passengers to Lebanon as hostages. Tax reform faded quickly. During the next weeks, some aides contended that Reagan's presidency hung in the balance.[24] Would this crisis paralyze the administration the way the Iranian hostage crisis had Carter's? Early on, one senior White House official confided to *Washington Post* columnist Lou Cannon that it was fortunate that tax reform would not come up for a vote in Congress until fall. Aside from whatever potential damage the hostage crisis might have on the president's public standing, tax reform had suddenly fallen from public view; and without active public support, it would face tough going in Congress. Then, nearly two weeks into the crisis, as those close to the negotiations realized that the hostages might be released soon, White House aides began voicing brighter prognostications for tax reform. One Reagan aide told Cannon that if the president "were successful in winning the release of the hostages, he would gain in public standing and use his increased popularity to become a more activist president." [25] The next day, before an audience in Illinois, President Reagan returned to the tax issue, stating with renewed enthusiasm that after Congress returned from the summer recess, "I'm heading out to the country—I'm going to campaign all across the nation throughout the fall for tax fairness." [26]

The promise of a "fall offensive" of public appeals was repeated frequently during the next few weeks. But it was turned off again when on

July 12 the president was admitted to Bethesda Naval Medical Center to remove a growth from his colon. Next to the president's health, the foremost political question was, if the president is unable to take to the hustings, what becomes of tax reform? Reagan pollster Richard B. Wirthlin cautiously answered one reporter's query by saying that the effect on tax reform depended upon "the speed and completeness of the recovery." [27] Meanwhile, *New York Times* columnist Tom Wicker was speculating that the public sympathy the president's illness could be expected to engender would give his legislative program a new boost.[28] Senator Pete Wilson sounded a cautionary note on tax reform, however, when during the president's convalescence he told a reporter that the "tax reform is losing rather than gaining momentum [in the country]." [29]

The president gives a prime-time address on tax reform, and it immediately soars to the top of the legislative agenda. Within moments, the chair of the House Ways and Means Committee in his own televised address promises action and exhorts the public for demonstrations of support. But when hostages are seized a couple of weeks later, the prospects of tax reform dim. Just as quickly, they brighten when the hostages are released. Then comes the president's operation and his speedy recuperation, tax reform once again waning and waxing in a two-week period. In a system such as ours where governing coalitions are formed by independent officeholders rather than by party teams, the personal skills and fortunes of the sponsor have always been a key ingredient in an issue's chances of success, but with the injection of public opinion into policy deliberation through grass-roots campaigns and the president's popularity, policy making promises to become more volatile.

The President's Agenda

Whatever their differences in personality—and they were considerable— Theodore Roosevelt and Woodrow Wilson shared one attribute that shaped their approach to leadership style as much as any other. Both men were Progressives. This meant that each envisioned a responsive federal government led by an energetic president actively promoting the collective interests of the country over the particular concerns of its political, geographical and economic subdivisions. Strategically, both men solicited demonstrations of public support for their program. They had to, since many of their Progressive reforms would strip power and its usufructs from those politicians who would be asked to enact them.

Compared with the access of modern presidents to the airwaves and to jet transportation, their opportunities to go public were truly modest. However handicapped, this strategy sometimes held more promise than did negotiations. When Wilson, as New Jersey's newly elected governor, was once pressed by reporters to explain how he could possibly hope to win political reforms from a state legislature dominated by solons loyal to their party organizations, he replied, "I can talk, can't I?" [30]

Neither president enlisted public strategies casually. The idea of continuous forays into the country to generate public support for their initiatives before Congress was plainly impractical. In their day, the imbalance between costs imposed by confining technology and benefits limited by firm institutional resistance would have made frequent public campaigns foolhardy. Roosevelt and Wilson regarded going public as a strategy appropriate for a limited set of issues. These issues were ones in which traditional bargaining could be expected to fail and for which the president could legitimately play the role of the national tribune against "the special interests" entrenched in Congress. By and large, these issues constituted the Progressive agenda. When these presidents expatiated on political reform, on the regulation of big business, and, for Roosevelt especially, on conservation, they spoke to the country as well as for it. On more fractious national issues—such as tariff reform, a bloated embodiment of Congress's particularistic urges—they refrained from enlisting public strategies. One Roosevelt biographer writes: "Significantly, Roosevelt reserved nearly all his opportunities as president for public persuasion—'a bully pulpit,' he called the office—for appeals to transcendent national interests and higher standards of personal conduct, rather than redress or justice to particular people or groups." [31] Woodrow Wilson recognized the necessary symbolic distinction when on the subject of regulation he asserted, "The present conflict in this country is not between capital and labor. It is a contest between those few men in whose hands the wealth of the land is concentrated, and the rest of us." [32]

The practices of Roosevelt and Wilson suggest that going public is more serviceable for some issues than for others. A president will enjoy his strongest claim to the public's attention and support when he can present his policies as uprooting unsavory particularism. This theme must be played off a backdrop of an unassailable public interest. For good measure, these appeals should, when possible, exploit Americans' deeply ingrained distrust of politicians. On these rhetorical criteria, the Progressive agenda was a motherlode to Roosevelt and Wilson.

With so many avenues for going public available to modern presidents, one finds them frequently appealing for public support more casually and frequently before the same "special interests" many Progressives held in open contempt. Nonetheless, the president's special legitimacy in going to the people to defend the public interest from private greed remains a powerful force today. Nor have the strategic implications been lost on the White House's recent occupants. Presidents Carter, Reagan, and, to a lesser degree, Bush couched their major legislative proposals as a struggle between public and private interests. When, early in his term, Jimmy Carter began a series of prime-time television addresses in behalf of his comprehensive energy program currently before Congress, he did not hesitate to conjure up the threat of rapacious special interests: "We can be sure that all the special interest groups in the country will attack . . . this plan. . . . If they succeed with this approach, then the burden on the ordinary citizen, who is not organized into an interest group, would be crushing. There should be only one test for this plan—whether it will help our country." [33]

President Reagan also cloaked his major legislative proposals in the public interest. Although his program differed diametrically from Progressivism in advocating the reduction of federal responsibilities to provide social services and to regulate industry, the imagery fit comfortably in that tradition. Chapter 5 examined Reagan's rhetorical style in his promotion of the budget and tax cuts of 1981. The following is an excerpt from his presentation of his tax reform proposal to a national television audience on May 28, 1985:

> The proposal I am putting forth tonight for America's future will free us from the grip of special interests and create a binding commitment to the only special interest that counts, you, the people who pay America's bills. It will create millions of new jobs for working people and it will replace the politics of envy with a spirit of partnership.[34]

For the rest of the year, Reagan would continue to sound this theme.[35]

The earlier two presidents engaged in public leadership to the degree they could because, despite their different party affiliations, each sought to enact a Progressive agenda over formidable opposition in Congress. What did Presidents Carter and Reagan have in common that led them to enlist similar rhetorical devices? Certainly, it was not Progressivism. I earlier noted their outsider status, which enhanced the credibility of their attacks on special interests. Presidents of this era portray special interests as being entrenched in the bureaucracy that doles out government funds ("puzzle palaces on the Potomac" administering the "social pork barrel") rather than in the party machines that extorted graft and dispensed patronage.

Even more important than their outsider status, these presidents share the modern facility to go public. For its first practitioners, going public was an invention inspired by a policy agenda that would fail if left to the traditional political process. The ends dictated the means. Today the situation may well be reversed. As modern presidents seek to exploit their strategic advantage in public opinion, they gravitate toward issues that endow them with the strongest claim to represent the "public interest." By its very nature, the policy program of the president's core constituency will be ill-suited for the kinds of appeals public strategies require. But no matter; presidents are no longer much beholden to these constituencies. Nor, in the setting of supply-side politics, are their policy options sharply circumscribed by the once great need to choose among policy ideas that had over time already attracted a sizable number of supporters in Washington. The profusion of think tanks, new-styled interest groups, and even the congressional caucuses offer presidents an ample supply of policy ideas from which to choose.[36]

When President Reagan mentioned in his 1984 State of the Union message that he would ask the Treasury Department to examine tax reform, his remark elicited tepid applause befitting its apparent insignificance. Little did the assembled members of Congress and other president watchers realize that by year's end, tax reform would emerge as the centerpiece of his second administration. With it he hoped to establish the Republican party as the new majority party of the country. That one of the principal authors of the Treasury bill had been a colleague of some of the early proponents of the "flat tax" proposal at the Hoover Institution illustrates the new, alternative sources of policy available to modern presidents.

As one looks to the future, the prospect for the continued use of going public as presidential strategy shines bright. The forces of technology and of an evolving political environment that set public campaigning from the White House on its current trajectory have not abated. Moreover, professional self-interest dictates that all participants in Washington's politics take going public into account as they plan their strategies. The president must as he decides which policies he wishes to promote. Would-be presidents must as they groom themselves and tailor their policy appeals for a future bid for the White House. So must White House correspondents as they evaluate the president's performance and as they weigh his rhetoric against their own and others' notions of reality. And so must all who do business with the president and are thereby vulnerable to his public appeals. The strategic adaptations these men and women are making will, as much as its original causes, guarantee that going public will occupy a prominent place in the strategic repertoire of future presidents.

Notes

1. The standards of performance Franklin Roosevelt established for his successors is the subject of William E. Leuchtenburg, *In the Shadow of FDR* (Ithaca, N.Y.: Cornell University Press, 1985).
2. Peter T. Kilborn, "The Key Democrat," *New York Times*, May 30, 1985, 15; and Hedrick Smith, "Analysis of Democrats' Strategy on Tax Reform? Yes—With Three Conditions," *Washington Post National Weekly Edition*, February 18, 1985, 28; and Steven V. Roberts, "A Most Important Man on Capitol Hill," *New York Times Magazine*, September 22, 1985, 44.
3. Alan Ehrenhalt, "Speaker's Job Transformed under O'Neill," *Congressional Quarterly Weekly Report*, June 22, 1985, 1247.
4. Julia Malone, "Party 'Whips' Lose Their Snap to TV and Voters Back Home," *Christian Science Monitor*, July 27, 1984, 16.
5. Steven V. Roberts, "Senate's New Breed Shuns Novice Role," *New York Times*, November 26, 1984, 15.
6. A recent example is the Department of Agriculture's grass-roots campaign to persuade Congress to adopt farm legislation it drafted. Ward Sinclair, "USDA's Farm Bill Lobbying Hit," *Washington Post*, October 1, 1985, A5.
7. Incidents such as this one are recounted in Edwin R. Bayley, *Joe McCarthy and the Press* (Madison: University of Wisconsin Press, 1981).

8. Ibid., 216-219; and Richard H. Rovere, *Senator Joe McCarthy* (New York: Harcourt, Brace, 1959).

9. Rovere, *Senator Joe McCarthy*.

10. Daniel C. Hallin, "Changing Conventions in Television Coverage of the Presidency, 1969-1985" (Paper delivered at the Annual Meeting of the Southern Political Science Association, Nashville, Tenn., November 1985). Technological advances—especially the introduction of the digital video effects machine—have had a hand in this change. Rather than an anchorperson editorializing during a video segment that may wander away from the subject, modern editing technology allows broadcast journalists to harness video footage to reinforce their message. For a discussion of the effects of modern broadcast technology, see Joan Bieder, "Television Reporting," in *The Communications Revolution in Politics,* ed. Gerald Benjamin (New York: Academy of Political Science, 1982), 36-48.

11. For a discussion of the Senate's special role in spawning presidential candidates and in the process incubating new policy issues, see Nelson W. Polsby, *Political Innovation in America* (New Haven: Yale University Press, 1984).

12. Martin Tolchin, "Baker Reported Planning to Quit Senate After '84," *New York Times,* January 11, 1983, A1.

13. Cited in Samuel Kernell and Dianne Kernell, *Congress: We the People* (Washington, D.C.: American Political Science Association, 1984), 90-91.

14. Timothy B. Clark, "Bankers' Opposition to Withholding May Leave a Bitter Legislative Aftertaste," *National Journal,* April 2, 1983, 700-703. Similarly, on the speedy passage of legislation providing federal incentive payments to states to strengthen enforcement of garnishing the wages of parents who are delinquent in child support payments, see Steven V. Roberts, "Political Survival: It's Women and Children First," *New York Times,* December 6, 1983, 10.

15. Ann Cooper, "Middleman Mail," *National Journal,* September 14, 1985, 2038.

16. For the background of this issue and a description of Kasten's floor maneuvers, see Clark, "Bankers' Opposition," 700-703.

17. One member targeted by the campaign, Philip Sharp of Indiana, calculated that he should have gotten 27,500 post cards according to the number of volunteer kits the Natural Gas Supply Association had distributed to his district. Instead, he received 1,125 post cards, and 200 of those had antidecontrol messages scribbled over the printed message. Cooper, "Middleman Mail," 2041. See also Milton R. Benjamin, "Natural Gas Lobby Organizes 'Grass-Roots' Decontrol Move," *Washington Post,* August 13, 1983, A1.

18. Two statements that arrive at much the same conclusion on this matter via quite different intellectual exercises are E. E. Schattschneider, *Party Government* (New York: Holt, Rinehart and Winston, 1942), 1-17, passim; and Anthony Downs, *An Economic Theory of Democracy* (New York: Harper and Row, 1957), 114-141.

19. Cooper, "Middleman Mail," 2037.

20. Nathaniel Beck makes precisely this point in his statistical analysis of recent administrations' macroeconomics policies. See his "Parties, Administrations, and American Macroeconomic Outcomes," *American Political Science Review* 76 (March 1982): 83-93.

21. Recent presidents have faltered in their popularity ratings more quickly and more seriously than their predecessors of the 1950s and 1960s. For evidence of this, see Samuel Kernell, "The Presidency and the People: The Modern Paradox," in *The Presidency and the Political System,* ed. Michael Nelson (Washington, D.C.: CQ Press, 1984), 253-256.

22. The volatility of popularity ratings is examined in detail in Chapter 7. See also Samuel Kernell, "The Presidency and the People: The Modern Paradox," in *The*

246 *Going Public*

Presidency and the Political System, ed. Michael Nelson (Washington, D.C.: CQ Press, 1984), 223-263.
23. Godfrey Hodgson so argues in *All Things to All Men* (New York: Simon and Schuster, 1980), 209-260.
24. Lou Cannon, "The Wait It Out Pitfall," *Washington Post,* June 23, 1985, A26.
25. Lou Cannon, "Reagan Agenda May Get a Lift," *Washington Post,* July 1, 1985, A19. For a more general treatment of the relation between the president's popularity and programmatic support, see Barry Sussman, "How Public Opinion Surveys May Bring Us a Fairer Tax System," *Washington Post National Weekly Edition,* June 24, 1985, 37.
26. Cannon, "Reagan Agenda," A19.
27. Jack Nelson, "Illness May Dim Outlook for President's Programs," *Los Angeles Times,* July 21, 1985, 1.
28. Tom Wicker, "After Surgery, What?" *New York Times,* July 23, 1985, 27.
29. Nelson, "Illness May Dim Outlook," 12. Senator Wilson's impressions were confirmed in Lou Cannon and Helen Dewar, "Tax Overhaul Hit in Poll, GOP Caucus," *Washington Post,* September 25, 1985, A3.
30. John Milton Cooper, Jr., *The Warrior and the Priest* (Cambridge: Harvard University Press, 1983), 173.
31. Ibid., 86.
32. Ibid., 126.
33. Jimmy Carter, "The Energy Problem" (address to the nation, April 18, 1977), *Public Papers of the Presidents of the United States, Jimmy Carter, 1977* (Washington, D.C.: Government Printing Office, 1978), 661-662. A year later when he kicked off his "three martini lunch" tax reform, he argued, "Average Americans foot the bill for the rich and others who mark off from their tax payments high-priced meals, high-priced theater tickets, ballgame tickets, first-class air travel, even country club dues.... And the ones who pay are the quiet, average American working family members" (Jimmy Carter, "Tax Reduction and Reform" [remarks concerning proposals submitted to the Congress, April 17, 1978], *Public Papers of the Presidents, 1978,* 755).
34. "Text of Speech by President on Overhauling the Tax System," *New York Times,* May 29, 1985, A18.
35. David E. Rosenbaum reports, "President Reagan has often succeeded in establishing himself as champion of the people and his political opponents as tools of 'special interest' " ("Momentum and the Tax Bill," *New York Times,* October 19, 1985, 8).
36. On the role of "think tanks" as the origin of ideas for the Reagan administration, see Dom Bonafede, "Issue-Oriented Heritage Foundation Hitches Its Wagon to Reagan's Star," *National Journal,* March 20, 1982, 502-507; Al Kamen and Howard Kurtz, "Theorists on Right Find Fertile Ground," *Washington Post,* August 9, 1985, A1; and Sidney Blumenthal, "Outside Foundation Recruited the Inside Troops," *Washington Post,* September 10, 1985, A1. On presidential-caucus relations, see Susan Webb Hammond, "Congressional Caucuses and Party Leaders" (Paper prepared for delivery at the Annual Meeting of the American Political Science Association, Washington, D.C., August 30-September 2, 1984).

Appendix

Chapter 4

To incorporate the research of William W. Lammers on the public activities of modern presidents, I adopted his coding scheme. I also consulted with Professor Lammers at the early stages of this study for his advice on how to code difficult cases. The present analysis, therefore, benefits from both his considerable research and good judgment.[1]

The three general categories of public activities presented in Figures 4-1, 4-2, and 4-3 are intended to be neither mutually exclusive nor together an exhaustive classification of all public behavior. Press conferences (examined in Table 3-2), purely ceremonial functions such as lighting the White House Christmas tree, vacation travel, and minor public activities such as White House receptions and brief remarks have been excluded from the analysis.

Addresses

Major addresses are those generally delivered in Washington, broadcast on television or radio, and focused on more than a narrow potential audience. Inaugural and State of the Union speeches are included in this group. Note that because of the extensive number of nationally broadcast radio addresses by President Reagan, I have separated his radio from his television addresses in Figure 4-1. Minor addresses are all nonmajor statements made outside the White House in which the president spoke more than 1,000 words. Question and answer sessions, even if conducted outside a formal press conference setting, are excluded.

Political Travel

To distinguish purely vacation travel from work-related travel, only those travel days that involved public political activity are included in Figure 4-2. Moreover, to be coded as domestic political travel, the president must do more than engage in brief conversation with reporters. To be coded as political foreign travel, the travel day must include comments exceeding 200 words, a meeting with a head of state, or attendance at an international conference, even if the president does not engage in public activity.

Appearances

Washington appearances take place away from the White House and the Executive Office Building and include all appearances in Washington and its surrounding suburbs. Brief comments with reporters are excluded from both Washington and U.S. appearances, but prepared remarks on arrival are included in the coding. Unlike Professor Lammers, who excluded President Carter's town meetings, I have coded them as constituting both days of travel and appearances.

Chapter 7

The coefficients reported in Table 7-4 are the products of an elaborate procedure to estimate well-specified models of partisan popularity for the seven presidents from Eisenhower through Reagan. Each stage of the statistical analysis of the popularity time-series presents choices that indirectly contribute to the strengths of the economic variables reported in Table 7-4. These choices concern variable specification and the implicit model of opinion change employed in the statistical analysis.

Specification of Variables

Deciding which variables should be included in the statistical analysis and how each should be operationally defined has important implications for the results. The omission or misspecification of noneconomic variables can bias the estimates of the economic variables. Generally, this phase of the analysis closely follows the procedures employed in earlier published research on presidential popularity. The reader is referred to those sources for a fuller discussion of the issues presented below.[2]

The dependent variables in the regression equations reported in Tables A-1, A-2, A-3, and A-4 are the percentages among respondents in each of the partisan subgroups who answered the monthly Gallup query "Do you approve or disapprove of the way ____ is handling his job as president?" with approval. If the president's popularity rating were to drop below 25 percent or rise above 75 percent, the "ceiling and floor effects" of variables expressed as proportions might bias the results. The president's overall popularity rating rarely exceeds these extremes, however, so that transforming them to adjust for ceiling and floor effects is normally unnecessary.[3] Estimating popular support for partisans, however, is a different matter. As indicated in Table 7-3, among those who identify with the president's party, support infrequently drops below 75 percent approving. And although the mean support levels of the opposition party's identifiers indicate that their support typically resides above 25 percent approving, the standard deviations indicate that it has sometimes declined below this threshold. To adjust for this potential bias, the regression equations in Tables A-1 and A-2 were also estimated with a logistical transformation of the popularity ratings. Since the relative strengths of the economic variables were unaffected by this procedure and the untransformed values are more readily interpretable, the results presented below and in Chapter 7 use the untransformed percentages.

The independent variables of principal interest in Chapter 7 are unemployment and inflation. A variety of statistical evidence suggests that citizens pay greater attention to *changes* in political conditions during a relatively brief time period than either to changes since the beginning of the president's term or to absolute conditions. As one of Reagan's political consultants averred, "It's far better to come into an election with a 9% unemployment rate that's falling than a 6% rate that is rising."[4] Accordingly, unemployment and inflation are defined as the percentage change in the unemployment rate and consumer price index over the preceding six months.[5] Finally, I have assumed that the public does not hold the president responsible for changing economic conditions during his first six months in office. The economic variables for this period were set at their respective mean values over the incumbent's term.

A number of dummy and real-value exogenous variables also appear in the four Appendix tables. Since presidents frequently begin their terms with a surfeit of popular support, an early-term variable was constructed by setting its initial value at 6 and decreasing it one unit each month until it reached a value of 0. A similar variable was constructed for those international events, typically crises, during which the president's overall rating appeared to surge temporarily beyond its normal level. Here, the dummy variable was set at 5 for the first observation after the onset of the rally event and decreased one unit per month until reaching 0. The following events were designated as rally events in Tables A-1, A-2, A-3, and A-4.[6]

Two long-lasting events that had a substantial negative effect on the public standing of Presidents Johnson and Nixon were the Vietnam War and Watergate, respectively. The first is measured with two indicators: the monthly figures of U.S. war dead and the log of the number of bombing missions over North Vietnam. Each measures a different aspect of the war's intensity, and Tables A-1 and A-3 show each to have been independently related to President Johnson's popularity. Watergate is represented by a simple dummy variable that assumes a value of 0 before the Senate Watergate Committee convened and a value of 1 thereafter.[7] Since political events and conditions are argued here to shape political evaluations to the degree they become political issues, I have weighted the Vietnam and Watergate variables by the percentage of Gallup Poll respondents who named this issue as "one of the most important problems facing the country

	Rally 1	Rally 2	Rally 3	Rally 4
Eisenhower	Korean truce	Sputnik	Lebanon	Khrushchev visit
Kennedy	Bay of Pigs	Berlin wall	Berlin crisis	Cuban missile crisis
Johnson	Dominican Republic	Bombing of North Vietnam	Glassboro summit	Tet offensive
Nixon	Vietnam peace agreement	—	—	—
Ford	Mayaquez	—	—	—
Carter	Camp David summit	Iran-Afghanistan	—	—
Reagan	Korean airliner	Grenada	—	—
Bush	Panama	Desert Shield	Gulf War	—

today."[8] A similar procedure was applied to the economic variables. Despite the variability of inflation and unemployment as major public concerns in recent years, this procedure had little effect on the coefficients. Therefore, to facilitate interpretation, I have retained the unweighted values for unemployment and inflation.

A Dynamic Model of Opinion Change

One may reasonably assume that events such as those presented above continue to have a residual effect on the president's popular support beyond the month in which they occur. This information must be incorporated into the analysis to obtain properly specified equations. How one estimates the residual effects of incremental opinion change depends upon the model of opinion formation under consideration. In recent years many specifications for the lagged effects of past events have been suggested in the literature.[9] Several approaches were tested before settling on an exponential decay function of past events on subsequent popularity ratings. By including the approval rating for the previous month on the right-hand side of the regression equation, I am stipulating that past events continue to have a lingering effect on the president's current popularity, and that they decay at the same rate for each exogenous variable.[10]

Inclusion of the president's popularity for the preceding month in the equation means that the coefficients for the other variables state their immediate effect on popularity. This explains why many of the coefficients in Tables A-1 and A-2 may appear to be unduly small and statistically

Table A-1 Effects of Political Conditions on Presidential Popularity among Party Groups: Eisenhower, Kennedy, and Johnson

	Eisenhower (N = 86)			Kennedy (N = 32)			Johnson (N = 50)		
	Same party	Independents	Opposition party	Same party	Independents	Opposition party	Same party	Independents	Opposition party
Intercept	27.9	23.8	20.3	37.1	21.8	17.2	58.5	43.1	22.9
Early-term	.4	1.2	1.8	.8	1.5	3.3	1.0	.8	-.1
Rally 1	.4	.4	1.0	1.3	1.2	1.2	.9	1.0	.4
Rally 2	.8	1.3	1.5	1.0	1.5	2.4	.7	2.0	1.5
Rally 3	.3	.1	.5	.1	1.9	-.2	.7	-.2	1.0
Rally 4	.4	.5	1.0	2.1	2.0	2.5	-.6	.5	-.5
VN bombings	—	—	—	—	—	—	-.001	-.005	-.0013
U.S. killed in VN	—	—	—	—	—	—	-.008	-.008	-.006
Unemployment	-3.1	-2.8	-4.2	-99.3	-137.8	-77.3	-523.6	-841.2	-247.1
Inflation	-290.2	-498.2	-715.6	—	—	—	-1,012.8	-2,225.1	-1,111.2
Lag of popularity	.68	.64	.59	.52	.61	.54	.23	.26	.56
Adjusted r^2	.61	.61	.64	.75	.76	.75	.87	.87	.92
Durbin's h	2.57	2.29	1.65	1.25	2.8	.82	-3.8	2.3	.90

Table A-2 Effects of Political Conditions on Presidential Popularity among Party Groups: Nixon, Ford, Carter, and Reagan

	Nixon (N = 6)			Ford (N = 21)			Carter (N = 40)			Reagan (N = 40)		
	Same party	Independents	Opposition party	Same party	Independents	Opposition party	Same party	Independents	Opposition party	Same party	Independents	Opposition party
Intercept	19.9	10.0	11.4	46.8	40.7	22.7	26.0	31.1	16.7	43.7	22.2	8.9
Early-term	.8	1.0	.7	-.5	-.1	.1	3.2	4.9	4.0	.8	1.3	1.2
Rally 1	.5	.8	.4	1.3	1.7	1.0	2.0	1.9	1.1	.9	1.2	1.6
Rally 2	—	—	—	—	—	—	3.1	3.2	3.0	.8	.4	.6
Watergate	-36.6	-35.1	-66.0	—	—	—	—	—	—	—	—	—
Unemployment	-46.4	-20.2	-175.9	-2.2	-19.0	-5.4	-26.8	-28.5	-37.6	-10.1	-16.6	-10.3
Inflation	-82.8	-48.3	-1.1	-132.6	-111.4	-101.2	-120.9	-199.1	-69.9	—	—	—
Lag of Popularity	.76	.81	.71	.34	.18	.42	.62	.44	.50	.46	.55	.65
Adjusted r^2	.92	.91	.91	.39	.33	.38	.81	.80	.76	.51	.72	.88
Durbin's h	3.38	3.30	1.40	2.77	.68	1.51	-1.04	-1.84	-1.40	-1.13	-1.21	-2.16

Table A-3 Long-term and Mean Effects of Political Conditions on Presidential Popularity among Party Groups: Eisenhower, Kennedy, and Johnson

	Eisenhower			Kennedy			Johnson		
	Same party	Independents	Opposition party	Same party	Independents	Opposition party	Same party	Independents	Opposition party
Early-term	1.3	.43	4.39	1.67	3.85	7.17	1.29	1.08	−.23
Rally 1	1.25	1.11	2.44	2.7	3.08	2.61	1.17	1.35	.91
Rally 2	2.5	3.61	3.66	2.1	3.85	5.22	.91	2.7	3.41
Rally 3	.94	.28	1.22	.32	.04	4.13	−.26	.94	2.27
Rally 4	1.25	1.39	2.44	4.38	5.13	5.43	−.78	−.68	1.14
Total rally (R1–R4)	5.94	6.39	9.76	9.6	12.1	17.39	1.04	4.31	7.73
VN bombings	—	—	—	—	—	—	−.0013	−.0007	−.003
U.S. killed in VN	—	—	—	—	—	—	−.010	−.011	−.014
Unemployment	−9.7	−7.8	−10.2	−206.9	−353.3	−168.0	−680.0	−1,136.8	−561.6
Inflation	−906.9	−1,388.9	−1,745.4	—	—	—	−1,315.32	−3,006.9	−2,525.5

Table A-4 Long-term and Mean Effects of Political Conditions on Presidential Popularity among Party Groups: Nixon, Ford, Carter, Reagan, and Bush

	Nixon			Ford			Carter		
	Same party	Independents	Opposition party	Same party	Independents	Opposition party	Same party	Independents	Opposition party
Early-term	3.33	5.26	2.41	-.76	-.12	-.17	8.42	8.75	8.0
Rally 1	2.08	4.21	1.38	1.97	2.07	1.72	5.26	3.39	2.2
Rally 2	—	—	—	—	—	—	8.15	5.71	6.0
Rally 3	—	—	—	—	—	—	—	—	—
Total rally	2.08	4.21	1.38	1.97	2.07	1.72	13.41	9.1	8.2
Watergate	—	—	—	—	—	—	—	—	—
Unemployment	-193.3	-106.3	-606.6	-3.33	-23.2	-9.3	17.9	-50.9	-75.2
Inflation	-345.0	-254.2	-3.79	-200.9	-135.9	-174.5	-318.16	-355.54	-137.8

Table A-4 Continued

	Reagan			Bush		
	Same party	Independents	Opposition party	Same party	Independents	Opposition party
Early-term	1.48	2.90	3.43	2.1	-2.1	-1.9
Rally 1	1.67	2.67	4.57	2.5	2.5	2.8
Rally 2	1.48	.89	1.71	1.6	2.6	1.4
Rally 3	—	—	—	3.6	7.4	6.5
Total rally	3.15	3.56	6.28	7.7	12.5	10.7
Watergate	—	—	—	—	—	—
Unemployment	-18.7	-36.89	-29.43	3.8	-9.8	10.4
Inflation	—	—	—	-253.0	-461.0	-297.0

NOTE: The main entries state the cumulative effects of the variables on the presidents' current popularity.

insignificant. A variable's long-term effect on popularity can be obtained with the following formula:[11]

$$\text{long-term effect of X} = \frac{bX_t}{1-cY_{t-1}}$$

where X_t is an exogenous variable and Y_{t-1} is the lag term of the dependent variable. The estimates presented in Tables A-3 and A-4 have been transformed to represent the long-term effects of the variables on popularity.

The coefficients have been transformed in another way as well. To compare the actual effects of variables that are based on different units of measurement, the coefficients have been multiplied by their mean values.[12] The relationships reported, therefore, in parentheses in Tables A-3 and A-4, and in Table 7-4, represent the long-term, "level" effects of the variables on the president's approval rating.

Notes

1. For the most comprehensive presentation of Lammers's work, see William W. Lammers, "Presidential Attention-Focusing Activities," in *The President and the American Public*, ed. Doris A. Graber (Philadelphia: Institute for the Study of Human Issues, 1982), 145-171.
2. Samuel Kernell, "Explaining Presidential Popularity," *American Political Science Review* 72 (June 1978): 506-522; and Samuel Kernell and Douglas A. Hibbs, Jr., "A Critical Threshold Model of Presidential Popularity," in *Contemporary Political Economy*, ed. Douglas A. Hibbs, Jr., and Heino Fassbender (New York: North-Holland, 1981), 49-72.
3. John E. Mueller was among the first to test for and dismiss these effects on the estimation of presidential popularity. See his "Presidential Popularity from Truman to Johnson," *American Political Science Review* 64 (March 1970): 18-34.
4. Rich Jaroslovsky, "Economic Upturn Aids President's Popularity, but It Is Not Panacea," *Wall Street Journal*, April 28, 1983, 1.
5. The unemployment and inflation variables have been annualized. The evidence for this specification is discussed fully in Kernell, "Explaining Presidential Popularity."
6. These events were identified by using criteria developed in Samuel Kernell, "Presidential Popularity and Electoral Preference" (Ph.D. diss., University of California, Berkeley, 1975); and in Richard A. Brody, "That Special Moment: The Public Response to International Crisis" (Paper delivered at the Annual Meeting of the Western Political Science Association, Seattle, Wash., March 24, 1983).
7. Kernell, "Explaining Presidential Popularity."
8. This procedure is suggested in the work of Charles W. Ostrom, Jr., and Dennis M. Simon, "Promise and Performance: A Dynamic Model of Presidential Popularity," *American Political Science Review* 79 (June 1985): 334-358.

256 Going Public

9. Among others is the distributed lag approach of Douglas A. Hibbs, Jr., "On the Reward for Economic Outcomes: Macroeconomic Performance and Mass Political Support in the United States, Great Britain, and Germany," *Journal of Politics* 44 (May 1982): 426-461. For shortcomings of this procedure, see Samuel Kernell, "Strategy and Ideology: The Politics of Unemployment and Inflation in Modern Capitalist Democracies" (Paper delivered at the Annual Meeting of the American Political Science Association, Washington, D.C., August 28-31, 1980). Kristen R. Monroe employs an Almon model of lagged effects of the economy in *Presidential Popularity and the Economy* (New York: Praeger, 1984). For a different (and somewhat iconoclastic) approach to this issue, see Helmut Norpoth and Thom Yantek, "Macroeconomic Conditions and Fluctuations of Presidential Popularity: The Question of Lagged Effects," *American Journal of Political Science* 27 (November 1983): 785-807.
10. After several tests, a standard exponential decay function for all independent variables appeared to be a reasonable one.
11. For a discussion of this procedure, see Potluri Rao and Roger LeRoy Miller, *Applied Econometrics* (Belmont, Calif.: Wadsworth Publishing Co., 1971), 45-46. Rao and Miller also provide a useful discussion (pp. 123-125) of Durbin's h, a statistic for testing serial correlation of the error terms in autoregressive models. Eleven of the 21 entries equal or exceed the values ± 1.645 indicating that the errors are serially correlated. An analysis (not shown) of the residuals suggested first-order autocorrelation. Reestimating the equations with an instrumental variable substituted for the lagged term eliminated the serial correlation. While the overall relationships are weaker than those reported in Tables A-3 and A-4, the relative strengths of unemployment and inflation with each other and across party groups were unaffected by this procedure.
12. This approach to causal interpretation of regression estimates is persuasively advocated by Christopher H. Achen in *Interpreting and Using Regression* (Beverly Hills, Calif.: Sage Publications, 1982), 68-77.

Index

Abelson, Robert P., 184-185n21
Abramson, Rudy, 184n14
Achen, Christopher H., 224-225n54
Acheson, Dean, 170, 185n32
Adams, Henry, 57
Adams, Sherman, 194
Albertazzie, Ralph, 118n20n25
Allison, Graham, 8n6
Alpern, David M., 150-151n20, 152n40
Alsop, Joseph, 46n18, 75, 118n31
Alsop, Stuart, 84n71
American Broadcasting Company
  (ABC), 158
Appropriations Committee, House,
  45n6
Arieff, Irwin B., 149n30
Armstrong, William, 134
Atlantic magazine, Stockman interview
  in, 198-199
Atwater, Lee, 149, 152n52
Ayres, B. Drummond, Jr., 51n49, 116n3

Babbitt, Bruce, 234
Baily, Robert Lee, 118n36
Baker, Howard, 135-136, 145, 231, 233
Baker, James, 127, 128
  negotiations with Israel, 157-158
  as Reagan Chief of Staff, 200
Balutis, Alan P., 82n17, 222n16
Banking industry, lobbying by, 235-236
Barnes, Fred, 86n84
Barry, David S., 61, 83n29
Barry, John M., 224n47
Bartlett, Charles, 75

Bay of Pigs invasion, 160
Bayley, Edward R., 244n7, 245n8
Beal, Richard, 126
Beck, Nathaniel, 245n20
Becker, Samuel L., 118n28n32
Beer, Samuel, 115
Benjamin, Milton R., 245n17
Bent, Silas, 58, 60, 83n21n23
Berman, Larry D., 223n37
Bieder, Joan, 245n10
Bingham, Worth, 85n65, 86n73n74
Binkley, Wilfred E., 82n7
Biznet, 29
Blum, John Morton, 48n23
Blumenthal, Michael, 216-217
Blumenthal, Sidney, 51n47, 126, 148,
  150n17n18, 151n26, 155n90, 246n36
Bodnick, Marc A., 151n23
Bohlen, Charles, 185n29n36
Bolling, Richard, 128, 152-153n53
Bonafede, Dom, 246n36
Boorstin, Daniel J., 68, 82n11, 84n56
Bork, Robert, 113
Bosler, Barbara, 223n33
Boyd, Gerald M., 86n79
Boyer, Peter J., 6n2, 119n41
Bradlee, Ben, 75
Brady, James, 126
Brandt, Raymond P., 83n19
Broder, David S., 9n11, 55, 153n64
Brody, Richard, 161, 183n7, 184n17,
  225n64
Broun, Heywood, 84n48
Brown, Jerry, 37, 234

Brown, Pat, 122
Brownell, Herbert, 197
Buchanan, Patrick, 37, 214, 234
Buchwald, Art, 103
Budget director, 198
Burke, Edmund, 238
Bush, George, 1, 37, 93, 107, 109, 117n13, 158, 163, 227-228, 242
  Desert Storm and, 158-159, 196, 218
  economic policies of, 214
  extent of political travels, 104-106
  on Israeli settlements and U. S. loan guarantees, 157-158
  issues confronting, as president, 206
  popularity of, 158, 159, 194, 218
  press relations of, 75, 77, 79-80, 87n86n87
  public opinion polling, 31
  public opinion strategy, 205
  relations with opposition Congress, 40-41, 42-45
  speaking engagements of, 99
  taxes and, 229-230
  television appearances of, 113
Byrd, Robert, 129
Byrnes, James, 170

Cable News Network (CNN), 79
Caddell, Patrick, 101
Cannon, Lou, 4, 7n12, 86n77, 123-124, 150n2n9, 240, 246n24n25n26n29
Capra, Frank, 191
Carter, Jimmy, 1, 37, 52n64, 99, 104, 107, 117n10n11, 118n38, 119n40, 131, 223n24, 225n61, 246n33
  effectiveness related to public opinion, 33
  energy policies of, 93, 189
  hostage rescue attempt, 160
  marginals strategy of, 216-217
  party approval and, 214, 216
  popularity of, 194, 200, 218
  and hostage taking, 163
  press relations of, 75, 77, 78, 91
  public appearances, 99
  public opinion polling by, 31
  public relations efforts by, 191
  relations with Congress, 38-39
  role of news media in public opinion of, 196
  Soviet Union grain embargo, 205
  on special interests, 242-243

  television use by, 112, 113
  as Washington outsider, 36, 123
Cater, Douglass, 16, 26, 47n9, 49n31, 56, 82n9, 117n8, 118n26
Catledge, Turner, 48n18, 118n31
Cavala, William, 51n60
CBS. *See Columbia Broadcasting System*
Chamber of Commerce, U. S., 28-29, 144
Chancellor, John, 81
Cheney, Richard B., 41, 51n, 57n62
Child support payment, 50n43, 247n14
Church, George J., 151n28, 152n46
Churchill, Winston, 107
Clapper, Olive Ewing, 82n2n5, 84n37
Clapper, Raymond, 84n49
Clark, Timothy B., 245n14n16
Cleveland, Grover, 83n27
Clines, Francis X., 154n75, 155n92n93, 184n14
Clinton, Bill, 37
Coalition building
  congressional caucuses in, 27, 29
  individualized pluralism and, 24-25, 238-240
  marginals strategy of, 212-217
  in presidential nominating process, 34
  presidential speechmaking for, 98-99
  protocoalitions, 13-14, 23-24
Cohen, Wilbur, 15
Cohen, William, 154n66
Cold War, origins in Truman Doctrine, 168-171
Columbia Broadcasting System (CBS), 112
Congress
  caucuses in, 27, 29
  constituent pressure on, 17-18
  midterm elections, 39
  opportunities to go public, 230-231
  opposition party president and, 39-41, 228
  outsider presidents and, 37-39
  presidential candidates from, 233
  press coverage of, 197, 222n16
  relations with president, 9
  relationships of members of, 12-13
  role of, 237-238
  role of leadership in, 15
  role of populist support for legislation, 235-238

structural changes in, 26-29
Congressional Arts Caucus, 27
Congressional Directory, 58
Conover, Paula J., 184n17
Consistency theory, 164-166, 168, 174-175
Conventions, Democratic Party reforms, 35-36
Cooke, Alistair, 155n87
Coolidge, Calvin, 65
  press relations of, 63-64
Cooper, Ann, 245n15n19
Cooper, John Milton, Jr., 246n30-32
Cornwell, Elmer E., Jr., 185n25, 222n16
Cowan, Edward, 154n77, 225n61
Crisis leadership, 159-168
Cuba
  Bay of Pigs invasion, 160
  missile crisis, 91
Cue giving, 13

Dahl, Robert A., 3, 6n5, 10, 47n1n3, 114, 119n45
Davenport, Walter, 67, 84n43n51n55
Davidson, Roger, 26, 49n32
Davis, Eric L., 49n28
Deakin, James, 78, 83n26, 85-86n71, 192-194, 196, 197-198, 221n6
Deaver, Michael, 80
Deaver, Richard, 126
Democratic Party
  black voters and, 214
  Democratic National Committee, 111
  Democratic Study Groups, 26-27, 49n33
  economic issues and, 207
  presidential nominations since 1972, 33-37
Democratic Study Groups, 26-27, 49n33
DeNardi, Lawrence, 146
Department of Agriculture, 14
Desert Storm, 158-159, 160, 163, 194, 218
Dewar, Helen, 154n78, 246n29
Dewey, Thomas, 175
Dicks, Norman, 131
Diehl, Jackson, 183n2
Dodge, Joseph, 198
Dole, Robert, 7n15

Domenici, Pete, 145, 153n55
Donnelly, Harrison, 116n3
Doonesbury, 124
Dowd, Maureen, 52n74
Downs, Anthony, 225n61, 245n18
Drew, Elizabeth, 150n17n19, 153n56
Duberstein, Kenneth, 30
Dukakis, Michael, 229

Early, Stephen, 66
Ebring, Lutz, 222n15
Economic issues. *See also Reagan, Ronald, budget negotiations; Tax issues*
  managing via general problem solving, 207-212, 217, 218-219
  managing via marginals strategy, 212-220
  in motivating electorate, 195
  nature of, 200, 207-208
  presidential popularity and, 217-221
  public opinion and presidential leadership in, 190, 208-212
Editor and Publisher magazine, 66
Education of electorate, foreign policy and, 177-178
Edwards, George C., III, 51n48, 86n81, 117n18, 184n18, 222n22
Ehrenhalt, Alan, 49n29, 244n3
Ehrlichman, John, 111
Eisenhower, Dwight, 13, 28, 36, 104, 107, 109, 118n30, 123, 150n6, 157
  budget director of, 198
  confrontation with press, 197-199
  importance of public opinion to, 202, 203
  popularity of, 194, 215, 219
  press relations of, 70-71, 75
Eizenstat, Stuart, 50n42
Elections
  in bargaining model, 11
  motivations of voters, 195
  nominee selection in Democratic Party, 33-37
  presidential popularity and, 202-203
  primaries/caucuses, 35
  primary, 9
  reforms in, 9, 33-39, 233-234
  role of political parties in, 10, 45-46
Employment issues, 207-217
Energy issues, public opinion and, 189
Equal time rule, 1, 111-112

Essary, J. Frederick, 60, 68, 83*n*24
Evans, Rowland, 89-90, 116*n*2

Farney, Dennis, 49*n*33, 154*n*80
Federal Communications Commission
 (FCC), 1, 111, 112
Federal Election Campaign Act, 28
Federal Election Commission, 28
Federal matching funds, 35
Federal Trade Commission (FTC), 28
Feinstein, Diane, 157
Feis, Herbert, 185*n*36, 186*n*39
Fenno, Richard F., 47*n*6, 85*n*57
Ferber, Mark F., 49*n*33
Festinger, Leon, 186*n*43
Fioriana, Morris P., 49*n*26
Fiske, Susan T., 185*n*22*n*24
Foley, Thomas, 126
Foote, Joe S., 119*n*44
Ford, Gerald, 39, 75, 112, 117*n*6,
 119*n*42, 152*n*46, 160
 Nixon pardon, 205
Foreign affairs
 Israel-U. S., 1991, 157-158
 role of public appeals in, 158
 Truman Doctrine, 168-183
Freeland, Richard M., 170, 171,
 185*n*30*n*33*n*35, 186*n*38
French, Blaire Atherton, 85*n*61
Friedman, Thomas L., 183*n*4
Fritz, Sara, 51*n*62
Fuerbringer, Jonathan, 9*n*15*n*18,
 154*n*75

Gallup Polls
 after Truman Doctrine speech, 172,
  178
 following Stockman interview, 198
 on "most important problem," 209
 during Reagan presidency, 126, 132,
  139-140, 152*n*45
Gelb, Leslie, 150*n*4, 154*n*72
George, Alexander L., 48*n*22
George, Juliette L., 48*n*22
Gephardt, Richard, 131
Gergen, David, 30, 127
Ginn, Bo, 131
Golden, David G., 225*n*64
Goldenberg, Edie N., 222*n*15
Goldman, Peter, 150*n*12,
 151*n*22*n*27*n*28*n*29*n*31*n*33*n*36
Gopoian, J. David, 50*n*37

Gorman, Joseph Bruce, 52*n*63
Gramm, Phil, 127, 151*n*23, 154*n*67
Gramm-Latta budget resolution, 127,
 151*n*23*n*32
Green, Theodore F., 17
Greenspan, Alan, 152*n*46
Greenstein, Fred I., 150*n*6, 185*n*24,
 202, 223*n*30*n*31
Greider, William, 152*n*44, 222*n*19
Grenada invasion, 162-163, 184*n*13
Gridiron Club, 60, 83*n*20
Grossman, Michael Baruch, 86*n*85,
 183*n*10, 221*n*3

Haberman, Clyde, 183*n*2
Hagerty, James, 72, 85*n*59, 109
Haight, Timothy, 225*n*64
Halberstam, David, 223*n*37
Hall, Ralph, 131
Hall, Robert, 50*n*43
Hallin, Daniel C., 87*n*85*n*88, 245*n*10
Hammond, Susan Webb, 50*n*34,
 246*n*36
Harding, Warren G., 63, 64, 65, 106
Harlow, Bryce, 203, 223*n*35
Hart, Gary, 36, 37, 234
Hebers, John, 183*n*9
Heclo, Hugh, 11, 47*n*2, 49*n*27
Helms, Jesse, 192
Herrington, John, 143
Hertsgaard, Mark, 86*n*77, 117*n*15,
 221*n*5
Hibbs, Douglas A., Jr., 224*n*50, 225*n*64
Hinckley, Ronald H., 183*n*8
Hodgson, Godfrey, 117*n*9*n*12, 118*n*27,
 246*n*23
Hollings, Ernest, 153*n*55
Hoover, Herbert, 63, 64, 65, 91, 99, 106
Hoover, J. Edgar, 15
Hoover Institution, 244
House, Karen Elliot, 153*n*56
Hovland, C.I., 184*n*21
Howard, Lucy, 116*n*3
Hubbard, Carroll, 131
Hubler, Richard G., 150*n*3
Humphrey, Hubert, 36
Humphrey-Hawkins bill, 216
Hunt, Albert R., 50*n*39
Hunter, Marjorie, 49*n*29
Hyde, Henry M., 84*n*45
Hyman, Herbert H., 187*n*52

Ickes, Harold, 67
Inaugural address, 91
Internal Revenue Service, 235-236
Irangate, 114
Irons, Peter, 82n13
Isaacson, Walter, 152n41, 154n66n73
Israel, Baker's negotiations with, 157
Iyengar, Shanto, 222n14

Jacobson, Gary C., 51n54, 82n17, 154n66, 222n16
Jagt, Guy Vander, 141
Jamieson, Kathleen Hall, 118n30
Jaroslovsky, Rich, 154n72, 223n25, 225n60
Jensen, Richard, 48n13
Johnson, Andrew, 57
  press relations, 60-61
Johnson, Haynes, 52n65n67
Johnson, Lyndon, 13, 15, 37, 79, 147, 159-160, 162, 203, 231
  background in Congress, 233
  policy-making vs. popularity of, 203-204
  popularity of, 194, 200, 219
  press relations of, 75, 77, 79
Jones, Charles O., 51n55
Jones, Jesse, 85n57
Jones, Joseph, 168, 185n26n28
Juergens, George, 61-63, 83n30, 84n33n34n35
Just, Ward S., 85n65, 86n73n74
Justice Department, 13

Kamen, Al, 246n36
Kasten, Robert, 236
Kefauver, Estes, 36, 52n63, 232
Kelley, Stanley Jr., 116n1
Kemp, Jack, 129, 137
Kemp-Roth tax bill, 127, 129-131
Kennan, George, 170, 185n31
Kennedy, Edward, 163, 216
Kennedy, John, 85n61, 86n73, 93, 111, 115, 119n46
  background in Congress, 233
  Bay of Pigs invasion, 160
  Cuban missile crisis, 91
  meeting with Kruschev, 101
  popularity of, 215
  popularity of, and international crises, 159
  press relations of, 70, 71-76

use of public support by, 6
Kennelly, Barbara, 50n43
Keogh, James, 86n81
Kernell, Dianne, 245n13
Kernell, Samuel, 52n64, 81, 82n17, 152n42, 154n66, 184n19, 185n24, 187n49, 221n9, 222n16, 223n38, 225n64, 245n13, 245n21n22
Kessel, John H., 223
Khrushchev, Nikita, 101
Kiewiet, D. Roderick, 221n10
Kilborn, Peter T., 224n44, 244n2
Kinder, Donald R., 184n16, 185n22n24, 195, 221n10n11n13, 222n14
King, Corretta Scott, 131
Kinsley, Michael, 50n35
Kirschten, Dick, 152n52, 154n75, 155n91n92, 225n56n58n59
Kissinger, Henry, 162, 183n9
  on public opinion and policy-making, 190
Kodak, 107
Kolko, Gabriel, 185n36, 186n39
Kolko, Joyce, 185n36, 186n39
Korean War, public opinion of, 181
Kraft, Joseph, 55
Kramer, Gerald H., 221n1
Kriesberg, Martin, 48n13
Krock, Arthur, 55, 67-68, 76, 84n48n52, 86n73
Kumar, Martha Joynt, 86n85, 183n10, 221n3
Kurtz, Howard, 246n36

Labor unions, 35, 36, 207
LaFeber, Walter, 178, 186n39n41, 187n47
Lammers, William W., 116n4n5
Lance, Bert, 198
Landon, Alfred, 68
Latta, Delbert, 127
Lau, Richard, 221n10
Lawrence, David, 55, 84n38
Lawrence, William, 72
Laxalt, Paul, 137-138
League of Nations, 2, 22
L'Enfant, Pierre, 55
Leuchtenburg, William E., 119n47, 244n1
Leviero, Anthony H., 197
Levinson, Daniel J., 187n54
Levy, David, 157-158

Lewis-Beck, Michael S., 223*n*36
Library of Congress, 112
Lindblom, Charles E., 3, 6*n*5, 10,
47*n*1*n*3, 114, 119*n*45
Lindley, Ernest K., 76
Lippmann, Walter, 55, 60, 83*n*25
Lisagor, Peter, 73, 76, 78
Lobbyists/lobbying, 28-29, 236. *See
also Political action committees*
affected by presidential popularity,
158
institutionalized pluralism and, 12
by Natural Gas Supply Association,
237
Lodge, Henry Cabot, 22
Long, Russell, 38
Lorenz, A. L. Jr., 85*n*58
Lott, Trent, 141, 155*n*93
Lukas, J. Anthony, 86*n*84

MacKuen, Michael, 222*n*15, 225*n*64
Madison, Christopher, 183*n*3
Magnuson, Ed, 9*n*10, 151*n*20,
152*n*47*n*48*n*49, 153*n*58, 155*n*93
Malone, Julia, 49*n*30, 244*n*4
Maltese, John Anthony, 87*n*89
Mann, Thomas, 25, 49*n*28*n*29
Mannheim, Jarol B., 86-87*n*85
Manning, George H., 84*n*32
Marer, Frank, 116*n*3
Markel, Lester, 73, 85*n*64*n*67, 115
Marshall, George C., 123, 170-171
Marshall Plan, 22, 49*n*24, 171, 172
Martin, John Bartlow, 6*n*1, 48*n*17,
85*n*63, 117*n*17, 118*n*34
Mathias, Charles McC., 184*n*14
Matthews, Donald R., 13, 47*n*5
Mayaguez, 160
Mayhew, David R., 224*n*42
McCarthy, Eugene, 36, 37
McCarthyism, 171, 181, 197, 202, 232
McClure Syndicate, 53, 82*n*3
McGillivray, Alice V., 150*n*5
McGinnis, Joe, 150*n*7, 221*n*5
McGovern, George, 36, 37
McGovern-Fraser Commission, 34
McIntyre, Marvin, 16
McKenzie, Ralph M., 83*n*20
McKinley, William
press relations of, 61
McLellan, David S., 48*n*24, 185*n*33
McManus, Doyle, 183*n*1*n*6

Meese, Edwin, 129
Merry, Robert W., 9*n*18
Michel, Robert, 49*n*30, 128, 134, 136,
143, 144, 155*n*93
Miller, Arthur H., 222*n*15, 224*n*40
Miller, Clem, 11, 47*n*4
Miller, Roger LeRoy, 225-226*n*65
Miller, Warren E., 184*n*16, 224*n*40
Mills, Wilbur, 13, 15, 129, 230
Minow, Newton N., 6*n*1, 48*n*17, 85*n*63,
117*n*17, 118*n*34, 119*n*42
Mitchell, Lee M., 6*n*1, 48*n*17, 85*n*63,
117*n*17, 118*n*34, 119*n*42
Moffett, Toby, 127
Moley, S., 84*n*38
Mollenhoff, Clark, 73
Mondale, Walter, 147
Monroe, Kristen R., 226*n*66
Montgomery, G.V. (Sonny), 141-142,
154*n*70
Morganthau, Tom, 152*n*41
Mothers Against Drunk Driving
(MADD), 29, 235
Moynihan, Daniel P., 153*n*55, 162
Mueller, John E., 177-178, 181, 184*n*20,
187*n*45*n*53, 225*n*64
Mulhollan, Daniel P., 50*n*34
Muskie, Edmund, 36

Nation, The, 82*n*14
National Automobile Dealers Associa-
tion, 28
National Broadcasting Company
(NBC), 112
O'Neill, Thomas P., Jr., 135
National Heritage Resources Act, 27
National Press Club, 54, 60, 234
Natural Gas Supply Association, 237
NBC. *See National Broadcasting Com-
pany*
Nelson, Jack, 6*n*7, 152*n*52, 153*n*56,
155*n*88, 246*n*27*n*29
Neustadt, Richard E., 3, 6*n*4, 14, 15,
19, 21, 31, 33, 47*n*7, 48*n*19*n*21, 49*n*24,
51*n*50*n*52, 114, 119*n*45, 185*n*37, 194,
221*n*7
New Congress, The, 25, 26
New Deal programs, 56
Nicaragua, 229, 240
Nielsen ratings, 113, 117*n*11,
119*n*42*n*43

Nixon, Richard, 1, 2, 71, 79, 85n63, 86n81, 99, 107, 109, 112, 113, 231, 233
  crisis leadership and public opinion, 161-162
  energy policies of, 189
  pardon by Ford, 205
  political travels of, 101-104
  popularity of, 194, 215, 219, 226n66
  press relations of, 75, 77-78
  public appeals of, 227
  public opinion polling by, 30
  public relations effort after Laos invasion, 89-90
  public relations efforts by, 191
  trip to China, 160
  use of television by, 98, 109, 111
Nofziger, Lyn, 126
Novak, Robert, 90, 116n2

Obey, David, 28
Olezek, Walter J., 52n70
On Bended Knee, 192
O'Neill, Thomas P., Jr., 39, 151n29, 152-153n53, 162, 230, 231
  Reagan budget proposals and, 126-131, 135-136, 141
Oppenheimer, Bruce I., 49n28n29
Oreskes, Michael, 52n74
Ornstein, Norman J., 49n28n29, 50n36, 151-152n39
Ostrom, Charles W., Jr., 225n64
Otten, Alan L., 85n68n70, 153n56

PACs. *See Political action committees*
Page, Benjamin I., 184n20
Parties, political
  decline of, 24, 45-47
  in divided government, 40-41, 45-47
  economic issues and, 207, 219-220
  in individualized pluralism, 238-239
  marginals strategy and, 212-215
  occupational class and, 209
  presidential problem-solving and, 208
  voter loyalty and economic issues, 217-218
  voters and, 10
Paullin, Charles O., 118n24
Pear, Robert, 225n56
Pearl Harbor, 160, 163-164
Pederson, Johannes, 187n46
Peffley, Mark, 221n13

Pepper, Claude, 169
Peretz, Paul, 224n51, 225n57
Perot, H. Ross, 234
Perry, James M., 184n13
Peters, Mark, 222n14
Pettit, Tom, 81
Pew, Marlan E., 84n46
Pierpoint, Robert, 71, 73-74, 85n60n70
Pluralism
  formation of public opinion in types of, 192
  going public and theory of, 3, 9
  individualized, 23-26, 46-47, 148, 192, 220, 235, 238-239
  institutionalized, 10-17, 25-26, 46-47, 54, 57, 76, 192
  outsider presidents and process of, 37-39, 235
  practiced in Congress, 233
  presidential bargaining in theory of, 15
  role of press relations, 55-57, 76
  role of public opinion, 17-23, 235
Political action committees (PACs), 26, 27-28, 29, 50n40
Politics, Economics, and Welfare, 10
Pollard, James E., 64, 83n27, 84n34n39n47n49, 85n68, 86n76n82
Polsby, Nelson W., 3, 6n6n8, 34, 49n27n33, 51n57n58n59, 82n15, 166-167, 185n23, 223n29, 245n11
Pompidou, Georges, 103-104
Porter, William E., 83n81
Poterba, James M., 225n64
Powell, Jody, 81, 200, 221n3
Presidency/Presidents. *See also specific President*
  appeals for public support, 1-6, 19-21, 22, 30-32, 39, 89, 166-168, 241-242
  aspirants to, 233-234
  bargaining model of, 3-4, 10, 195
  calculating public support, 201-208
  campaign for, coalition building in, 238-239
  coalition building, 13-15, 23, 24-25, 98-99, 206, 212-217
  crisis leadership, 159-164
  economic performance and public opinion, 217-221
  electoral process for, 9

evolution of press coverage of, 197-199
future sources of candidates for, 234
influence of public opinion on, 18-21, 183n8, 199-201
in institutionalized pluralism, 14-15
leadership styles, 114-116, 241-242
managing economic issues via general problem solving, 207-212
via marginals strategy, 212-217
nominee selection, Democratic Party process, 33-37
with opposition party in Congress, 39-41, 228
outsiders as, 37-39, 123
popularity of, and support for policies, 164-168, 173-174, 177, 239-241
press coverage of, vs. Congress, 197
press relations and, 55-57, 60-64, 76-79, 80-81, 192-199
prestige as negotiating tool, 32-33, 229
problem-solving and popularity of, 189-191, 205-212
public appearances, 99-101
public relations efforts by, 191-199
publicity from political travels, 101-106, 109, 203
relations with Congress, 15-17
relations with political party, 208
speeches to raise public support, 91-99
trends in going public, 227-228
types of problems facing, 206-207
Presidential Power, 14-15
Press conference
in Bush administration, 79-80
development of, 63-65, 70-71, 110, 233
frequency, 75, 79, 93-95
under Kennedy, 71-75, 111
television in, 71-74, 76, 111
Eisenhower confrontation at, 197-199
Press corps
Bush and, 79-80
competition in, 64-65
coverage during international crises, 161-164
coverage of first Reagan term, 142
development of, 57-60, 77, 83n19, 220, 231-233
effect of television on, 73-74, 85n

Eisenhower and, 71
evolution of presidential coverage, 197-199
Franklin Roosevelt and, 53-54, 56-57, 65-70, 82n6
Kennedy and, 71-76
during McCarthy era, 232
presidential attacks on, 192
in presidential public relations efforts, 192-196
presidential relations, 60-64, 75-79, 80-81
presidential vs. congressional coverage, 196
role of, and pluralist president, 55-57
Truman and, 70-71
Press Gallery Correspondents Association, 60
Pressler, Larry, 50n39
Price, H. Douglas, 82n15
Primaries, Democratic presidential, 35
Public opinion. *See also Gallup Polls*
affected by Washington political opinion, 192-196
cost/benefit of obtaining presidential popularity, 201-204
early conceptions of role of, 237-238
economic performance of presidents, 217-221
employment/economic issues, 208-212
factors in formation of, 237
following Stockman interview, 198
general problem-solving approach and, 208-212
during Grenada invasion, 162-163, 184n13
importance in divided government, 42
managing as resource, 204-208
news media in shaping, 194-196, 199
policy formulation and, 234-236, 239-240
polling by politicians, 18-19, 30-31, 199-201
presidential problem-solving and, 189-191, 199-201, 205-212
presidential public relations efforts, 191-196
president's popularity related to support for policies, 164-168, 173-174, 177, 191-195, 239-241

of Reagan, during early presidency, 126, 132
role of, in influencing Congress, 17-18
role of personal circumstances in, 195
role of rally events in, 160-168
Truman Doctrine and, 168-183
Pueblo, 160, 162

Rabushka, Alvin, 50*n*43
Rafshoon, Gerald, 93, 117*n*10, 119*n*, 191
Ragsdale, Lyn, 221*n*3
Raines, Howell, 116*n*3, 152*n*50, 153*n*60*n*63
Randolph, Jennings, 49*n*29
Ranney, Austin, 49*n*26
Rao, Potluri, 225-226*n*65
Reagan, Ronald, 9, 29, 37, 86*n*79, 98-99, 115, 116*n*3, 117*n*11*n*15*n*16, 118*n*19, 118-119*n*38, 150*n*3*n*5*n*7, 152*n*43, 153*n*56, 155*n*88*n*93, 184*n*13, 227
  appeals for public support, 4-6, 126-127, 128, 130-131, 134-135, 136, 138, 146-147, 240
  assassination attempt on, 126, 239
  bargaining strategies, 151*n*23
  budget negotiations, 124-125, 237
  1981, 125-134
  1982, 134-139
  1983, 139-146
  campaign tactics, 1983, 203, 212
  campaigning in office, 148-149
  career before presidency, 122-124
  Grenada invasion, 162, 184*n*13
  leadership style, 228
  major speeches of, 91-93, 126-127, 128, 130-131
  marginals strategy of, 215-216
  Nicaragua and, 229
  political travels of, 101, 104, 203
  popularity of, 194, 200, 202, 203-204, 215
  press relations of, 75, 77, 78, 79, 149
  as Progressive, 242, 243-244
  public opinion polls, 31, 126, 132, 139-140, 152
  public relations efforts by, 90, 191, 237
  relations with Congress, 121
  Saudi Arabia AWACS sale, 150*n*11
  Stockman and, 197, 198-199

  tax reform campaign, 1985, 240-241
  television use by, 1-2, 112-113, 113-114, 125, 126-127, 128, 130-131, 148, 167
  as Washington outsider, 36, 122-124
  Watt and, 205
Reciprocity, in congressional bargaining, 13
Reed, Thomas B., 34
Regan, Donald, 130-131
Republican Party
  economic issues and, 207
  rejection of Bush budget compromise, 1990, 43-44
  Republican National Committee, 118-119*n*38
Reston, James, 55, 72, 75, 76, 197, 222*n*18
Reuss, John W., 48*n*24, 185*n*33
Rice, Stuart A., 83*n*22
Rice, Tom W., 223*n*36
Richards, Robert W., 222*n*18
Riker, William H., 225*n*55
Roberts, Chalmers, 82*n*1*n*4, 84*n*44
Roberts, Steven V., 49*n*29, 50*n*43, 131, 150*n*1, 151*n*38, 154*n*66*n*68*n*71, 154-155*n*82, 155*n*84*n*86*n*89*n*93, 244*n*2*n*5, 245*n*14
Robertson, Pat, 234
Robinson, Michael, 25, 26, 49*n*30, 222*n*14
Robinson, William A., 51*n*56
Roemer, Buddy, 141
Rollins, Edward, 135, 138, 141, 149, 152*n*52
Roosevelt, Franklin D., 16-17, 48*n*16, 82*n*6*n*7, 84*n*43*n*48*n*55, 85*n*57, 93, 99, 107, 115, 117*n*8, 118*n*27*n*32, 244*n*1
  compared to Reagan, 124
  court packing attempt, 19, 48*n*18, 110
  fireside chats, 2, 115
  leadership style, 228
  Pearl Harbor attack and, 160, 163-164
  popularity vs. policy-making of, 203-204
  press relations, 53-54, 56-57, 65-70, 75, 82*n*6
  public opinion polling by, 18-19
  on television, 192
Roosevelt, Theodore, 2, 64, 123, 241-242

press relations of, 61-62
Rosellini, Lynn, 150*n*14
Rosen, Carey, 184*n*18
Rosenbaum, David E., 9*n*17*n*18, 52*n*73, 246*n*35
Rosenstone, Steven J., 184*n*16
Rosenthal, Andrew, 87*n*86
Rosentiel, Thomas B., 86*n*78*n*80, 87*n*87
Rossi, Eugene J., 184*n*20
Rosten, Leo, 65, 68, 84*n*42*n*45*n*48*n*54
Rostenkowski, Dan, 129, 130, 146, 230-231
Roth, William, 129
Rovere, Richard H., 245*n*8*n*9
Rowe, James, 47-48*n*10, 52*n*71, 85*n*61
advice to Truman, 41-42
Rowen, Hobart, 225*n*62
Rules Committee, House, 143
Rusk, Dean, 50-51*n*44
Rutkus, Denis Steven, 118*n*35*n*36*n*37
Ryan, Pauline, 50*n*43

Salant, Richard S., 85*n*63
Salinger, Pierre, 71-72, 75, 85*n*61, 117*n*9
Scammon, Richard M., 150*n*5
Schattschneider, E. E., 201, 223*n*28, 245*n*18
Schick, Allen, 151*n*38
Schlesinger, Arthur, Jr., 115, 117*n*12, 119*n*46
Schlozman, Kay L., 50*n*41, 221*n*12
Schneider, Frederick, 226*n*66
Schudson, Michael, 83*n*25
Sears, David O., 186*n*40, 221*n*10
Selling of the President, 192
Selznick, Philip, 82*n*12
Semple, Robert B., Jr., 6*n*3, 119*n*39
Seniority, congressional, 11
Shamir, Yitzhak, 157-158
Shapiro, Margaret, 7*n*14
Shapiro, Robert Y., 184*n*20
Sharp, Harry Jr., 85*n*62
Sharp, Philip, 245*n*17
Sharp, Willis, 63-64, 84*n*36
Shribman, David, 9*n*18
Sigel, Roberta S., 185*n*24
Sigelman, Carol K., 184*n*18
Sigelman, Lee, 184*n*17*n*18*n*19
Silk, Leonard, 224*n*47*n*48
Simon, Dennis M., 225*n*64
Sinclair, Barbara, 29-30, 50*n*44, 51*n*46

Sinclair, Ward, 244*n*6
Skelton, George, 150*n*15, 223*n*32
Smith, Anthony, 65, 84*n*41
Smith, Hedrick, 7*n*9*n*14, 52*n*68, 86*n*72, 116*n*3, 118*n*19, 153*n*60*n*61*n*64, 154*n*74*n*72, 155*n*V*n*89, 183*n*11, 184*n*14, 244*n*2
Smith, Howard K., 90
Sorensen, Theodore, 72, 76
Soviet Union
Afghanistan invasion, 1980, 163
grain embargo, 1980, 205
U. S. relations under Truman, 168, 170
Speechmaking, presidential, 91-99, 233
Sperlich, Peter, 47*n*8, 51*n*50, 52*n*66, 185*n*24
Sprinkel, Beryl, 207
Sputnik satellite, 160, 186*n*40
Stanton, Frank, 112
State of the Union address, 91, 112, 143
Steele, Richard W., 19, 48*n*16
Stenholm, Charles, 142, 154*n*70
Stevens, Arthur G. Jr., 50*n*34
Stevens, Ted, 134
Stevenson, Adlai, 118*n*30
Stimson, James, 223*n*34
Stockman, David, 127, 132, 151*n*24, 152*n*45, 197, 198-199
Stouffer, Samuel, 187*n*51
Strout, Richard, 55, 222*n*18
Sudman, Seymour, 116*n*3
Sullivan, Mark, 64, 84*n*49
Supreme Court, 19, 110
Sussman, Barry, 184*n*13
Sussman, Leila A., 48

Taft, Robert, 169
Tarbell, Ida M., 61
Tate, Dale, 152-153*n*53*n*55
Tax issues. *See also Reagan, Ronald, budget negotiations*
bank industry lobbying, 235-236
in Bush 1990 budget compromise, 43-44
Carter reforms, 246*n*33
flat tax proposals, 234
Kemp-Roth bill, 129-131
politicians and, 229-230
Reagan campaign for reform, 240-241, 243-244
Taylor, Stuart, 183*n*12

Technology
  broadcast, 245*n*10
  communications, 9, 24, 25, 70, 77,
    103, 106, 107-109, 113, 237
  in growth of going public, 106-109,
    192
  transportation, 9, 24, 103, 106-107
Teeter, Robert, 149
Television
  coverage of press conferences, 71-73,
    85*n*59
  decline in viewing of presidential ad-
    dresses, 113-114, 117*n*11, 119*n*42
  F. Roosevelt on, 192
  fairness doctrine, 1, 111-112
  network broadcasting policy, 112-113
  presidential use of, 85*n*61*n*63, 93-95,
    107-109, 111, 125
  Reagan use of, 1-2
  in scheduling presidential travel, 101,
    103-104
Tennesee Valley Authority, 56
terHorst, J. F., 118*n*20*n*25
Theoharis, Arthur, 178, 186*n*39*n*41,
  187*n*47
Thurow, Lester, 207, 224*n*45*n*46
Tierney, John T., 50*n*41
Tolchin, Martin, 153*n*57, 155*n*83,
  245*n*12
Truman, David, 17, 48*n*12
Truman, Harry S., 18, 22-23, 30, 68, 99,
  104, 108, 109, 110, 111-112, 186*n*42,
  197
  See also Truman Doctrine
  popularity of, 240
  press relations of, 70-71
  on public opinion, 202
  relations with opposition Congress,
    41-42
Truman Doctrine, 22, 48-49*n*24
  anticommunist fear aroused by, 168-
    171, 178-182
  mobilizing popular support for, 168-
    183
Tsongas, Paul, 37, 234
Tufte, Edward, 208, 209, 221*n*1,
  223*n*27, 224*n*52
Tumulty, Joseph, 63
Tumulty, Karen, 9*n*15

Vandenburg, Arthur, 22, 48*n*24, 68,
  170, 171

Verba, Sidney, 221*n*12
Vietnam War, 1, 78, 79, 111, 159-160,
  178, 191, 194, 200, 204, 223*n*37, 231
Villard, O.G., 84*n*38

Waldo, Richard, 53-54, 82*n*3
Wallace, Henry, 169, 175
Walters, Barbara, 90
Watergate, 78, 104, 162, 215
Watt, James, 205
Wattenberg, Martin P., 49*n*26
Ways and Means Committee, House,
  129
Weatherford, M. Stephen, 221*n*10
Wehr, Elizabeth, 151*n*32*n*34
Weinberger, Caspar, 145
Weinraub, Bernard, 7*n*13*n*14*n*16,
  150*n*10, 155*n*88
Weisman, Steven R., 51*n*45, 155*n*85*n*89
Weiss, W., 184*n*21
Where's the Rest of Me?, Reagan auto-
  biography, 122
White, Graham J., 82*n*7, 84*n*55
White, William S., 17, 48*n*11, 50*n*38
White House Correspondents Associa-
  tion, 60, 63-64
Wicker, Tom, 241, 246*n*28
Wiebe, G.D., 52*n*63
Wildavsky, Aaron, 6*n*6, 34, 51*n*57,
  185*n*24*n*25
Willey, Malcolm M., 83*n*22
Williams, Dennis, 116*n*3
Williams, J. T., 221*n*13
Williams, Juan, 154*n*75*n*78*n*79
Wilson, Pete, 241
Wilson, Woodrow, 2, 22-23, 56, 64, 65,
  106, 107, 241-242
  press relations of, 62-63
Wines, Michael, 117*n*13
Wirthlin, Richard, 116*n*3, 126, 130, 138,
  149, 153*n*56*n*60, 215, 225*n*56, 241
Wise, Daniel, 223*n*23
Witcover, Jules, 85*n*69, 86*n*72*n*83
Wooten, James T., 117*n*14
Worsthorne, Peregrine, 90
Wright, James, 128, 230

Yang, John E., 183*n*5
Young, Andrew, 131
Young, James Sterling, 82*n*8

Zeidenstein, Harvey G., 221*n*4